EMBATTLED GARRISONS

EMBATTLED GARRISONS

COMPARATIVE BASE POLITICS
AND AMERICAN GLOBALISM

Kent E. Calder

PRINCETON UNIVERSITY PRESS   PRINCETON AND OXFORD

Published by Princeton University Press, 41 William Street, Princeton,
New Jersey 08540
In the United Kingdom: Princeton University Press, 3 Market Place,
Woodstock, Oxfordshire OX20 1SY
All Rights Reserved

Library of Congress Cataloging-in-Publication Data

Calder, Kent E.

Embattled garrisons : comparative base politics and American
globalism / Kent E. Calder.
p. cm.
Includes bibliographical references and index.
ISBN 978-0-691-13143-6 (hardcover : alk. paper) —
ISBN 978-0-691-13463-5 (pbk. : alk. paper)
1. Military bases, American—Foreign countries.   2. Military bases,
American—Political aspects.   I. Title.
UA26.A2C35   2007
355.7—dc22
2007023217

British Library Cataloging-in-Publication Data is available
This book has been composed in Sabon

Printed on acid-free paper. ∞

press.princeton.edu

Printed in the United States of America

1 3 5 7 9 10 8 6 4 2

To the memory of Grant H. Calder

Contents

List of Figures

List of Tables

My personal experience with American military bases goes back a long way. My father was a retired U.S. Naval officer, medically discharged from active duty during World War II, who loved to travel. Posted overseas in Southeast Asia and Africa, on contract projects with the Ford Foundation and U.S. AID, he thought up all sorts of outlandish car trips, often with a European or a North African angle. And as a retired officer, he liked nothing better than to ferret out a military base along the way, and have a good American steak at the local Officers' Club.

In the course of our wanderings, we passed through Officers' Clubs and BOQs from Wheelus Field in Libya, Kagnew Station in Ethiopia, and Nouassir in Morocco to Berchtesgaden, Ramstein, and Wiesbaden in Germany, with Rota, Spain, Hellonikon, Greece, and Verona, Italy, along the way. Travelling tortuously by car from Cairo to Casablanca, then across the Pillars of Hercules and throughout Europe, we also saw a fair amount outside the gates. The contrasts—between the spacious, confident world within, and the poorer, more turbulent and tortured world outside the gates—left a strong impression on me.

Years later, as a U.S. State Department official serving as Special Advisor to the U.S. Ambassador to Japan, I had cause to frequent bases once again—this time predominantly in the Far East. In the course of my government work, I visited Okinawa sixteen times, and passed through every American military facility in Japan, as well as most in South Korea. Once again, the contrasts between the world inside the checkpoint and the world beyond—their different economic and cultural circumstances, and their difficulties at communication—struck me powerfully as evocative micro-symbols of the grassroots challenge to the foundation stones of America's global leadership, and prompted flashbacks to my childhood travels three decades before. I resolved to write about it all someday.

Among the first to encourage me in all this was Toshiko Calder. In days and nights of incessant discussion—indeed, frequently debate—she pointed to the central role of bases in U.S.-Japan relations, to their linchpin status in a fateful bilateral equation at the point of historic transition, and to the unusual perspectives that I, as an academic Japan specialist with an additional inside view as a government official, could bring to a topic such as base politics. She also encouraged me to view this subject comparatively.

An unforgettable catalyst to this work was my policy task force on U.S. bases in Japan at Princeton's Woodrow Wilson School for International

Affairs in the fall of 2000. Eight students, Toshiko, and I spent a week in Okinawa, roaming about in a decrepit old microbus. We traveled, in one single, memorable day, from the dank war-time caves where thousands of Okinawan civilians died, to a dissenter's hut on the sandy beach at Henoko, to the control tower of the Marine Corps Air Station at Futenma—and then we returned to Princeton to debate what we had seen. In the fall of 2001, Ivy Esguerra, the Senior Commissioner for the task force, with a passion for the Filipino struggle about the bases, became my first research assistant on this project, followed later by another task-force member, Benje Kwak.

Min Ye, then a fledgling Ph.D. student at Princeton, joined this project in the spring of 2002, and persisted with it, in various roles, for nearly four years. Min's strong sense for theory, her computer skills, and her unerring eye for the obscure but evocative factoid have contributed enormously to this book. She can see her handiwork here, however unknown it may be to others, and I am grateful to her.

Yukie Yoshikawa, who, after completing her M.A. at Columbia University, joined the Reischauer Center for East Asian Studies in 2005, has been my indispensable assistant in pulling this book together over the past two years. Her insightful creativity, impeccable sense for logic, and refreshing irreverence have greatly improved this product. She has contributed enormously to the graphics and the use of Japanese-language materials.

Chang Boo-Seung, a Ph.D. candidate at SAIS who also serves in the Korean Foreign Ministry, also contributed greatly to this project. A former KATUSA liaison officer with the U.S. military in Korea, he helped make this project much more systematically comparative. Apart from his expertise on Korea, his comparative work on Spain, and his assessment of how population density affects base politics, contributed importantly to the final product.

On three occasions since the spring term of 2004, I have taught seminars on "The Comparative Politics of Forward Deployment" at SAIS. I am enormously indebted to my students in those seminars, from whom I have learned a tremendous amount. Heather Leavey, Michael Maughan, and Andrew Rhodes, in particular, have gone beyond the call of duty, and offered commentary, grounded in their own background of military service, that has been useful to this research.

Any project of this sort is the product of many hands: Ted Baker, Susan Basalla, Jim Blaker, Lincoln Bloomfield, Jr., Frederick Z. Brown, Kurt Campbell, Eliot Cohen, Paul Choi, Rust Deming, Tom Drohan, Jessica Einhorn, Francis Fukuyama, Robert Gilpin, Bill Grimes, John Harrington, John Hill, Andrew Hoehn, Karl Jackson, Chris Johnstone, Charles

Jones, Tom Keaney, David Lampton, Sook-Jong Lee, Eunjung Lim, Marisa Lino, Michael Mandelbaum, Don Oberdorfer, Michael O'Hanlon, Jin-Hyun Paik, Susan Pharr, Yukio Sato, David Shear, Ruth Wedgewood, Bill Weiss, Lynn White and Bill Zartman are just a few of the many officials, former officials, and colleagues who have contributed important ideas; seminar discussions at the U.S. Air Force Academy, Harvard University, Princeton University, RIPS, and Seoul National University also deepened the analysis. Chuck Myers has been a most patient, sympathetic, and insightful editor for more than four years, while Deborah Tegarden has deciphered my continued scribblings at the production stage with remarkable good cheer. I am pleased to be working closely on a second book with Peter Dougherty. I am also enormously grateful to the Japan Foundation; its Center for Global Partnership; the Abe Fellowship Program, administered by the Social Science Research Council; and the Korea Foundation for their financial support at different intervals. Responsibility for the final product, warts and all, is mine alone.

Kent E. Calder
Washington, D.C.
February 2007

List of Abbreviations

AFTAC	Air Force Tactical Air Command
BIOT	British Indian Ocean Territory
BRAC	Base Realignment and Closure Commission
BSR	Base Structure Report
CENTCOM	Central Command (Middle East)
CFC	Combined Forces Command (U.S.-Korea)
COMLOG-WESTPAC	Commander, Logistics Group, Western Pacific (Singapore)
DFAA	Defense Facilities Administration Agency (Japan)
DOD	Department of Defense
EUCOM	European Command
FMP	Foreign Military Presence
FOB	Forward Operating Base
FOL	Forward Operating Location
HNS	Host-Nation Support
ICBM	Intercontinental Ballistic Missile
IFOR	Intervention Force (Bosnia)
IRBM	Intermediate Range Ballistic Missile
ISAF	International Security Assistance Force (Afghanistan)
JCS	Joint Chiefs of Staff
JDA	Japan Defense Agency
MCAS	Marine Corps Air Station
MOD	Ministry of Defense
MNC	Multinational Corporation
MND	Ministry of National Defense (South Korea)
NATO	North Atlantic Treaty Organization
NGO	Nongovernmental Organization
NMPC	National Monitoring and Planning Center
NSC	National Security Council
ODA	Overseas Development Assistance
OSCE	Organization on Security Cooperation in Europe
PRV	Property Replacement Value
RDJTF	Rapid Deployment Joint Task Force
RMA	Revolution in Military Affairs
ROK	Republic of Korea (South Korea)

SAC	Strategic Air Command
SACEUR	Supreme Commander-Europe
SACO	Special Action Committee on Okinawa
SCAP	Supreme Commander Allied Powers (Japan)
SDA	Self-Defense Agency (Japan)
SDF	Self-Defense Forces (Japan)
SIGINT	Signals Intelligence
SOFA	Status of Forces Agreement
TGS	Turkish General Staff
UNAMA	U.N. Assistance Mission in Afghanistan
USFJ	U.S. Forces Japan
USFK	U.S. Forces Korea

EMBATTLED GARRISONS

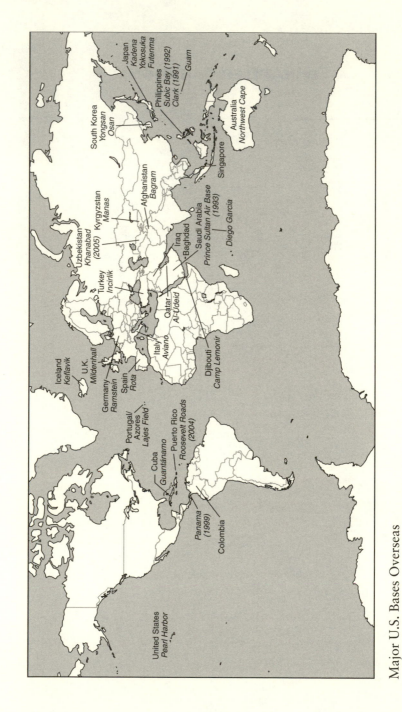

Major U.S. Bases Overseas

Note: The sites of representative current U.S. bases are in italics; parenthetical years indicate the date of closure of an inactive base.

INTRODUCTION

THE PRESENCE OF FOREIGN troops on the soil of independent nations has traditionally been at once an unusual and an uncomfortable reality. Historically overseas military bases have almost invariably been the product of empires, and have disappeared with the liberation of their peoples. For the citizens of the United States, they were for the first century of the Republic and beyond a particularly noxious form of foreign entanglement. Only from the late 1930s, as the storm clouds of World War II began to deepen, did overseas military bases in other sovereign nations gradually become a more acceptable reality, for both Americans and others.[1]

Since World War II, foreign bases have come to seem commonplace, and even natural—especially to Americans—despite their earlier historic uniqueness. As we will see, bases have come to perform important roles in international affairs: deterring aggression, reinforcing alliance relations, inhibiting balance-of-power conflict, providing formidably efficient global logistics networks, assuring smooth resource flows, and helping most recently to combat terrorism. Overseas bases have become the very sinews of an American globalism that in any other age would be known as empire.[2]

Yet these global guardians are also themselves both vulnerable and often controversial. However omnipotent the power of American arms may be in technical and geopolitical terms, it must also, like the military of other great powers past and present, contend with the domestic political context of host nations and indeed, often with dissent at home. Other great powers, such as Russia, Britain, and France, have already, by and large, lost their global basing networks, under a range of economic and political pressures. And since 9/11, the United States has also come to face an increasingly complex political basing problem. As the struggle against terrorism has broadened into a global "arc of instability" within the developing world, and as even America's industrialized allies have grown skeptical and weary, the pressures on America to retrench have deepened once again, from Saudi Arabia to Turkey, South Korea, and beyond. Something much larger than an "Iraq War syndrome" is at work, although Iraq has proven to be an important catalyst.

In some countries, to be sure, the broad skepticism and antagonism about foreign bases have been arrested, at least for a while. In some few instances, both past and present, foreign troops are greeted as liberators rather than agents of empire. Yet those instances are rare, and the felicitous conditions they create fleeting and difficult to sustain.

Foreign bases, in short are thus *embattled garrisons*, and are likely to be increasingly so as America's turbulent involvement in the Middle East is steadily redefined. Overseas bases often fill important military roles, not only in the Middle East, but around the world, yet they are increasingly difficult to sustain politically. How and where to best keep them are issues of crucial importance for policy. Similarly understanding the comparative politics behind host-nation response ranks as an important question for middle-range social science theory, as well.

This volume, in the social science tradition, approaches the world around us from the perspective of causal explanation; it struggles to answer the persistent question, Why? Like all social scientists engaged in that process, we confront the continuing dilemma of how to strive simultaneously for universalism and realism. As policy-oriented students of social science, we face an additional challenge—how to produce generalizations that have both predictive and prescriptive relevance for the future.

The response that we propose to the multiple analytical challenges confronted here is threefold: (1) to develop and test falsifiable generalizations about why military bases come and go; (2) to employ the more viable ones in probabilistic fashion to provide a prognosis for existing and anticipated basing configurations; and (3) to suggest prescriptions for future policy on the basis of past historical experience. Broadly speaking, this approach leads us to see clearly that overseas bases have over the past half century developed important stabilizing functions in the global system, but that they are historically and institutionally contingent; that their prospective political viability in host nations varies considerably, if in predictable fashion; and that public policy can critically affect that viability. In sum, it argues that there can be a policy science of basing, and presumes to diffidently suggest how that science might evolve.

In an attempt to initiate a more systematic study of base politics, I begin this volume in chapter 1 with a historical survey of foreign basing—since the concept of "bases outside of empire" emerged in the late 1930s—that illustrates the important strategic functions that forward deployment has come to perform.[3] In chapter 2 I summarize the current state of American overseas basing in comparative historical and cross-national perspective, emphasizing the political and technological forces affecting its long-term viability, and the policy challenges that those long-term forces create. Chapter 3 conceptualizes base politics in more theoretical fashion.

Chapters 4 through 8 outline in greater detail, through subnational analysis, the varied yet generalizable patterns that host-nation base politics typically assume. They show the primary importance of understanding the analytical structure of base-related conflicts, before getting trapped by their details. They clearly illustrate that there are definite patterns of success and failure in stabilizing the presence of overseas bases, and making them consistent with the aspirations of local inhabitants. Yet amidst the nuance, the difficulties of sustaining bases in the absence of large-scale financial support, and those of transforming base presence even in the presence of such support, come through clearly.

Chapters 9 and 10, in conclusion, consider what the United States should do about the detailed, real-world circumstances previously presented. Chapter 9 outlines emerging options for policy, beyond the details of current conflicts, while chapter 10 is more normative, presenting concrete policy recommendations and implications for further research. Given the strategic importance that these embattled garrisons have assumed over their short lifetime of but three score years and ten, it concludes that policy should attempt to sustain some core functions and locations on a global basis. Yet substantial retrenchment, relocation, and sensitivity to local politics are emphatically in order, as recent developments in the Islamic world make clear. Also important is more systematic analytical attention to the forces that support and erode foreign basing, toward which end this volume hopefully provides a useful start.

CHAPTER ONE

THE HERITAGE OF HISTORY

TEN MILES SOUTH of Korea's Demilitarized Zone (DMZ), sandwiched between eight thousand North Korean artillery pieces and Korea's capital, Seoul, with its more than ten million people, stands Camp Sears. Home for nearly half a century, since the guns of the Korean War went silent in 1953, to the U.S. Army's Second Infantry Division, it now stands abandoned, save for solitary sentries guarding the gate. Since 2005, the camp has been silent—its soldiers redeployed, many to the Middle East.

Camp Sears, and fifty-eight other garrisons like it, from which American troops are withdrawing under 2004 transformation accords, present in microcosm the deepening dilemmas that America's military confronts around the world today, far beyond any particular fleeting conflict. The operational demands for their presence are many, and rising. Yet so are the host-nation pressures that they confront.

Almost the only strident claims commonly heard in the vicinity now, with distant, martial North Korean loudspeakers across the DMZ recently silenced, are those of Green Korea United's environmental protest, continuing since the pullout proposal was adopted in 2004. American troops, when they vacated the camp, cleaned up to the standards of the bilateral U.S.-Korea Status of Forces Agreement.[1] Those criteria, however, do not meet the strictures of Korea's new environmental laws, enacted in the flush of democratic reform, four decades after the base itself was originally built. Recent estimates are that the incremental cost of meeting the higher Korean standards would be over $600 million—nearly nothing compared to the trillion-dollar ultimate costs of the Iraq War, but a substantial piece of change by most other calculations.

Twenty-five miles south of Camp Sears, in the heart of Seoul, stands Yongsan—literally "Dragon Mountain"—home of the U.S. Forces in Korea (USFK) command. Yongsan has been host to foreign military garrisons in Korea since 1882, when troops of China's Ching Dynasty seized this strategic site, lying between the Han River and the Korean royal court. "Whoever rules Yongsan rules Korea" has been the historic refrain.

In 2007 Yongsan remained host to over four thousand American troops. Yet their prospects for staying were highly uncertain. The Korean Ministry of National Defense (MND) lay right across the street, making coordination with the headquarters of USFK, and its commanding four-star general, with his direct links to the Pentagon, logistically easy. The proximity of the massive American presence in Yongsan to Korean government agencies, including MND, has long allegedly been a powerful deterrent to a North Korean attack on Seoul.

Yet strategic calculations have changed and political pressures for relocation have deepened since the advent of democracy two decades ago. An American pullout from Yongsan, after all, would provide 656 acres of green space to the people of Seoul, a city where parks have been sacrificed to the building of the world's twelfth-largest economy; 250,000 potential buyers have already put down $6 billion in deposits for 629 apartments, or 141 offices, in just one corner of the Yongsan complex.[2]

The United States first agreed to leave Yongsan in 1988, and the day of reckoning was long in coming. But at last, irresistible pressures for departure were building, with Seoul's long-time mayor Lee Myung Bak, tempted by presidential ambitions, and veteran Foreign Minister, and U.N. Secretary General, Ban Ki Moon, author of early-withdrawal plans fifteen years earlier, also having a stake in bringing the relocation plan to fruition.

Forty miles south of Yongsan, at Camp Humphreys, near the town of Pyeongtaek, matters are livelier still. Ringed with barbed wire, 3.6 square miles of land was surrounded by a 29-kilometer-long wire fence during the spring of 2006 in preparation for a tripling in the scale of Camp Humphreys so as to accommodate one of the largest and most technologically advanced U.S. Army bases in the world.[3] With detachment impossible along the DMZ, highly mobile American forces would be capable from Pyeongtaek of responding flexibly to any Korean crisis, or, prospectively, to emergencies far from the peninsula as well.

Technologically, the new base is a modern marvel, with state-of-the-art communications and transportation. Yet it, too, is beset by political challenges in both the domestic and the foreign-policy realms. Pyeongtaek's rice farmers, appeased by subsidies of $15,000 per household—the first such payments offered in Korean history to landowners displaced by the military—were relatively quiescent. From the time that the U.S. military's prospective move to Pyeongtaek was first announced, however, that development inspired a continuing wave of protests. They were led by the "386" generation activists from Seoul, raised in the struggle for democracy against military regimes of the 1980s, with which the United States had been once allied.[4]

Many of Korea's powerful new nongovernmental organizations (NGOs), such as People's Solidarity for Participatory Democracy (PSPD) and Green Korea United, have been stridently aligned against the bases. And public sympathy has been thin for those bases since the tragic deaths in the summer of 2002 of two young Korean schoolgirls, crushed in a military road accident later graphically publicized over the Internet. Korean feelings toward the bases have also been cooled by trends in geopolitics—especially deepening ties with China, a traditional benefactor, and, since the June 2000 Pyongyang summit, the remarkable assumption of a benign North Korea, its nuclear and missile tests notwithstanding. Most observers doubt that Korean politics would smoothly allow the deployment of the troops based at Pyeongtaek anywhere outside the Korean peninsula, let alone to nearby strategic yet politically contentious locations like the Taiwan Straits.

In several Seoul opinion polls of 2004–2005, George W. Bush ranked as more of a threat to Korean security than Kim Jong-II—a novel development to American eyes and one that has not helped base relations. Behind this sentiment lies a complex of factors far beyond simple anti-Americanism: a sense of U.S. abandonment due to troop redeployments to Iraq and troop withdrawals from the DMZ; a sense of generational resentment by young, activist supporters of democracy; alleged American complicity in the 1980 Kwangju massacre by the prior military dictatorship; and a growing belief that America, through its military presence, has been perpetuating the division of Korea.

As if pressures from politics and economics were not enough, America's embattled garrisons in Korea are under siege from the cinematic world as well. One of Seoul's recent monster movies, *Guimul* (*The Host*), which drew a record audience of six million (one in eight South Koreans) in its first eleven days, has U.S. bases as its theme. It concerns a child-snatching mutant that rears up into Seoul out of the Han River, spawned by noxious gases generated by toxic fluid carelessly discharged from an American military base.[5]

Unfortunately the movie has a tiny, albeit badly distorted and sensationalized, basis in fact. The director of *Guimul*, Bong Joon-ho, claims to have based it on an incident in 2000 in which a mortician with the U.S. military was arrested over a discharge of formaldehyde into the Han. Although the incident was unfortunate, there was no lasting pollution—not to mention monsters. Yet the distortions, and the popularity of the film, are a sign of the times. Even Korea's environmental minister, Lee Chi-beom, was worried that the sentiments evoked by the movie might resonate with the protests of Green Korea United, and make it still harder to reach an environmental agreement on the newly vacated bases along the DMZ, such as Camp Sears.

To a remarkable degree, in sum, U.S. bases in Korea, as the Cold War finally winds down, have become embattled garrisons—besieged not by North Korean legions, their traditional foe, but instead by host-nation environmentalists, irate moviegoers, students, and even real estate developers coveting their choice urban land. The bases also endure crossfire between Washington and Seoul—between Pentagon strategists prioritizing defense transformation, and schizoid Korean politicians decrying American unilateralism while fearing abandonment. How long these Korean bases can survive and prosper in this frustrated whirlpool of conflicting emotions and judgments, as the memories of a common U.S.-Korean battle partnership fade and the dividends of bilateral interdependence yield to the greater attractions of China, is a deepening question—one that mirrors the lengthening shadows over America's embattled garrisons in the broader world.

BASES AS AN OUTGROWTH OF EMPIRE

Military bases on foreign soil, both in Korea and elsewhere, have a venerable history as an outgrowth of empire, dating back over two thousand years. Thucydides, for example, wrote of basing issues that emerged during the Peloponnesian Wars of the fifth century B.C.[6] The Persians and the Romans both prized bases controlling land-access routes to strategic locations as crucial to their imperial power, while the classic maritime empires, including Venice, Portugal, Spain, and Holland, likewise valued them, and vociferously fought over them.[7]

With the coming of the Industrial Revolution, and the supersession of sailing ships by steamers, the major powers became increasingly dependent on bases—again in the context of empire—as coaling stations for their fleets, and the era of transnational basing networks was born. The British, in particular, placed special priority on overseas bases as the linchpin of Pax Britannica. That mighty imperium ruled the waves for a full century, from the Napoleonic Wars through World War I.

As an island, seafaring nation, with over half of the registered shipping tonnage in the world by 1890,[8] and with far-flung colonies, Britain was critically dependent on control of the seas to sustain its imperial dominion. And naval bases—at Gibraltar, Simonstown at the Cape of Good Hope, Suez, Aden, Singapore, Heligoland, and Hong Kong, not to mention Portsmouth—were critical to that dominion. They were, in the words of First Sea Lord Sir John Fisher, "the keys that locked up the world."[9]

Apart from their role as strong points, quietly controlling the movement of rival fleets, bases were also important to the British in sustaining logistical and communications networks. These global networks imposed clear financial burdens, to be sure.[10] Yet they also allowed Britain to concentrate the Crown's capabilities at strategic points, and to draw on the considerable political-economic resources of colonies and allies to leverage its own strength.[11]

As geopolitical competition became global during the nineteenth and twentieth centuries, the nations that *lacked* extensive basing networks, while harboring great power aspirations, such as Russia and Germany, clearly suffered as a consequence. Without broadly dispersed naval ports, coaling stations, and ultimately airfields, it was hard for them to meet military strategist Carl von Clausewitz's prescription for victory: bring overwhelming force rapidly to bear.[12] Imperial Russia's absence of an adequate basing network was central, for example, in its historic loss to Japan at Tsushima in 1905, despite the czar's demonstrably greater underlying capabilities.[13] Imperial Germany's lack of a dominant fleet, despite its possession of a powerful army, was similarly responsible for the early loss of its African and Pacific colonies in World War I, echoing the colonial setbacks of the land-based French in the Napoleonic Wars a century earlier.

Until World War II, military bases existed almost exclusively within the context of formal empire. As Robert Harkavy points out, prior to that point there was little if any long-term stationing of forces by major powers on their allies' soil—even of naval and air bases. Some German use of Spanish and Italian bases in the late 1930s and early 1940s, together with Japanese access to Thai facilities, were among the rare exceptions.[14] The problem of base politics presented here, focusing as it does on the naturally delicate interaction of independent political systems on a matter of major strategic importance between them, is thus very much a contemporary one.

THE CHANGING STRATEGIC ROLE OF BASES

Over the centuries, foreign bases have filled a changing series of strategic and geopolitical functions. Beginning with simply assuring territorial control, they gained additional value in providing maritime supremacy. Then, as global communications and transportation improved, they played a crucial role in allowing world powers to flexibly and rapidly concentrate resources from diverse locations for national advantage on land, at sea, and, ultimately, in the air.

Following World War II, bases took on new political-economic functions, stabilizing national ties across both the Atlantic and the Pacific in ways that promoted trade and investment interdependence, as well as political-military alliance relations. During the Cold War, bases both supported nuclear deterrence and improved global communications and intelligence for the emerging space age. As America and its allies have grown ever more dependent on imported oil and resources, particularly since the 1970s, bases have helped to safeguard those flows. And since 9/11, new types of bases have become central to the deepening struggle against terrorism as well.

Historical experience suggests, as the following discussion indicates, that even though the narrow strategic and geopolitical functions of bases have changed greatly over time, they have consistently had an important—indeed, increasingly important—impact on political-economic life as a whole, especially in the industrialized world, and particularly since World War II. Bases in Europe and Northeast Asia have become a discreet, neglected, yet indispensable linchpin of global interdependence, reinforcing common expectations of the political-economic future. They do so by arresting, often subtly and imperceptibly, the primordial geopolitical and geoeconomic rivalries that have historically fueled cross-border suspicions and antagonism, and that in the absence of bases might well do so once again. This stabilizing impact on trade, investment, and broader cooperative interactions—particularly among the industrialized nations of North America, Europe, and Northeast Asia—is a key reason why overseas basing has persisted so long in the postwar world, and why bases in some form, and in some locations, have a potent long-term logic, in both strategic and political-economic terms.

DEEPENING DOMESTIC COMPLICATIONS

Yet there is a troubling domestic political shadow hanging over forward deployment, both in America and in host nations beyond our shores, especially in the developing world. The Korean case presented earlier in this chapter is only one sobering illustration. That shadow grows longer and deeper as memories of early postwar American magnanimity to host nations fade, and as resentments of American unilateralism correspondingly rise. Foreign bases, for all their importance in securing the complex fabric of global interdependence, involve the presence of one nation's military on another nation's soil, and are almost invariably unpopular at the grassroots for that reason. For average host-nation citizens, foreign bases present inconvenience, civic nuisance, and occasionally danger. For ordinary inhabitants in nations that themselves deploy troops abroad, sustaining such overseas outposts represents all too often a costly investment of blood and treasure, as recent American deployments in Iraq and Vietnam have made tragically clear.

Bases are also often vulnerable at the national political level, especially in developing nations where, since 9/11, they have grown ever more heavily concentrated.[15] This dualistic theme of strategic importance and political vulnerability—making bases truly "embattled garrisons"—is central to this volume as a whole.

This chapter has three objectives: (1) to illustrate the important yet changing geopolitical implications of forward deployment; (2) to clarify the embedded yet obscured institutional legacy for the world that basing networks create, which policymakers must now confront; and (3) to review lessons that history teaches regarding basing. The present chapter focuses particularly on the legacy for today's basing profile of empire, war, foreign occupation, and technological advance across the first nine decades of the twentieth century. That heritage of history profoundly shapes the challenges of post–Cold War and post–9/11 base politics that American decision makers, in particular, must now confront. In presenting that history of basing, this chapter illustrates the powerful ways in which the distant origins of foreign military presence, even if far removed in time, continue to shape the disposition of host nations to tolerate or oppose that presence long after the original catalytic events are past.

This chapter argues strongly that basing-nation strategy, driven by perceived geopolitical context, has a powerful hand in creating basing profiles at their outset.[16] Yet it also maintains that strategy becomes increasingly compromised by host-nation politics, both conservative and revolutionary, as the base life cycle proceeds. Even where technology and changing world conditions mandate more dynamic and flexible approaches, local concerns, ranging from embedded economic interests and fears of abandonment to demands for environmental clean-up, often make military base–transformation politically difficult. And strategy, however elaborately conceived and implemented, rarely anticipates the critical junctures, like the Korean War, the fall of the Berlin Wall, and the 9/11 terrorist attacks, that so profoundly shape the short-term political context within which long-term military decisions must inevitably be made.

BUILDING ON AN ANGLO-AMERICAN IMPERIAL FOUNDATION

The foundations of the contemporary global basing structure were laid most fatefully in London, two centuries ago and more. Britain, the first nation to maintain a truly worldwide military-basing network, desired forward garrisons in control of the seas, on which its leaders perceived their nation's economic livelihood—not to mention sovereignty itself—to depend. Britain is, after all, both an island, detached from the European continent by the moat of the English Channel, and a trading nation dependent on imported food and raw materials, paid for by exported manufactures. A global network of bases commanding the major approaches to strategic waterways was a natural objective of the British Empire, and a bulwark of Pax Britannica in its heyday.

Although the residue of the classic empires has in geopolitical terms largely dissipated, the physical heritage of British imperial basing decisions

still endures to a remarkable degree, centering on some remaining possessions of strategic significance. The massive Rock of Gibraltar still lies in
British hands, as it has since 1713; so do several tiny outposts of empire in
the South Atlantic, where the Union Jack landed during the Napoleonic
Wars, or soon thereafter.[17] Akrotiri and Dhelelia in Cyprus for nearly a
half-century post-independence have continued to play important logistical roles in supporting British Middle Eastern involvement, including the
extended 2003–2007 troop presence in southern Iraq.[18] Diego Garcia, a
British colony originally seized from Napoleonic France, now hosts one
of the most strategic American bases in the world, more than three thousand miles south of the Persian Gulf. Despite its location deep in the
Indian Ocean, Diego played crucial roles in the Gulf, Afghan, and Iraq
Wars—delivering 65 percent of all the ordnance dropped in the Afghan
conflict, for example.[19]

Perhaps the most important heritage of the British imperial preoccupation with basing was its strategic bequest to a wayward yet predestined
one-time colony: a tradition and a physical infrastructure to support the
massive American global presence that followed the United Kingdom's
own decline. America had the unique advantage, relative to Russia, Germany, Japan, and other substantial powers, of building on Britain's prior
basing structure—an often-neglected jump-start to Washington's sudden
postwar emergence as a global superpower.

Outside the British Isles, British facilities became a crucial backbone
for the American postwar basing network.[20] Of central and continuing
importance also, of course, were bases in the United Kingdom itself, dating from America's move to Britain's defense amidst the German Blitz of
World War II. After the war's end, such facilities as Mildenhall, later a
key Strategic Air Command (SAC) base, and Tylingsdale, the initial overseas station on the Distant Early Warning (DEW) Line, became crucial
links in the American system of global nuclear defense.[21]

Britain's bequest was made easier and more effective by the symmetry—
indeed, virtual congruence—in Anglo-American strategic goals. Both nations wanted a stable, open global order, with transcendent, transparent,
and predictable international rules, in which trade and cross-border investment could flourish.[22] A global basing network supports this essentially political-economic vision in many ways, as will be seen.[23]

Apart from Diego Garcia and bases in the British Isles, the United
States also inherited multiple British facilities in the Caribbean. These
were ceded by the British in 1940, to support Atlantic defense, providing
America with its first enduring overseas bases on purely foreign soil. In
return, the United Kingdom received fifty over-age destroyers and Lend-
Lease aid. The American facilities in Bahrain, Singapore, and Ascension,

where the United States long had a space-tracking station, were all like-wise descended from those of the British.

Other core American bases are directly descended from this country's own imperial experience. It began, like that of the British, with an important period of informal empire, primarily in the Pacific: expeditions to open Japan and Korea to foreign trade, together with the subsequent acquisition of Jarvis, Baker, and Howland Islands as coaling stations in 1857–58, and Midway in 1867. In another fateful development, the United States in 1884 acquired exclusive rights from the Hawaiian Kingdom to Pearl Harbor for use as an American naval base.[24] In all these cases, middle-range logistical and economic concerns appear to have been more important than grand strategy, which decisively emerged only much later, in driving American policy.

More formal efforts at establishing an American Empire date essentially back to the Spanish-American War of 1898.[25] Through that conflict, the United States acquired the Philippines, Puerto Rico, and one of the finest deep-water ports in the Caribbean, at Guantanamo Bay in Cuba. The war also provided impetus for the annexation of Hawaii, American Samoa, and Wake Island.[26] Five years later, in December, 1903, Theodore Roosevelt acquired rights to build the Panama Canal, with the option of building major bases in the vicinity to defend it. The American quest for empire was growing more articulate and strategically driven, spearheaded intellectually by Alfred Mahan, and politically by Theodore Roosevelt.[27]

Over the ensuing eighty years, as will be recounted elsewhere in this volume, the United States built the Philippine bases into one of its largest and most important military complexes anywhere in the world, employing nearly 70,000 Filipinos and 13,000 U.S. servicemen. Clark Field, established in 1903, grew to become the second largest U.S. airbase on earth, with an aviation-fuel storage capacity equivalent to that of Kennedy Airport in New York. Subic Bay, in turn, emerged as the largest American naval facility outside the United States.

In the Caribbean, meanwhile, the United States also developed a very substantial basing presence in Panama, involving 134 military installations and 69,000 U.S. troops at its peak in 1943.[28] Following World War II, the Truman administration desired to retain thirteen of these new bases, provoking riots in Panama City, and an unanimous rejection by the Panamanian National Assembly, as ambitious geostrategy ran headlong into resentful host-nation politics. Under continuing local nationalist pressure, fueled by Nasser's nationalization of the Suez Canal continents away, the American Canal Zone presence itself gradually receded to eleven bases by 1977, when an agreement to return the Panama Canal itself to Panama by the end of 1999 was signed.

The United States, of course, also maintained facilities in Puerto Rico, taken as a possession in the Spanish-American War, as well as the Guantanamo Naval Air Station in Cuba. After U.S. relations with Cuba deteriorated sharply following Castro's revolutionary triumph in 1959, Washington continued to pay rent to the Cubans. Yet it sharply refused Cuban calls for withdrawal, citing treaty rights to lease the base in perpetuity that it had voluntarily relinquished in the Philippines, for example. After the 9/11 attacks, as is well-known, the United States has used Guantanamo extensively and flexibly, and beyond the constraints of its own legal tradition, as a detention center for accused terrorists captured in Afghanistan and elsewhere. Complete host-nation rejection of normal base relations thus ironically proved useful to the Bush Administration in furthering its strategic purposes in the struggle against terrorism.

World War II and Base-Network Expansion

The massive American overseas basing presence of the present also has important roots in World War II, as well as in empire. The wartime origins appear to have been consistently strategic, although there was an important evolution from narrow political-military objectives at the outset to broader "milieu goals" as the war progressed. From the outbreak of the war in Europe, well over a year before the Japanese attack on Pearl Harbor, President Franklin D. Roosevelt feared German encroachment across the Atlantic, together with the more distant prospect of Nazi subversion in South America's Southern Cone. He strongly backed the establishment of American bases on eight British possessions in the Caribbean during 1940, and then additional facilities in Greenland (April 1941), and in Iceland (July 1941) following the German occupation of their mother country, Denmark, in the spring of 1941.[29] In 1943 Britain, and in 1944 the United States, also secured access to bases in the Portuguese Azores.[30]

Although Roosevelt's early strategic concerns initially centered on the Atlantic, he began to show much broader—indeed, global—strategic interests, not long after America's formal entry into the war. As early as December 1942, only a year after the attack on Pearl Harbor, Roosevelt began pressing the Joint Chiefs of Staff (JCS) to prepare proposals for an extended global network of bases for a prospective International Police Force with a strong American role, to be established at the end of the war.[31] As the prospect of America's postwar global dominance grew, so, too, did Roosevelt's perception that bases could be a stabilizing element in the emerging political-economic equation of both Europe and Asia, as well as a guarantor of an open, interdependent political-economic order, and a support for American aviation interests. By early 1945, Roosevelt appears to have understood the emerging strategic need for an American Middle Eastern presence to assure the global flow of energy resources as well.[32]

Among the most important strategic rationales for global basing over the past two centuries, as noted previously, has been the capacity it creates to rapidly and flexibly concentrate military resources at a desired "point of decision." This capacity proved important centuries ago at sea, as manifest in Britain's historic naval triumphs at Trafalgar and Jutland. Thanks to the presence of its warships at multiple dispersed points within sailing distance of one another, the Royal Navy was able to mass the overwhelming power needed to vanquish its most potent rivals of the day.

Basing grew even more vital in the air age, demonstrably so during World War II, as Roosevelt and his strategic advisors no doubt realized. Anglo-American victory prospects at el-Alamein, Normandy, and Okinawa, not to mention campaigns in later struggles, all were enhanced by the ability created by a global basing network consolidated during the war to concentrate worldwide military resources at the points of decision—from Midway and el-Alamein to Stalingrad, where they could prove crucial to victory. This global logistical capacity had broad implications that lingered long thereafter, in campaigns ranging from the Yom Kippur War of 1973 and the Gulf War of 1991 to the Iraq invasion of 2003 and the Sumatran tsunami relief operation of 2005.

Apart from its impact on the intellectual evolution of American leaders, the course of World War II also propelled new physical realities: actual creation of the global basing infrastructure about which Roosevelt and the JCS strategized, extending the physical reach of the U.S. military worldwide. Continuing the wartime process of global basing-network expansion, "island hopping" across the Pacific, en route to victory against Japan, generated many new bases. That network was augmented at Guam, Saipan, Tinian, and then Okinawa so as to support the intensive bombing of Japan itself. By 1945 more than 44 percent of all American overseas military facilities worldwide were in the Pacific.[33]

Despite Roosevelt's early strategic bias toward the Atlantic, the exigencies of war had thus led to a nearly equivalent U.S. basing presence in the Pacific as well. This was enhanced further in the early postwar period by the American acquisition of former Japanese bases throughout the region, including major facilities at Truk, as Washington assumed custody of the Strategic Trust Territory of the Pacific Islands. The United States also established major bases in Japan and South Korea, connected with its occupations there.

The global reach of American forces and their basing network at war's end was stupendous. The United States had custody of over thirty thousand installations, located at two thousand base sites, in around one hundred countries and possessions, stretching from the Arctic Circle to Antarctica.[34] It deployed well over ten million troops at these facilities.

Matching the global sweep of America's military presence as the war wound to its turbulent close was an expanding conception of America's postwar international role. Roosevelt, despite a more subtle strategic sense than has often been appreciated, had consigned the maintenance of global order to the "Four Policemen" of the U.N. Security Council—the United States, Britain, Russia, and China—within their respective regional spheres. Truman, who succeeded Roosevelt in April 1945, believed more explicitly in American preeminence than did Roosevelt. The weakness of China and Britain, coupled with the truculence of Stalin's Russia, gave Truman little alternative.[35]

The emergence of international institutions, following the Bretton Woods Conference of 1944, strengthened the economic argument for overseas basing. Global institutions and an open world required an end to the bitter geopolitical rivalries in Europe and Asia that had fueled prewar mercantilism, and overseas American basing helped suppress those rivalries.[36] The deployment of American troops in Germany and Japan had the dual geo-political merit of reassuring those nations against traditional antagonists in Russia, France, and China, while conversely also moderating the apprehensions of those latter nations about Axis revanchism.

The official American early postwar stance toward the suddenly massive U.S. basing network of that period, intensified by nascent rivalry with the Soviet Union, was clear: that the network should be retained to the extent possible in order to support global system stability, and that further bases should also be acquired. Indeed, at the Potsdam Conference President Harry Truman explicitly endorsed the notion of a forward-deployed base network: "Though the United States wants no profit or selfish advantage out of this war, we are going to maintain the military bases necessary for the complete protection of our interests and of world peace. Bases, which our military experts deem to be essential for our protection, we will acquire. We will acquire them by arrangements consistent with the United Nations Charter."[37]

American geopolitical standing in world affairs had been transformed: from that of a middle power with narrow national interests to that of a great-power guarantor and guardian for global peace and stability. In that ambitious latter role, Washington needed foreign bases as never before—not only to defend strong points and handle military logistics, but also to inhibit traditional rivalries in Europe and Asia, ensure domestic stability there, assure access to needed raw materials, and guarantee an open world economic order.[38] Global basing had gained new political-economic functions, amplifying their strategic role, that were to have fateful long-term importance, especially in the trilateral world of advanced industrialized nations.

Postwar Retrenchment and Transformation

Despite the new ambitions of American diplomats and military strategists, however, the massive U.S. overseas basing presence of mid-1945 began to recede rapidly at war's end for three key reasons: other key allies, notably Labourite Britain, failed to support the concept, American domestic budgets were tight, and several prospective host nations declined to cooperate. Denmark in December 1946, for example, rejected American overtures to buy Greenland for basing purposes.[39] Iceland, where Left-oriented labor groups were strong, insisted, also late in 1946, on limiting American military forces' use of the Keflavik International Airport, which was simultaneously open to civilian traffic, to a strictly bounded tenure of only five years.[40] And the Panamanian National Assembly unanimously rejected proposals for a large expansion of American basing a few months later.[41]

Half of the American wartime basing structure was gone within two years of V-J Day, and half of what had been maintained until 1947 was gone by 1949.[42] As indicated in figure 1.1, the number of U.S. overseas base sites fell sharply, from 1,139 to 582, in just two postwar years of retrenchment: 1947–1949. In some parts of the world, including particularly Africa, the Middle East, and South Asia, vast wartime basing networks virtually disappeared, not to reemerge, if at all, until after 9/11.

The evolution of basing in the Middle Eastern, African, and South Asian regions, which were important in wartime desert, jungle, and submarine warfare, respectively, illustrate most clearly this dramatic retrenchment and transformation in the U.S. basing network. During the early stages of World War II, North Africa had been a major battlefield, with epic struggles at Tobruk, el-Alamein, and the Kasserine Pass being crucial way stations on the path to ultimate Allied victory. West Africa, like the Caribbean, was important in the "Battle of the Atlantic" against Axis submarines. Indian bases helped resupply China over the Himalayan "Hump," and also arrested Japanese westward expansion toward the Middle East. Similarly, Latin America was viewed as a potential collaborator in Nazi efforts to leapfrog the Atlantic.

After the war, however, such far-flung American outposts in developing nations were rapidly closed. As illustrated in figure 1.1, the number of U.S. bases in Africa, the Middle East, and South Asia *combined* fell by nearly 80 percent in only two years, from 177 in 1947 to just 30 in 1949. By 1953 they had dropped to only 17, and did not exceed that number

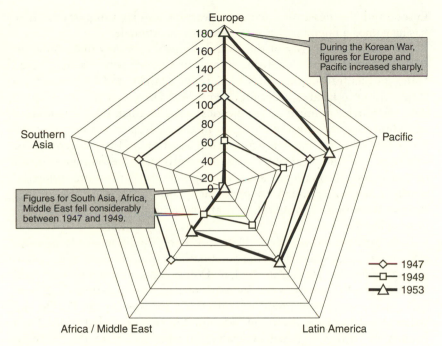

Figure 1.1. Transformation of the U.S. Overseas Base Structure,
1947–1953
Source: James R. Blaker, *United States Overseas Basing*, p. 32.

until after 9/11. Latin American bases likewise diminished in number
and importance.

Early postwar American strategists did, to be sure, see some value in
Third World bases, especially in India, the Middle East, and adjacent to
the Panama Canal.[43] Host-nation politics, however, made such bases
along the soft underbelly of the Soviet Union difficult to obtain. The
United States did indeed reopen Wheelus Air Base in Libya in December
1947, and retained its presence in Dhahran, Saudi Arabia. Yet it was
forced to relinquish prospects in India, Pakistan, and Burma, amidst
British Labourite opposition, and the turbulent transition of South Asia
to independence.

Occupation and its Residue

As figure 1.1 suggests, early American postwar strategy thus shifted decisively away from the developing world, despite some modest interest in the
Middle East.It prioritized instead the industrialized yet troubled nations of

Europe and Northeast Asia, where its wartime foes lay vanquished. There basing gained a fateful new political-economic rationale.

The current prosperity of the global political economy owes much to the remarkable transitions from enmity to alliance between the United States and its transoceanic foes in Germany, Japan, and Italy that were forged in this crucial half-decade after 1945. The predictability of those new yet crucial political-economic ties rests, in turn, on a foundation of military bases, with their origins in the early postwar occupations. Bases providing the implicit geopolitical sanction and reinforcement for otherwise abstract legal obligations have grown to become key sinews of transnational interdependence throughout the democratic industrial world. They have gained an enduring political-economic importance distinct from more ephemeral, and at times misguided, involvements in developing nations.

Early postwar basing developments were especially fateful in one distinctive group of countries—the four nations that the Americans occupied for extended periods in the late 1940s: Japan, Germany, Italy, and South Korea.[44] Each of these occupations had a highly strategic dimension, as the nations in question collectively constituted the Pacific and Atlantic pillars of the emerging Washington-focused global order. Each occupation, involving a historic transition from enmity to alliance, continued for at least three years, with enduring implications for both base politics in each nation and for the long-term U.S. global role.

Bases established through the occupations of Germany and Japan, in particular, were fateful geopolitically for their "dual containment" effects: neutralizing a potential security threat to the United States and surrounding neighbors, while also leveraging the U.S. role in relation to potential third-party adversaries. Bases in nations like Japan and Germany were geopolitically important to the overall stability of America's Atlantic and Pacific alliances—indeed, were a major factor in sustaining them—because they simultaneously reassured allies, raised the costs of alliance defection, and deterred serious military assault by third parties such as Russia and China.

As will be noted in chapter 2, very major shares of American base-facilities investment worldwide during the Occupation and Cold War periods—roughly half of all base investments in the entire world, war zones excepted—were made in Germany and Japan. Both countries, after all, were at once both past and prospective world powers. They had led the Axis challenge to Anglo-American global supremacy in World War II and were natural rivals to communist Russia and China, whom they had also fought bitterly in that global conflict. This chapter provides a short chronicle of the fateful evolution of basing structure in Germany and Japan during the Occupation period; a more detailed comparative assessment of the long-term implications of Occupation for base politics in each nation is provided in chapter 5.

Despite the fateful geostrategic significance of the early postwar Occupations and the basing structure they engendered, particularly in creating the physical presence that later stabilized political-economic ties among the core noncommunist industrialized nations, those occupations initially coincided with a major drawdown of American forces abroad. Even after relations with the Soviet Union began to deteriorate during 1946–47, and even after State Department Policy Planning Director George Kennan enunciated the initial doctrine of containment, America's strategic emphasis continued to focus on limited "strong points"—shaping a positive balance of power in key areas of the industrialized world—rather than on extensive perimeter defense.[45] Even on the very borders of the communist world, the U.S. basing posture—and, indeed, American aspirations to sustained offshore presence in the late 1940s—was, by later Cold War standards, remarkably minimal, the April 1949 establishment of NATO notwithstanding.

The modest and hesitant early postwar development of a U.S. military presence in Europe, contrasting so strangely to expansive, globalist notions of the wartime years, was a striking manifestation of this minimalism. It also contrasted incongruously with the clear priority that both defense planners and diplomats ascribed to stability and prosperity on the Continent. General Carl Spaatz, commander of the U.S. Strategic Air Forces in Europe, for example, was a strong advocate of European bases within the government from 1944 onward, but he was restrained from public expression of his views by superiors, who feared diplomatic complications, especially with the Soviet Union.[46]

Secretary of State James Byrnes did announce in September 1946 that American troops would remain in Germany, where their presence was not diplomatically controversial, for an extended period. Yet the broader trend on the ground was toward numerical retrenchment. The concept of an interdependent economic order, the notion of powerful forward-deployed forces in Europe to assure it, and the idea of a trans-Atlantic alliance to legitimate such novel arrangements had not yet emerged.

On V-E Day in May 1945, the United States had sixty-nine divisions on German soil, totaling more than two million men.[47] With the Pentagon calculating that three quarters, or 1.5 million, should be transferred to the Pacific to assure the defeat of Japan, drawdown in Europe began almost immediately. And that drawdown continued steadily until mid-1950, the Berlin Blockade, the Czech coup, and the formation of NATO notwithstanding.[48]

By June 1950, the American military presence in Germany had thus been reduced to a skeleton force of 75,000—less than one-twentieth of its strength only five years earlier. That minimal garrison was mainly engaged in residual de-Nazification and local government-promotion efforts. Indeed, the United States saw its prospective future military role within NATO largely as providing air and naval forces in an emergency, with the Europeans, predominantly the French, responsible for ground forces.

With respect to Asia, America's early postwar vision was also remarkably limited. Top U.S. military leaders, including both Joint Chiefs of Staff Chairman George Marshall and Supreme Commander of the Allied Powers Douglas MacArthur, did have a strong early priority: American bases in the Ryukyu Islands, particularly Okinawa, as a means of maintaining influence over Japan, and indeed across the Western Pacific as a whole.[49] George Marshall foresaw potential turbulence around the Yellow Sea, which washes the shores of Shandong and the Korean peninsula, and stressed the potential value of an enduring American presence in the Ryukyus as early as July 1945, less than a month after hostilities ended there.[50] By October 1945 the JCS collectively also made clear that Okinawa and all Japanese mandated territories, for control of which American troops had fought so bitterly only months before, would remain under U.S. "strategic control."[51] Yet neither Marshall nor any other major American military strategist mentioned permanent bases on the home islands of Japan.

The State Department did not even foresee the prospect of bases in the Ryukyus. Its first draft of a possible peace treaty with Japan, completed in March 1947, made absolutely no provision for bases in either the Japanese home islands or Okinawa.[52] As with respect to Germany, State envisioned a short, punitive period of occupation. This was to involve an extensive purge of those complicit in the war effort and a clear dismantling of the Japanese war machine, followed by a restoration of independence once those transformational objectives were achieved. MacArthur, effectively the viceroy of Japan, spoke of making it the "Switzerland of the Pacific," and imposed a radical "no-war" constitution to further that idealistic aim.

State Department and Pentagon advisors in Washington began to gradually embrace the notion of defensive bases in Japan from 1947–48 on. Yet MacArthur would not even consider the notion of permanent bases there until after the fall of China in late 1949. By December 1949 President Harry Truman had agreed to the concept of a Japanese peace treaty without Soviet participation; by removing a crucial prospective veto, this in turn opened the clear possibility of long-term Japanese bases. Even then, the notion of exactly what concrete American basing presence might be politically viable in Japan remained in flux when communist forces crossed the 38th Parallel in June 1950.

Curiously, in the hindsight of history, the United States did not entertain the prospect of a permanent military presence—or any major presence at all—in Korea. Indeed, in April 1948 President Harry Truman explicitly endorsed the JCS assessments of the previous fall that the United States had "little strategic interest in maintaining its present troops and bases in Korea," noting that the Occupation forces "could well be better used elsewhere."[53] In October 1948, George Kennan emphasized at the National War College that positions on the Asian land mass were not fundamental to U.S. national security, whose principal concern needed to be the industrial rim lands of Eurasia: Western Europe and Japan.[54] As the culmination in this line of thinking, Secretary of State Dean Acheson's explicit exclusion of Korea from the U.S. defense perimeter in January 1950, months after European defense configurations were clearly cast with the foundation of NATO, is often viewed as having provided implicit encouragement for Kim Il-Sung to launch the Korean War itself.

Enduring Shadows of the Korean War

It may well have been that World War II made the United States truly a global military power, as also that the British Empire had created the skeleton for America's global presence. Yet it was the Korean War, combined with the intellectual framework provided by State Department Policy Planning Director Paul Nitze's fateful National Security Council (NSC) memorandum 68, which added real scale to U.S. Cold War forward deployment. That fateful conflict also linked forward deployment firmly to the emerging notions of postwar alliance, and began to make an interdependent political-economic order a reality among the noncommunist industrial nations.

On June 25, 1950, the North Korean People's Army punched across the 38th Parallel, beginning a three-year conflict in which U.S. forces suffered 140,000 casualties, including 33,000 dead.[55] This sudden surprise attack, coming in the midst of the sweeping global drawdown in American troop strength just described, triggered a full-fledged reassessment of the minimalist notions of U.S. overseas military presence that had previously prevailed. It also forced a rethinking of how forward deployment was linked to the stability and prosperity of the broader political-economic order. Preconceived force deployment strategies seemed of little use at this critical juncture, opening the way for politics, in both host and basing nations, to play new and unexpected roles in transforming base configurations.

The Korean War consolidated the global framework of American forward deployment in two important ways. First, it emphatically resolved previous debates, discussed earlier, as to whether the United States should protect only vital "strong points," as Kennan had maintained, or oppose communism on every front, as Nitze had insisted—in favor of Nitze. More generally, the Korean War also established that there could be conventional war in the nuclear age, a sobering realization that once again turned the attention of American strategists to overseas ground-force deployments.[56] Yet the outbreak of war unfortunately did not provide a clearly articulated, forcefully argued, or operationally plausible framework for dealing with the grave emerging crisis.[57] And many, including President Harry Truman, perceived that crisis, especially following the massive Chinese intervention of November 1950, potentially to be the onset of World War III.[58]

Just as importantly, from a political-economic standpoint, the Korean War, and the NSC-68 interpretation of its significance, triggered creation of the "San Francisco System" of asymmetric economic relations. This new framework bound the major East Asian allies of the United States, like those in Europe, to Washington by opening the U.S. market to the products of American allies, and by conversely encouraging American investment in their promising industrial futures. One of the key quid pro quos was acceptance of U.S. bases, a development which also consolidated investor interest in the fragile yet promising political economies of Europe and Northeast Asia.[59]

NSC-68 was ultimately to play that crucial role of rallying the country and giving its new cause operational definition. This sixty-six-page, single-spaced document, completed April 4, 1950, was drafted by a small, ad hoc committee of State and Defense Department officials, chaired by Paul Nitze. It nominally adhered to Kennan's pragmatic containment doctrine, yet it fatefully redefined the concept. While Kennan had argued that keeping major centers of military-industrial capacity out of adversarial hands was the only prerequisite to maintaining a favorable global balance of power in the world, NSC-68 argued, in contrast, that any substantial expansion of unfriendly power *at all* was dangerous.[60]

NSC-68 called, in a word, for the globalization of containment, with the observation that "a defeat of free institutions anywhere is a defeat everywhere."[61] The notion echoed across the years, to the inaugural address of John F. Kennedy and beyond to the collapse of the Berlin Wall, becoming a classic statement of American Cold War ideology. In this sense, NSC-68 was also the intellectual underpinning of the expansive concept of American security responsibilities that led to global basing in later years.

In laying the strategic basis for later large-scale U.S. foreign deployments, and for a related deepening of transoceanic-alliance ties, NSC-68's contribution is important to our story here. Its most persuasive argument was a two-part contention: that Soviet political-military capacities were rapidly rising, and that they would soon enable the U.S.S.R. to intimidate, or potentially even attack, American allies, should Allied capabilities themselves not sharply rise. NSC-68 projected, for example, that the Russians by 1954 would possess enough atomic bombs to devastate the United States. Moscow could thereby achieve overwhelming conventional weapons superiority in the Cold War, absent a substantial new Allied buildup combined with a comprehensive perimeter defense of Allied positions.[62]

The brutal, sudden North Korean thrust across the 38th parallel in mid-1950 gave immense new credibility to NSC-68. That brief but forceful document had previously been highly controversial within the U.S. government, as it appeared to confirm a dark yet debated view of communist expansionist tendencies. The combined effect of the war—which many saw as the opening shot of World War III—and the hawkish, controversial new strategic document penned by Nitze and his colleagues was to send military spending sharply upward, and to stimulate serious thinking about ambitious new American deployment patterns overseas. The final congressional defense authorization for fiscal 1951, for example, swelled to a massive $48.2 billion—a 257 percent increase over the original Truman Administration request of $13.5 billion.[63]

NSC-68 had an especially powerful impact on strategic thinking regarding European deployments, and their relation to the NATO alliance, because it so starkly and persuasively presented the challenge of rising Soviet nuclear and conventional capabilities along that crucial front. American troops in Europe were a crucial means of cementing alliance collaboration against this Soviet threat, while also containing a resurgent Germany. The American presence was, in a word, a means of "keeping the Russians out, the Americans in, and the Germans down."[64] It also had a political-economic dimension, in helping reduce the risk to global investors willing to bet on Europe's uncertain future. Forward deployment in Europe thus played a key role in creating the dynamic capital flows that have been at the heart of post–World War II global economic recovery.

Beyond the arcane details of strategy and finance, there is no question that, at the elemental public level, the dramatic events of June 1950 had a catalytic effect throughout the Western world. "Korea," as John McCloy put it, "brought Europe to its feet."[65] New European anxieties resonated deeply with those in Washington.

After the Senate's "Great Debate" on global security in the winter of 1950–51, four additional divisions were dispatched to Europe to strengthen NATO—the beginning of an expanded troop commitment that continues to this day, although one that has been gradually modified by defense transformation.[66] In February 1952, the Lisbon meeting of the North Atlantic Council pledged a NATO expansion to eight-nine divisions by the end of 1954. Although never achieved, this decision signaled a commitment to European rearmament, in response to the Korean experience, which reinforced the growing American trans-Atlantic presence, both military and economic, as a counterweight to the Soviet Union.

In the Pacific, the Korean War had four major implications for U.S. base presence, apart from the global considerations discussed earlier. Most importantly, it confirmed Japan as the fulcrum of U.S. policy in the region.[67] Even before the war began, American policymakers such as George Kennan and Joseph Dodge had decided that both U.S. security and American economic interests required an economically strong Japan, rather than a broken, subjugated society. The Korean conflict reinforced that notion, and aided Japan's revival through massive wartime procurements and support for its economic recovery through access to the U.S. market.[68] In addition, American bases played an important supporting role in the war, obliterating earlier sentiment for abandoning them.

The Korean War also reinforced the earlier Pentagon emphasis, dating back to 1945 and even before, on Okinawan bases. During the war, the United States extensively developed such bases, taking over 40,000 acres, or 13 percent of Okinawa's total land area, for that purpose.[69] As in mainland Japan, the basic profile of U.S. bases in Okinawa was established during this period. And it proved to be even more enduring.

Thirdly, the Korean War led to direct American involvement in the Taiwan Straits. Soon after the war began, the United States sent the Seventh Fleet into the Straits, preventing a communist attack on Taiwan. The Korean conflict thus indirectly resolved disputes within the Truman administration about American support for Chiang Kai-Shek, leading toward direct defense commitments to Taiwan.

A final impact of the Korean War in the Pacific was to give birth to the "hub-and-spokes" alliance structure of bilateral security treaties, which established the international legal foundation for U.S. base access. The war provoked early conclusion of the San Francisco Peace Treaty, embedding strong, asymmetrical economic support measures for Japan's recovery that later broadened to other Asian allies, and interacted synergistically with base presence to promote trade, investment, and prosperity. In 1951 the United States also signed treaties with Japan, the Philippines, Australia, and New Zealand.

These understandings were followed by similar treaties with South Korea in 1953, and with Taiwan in 1954.[70] Although security-oriented, these treaties also strengthened the broader framework of trans-Pacific political-economic integration, of which the bases were a linchpin. By reassuring both allies and potential adversaries, while simultaneously encouraging the revival of transnational trade and investment, the bases and the security treaties in combination thus played a fundamental role in stabilizing the postwar global political-economic order.[71]

The onset of war in Korea also gave new reality to another function for American bases: strategic deterrence.[72] Spurred by an increasingly visible communist challenge, the United States began systematically building Strategic Air Command (SAC) air bases around the rim of the U.S.S.R—in Europe, the Arctic regions, the Pacific, and the Middle East.[73] During the ensuing decade, Washington concluded twenty-one strategic air base agreements with Allied nations, to secure bases in far-flung areas including Morocco (1950); Greenland (1951); Saudi Arabia and Libya (1951); Japan and Norway (1952); Greece, Turkey, and Spain (1953); Italy (1954); and Iceland (1956).[74] The number of U.S. overseas SAC bases soared from one in 1950 to thirty by 1957, before declining to twenty in 1960, as strategic bombers began to be replaced in the American arsenal by intercontinental ballistic missiles (ICBMs).[75]

The rationale for the proliferation of American strategic bomber bases overseas during the 1950s was clear: strategic bombers had the longest operating radius of any American weapon. They could strike the prospective Soviet enemy more rapidly and destructively than any other military force.[76] During the early Cold War period, only intermediate-range bombers such as the B-47, with a range of just over 4,000 miles, could reach the interior of the U.S.S.R., and they could do so from European, East Asian, and Middle Eastern bases. The urgency of this task and the life-and-death importance of deterring the Russians, were intensified by the mammoth scale of the Red Army, comprising 175 divisions in the early 1950s, or 3 to 6 million soldiers, many poised in Central Europe.[77] Its scale dwarfed that of U.S. forces, which were, in addition, simultaneously at war in Korea, which the Soviets were not. A nuclear deterrent—made credible by the existence of SAC bases within striking distance of the Soviet Union—was thus the crucial equalizer, especially during the "New Look" years of pessimism regarding the East-West conventional balance, before the Sino-Soviet split, and before NATO mobility and alliance structure had been fully consolidated.[78]

Safeguarding Resource Flows

The steady decline in America's Third World basing between 1945 and 9/11, interrupted episodically by the Korean and Indochina Wars, disguised a deepening U.S. involvement in the Middle East. Although the United States did not itself become a major oil importer until the 1970s, concern for the energy security of European and Japanese allies—not to mention the welfare of American multinational corporations that supplied them—was a dominant concern from the beginning. And in the early postwar years the military had a stake also: between 30 and 42 percent of the petroleum products moved by the U.S. Navy during 1946–50 came from the Persian Gulf, which also fueled America's military during the Korean War.[79] This resource dependence, together with President Harry Truman's concerns about a possible Soviet drive toward the Gulf, led to the 1947 establishment of the U.S. Navy's base at Bahrain, also the site of America's most venerable Middle East oil concession, and the Navy's main outpost in the region to this day.

American firms have been centrally involved in mediating both the substantial oil flows from the Middle East to Europe and Asia, as well as energy shipments directly to the United States itself. Although the British were preeminent politically in the Persian Gulf until well after World War II, American oil companies were active in Bahrain, Saudi Arabia, Kuwait, and Iraq by the early 1930s, and the U.S. government actively supported them in gaining economic access.[80] Although British-dominated Iran remained the source of two-thirds of Persian Gulf oil, American participation in the Iraq Petroleum Company and control of Bahraini and Saudi concessions, showed a powerfully growing American economic interest in the region.[81]

The economic scale of the Middle Eastern oil industry grew rapidly from the late 1930s, with Persian Gulf refinery capacity growing 89 percent between 1938 and 1944. American strategic understanding that Middle Eastern oil would be important in the postwar world, however, lagged considerably behind emerging economic realities, and seems not to have surfaced clearly until 1943–44. In February 1944, a Petroleum Administration for War (PAW) technical report, for example, labeled the Persian Gulf "the center of gravity" for future global oil development— one of the early such manifestations of geoeconomic consciousness in Washington.[82] The State Department similarly called for the "conservation of Western Hemisphere petroleum reserves," concurrent with the substantial and orderly expansion of Middle Eastern production, in late 1943 and early 1944.[83]

The first linkage between American strategic consciousness of Middle Eastern oil and actual Middle Eastern basing occurred during February 1945, when President Roosevelt's shipboard meeting with King Abdul Aziz of Saudi Arabia on the U.S. heavy cruiser *Quincy* laid the groundwork for the American air base at Dhahran. This President Truman explicitly approved in September 1945. Originally intended as a link between Cairo and Karachi in the redeployment of American forces to the Far East after the defeat of Germany, Dhahran grew and prospered as a SAC base for bombing runs against the Soviet oil fields in Baku and also demonstrated American military support of the vulnerable, but oil-rich, Saudi regime.[84]

The JCS, to be sure, in February 1946 advised avoiding Middle Eastern military commitments, despite Soviet pressure on British positions in the region.[85] But the Sixth Fleet was created to show American presence in the eastern Mediterranean later the same year. Truman's concerns about a possible Soviet drive toward Middle Eastern oil—intensified by the 1946 Iran crisis—also rapidly triggered establishment of the naval base at Bahrain, as noted above.

America's appreciation of the strategic importance of Middle East oil deepened rapidly during 1947–48, as domestic energy shortages began to emerge in the United States itself, due, ironically, to heavy exports to war-ravaged, but recovering, European nations. Secretary of the Navy (and later Defense) James Forrestal played a key role in catalyzing this new strategic sentiment, arguing that Middle Eastern oil would be important not only in wartime, but in peacetime as well. The Marshall Plan for Europe, he contended, could not succeed without Middle East oil, and the United States would find itself short two million barrels a day if a World War III were to break out.[86]

For nearly two decades after World War II, American strategic interest in Middle Eastern bases, apart from the resource dimension, was strengthened by their proximity to the Soviet Union. Dhahran in Saudi Arabia, together with bases such as Incirlik in Turkey,[87] provided unparalleled access to the U.S.S.R.'s vital but vulnerable underbelly in the oil fields of Azerbaijan and Ural industrial sites, for both potential military action and also surveillance. Indeed it was to that southern Turkish base that Gary Powers was scheduled to fly on his ill-fated U-2 espionage flight of May 1960, when he was shot down over Sverdlovsk. Only with the coming of ICBMs, like the Atlas missile, and satellite surveillance during the 1960s, did this strategic function of American Middle Eastern air bases in the Cold War conflict begin to decline.

American dependence on imported oil began to rise sharply in the early 1970s, as indicated in figure 1.2, while the macroeconomic effects of this increased dependence intensified sharply during 1973–74 via a tripling in the price of oil. This "oil shock," and the concomitant Yom Kippur War, where U.S. forces encountered unprecedented logistical and political difficulties resupplying a newly endangered Israel, led to major intensification of American interest in a Middle Eastern strategic presence. In 1967, following the Six Day War, the United States had home-ported its Sixth Fleet flagship in Gaeta, Italy;[88] it sharply augmented this presence by moving to "home-port" elements of the Sixth Fleet, including an aircraft carrier, in Piraeus, Greece, during the early 1970s, as it did simultaneously in Yokosuka, Japan.[89]

Figure 1.2. America's Rising Oil Import Dependence: Stimulus to Deepened Middle East Commitments?

Sources: U.S. Department Of Energy, *Energy Statistics Of OECD Countries*; and Anthony H. Cordesman, "The USCENTCOM Mission and History," Washington, D.C.: Center for Strategic and International Studies, April 1998.

The Pentagon also accelerated construction of the Diego Garcia airbase and logistics port in the Indian Ocean during the 1970s, clearly driven by the increasing strategic importance of resource security. Diego, after all, lies only 3,000 miles south of the Persian Gulf. The Nixon administration's major efforts to enhance resource security in the Middle East, however, were focused narrowly on promoting the Shah of Iran as a regional proxy for U.S. power. Washington concentrated initially on arming his forces, as proxy guardians of U.S. interests in the Gulf, rather than developing an independent American–Middle Eastern basing network to directly protect the flow of oil.

Three critical junctures, however, forced a sharp revision in this indirect approach during the Carter administration. The Iranian Revolution of early 1979, followed closely by the Soviet invasion of Afghanistan, and another spiraling of global oil prices all led to a sharp American strategic reassessment of how it might best assure national security in an increasingly turbulent, yet geoeconomically vital, Middle East.[90] With the Shah gone, and the Soviets threatening, President Jimmy Carter in

January 1980 declared that "any attempt by an outside force to gain control of the Persian Gulf region will be regarded as an assault on the vital interests of the United States of America."[91]

To back up the new Carter Doctrine, President Carter explicitly called for the establishment of additional basing facilities in the Gulf to protect the flow of oil, setting the stage for the extensive American basing network that now characterizes the region. The Rapid Deployment Joint Task Force (RDJTF) was established at McDill Air Force Base in Tampa, Florida, later in 1980 to augment rapid power-projection into the region. It was supplemented institutionally by creation of the United States Central Command (CENTCOM), also based at McDill, in 1983.

The Navy, as noted earlier, has traditionally been the heart of the Pentagon's Middle Eastern presence, ever since the establishment of the first U.S. naval base at Bahrain in 1947. The strategic importance of energy sea-lanes, the tactical flexibility of a naval presence, and the Navy's low political profile—an important factor in the region, given the political delicacy of U.S.-Arab relations since the birth of Israel—have all contributed to this naval prominence. After the fall of the Shah, naval power grew even more important as a tool of American power-projection in the Gulf insofar as the U.S. presence was distinctly limited on land. During the Iran-Iraq War of the 1980s, force levels of the Bahrain-based Middle East Force were increased substantially, from five to as many as forty naval vessels during Operation Earnest Will, a reflagging campaign of 1987–88.[92] This sort of long-distance power-projection proved to put substantial logistical strain on American naval forces, however, prompting increased Pentagon interest in expanded basing within the Middle East itself.[93]

After the Gulf War, with the increased regional legitimacy that America's liberation of Kuwait and the continuing threat of Saddam Hussein created within the Islamic world, the United States substantially expanded its direct Middle Eastern presence, as its overall energy-import dependence steadily rose. By 2000 there were typically 20,000–25,000 American military personnel present in the CENTCOM operational area at any given time, manning the no-fly zone over Iraq, detailed at sea with carrier battle groups, and otherwise deterring Iraq and Iran. These service people included 4,000 personnel at Prince Sultan Air Force Base, about sixty miles southeast of Riyadh, and 3,000 troops at Camp Doha in Kuwait. The U.S. ground presence was supplemented by an active program of joint exercises with Gulf Cooperation Council (GCC) states, and extensive prepositioning of war-reserve materials in Oman, Qatar, Kuwait, the UAE, and Bahrain.

The American Middle Eastern presence has been greatly enhanced, of course, since 9/11. The struggle against terrorism clearly led to overt

American intervention in Afghanistan, together with support activities in Uzbekistan, Kyrgyzstan, and elsewhere in Central Asia. Terrorism, in its potential relation to weapons of mass destruction, was nominally a major reason for intervention in Iraq, although the direct linkages have never been plausibly demonstrated. What can be clearly said is that oil provides a long-term geoeconomic rationale for a substantial network of bases in the Middle East, regardless of how the terrorist threat evolves.

Natural gas provides another energy-related reason for American political-military involvement in the Middle East. Qatar presents a striking case of bases protecting energy extraction and flows while also filling broader strategic functions: since March 2002, it has been the operational headquarters of all American military forces in the Middle East. Qatar hosts the state-of-the-art al-Udeid Airbase, built at a cost of $1.4 billion in the late 1990s, with a 14,760-foot runway, hardened concrete bunkers for 120 warplanes, and advanced telecommunications. Qatar also hosts the U.S. Army's largest stockpile of prepositioned war materiel anywhere in the world at Camp as-Sayliyah.[94] This facility simultaneously served as forward headquarters for General Tommy Franks, CENTCOM commander during the Iraq War of 2003.[95]

Together with being the literal heart of America's strategic presence in the Middle East, Qatar also lies astride the largest natural gas field in the world—the massive North Field of 900 trillion cubic feet.[96] It shares this field with Iran. Apart from this uncomfortable interdependence with the ayatollahs, Qatar's emir has ample reasons to want American bases nearby: his country has a population of only 800,000, including fewer than 200,000 Qatari citizens, and also a disputed border with well-armed Saudi Arabia. As the largest LNG producer in the world, with plans to produce nearly half as much energy by 2010 as Saudi Arabia,[97] at the massively capital-intensive Ras Laffan gas liquefaction complex, Qatar has at once immense potential and considerable vulnerability. Hence the logic—for both the United States and Qatar—of a large, risk-reducing American military presence that can simultaneously calm global energy markets and spur investment in the massive facilities that the modern, globalized LNG industry of the twenty-first century clearly requires.

THE INSTITUTIONAL IMPRINT OF THE COLD WAR AND RISING RESOURCE DEPENDENCE

The Korean War, as suggested above, led to a "globalization of containment," and a consolidation of America's Atlantic and Pacific alliances, in both their military and political-economic dimensions. Rising European and Northeast Asian resource dependence on the Middle East that in return relied upon sea-lanes defended by the United States intensified the community of interest among the industrialized democracies. These developments collectively meant a substantial, worldwide, and previously unanticipated buildup of U.S. forces overseas by the mid-1950s, accompanied by deepening trade and financial interdependence, that grew even more pronounced as reliance on Middle Eastern oil rose during the 1970s. To what extent have these buildups and transformations proven to be enduring? To what extent do they continue to shape the profile of U.S. forces overseas, and America's options for the future?

The sharpest effect of the Korean War on U.S. force strength, ironically, was in Europe, especially in Germany, rather than in Asia, where the armed conflict was actually taking place. By early 1950, as noted above, American troops in Germany had been reduced to 75,000, down from a full two million on V-E Day in 1945.[98] By 1952, following the outbreak of hostilities in Korea, these numbers had more than tripled from the meager pre-Korea base, and rose further, to 292,000 by 1961, as troops in Europe became more and more central to the Cold War trans-Atlantic alliance.

The U.S. troop presence in Europe declined marginally during the 1960s, especially following the outbreak of the Vietnam War. The United States redeployed forces to Asia, attempting to preserve deterrence on the European front through a dual-basing strategy (CONUS and Europe), involving major airlifts. Under the REFORGER exercises, which began in 1969 and continued until 1993, for example, the United States airlifted 50,000 men and 100,000 tons of equipment and supplies across the Atlantic in as little as sixty-two hours.

Changing communications and transportation technology began to subtly change the function and character of overseas bases during the late 1950s and the 1960s. As the world entered the space age, small, often unobtrusive communications ground stations and monitoring facilities—increasingly unmanned—became strategically important, and a new politics of concealment and unmasking emerged.[99]

SAC airbases in such locations as Saudi Arabia and Morocco, so vital to nuclear deterrence as long as America lacked alternative delivery systems, became, conversely, more dispensable, with the transition to long-range bombers like the B-52, submarine-launched ballistic missiles (SLBMs) beyond the Polaris, and the Atlas ICBM.[100] Flexible movement among bases, and distributing functions across plural facilities, became more possible, making the quality of the overall basing network more important, and any one facility within it less so.

Changing technology did, to be sure, give birth to new political-military complexities. European allies, fearing both abandonment and entrapment, were ambivalent about mobile American capabilities, and fluctuating "on-the-ground" commitments that evolving technology made increasingly possible. In the interest of alliance credibility, the United States thus continued to station well over 200,000 troops in Europe—as it had for four decades—until redeployment to the Middle East under Operation Desert Shield in 1990. Thereafter more than half of these troops returned stateside, with the Gulf War, rather than strategy per se, providing the political-economic catalyst for change in deployment patterns. American power-projection in the Middle East was largely provided by naval forces—the Gulf War interlude aside—until the fateful Afghan, Central Asian, and Iraqi interventions in the wake of 9/11.

The institutional heritage of the Korean conflict for the American military was broadly similar in Asia. On the eve of that bitter struggle, the United States had less than 150,000 troops deployed in the Far East as a whole, of which more than 115,000 were in Japan, and only a miniscule 510 in South Korea. The political-economic framework undergirding America's military presence lay undefined.

A mere three years later, at the end of the war, the United States had over 629,000 men deployed in East Asia. This included 326,800 in Korea and 185,000 in Japan.[101] And Washington had established, through the San Francisco Treaty, commerce and navigation arrangements, and related aid programs a comprehensive political-economic order to both cement long-term relations and stimulate economic revival.

The major U.S. land commitment in Korea itself, of course, has continued to this day, although the number of American troops deployed has been gradually reduced.[102] So, too, has the air and naval presence in mainland Japan, reinforced by the only aircraft carrier deployed outside American territory. And a major rapid-deployment presence remains in Okinawa as well.[103] Together, these forces serve as a major stabilizing element in the geoeconomic profile of the Pacific Rim as a whole.

Ironically the U.S. military presence in the Japanese homeland, which had never been seriously contemplated by American strategists before the Korean War, has become one of the most stable, substantial, and strategically important American offshore military deployments in the world. By September 2005, the replacement value (PRV) of U.S. bases in Japan had reached over $34 billion—the most of any nation in the world except Germany and the United States itself.[104] And the scope of their operations had become global, reaching to Diego Garcia, Afghanistan, Iraq, and beyond. How that remarkable configuration came to be, and what it means for global affairs, is a matter of fateful worldwide geopolitical and strategic importance, to which we will return in future chapters.

IN CONCLUSION: LESSONS FROM HISTORY

Apart from the enduring institutional heritage that history has bequeathed to contemporary base politics, it offers important lessons for the conduct of future base politics as well. Some of the most important include these maxims:

1. INDIVIDUAL BASES HAVE MULTIPLE POTENTIAL STRATEGIC FUNCTIONS, AND THE RELATIVE IMPORTANCE OF GIVEN FUNCTIONS SHIFTS OVER TIME. In Roman days, for example, territorial control was the principal function of bases. For the British in the nineteenth century, by contrast, control of the seas was preeminently important. For the U.S. military in the Cold War, bases filled dual functions, as operational *staging areas,* and as tools of *strategic deterrence.* From the 1970s onward, assuring the security of resource flows, especially from the Middle East, has become vital. And since 9/11, the role of bases as staging areas and support locales for antiterrorist operations has grown increasingly important also.

2. THE EVOLVING STRUCTURE AND FUNCTION OF BASES ARE SHAPED PROFOUNDLY BY THE SYSTEM STRUCTURE OF THE INTERNATIONAL POLITICAL REGIME. In an era of bipolar rivalry—U.S.-Soviet during the Cold War, or British-German before World War I, for example—the geopolitical role of bases in establishing control of the air and sea can be crucial. For Britain, for example, bases at Gibraltar after 1713, or Heligoland after 1866, were important in sustaining its global strategic position, just as bases in Greenland, Iceland, or the Fulda Gap in Germany reinforced the American strategic position in the Cold War after 1950. During the post–Cold War period, by contrast, sea and air control (or denial) have become relatively less important, in military terms, than they were previously. Instead, a capacity for *rapid intervention* has become increasingly crucial due to antiterrorist concerns. The revolution in military affairs (RMA) also, of course, affects the utility of individual bases. Broadly speaking, there is a need for more and "lighter" bases, with many distributed across remote, sparsely governed parts of the developing world.

Some high-tech coordinating centers, such as the Combined Air Operations Center (CAOC) at Prince Sultan Air Base in Saudi Arabia during the Afghan War, or the Qatar Joint Operations Center during the Iraq War, have clearly become more vital.[105] Static defense facilities in relatively peaceful parts of the world, by contrast, have grown less active, although not necessarily less important. Yokota Air Force Base, in the suburbs of Tokyo, presents a good example of how changes in global system structure can preserve the importance of even a militarily obsolete base, provided that base personnel and their commanders are alert to the potential for functional change.

Originally a requisitioned Japanese Imperial Army facility, converted to U.S. military use within three weeks of Japan's surrender, Yokota played a major role during the Korean War as a primary staging point for B-29 bombers, reconnaissance squadrons, and fighter planes.[106] In November 1974 Yokota became the headquarters of both U.S. Forces Japan (USFJ), the command center for all branches of the U.S. military in Japan, and of the U.S. Fifth Air Force, controlling U.S. air power in both South Korea and Japan. The air base was refurbished in 2001–2002, at a cost of roughly $40 million to the Japanese government.[107] Yet its military role has become marginal, relative to such other major facilities as the nearby Yokosuka Naval Base, homeport to a U.S. aircraft carrier, or to Kadena Air Force Base in Okinawa.

Yokota Air Base remains a vital U.S. military facility, however, due to the *administrative* and *diplomatic roles* that it plays. Apart from its central role in interservice coordination within the U.S. military in Japan, Yokota is within a half hour by helicopter of the Japan Self-Defense Forces headquarters and the U.S. Embassy in Tokyo. It is also a convenient refueling stop for members of Congress and other high-ranking U.S. government officials en route from Washington, D.C., to various parts of Asia on U.S. government aircraft, giving it important educational and networking functions in U.S.-Japan relations as well.

3. CRITICAL JUNCTURES CRUCIALLY SHAPE BASING PROFILES—OFTEN FOR LONG PERIODS AFTER THOSE FLUID PERIODS OF INSTITUTIONAL AND POLICY CHANGE HAVE COME TO AN END. Of all the fateful critical junctures of the past century, the 1943–45 and 1950–53 periods probably shaped global basing profiles most profoundly, with consequences that persist to this day. As has been noted, during these fateful periods, the core of the current U.S. basing network, including beachheads in continental Europe and Northeast Asia, was established for the first time. The 1943–45 period, at the climax of World War II, also gave rise to the massive Soviet forward-deployed presence in Eastern and Central Europe. That presence would persist largely undisturbed, as the fruits of a pyrrhic victory, for more than a half-century thereafter. The post-9/11 years are also transforming the American overseas-basing presence in important ways, as evidenced by both the Afghan and Iraqi Wars, and the Bush administration's August 2004 global force-transformation proposals.[108] Those initiatives are both realigning American forces in key allied nations, to enhance deterrent capabilities, and also bringing large numbers of troops home from overseas deployments outside the Middle East.

4. DEPLOYMENT PATTERNS TEND TO BE CONSERVATIVE. Once overseas bases are established—normally during a war, or in its immediate aftermath—they tend to be remarkably durable, regardless of how the actual functions of those bases evolve. Even when military technologies, economic capacities, or geopolitical alignments change, bases and the prerogatives embedded with them tend to remain, at least in the short term. Only host-nation regime shifts typically produce major short-run changes in deployment patterns, although changes in international system structure create pressures for change in deployments—post–Cold War downsizing, for example—over longer periods of time.

History provides numerous examples of the remarkable persistence of basing facilities, even where local populations are ambivalent regarding their presence. U.S. bases have remained in Iceland, for example, for the better part of six decades since 1941, despite frequent motions of disapproval in the Althing, or local parliament, and despite the obsolescence of the bases' long-time mission of antisubmarine warfare. Similarly, the U.S. Marine presence has persisted in Okinawa since 1945, with substantial ongoing Japanese government financial support, despite considerable local opposition and a strategic mission that could be performed more efficiently from a large number of alternate locations.

Transformation in basing patterns, in sum, is never easy, absent major host-nation political upheavals—even when the technological rationale for change may be strong. There are exceptional cases, to be sure, when the patterns of the past are suspended, but they are truly rare. It is thus generally within the straitjacket of history, and the institutions it bestows, that statesmen must work to fashion better policies for the future. It is far easier to change functions at existing bases than to move bases themselves.

CHAPTER TWO

DEEPENING VULNERABILITY

CHANGING PROFILES OF FORWARD DEPLOYMENT AND IMPLICATIONS FOR POLICY

MILITARY BASING, as history demonstrates repeatedly, tends to have a conservative bias. Once bases are established, generally in the heat of major conflict, they tend to remain for long periods of time. Inertial bureaucratic and political forces, operating on a logic akin to Newton's second law of thermodynamics, cause bases to continue in motion, once conflict has initiated or rationalized them, until stopped by some more powerful outside force.

Yet foreign bases are buffeted by winds of change, their physically unassailable profile notwithstanding. This chapter surveys those pressures, and the transformations they impel, especially developments of the momentous post–Cold War years. It does so in an effort to better weigh the policy challenges and choices now emerging.

Focusing ultimately on emerging options for the United States, this chapter begins with a more general comparative perspective. That panorama places America's current dilemmas in sustaining and reordering its basing empire in the context of broader global trends. America's embattled overseas garrisons, after all, stand to benefit from the wisdom and experience of others. While chapter 1 has outlined the institutional constraints that history imposes upon America's overseas basing, we now consider the converse process. We will survey how emerging political and technological pressures challenge the institutions of the past, creating new policy imperatives, like military transformation, together with subtle political barriers to their realization that need to be better understood.

THE SUNSET OF EMPIRE? COMPARATIVE PERSPECTIVES ON FOREIGN MILITARY BASING

Overseas basing, as noted in the previous chapter is, outside of the colonial context, largely a post–World War II phenomenon: it is historically rare for one nation to base military forces on another independent nation's territory. The Axis powers, to be sure, pioneered intra-alliance basing relationships on the eve of World War II in Italy, Spain, and Thailand.[1] The United States itself did begin to create its own transimperial basing network, of course, with the Anglo-American Lend-Lease agreement of 1940. Yet the sweeping transformation that truly gave birth to America's current global presence really came between then and the Korean Armistice of 1953.

The dimensions of America's postwar overseas military presence have been shaped by two powerful forces. Most obvious and well-remarked-upon has been a cycle of war and peace, determined by the contingencies of American foreign-policy strategy outlined in chapter 1. In wartime the basing network has expanded, and in peacetime it has contracted.

Yet there has also been a more subtle and, to some, more subversive dynamic—a long-term downsizing trend—which has affected the basing of all great powers in the post–World War II world. Foreign bases—especially the large, high-profile variety involving large numbers of troops interacting intimately with local societies—have grown increasingly vulnerable politically, as economic development and democratization have progressed worldwide. Even U.S. forward deployments have been periodically affected. Between 1945 and 1950, for example, the American offshore military presence contracted sharply, from over 12 million to less than 1.5 million personnel, driven by the postwar U.S. demobilization of that period.[2] The number of foreign bases fell by more than half. American troop deployments abroad surged again to more than 1.6 million men at the height of the Korean War, however, and rose close to those levels once more during Vietnam. The number of bases also increased, although by lesser magnitudes.

Apart from these wartime surges, however, the dominant long-term pattern was one of retrenchment. From the end of the Korean conflict until the fall of the Berlin Wall, the number of U.S. troops deployed abroad fell steadily, and bases outside Europe declined by more than two hundred. The British also withdrew from most of their bases "east of Suez" by 1976,[3] while the Soviet Union pulled out of its former satellites in the early 1990s.[4]

The general long-term decline in great-power overseas military deployments accelerated following the fall of the Berlin Wall in November 1989. Indeed, total UN P-5 foreign deployments fell 40 percent in less than a decade, from 650,000 in 1990 to under 260,000 ten years later, as shown in figure 2.1; bases also declined sharply in number. Despite some important cross-national nuances, this downsizing was common to all the major nations possessing foreign military bases: Britain, France, Russia, and United States. It continued relentlessly from the end of the Cold War until the terrorist attacks of 9/11.

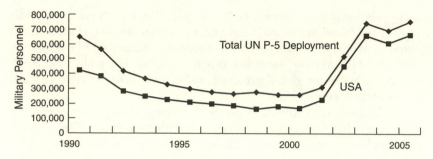

Figure 2.1. Post–Cold War Fluctuations: Trends in UN P-5 Overseas Deployment

Notes: "UN P-5" refers to members of the United Nations Security Council: the United States, France, the United Kingdom, Russia, and China. Calculation of the 2005 personnel figure for the U.S. military includes numbers for the Pacific and Atlantic fleets unavoidably based on 2004 figures; *The Military Balance*, 2005–2006 edition did not provide updated statistics in those two categories.

Source: International Institute for Strategic Studies. *The Military Balance*, 1990–2005 editions.

Post–Cold War Downsizing

Following the collapse of the Soviet Union at the end of 1991, the major powers of the world downsized their basing structures—at different rates, and for different reasons, but all in a common direction. Broadly speaking, the global base networks of Russia, Britain, and France largely collapsed, although again at different rates and for different reasons. That of the United States remained, however, and grew steadily more indispensable to broad global political-economic stability, as the other major powers retrenched. America experienced parallel political-economic pressures within host nations for downsizing to those that the other P-5 members confronted.

To understand these divergent, and yet related, national paths, it is useful to summarize our historically grounded discussion of the strategic roles that bases have played in the postwar world. The central point, presented clearly in figure 2.2, is that the United States has filled, and continues to fill, all the major strategic functions of overseas basing. The concerns of other powers, by contrast, have grown narrower, and their incentives for downsizing correspondingly greater, given their more limited systemic roles in world affairs.

In the post–Cold War world, American forces, for better or worse, have become global guardians, and the other P-5 nations, beset by mounting pressures at home and abroad, have assumed more specialized roles. Yet America's garrisons, too, are embattled, this nation's awesome military

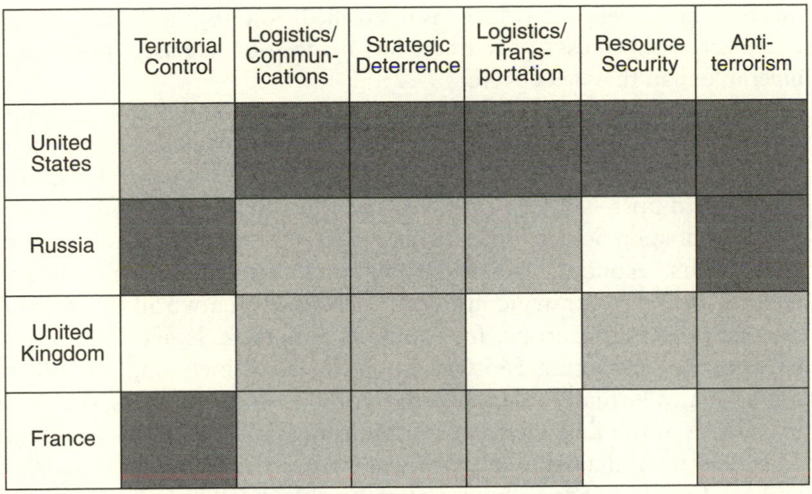

	Territorial Control	Logistics/ Commun- ications	Strategic Deterrence	Logistics/ Trans- portation	Resource Security	Anti- terrorism
United States						
Russia						
United Kingdom						
France						

Figure 2.2. Strategic Roles for Basing: Comparative Perspectives

Note: The darker the shading, the more salient the factor.

power notwithstanding, by both global and local forces whose contours and consequences remain imperfectly understood. In a volatile, finely poised world of growing interdependence, their stabilizing tasks are clear and enormous. Yet the prospects for success remain much more problematic.

A word of elaboration is in order regarding the categories presented in figure 2.2. The classic function of basing in empires, from time immemorial, has of course been "territorial control." That function endures, particularly with respect to Russian and French basing.

"Logistics/transportation," "logistics/communications," and their correlate, "resource security," are political-economic functions of concern to all major powers dependent on international trade and investment, but they are performed in their military dimensions primarily by the United States. "Strategic deterrence" is an imperative in the nuclear age, and also a special American responsibility in the post–Cold War world. "Antiterrorism," including related proactive interventionism in the Middle East and Central Asia, is an especially prominent function of bases since 9/11, performed by all the major powers, but especially by the United States and Russia.

As we shall see, powerful global tides have been tearing at the foundations of forward deployment for two decades, even as bases grow more central to global political-economic stability. Regime shifts, most prominently democratization, and the related mobilization of mass social groups into politics, have been among the most prominent challenges. Economic costs have also risen. Terrorism has intensified. And technological change, particularly rising missile accuracy, has made foreign bases much more vulnerable than they once were.

All the P-5 nations, with the partial exception of the United States, have grown less ambitious in forward deployment over the past generation, responding to the powerful new challenges by scaling back. The trend toward post–Cold War downsizing was initially most pronounced in nations hosting Soviet forces, where it was closely related to domestic regime shifts, economic costs, international agreements, and, behind them, the declining strategic utility of such bases in a world of declining tensions. In Eastern Europe, for example, a massive Soviet foreign military presence numbering 565,000 troops in 1988, including 380,000 in East Germany, virtually disappeared over the ensuing six years, driven by the collapse of the East German communist regime. The Soviet presence of 116,000 in Afghanistan in 1988 was abruptly reduced to a miniscule number of advisors the following year, and the 65,000 Soviet troops in Mongolia were also suddenly withdrawn in early 1993, following local political transitions in both cases.

By the mid-1990s, the Russian forward-deployed presence overseas was thus reduced largely to a "combat brigade" and an intelligence communications-monitoring station in Cuba, together with some small facilities in Vietnam. Yet even the Cuban outposts were dismantled by late 2001, and those in Vietnam less than a year later, two years ahead of schedule. In mid-2007 the Russians had no significant foreign military presence outside eight "near-abroad" republics of the former Soviet Union, although rising Islamic fundamentalism, and resurgent great-power consciousness, did provoke them to an expanding presence in several of those nearby areas, such as Georgia and Kyrgyzstan, after 1997.[5]

Britain experienced the second most drastic long-term downsizing of its foreign military presence among the powers considered here, with costs, host-nation regime shifts, and declining strategic utility again being prominent reasons. In 1940 Britain had the most extensive overseas basing network in the world. As late as 1952 its global presence still remained second only to the United States. Yet in 1968 Prime Minister Harold Wilson announced Britain's total withdrawal "east of Suez," which was finally realized by 1976.[6] This strategic reconfiguration led to withdrawal from Singapore and Malaysia after confrontation between Indonesia and Malaysia ended in the late 1960s, and from Belize in 1994. Today Britain, once the world's preeminent imperial power, retains bases only in Germany, a few strategic colonial locations like Gibraltar, the Falkland Island, and Diego Garcia, and in a few former colonies such as Brunei, Cyprus, and of late Iraq.[7]

France has downsized its foreign military presence somewhat less in the past half-century than have Britain and the Soviet Union, partly because its bases appear to have more intrusive, political-economic functions than in the British case, and partly because France retains more ambitious pretensions of independent global standing than does Britain. Paris retains the second most extensive overseas base network in the world, despite its relatively modest standing as the world's fifth largest economy.[8] Most remaining French bases, however, are concentrated in former African colonies where France retains significant economic interests, such as Ivory Coast, Djibouti, Senegal, and Gabon, or in current French possessions in the Caribbean and the Pacific, where they give French military forces global strategic capabilities they would otherwise lack.[9]

The United States, of course, remains the one nation with global military capabilities, and a basing network to match, as noted in figure 2.2, despite the powerful pressures for downsizing that confront all the major powers. America is also the nation whose basing network has shown the most substantial two-way fluctuation in size over the period under study, reflecting changing notions of security in American political life and their relation to forward deployment.

The United States downsized and significantly consolidated its overseas forces in the half-century following World War II. The overall number of foreign bases fell by the year 2000 to one-third of its 1945 total, and the number of troops deployed abroad from well over ten million to less than 200,000, although this downsizing has been periodically reversed by conflicts such as the Korean, Vietnam, Afghan, and Iraqi wars.[10] The fluctuation is mitigated to some degree by the stable growth of mobile amphibious forces based on U.S. aircraft carriers, which are performing significantly more important strategic functions in the Middle East and East Asia than was true prior to the 1970s.

Today, the Fifth Fleet, covering mainly the Middle East, usually has twenty-plus ships, with about 1,000 personnel ashore and 15,000 afloat. It includes a Carrier Battle Group, Amphibious Ready Group, combat aircraft, and other support units and ships. After its disestablishment in 1947, the Sixth Fleet, primarily responsible for the Mediterranean, was secondarily covering the Middle East until the reestablishment of the Fifth Fleet in 1995, under CENTCOM.[11]

Fluctuations in American land-based overseas military presence have been especially striking over the past two decades. With the waning of the Cold War, the number of forward-deployed U.S. forces abroad declined sharply in many areas, especially Europe, as alliance-reassurance functions grew less pressing. From over 244,000 in 1990, U.S. troop strength in Germany, for example, fell by more than two-thirds by the year 2000.[12] The number of American troops abroad rose in connection with wars in Afghanistan and Iraq, of course, but declined again following the fall of Baghdad and the collapse of Saddam Hussein's strategic threat, the subsequent, extended Iraqi insurgency notwithstanding.

American military presence abroad surged sharply again, of course, following 9/11. The highpoint, as noted in figure 2.1, was in late 2002, with Afghanistan operations still underway, and U.S. forces simultaneously preparing for the invasion of Iraq. In 2004–2005, America's deployments abroad once again declined slightly, despite the persistent Iraqi insurgency, as withdrawals from Europe to the continental United States accelerated, and as American troops in Iraq turned more and more security functions over to the Iraqi military; yet they accelerated again during 2007.

Some important basing changes, it is vital to note, have had more to do with host-nation politics than with global American strategy. The U.S. forces withdrew totally from the Philippines during 1990–92, in the largest and probably the most important peacetime redeployment since World War II—one deeply related to the regime shift from Ferdinand Marcos to Corazon Aquino. Under Marcos, base-lease negotiations had proceeded fairly smoothly, in part because Marcos maintained tight personal control of them. Under Aquino, the process was much more open, fluid, and indeterminate, with resentment strong on the Filipino side at previous American favoritism toward the dictator Marcos. The two sides had difficulty anticipating and responding to each other's political requirements, a problem complicated by the eruption of Mt. Pinatubo, which buried Clark Field.

In the end, the two sides grudgingly reached an agreement. Yet they did so only after a bitter process that gravely undermined the legitimacy of the bases in the Philippines, as well as American conceptions of their utility, and the value of conciliating the nationalistic Philippine government. When the hard-won draft base treaty was rejected in the Philippine Senate, the United States abruptly announced its intention to leave.[13]

Clark Air Base, employing 9,000 U.S. service personnel, had been operated by the U.S. Air Force since 1903, and was the largest U.S. air base ever closed. Subic Bay, employing 6,000 service personnel, was the fourth-largest U.S. naval base ever closed.[14] Clearly it was politics much more than strategy that caused the United States to leave the Philippines, thus contributing to the long-term downsizing trend worldwide. Clearly even America is sometimes buffeted by the powerful populist political pressures for downsizing that are operating in world politics more generally.

Political Change and the Profile of Forward Deployment

Forward deployment itself, as noted in chapter 1, is a historically unusual phenomenon outside the context of formal empire. It rarely occurred in noncolonial areas prior to World War II.[15] Following that global conflagration, there was a period of prominence for forward deployment as the Cold War intensified, and the practice grew more strategically important. Decolonization also situated preexisting bases in suddenly independent lands, although this triggered anti-imperial sentiments that led foreign basing by middle-range powers like Britain and France to once again recede in prominence.

The United States, with its preeminent global role, was of course a partial exception to this downsizing, as we have noted. Yet between the fall of the Berlin Wall and 9/11, it, too, found its global military presence declining along three important dimensions: (1) the number of countries hosting U.S. military bases; (2) the absolute number of overseas bases themselves; and (3) the number of U.S. troops permanently deployed abroad. These trends were especially pronounced during the first post–Cold War decade (1991–2001), as shown in figure 2.1. American garrisons, too, were vulnerable and embattled, despite America's political-military standing as a superpower. Indeed, that seeming omnipotence itself was one of several factors spurring intensified opposition to U.S. bases abroad.

What did host-nation politics contribute to the sharp decline in the overseas political-military presence of the great powers—the case of the United States, partially excepted—over the last third of the twentieth century? And what implications do the patterns of that period have for American foreign policies of the future? figure 2.3, detailing the fate of major long-term UN P-5 foreign military deployments of the past half-century, sheds important light on these two crucial questions.[16]

The central issue considered in figure 2.3 is what happens to the UN P-5 basing nation presence in a host country when a "regime shift" occurs.[17] As is graphically clear from the table, the probability is more than 80 percent that foreign forces in such a case will withdraw, either voluntarily or under duress. As is clearly shown in figure 2.3 and figure 2.4, this historical pattern applies not only to European troop presence, but to American as well, although the United States has been able to insulate itself from the impact of regime shifts on its foreign base presence marginally better than other great powers.

Some historical regime-shift catalysts for foreign withdrawal have included *populist military coups* (Nasser's Egypt, Kassem's Iraq, or Qadaffi's Libya); *decolonization* (Indochina, Algeria, and Hong Kong); and *democratization* (the Philippines during 1986–91, or Eastern Europe during

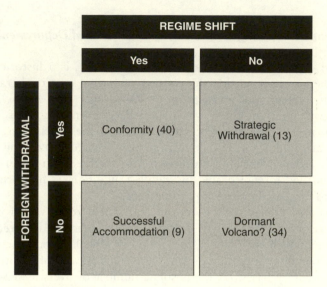

Figure 2.3. UN P-5 Base Presence and Host-Nation Domestic Political Change, 1951–2006

Source: Data is from David Lea and Anna Marie Rowe, *Political Chronologies*. London: Europe Publications, Ltd., 2001, and supplementary press data.

1989–90). Popular rule, it is important to reiterate, has not been a particular friend of foreign base presence, even where, as in the American, British, and French cases, the basing nation itself has been a liberal democracy, and thus ostensibly a defender of liberal values. The epic process of political-economic transformation that has convulsed the developing world since the 1950s and 1960s—and that poses fresh challenges to American basing also, as it expands back to the volatile developing nations in the wake of 9/11—appears to destabilize base presence, except under highly specialized circumstances of "liberating occupation" that will be discussed in greater detail in chapter 5.

It is still too early to conclusively judge the prognosis for American bases in Iraq, Central Asia, and Afghanistan in the wake of post-9/11 interventions. Yet the implications of figure 2.3 are not encouraging. Even when democratization occurs—indeed, *especially* when democratization occurs—regime shifts often lead to forced withdrawal. Even where bases remain in the face of democratic transition, as in South Korea, Spain, Greece, and Kyrgyzstan, they face strong pressures to downsize, constrain base operations, raise rental payments, and conclude new status-of-forces agreements(SOFAs). Only where anchored by strong alliance relationships do they typically remain. To make matters worse, in the Islamic world and many other developing nations, cultural factors, including strong intra-national communalism, also frequently complicate the base politics equation.

The complex pressures typically unleashed against foreign base presence by democratization were clearly evident in Iraq, following the end of the formal Coalitional Provisional Authority occupation there in June 2004; well over 70 percent of Iraqis have since consistently favored setting a timeline for withdrawal of American forces,[18] and their fervor has typically intensified with proximity to democratic elections. Fearing sectarian violence, only a few leaders of the Sunni minority—a group that are themselves ironically the ethnic backbone of the insurgency—have been willing to even tacitly consider an extended American presence.[19] The Iraqi case does thus *not* appear to demonstrate the often-argued proposition that democratization leads to greater support for American military presence. Indeed, the reverse is apparently the case in Iraq, as it was previously in the Philippines and many of the other nations indicated above.

The political forces driving foreign withdrawal have, in the final analysis, typically been rooted more in the domestic politics of the host country rather than in those of the basing nation. Great powers typically strive to retain the trappings of global status that foreign bases confer, and it is host-nation resistance or ambivalence that ultimately terminates their presence. In figure 2.3 cases of "Conformity," which include the Philippines (1991), Iran (1979), and South Vietnam (1975), are instances in point.[20] Neither great-power strategy nor the shifting fortunes of the Cold War can adequately explain the transformation of foreign basing without reference to the volatile, and often uncertain, aspirations of the host nations themselves.

Regime shifts, in particular, have contributed significantly, in the aggregate, to downsizing the great-power foreign military presence in the world over the past half-century. Yet as figure 2.3 also indicates, they have not been the only factor at work, despite the powerful impact so evident in the Philippines, Iran, and elsewhere. In more than a quarter of the cases of foreign withdrawal in our UN P-5 sample, the basing nation withdrew despite a continuation of the host-nation regime—essentially at its own volition. These cases of "strategic withdrawal" include such instances as the United States leaving Taiwan after the Shanghai communiqué (1973); pulling out of Saudi Arabia after the initial Allied victory in Iraq (2003); the Russian departures from Cuba and Vietnam following the end of the Cold War (2001); and the British withdrawals "east of Suez" during the late 1960s and the 1970s.[21]

As suggested in figure 2.4, among the great powers, Britain has clearly been the most prone to "strategic withdrawal." Its forces have pulled out fully 40 percent of the time that they have withdrawn without the

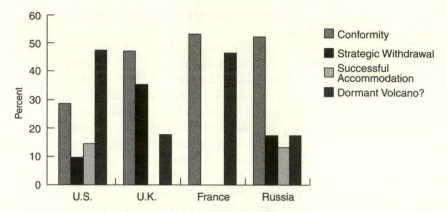

Figure 2.4. Basing Nations and the Regime-Shift Hypothesis

pressure of a host-nation regime shift. In more than two-thirds of the country cases unrelated to decolonization where Britain has withdrawn, it has done so proactively, rather than in response to host-nation political demands. France, conversely, has *never* been so pragmatic. Its forces leave *only* when political regimes change, in which case, like the British, they invariably disappear.

The reasons for the striking contrast in British and French base-policy responses are not fully clear, but may well flow from contrasting linkages to host-nation political economies. British subnational interests, due to the institutional heritage of colonial indirect rule, have not traditionally had strong economic stakes in the political orders of nations where British troops are based, especially during Labour administrations in Britain. The opposite pattern has been dominant in France.

Both figure 2.3 and figure 2.4 suggest that foreign military presence *can,* in specialized circumstances, survive host-nation regime shifts. One requirement seems to be that the basing nation be a true superpower; neither Britain nor France, for example, has achieved "successful accommodation," while Russia has achieved it only in six of fourteen former Soviet republics of the "near abroad." And in two of those cases (Georgia and Moldova), Russian troops remain in a geographically limited portion of the nation in question, on debatable security-related grounds, against the explicit wishes of the host government.[22] Russia's forces were compelled to withdraw from *all* of its nominally independent former satellites in Eastern Europe following the fall of the Berlin Wall.

Even powerful and affluent America, as figure 2.3 suggests, has had trouble retaining a foreign military presence in the face of host-nation regime shifts, suggesting the potency of these fateful transitions. Indeed,

U.S. forces have withdrawn in nearly *two-thirds* of the cases where such regime shifts occurred. The United States has succeeded in retaining its base presence only where that was secured by a major alliance relationship—in four of six cases, by NATO itself. Thus U.S. conformity to the regime-shift hypothesis is surprisingly high, given America's superpower standing, although moderated by its unusual wealth and web of alliance relationships.

Even where the United States has not been forced to withdraw in the wake of regime shifts or major leadership changes, it has generally been forced to accept sharp increases in local base rentals, as will be elaborated in chapter 8.[23] It has also often been compelled by new regimes to accept major operational constraints on the deployment of its forces. Limits on the deployment of nuclear-capable forces; restrictive SOFAs; constraints on transit rights to third countries, such as Israel; and cutbacks on deployments to urban or suburban areas (Yongsan, South Korea; Torrejon, Spain; or Hellenikon, Greece, for example) are among the restrictions typically placed on U.S. forces locally in the wake of regime change within the nations in question.

Base politics can also operate to support preexisting base presence, albeit only when specialized conditions prevail. Interestingly, as chapter 5 will show in detail, the key seems to be historical: that is, whether the basing nation is perceived to have arrived in the host nation as "imperialist" or as "liberating occupier." Where bases are seen as the heritage of empire, they invariably disappear; when they are seen as the product of "liberating occupations," as in Germany, Japan, Italy, or, arguably, more recently in Bosnia or Afghanistan, they have much better prospects, and host nations tend to respond more positively to foreign forces than elsewhere.

Available evidence suggests, in summary, that host-nation politics profoundly affects patterns of great-power overseas deployment, including that of American forces. Foreign bases lie on the fragile frontier of host-nation political acceptance. And that can vary sharply, both cross-nationally and over time.

Two strikingly different patterns are thus discernable. For nations in social transition—especially after regime shifts occur—base politics are often turbulent and uncertain, with foreign withdrawals or imposed operational constraints frequent. Base relations are especially troubled when the bases themselves are perceived as neocolonialist in character. Conversely, where local politics are stable and compensation-oriented, and the basing nation has a positive reputation as a former liberator, base politics tend to be more predictable also, particularly as long as the financial flows to base-related constituencies continue.

The steady decline of foreign basing—wartime periods aside—suggests that the volatile former pattern of base politics, typical of developing nations, is more pervasive than the latter. Yet the enduring presence of bases in important core areas like Japan and Germany, where American military assets are concentrated, also indicates that the stable latter pattern is possible, and remains highly consequential in global strategic terms. Base-politics outcomes, in a word, are varied, and they have fateful implications for America's future global role that need to be better understood.

The Winds of Technological Change

Beginning in the 1960s, but gaining particular force during the first post–Cold War decade, technology has been quietly transforming the profile of forward deployment, and the strategic role of bases in military affairs. We saw these effects to some extent in chapter 1, and will return to them in greater detail later. Revolutionary technological change has had dramatic impact on military logistics, helping to make military forces increasingly mobile. Technology is also revolutionizing intelligence-gathering and power-projection, with major implications both for base configurations and, ultimately, also for base politics, as manifest in both American policies of strategic transformation and in the mixed host-nation response to them.

The logistical requirements of U.S. soldiers have been steadily rising over the decades. During the Civil War horse fodder and ammunition made the average soldier's daily requirements about thirty pounds. By World War II those requirements had doubled in weight, and today they have reached about 400 pounds.[24] Between 1990 and 2002, the share of defense dollars going to logistical support rose from around 50 to about 60 percent, while the ratio allocated to combat units fell from around 48 percent to 40.[25]

Although per capita logistical requirements have been rising, so, too, have lift and supply-chain-management capacity, aided by the computer and the Internet revolutions. During the first three weeks of the American buildup to the Gulf War, the United States moved more troops and equipment than in the first three *months* of the Korean War.[26] It was able to do so even more rapidly in the case of Iraq, twelve years later.

Due to efficient supply-chain-management systems, greatly facilitated by the coming of the Internet, it is also increasingly feasible to preposition an adequate amount of equipment and supplies at all times, both wartime and peacetime, to facilitate rapid reaction. As a consequence, the number of prepositioned supply ships the U.S. military has stationed around the world rose during the first post–Gulf War decade from twenty-five to forty-one.[27] In addition, substantial military supplies are now prepositioned at a variety of new "shadow bases" filled with such equipment—in Singapore, for example. The role of these facilities is discussed more extensively later in this volume.

Intelligence-gathering has also been revolutionized by technological change, leading to a rapid proliferation, dispersion, and, in many cases, concealment of such facilities throughout the globe.[28] Many, such as the strategic Pine Gap satellite intelligence base in Australia, are nominally under the authority of other nations, but nevertheless managed by the United States.[29] Others, including many listening and retrieval posts, are reportedly located on foreign military installations but staffed by U.S. military and intelligence personnel.[30]

As the Information Revolution proceeds, space-based facilities are gaining increasing capacity to handle important military and political signals-intelligence (SIGINT) functions. Yet ground stations and processing facilities abroad remain important, especially for tactical intelligence requiring rapid reaction times and to provide reassuring redundancy. Among the intelligence systems requiring what Robert Harkavy terms "foreign military presence" (FMP) are the Sound Surveillance System (SOSUS) of antisubmarine warfare monitoring;[31] Air Force Tactical Air Command (AFTAC) nuclear detection devices;[32] and strategic early-warning mechanisms, such as the SAGE and the North Warning Systems.[33]

In the signals-intelligence area, overseas facilities appear to be important with respect to two particular types of telecommunications intelligence. First, they are capable of monitoring telephone calls, faxes, e-mails, Internet communications, and so on. The scale of these communications is, of course, both huge and rapidly growing, yet nevertheless surprisingly amenable to monitoring. The volume of international telephone traffic alone rose from 38 billion to over 100 billion minutes a year over the course of the 1990s,[34] but can reportedly still be monitored to some extent using known telephone numbers and computer-based recognition mechanisms. Short wave and Very High Frequency (VHF) communications surveillance is also possible, although the curvature of the earth makes this more difficult for ground-based systems.

The world of surveillance and intelligence-gathering is obviously a complex, secretive, and rapidly changing one, largely tangential to this research. It is, however, important to note in passing its dynamic, rapid, and discontinuous development. The impact of new, interactive technology on the role of more conventional bases in global strategic affairs is also important to understand. Far from rendering bases obsolete, technological change in communications, intelligence, and logistical systems is making them both more flexible and more capable of reacting quickly to novel military challenges. Flexible, high-speed communications are also facilitating the emergence of highly differentiated and interactive

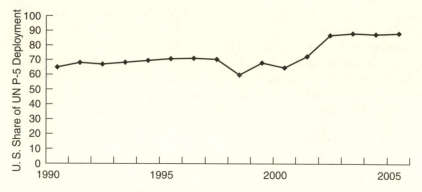

Figure 2.5. U.S. Shares In UN P-5 Overseas Deployment

Source: International Institute of Strategic Studies. *The Military Balance*, 1991–2005 editions. London: IISS, 1991–2005.

Note: In calculating figures for the overall 2005 U.S. military deployment, it was necessary to use the 2004 figures for the Pacific Fleet (140,400) and the Atlantic Fleet (108,000), because analogous figures for 2005 were not reported in the 2005–2006 edition of *The Military Balance*.

global basing systems, in which highly specialized functions of the overall system, such as intelligence, logistics, and power-projection, can be handled seamlessly from widely disparate locations.

One of the most important challenges on the horizon, of course, is missile defense. The rising accuracy of even intermediate-range missile technology has rendered overseas bases vulnerable in many parts of the world—including Europe, Northeast Asia, and the Middle East.[35] To maintain the credibility of deterrent and power-projection capabilities related to forward deployment, introduction of point and limited-area missile defenses, mobile or otherwise, may well be an increasing imperative.

The Impact of 9/11

Following nearly a decade of post–Cold War downsizing, the United States sharply reinforced its overseas military presence after the terrorist attacks of September 11, 2001, as is indicated in figure 2.1. As can be seen in figure 2.5, America's military initially expanded its offshore deployments considerably faster than that of any other UN P-5 nations, responding vigorously to the 9/11 attacks on its own soil. This powerful response caused the U.S. share of total P-5 offshore deployments to rise sharply, from 65 percent of the total in late 2000 to 88 percent in 2005.[36] Global base politics increasingly became an issue for the world's lone remaining superpower.[37]

By early 2002 the United States had close to 70,000 troops at thirteen bases in nine nations of the Middle East and Central Asia, together with five aircraft carriers in the Arabian Sea.[38] By mid-2003, eighteen months later, it had around 150,000 troops in Iraq alone.[39] In addition, the U.S. retained roughly 100,000 forward-deployed troops in each of its European and Pacific commands. In total, U.S. overseas deployments by the end of the Iraq War in the spring of 2003 were more than triple those on the eve of the 9/11 terrorist attacks. And they were continuing to broaden in politically volatile areas, such as Africa, Central Asia, and the Persian Gulf, giving issues of base politics increased prospective salience in American diplomacy and international security policy for the foreseeable future.

Since 2003 the American presence in Iraq has fluctuated, in a volatile, changing pattern, complemented by substantial deployments elsewhere in the Middle East and some retrenchment in Europe.[40] Russian deployments in the "near abroad" have risen, as the French foreign presence has fallen, leading to rough stability in America's remarkable share of UN P-5 overseas deployments, as noted in figure 2.5. Over time, it remains to be seen whether the United States, despite its unchallenged military might, will resist the subtler political undertow that has already forced other major world powers to retrench over the past three decades. The bitter Iraq experience suggests that the short-term pressures for major reductions could be strong.

Broadening U.S. Commitments: Return to the Developing World

The geographical profile of overseas American deployment patterns in the wake of 9/11 is profoundly different from that of the Cold War years. In the aggregate, over half of U.S. overseas bases today are in developing nations, many of them politically volatile, with more than a third in the Islamic world alone. By 2005 the United States was deploying 18,000 troops in Afghanistan, 121,600 in Iraq, and 25,250 in Kuwait, totaling 176,000 in the Middle Eastern/Central Asian region as a whole.[41] In 2006 the United States deployed new troops to Qatar (6,540), the United Arab Emirates (1,300), Bahrain (3,000), and Saudi Arabia (300) while the troop levels for Afghanistan, Iraq, and Kuwait remained roughly the same, until the 2007 surge. Some of the most important, such as CENTCOM's regional operations center at al-Udeid Air Base in Qatar, were clearly there. The dominant overall share of American bases in developing nations today compares with less than 6 percent of total global bases in such countries, and less than 1 percent in the Islamic world, before the Berlin Wall fell in late 1989.[42] In terms of troops deployed, America's

Figure 2.6. Shifting U.S. Troop Deployment Patterns toward the Islamic World

Sources: U.S. Department of Defense, *World Manpower Distribution by Geographic Area*; *International Institute of Strategic Studies*; *The Military Balance*, 2003 and 2004 editions; London: IISS, 2003–2004.

Notes: Nations included as NATO members here are the traditional members as of 1991 (before the recent expansion): Belgium, Denmark, France, Germany, Greece, Greenland, Iceland, Italy, Luxemburg, the Netherlands, Norway, Portugal, Spain, Turkey, and the United Kingdom. U.S. troops deployed to Iraq from NATO nations are excluded from 2003–2004 figures for NATO; these troops include 3,000 First Infantry Division personnel from Germany and 1,000 members of the 173rd Airborne Brigade from Italy. Because figures for U.S. troops in Afghanistan during 2003 and 2004 were not available at *World Manpower Distribution by Geographic Area* (2003 and 2004 editions), the numbers presented in *The Military Balance* were used.

commitment in Muslim developing nations, beginning with Iraq, Afghanistan, and Kuwait, is of course much larger still (figure 2.6).

America's political-military presence has expanded significantly since 9/11 in six major regions of the world: Central Asia (including Afghanistan); the Persian Gulf (including Iraq); "New Europe" (mainly formerly communist Eastern Europe); Africa; Southeast Asia; and Latin America. None of these areas were regions of major U.S. military commitment before the World Trade Center and Pentagon terrorist attacks. Yet *all* lie within or border the "arc of instability" stretching across the developing world that has become a major focal point of U.S. Defense Department strategic attention since 9/11.[43]

In each area, the war on terrorism has been the nominal catalyst for newly expanded U.S. commitments. Yet the commitments themselves have much broader geopolitical implications. Most importantly, they help provide the security necessary to increase economic and social connectivity between the core areas of the global political economy, on the one hand, and the "nonintegrating gap," stretching across Africa, the Middle East, and parts of Southeast Asia and Latin America, on the other.[44]

The new U.S. basing presence appears in five basic types of facility:[45]

1. MAIN OPERATING BASES (MOB). These are locations of enduring strategic value, where troops are expected to be deployed for long periods of time, as has been traditional during the Cold War in Western Europe and Northeast Asia. These MOBs are envisioned as the common anchor for the smaller forward-operational bases within an area of operational responsibility. Examples could include facilities like Ramstein Air Force Base in Germany, or Kadena Air Force Base in Japan, with such substantial infrastructure that they would be prohibitively expensive to rebuild, and where troops will likely be stationed with their families in future.

2. FORWARD-OPERATING SITES (FOS). These are barebones facilities that can be expanded as needed. These bases would, in principle, be home to rotational forces without families for tours of three to six months. Examples are Camp Bondsteel in Kosovo; Moron Air base in Spain; Libreville, Gabon; and Dakar, Senegal.[46] The nature of these facilities would prohibit the housing of dependents on them or in surrounding areas, as they are expected to be established largely in less developed parts of the world.

3. COOPERATIVE-SECURITY LOCATIONS (CSL). These are host-nation facilities with little or no permanent U.S. presence, although CSLs do require periodic service, contractor, and/or host-nation support. They provide contingency access, such as might be required in combating terrorist incidents, including hostage cases, and are a focal point for security cooperation activities. They are rapidly expandable to FOS scale, and are located mainly in "arc-of-instability" nations.

4. JOINT PREPOSITION SITES (JPS). These facilities are set up as large storehouses where incoming units can quickly pick up equipment without being compelled to rely on scarce airlift capabilities, "capitalizing on the strategic advantage of being an 'ocean closer' to engagement, conflict, and influence."[47] JPS facilities of this type exist in Qatar, Benelux, and Kuwait, for example.[48]

5. EN-ROUTE INFRASTRUCTURE (ERI). These are strategically located, enduring assets with infrastructure that provides the ability to rapidly expand, project, and sustain military power during times of crisis and other contingencies. ERI bases serve as anchor points for throughput, training, engagement, and U.S. commitment.[49] Examples of ERI can be found in Poland, Georgia, and Bulgaria.[50]

Apart from the foregoing, the U.S. military also supplements its formal facilities with contingency support from private contractors and from a network of standby understandings with foreign governments. Following the Gulf War, the U.S. Government concluded, for example, a number of agreements to establish "joint cooperative security locations" corresponding to the CSL and JPS facilities discussed above, in Qatar and Oman. These agreements involved contracts with private firms to keep bases in good condition to be used on short notice, even though U.S. troops were not deployed on a large scale. Since 9/11, the United States has also concluded a series of ERI base agreements, particularly in Africa, which establish legal procedures for handling the rapid transport of goods and military staff in locations where troops might not routinely be deployed, but where they might desire to train or transit to or from in an emergency.[51]

In the new nations of Central Asia, most of them republics of the former Soviet Union, U.S. military forces had no basing presence whatsoever prior to 9/11. That has sharply changed. Within months of the World Trade Center and the Pentagon attacks, the United States established major new bases at Khanabad in Uzbekistan, as well as at Manas in Kyrgyzstan—less than 250 miles from the Chinese frontier—as well as a multitude of smaller operational facilities elsewhere in the region.[52]

All these new bases were directly related to the war against the Taliban. Yet their location in the heart of Central Asia was invested with considerable geopolitical significance, as well. Geographically the region lies near the epicenter of the Eurasian continent, making it accessible by conventional, nonrefueled flights to virtually all points of that huge land mass, as well as to three-quarters of Africa and offshore Southeast Asia. Being halfway around the world from the U.S. East Coast, Central Asia is also an ideal site for "contingency basing," allowing American forces to flexibly cover the globe, in response to sudden crises or disasters, from the smallest possible number of locations.

The strategic location of the post-9/11, U.S. Central Asian bases, so close to sensitive frontiers, as well as globally significant, has naturally stirred complex, if discreet, reactions in both Russia and China. The local economic significance of U.S. bases, many of them also used by the International Security Assistance Force (ISAF) in Afghanistan, is substantial, however, creating strong local incentives to encourage the United States to stay.

American military spending related to the Ganci Air Force Base at Manas alone, for example, amounted to 5 percent of Kyrgyz national GDP in 2003.[53] Its local economic importance has subsequently expanded further still. In 2006, President Bakiyev demanded a one-hundredfold rent increase for Ganci, from $2 million to $200 million a year, while settling in the end for $150 million annually in general economic assistance.[54] With strategic withdrawal from Uzbekistan at the end of 2005, the United States had little choice but to make substantial concessions in the 2006 negotiations with Kyrgyzstan.

In the Persian Gulf and the Middle East more generally, the U.S. base presence has, of course, expanded massively since 9/11, and especially since the buildup to the Iraq War of 2003. The United States has, to be sure, withdrawn its 10,000-troop presence from Saudi Arabia, established since just before the Gulf War. It has likewise downsized its presence in Turkey, following the elimination of "no-fly zones" above Iraq.

Yet the United States has also established a new, massive, state-of-the-art regional command center at al-Udeid Air Base in Qatar. And it has maintained a major, if receding presence in Iraq, since the euphoric aftermath of the 2003 war. U.S. strategic planners reportedly contemplated at that point a long-term presence there, involving several major air bases.[55] Yet how these plans will be affected by the course of the Iraq conflict itself, and the retrenchment program of 2006–2007, remains to be seen.

In Central and Eastern Europe, the American military moved beyond the basic presence in Bosnia, Hungary, Macedonia, Albania, and Kosovo that it had maintained since 1999, revolving around Camp Bondsteel in Kosovo. It has also established operational basing and training relationships with Bulgaria, Romania, and Poland. U.S. forces used the Constanta port in Romania and the Burgas air field in Bulgaria to support Operation Enduring Freedom operations in Afghanistan, and to provide KC-135 Stratotanker in-flight refueling support for U.S. operations against Iraq.[56] Since 9/11 the U.S. European Command (USEUCOM) has also begun to use training facilities in Poland for major training exercises, such as the annual Victory Strike war games, due to restrictive training conditions at higher local-cost facilities in Germany.[57]

With the New Europe of Poland, Romania, Hungary, and Bulgaria, among others—markedly more supportive of Bush administration strategic purposes than the "Old Europe" further west—and with the costs of "New Europe" also being highly competitive, the United States after 9/11 seriously considered a deeper partnership with the new, involving the establishment of new forward-operation locations (FOLs) and training locations in the East. In connection with the redeployment plan announced by President George W. Bush in August 2004, two heavy divisions now formally based in Germany were scheduled to return to the United States.[58] New short-term deployments to forward-operation bases (FOBs) and FOLs in Eastern Europe are also emerging. Both Bulgaria and Romania, in particular, cut deals in 2005–2006 to host American military forces on their territory, and have been eager to expand the presence of U.S. forces.[59] Bulgaria agreed in March 2006 to host 2,5000 American troops at a time, with the first group scheduled to arrive in Bulgaria by late 2007. Romania will host 1,500 troops.[60]

Before 9/11, Africa was never the site of major U.S. military deployment, save for brief periods during World War II. Yet since 9/11, it has become a significant focal point of American antiterrorist military activity. Camp Lemonier, in the Horn of Africa at Djibouti, only an hour's boat ride from Osama bin Laden's ancestral homeland of Yemen, hosts 1,800 U.S. troops,[61] while since 2002 Kenya has hosted a small contingent of Marines.[62] The U.S. State Department has helped initiate important new cooperative security frameworks that also substantially engage the U.S. military, such as the 2002 Pan-Sahel Initiative and the Trans-Saharan Counter-Terrorism Initiative. Through these projects the United States is aiding local North and West African authorities in coordinated efforts to suppress local terrorism across ill-marked national boundaries in their region.[63] In early 2007 it also announced plans to establish an Africa Command (AFRICOM).

A sixth area of recent, and relatively novel, U.S. security concern has been Latin America. In 1999 the U.S. military closed its most important bases in the region as it evacuated the Panama Canal Zone. Thereafter, however, the U.S. military moved its regional headquarters to Puerto Rico. It began, especially after 9/11, to expand its basing presence in the region once more, as a combined antiterror and antidrug operation. Under "Plan Colombia," aimed at insurgent forces in Colombia and Ecuador, the United States has established new military bases at Manta, Ecuador; Aruba; Curaçao; and Comalpa, El Salvador, as well as more military sites in Colombia itself.[64]

The Broadening Profile of Overseas Bases

Although we have witnessed a recent trend of broadening American military commitments in developing countries, as noted above, the asset value of overseas bases still remains concentrated within NATO and Northeast Asian allied nations. Table 2.1 presents the general profile of America's forward-deployed global presence as of September 2005, expressed through four key indicators, for the nineteen nations with the largest American overseas troop presence.

In total, including figures for the nineteen nations detailed above, the U.S. military had over 290,000 personnel formally assigned abroad, and the overall American defense community outside the United States totaled more than 590,000.[65] The replacement value of U.S. military assets abroad was about $118 billion.[66] And the United States was spending more than $60 billion annually to sustain its military forces overseas,

TABLE 2.1.
The Stakes of Base Politics: Beyond Iraq

Country	U.S. Troops Deployed		P.R.V.[a] ($ million)	Resource Flows (vs. U.S. Gov't)	Offsets (%) (vs. 2002)
	Military	Total DoD[b]			
Germany	58,118	176,969	39,920.3	−0.86	33
Japan	33,871	115,568	34,044.2	4.61	75
South Korea	30,683	62,804	13,123.2	+0.32	40
Kuwait	25,250[c]	—	3.8	−0.25	58
Afghanistan	18,000[c]	—	—	—	—
United Kingdom	10,052	28,931	5,367.3	−0.13	27
Italy	8,841	29,756	5,135.3	0.32	41
Spain	1,680	5,953	1,938.5		58
Bahrain	1,641	2,089	409.6	−0.03	—
Belgium	1,386	4,708	757.3	−0.05	24
Iceland	1,270	3,178	2,586.1	—	—
Portugal	970	3,426	1,123.8	—	4
Kyrgyzstan	950[c]	—	—	—	—
Djibouti	622	625	—	—	—
Qatar	6,540[c]	—	347.0	−0.10	61
Turkey	380	3,547	1,337.5	+0.36	54
Bosnia and Herzegovina	263	270	—	—	—
United Arab Emirates	1,300[c]	—	—	—	—

Sources: U.S. Department of Defense, *Base Structure Report*, September 2006 edition; Department of Defense, *Worldwide Manpower Distribution by Geographical Area*, 2005 edition; U.S. Department of Defense, *Report on Allied Contributions to the Common Defense*, 2004 edition; and International Institute of Strategic Studies. *The Military Balance*, 2005–2006 editions, London: IISS, 2005–2006.

Notes:

a. As the figures for Iraq were subject to dramatic fluctuation during the writing of this book, data for Iraq is intentionally excluded from the table. The figure for total DoD personnel was 243,200, according to *The Military Balance*, 2005–2006 edition, and the approximate number for U.S. troops deployed there was 134,000. This surged to over 150,000 during 2007, with provisions for subsequent decline.

b. PRV denotes "Plant Replacement Value," or the prospective cost of replacing the facility in question.

c. DoD figures indicate both military and civilian employees of the Department of Defense, plus dependents. All personnel figures are for September 2005.

d. These figures are drawn from *The Military Balance*, 2005–2006 edition.

although about $8.5 billion of this amount was offset by allied contributions, either monetary or in kind.[67]

In reviewing the profile of U.S. forward deployments by country, two features are striking: (1) the scale of existing American facilities and long-term U.S. commitments in NATO and Northeast Asia, together with the cost of replacing them if American forces were to leave; and (2) the heavy U.S. military manpower buildup in the Islamic world. The latter dimension is new, but well known, and a piece of the larger shift toward forward basing in the developing world that will be a major analytical concern of this volume. The American stakes in Europe and Northeast Asia—three-quarters and more of the value of U.S. military assets overseas, with sophisticated deployment capabilities and the financial ability to support U.S. purposes globally—are less well understood by the general public, despite their long history.

AMERICA'S MASSIVE INFRASTRUCTURAL STAKES IN JAPAN AND GERMANY. Especially striking, when one considers the embedded dimensions of America's foreign base presence, and their prospective implications for the future, are the scale of existing facilities in Germany and Japan. As indicated in figure 2.7, 65 percent, by value, of the total U.S. Army facilities located outside the United States are located in Germany. South Korea, in second place, has only 17 percent of the total.

The ratios for Japan are even more striking, and prospectively more important for the future of global base politics. Most surprisingly, perhaps, the value of American Navy and Air Force assets in Japan is now greater than that in any nation outside the United States, having briefly surpassed the overall value of all facilities in Germany during 2004, according to official Pentagon data.[68] Over 99 percent of the total value of U.S. Marine Corps, 44 percent of U.S. Navy, 33 percent of U.S. Air Force, and even 7 percent of permanent U.S. Army facilities worldwide located outside the United States are in Japan.

Kadena Air Force Base, with a replacement value of more than $4.6 billion, was the most "expensive" American offshore facility in 2005, while Yokosuka Naval Base outside Tokyo, home of the only U.S. aircraft carrier home-ported outside the United States, was second. To be sure, U.S. deployments in Iraq were much larger in numerical terms than those in the old Axis nations, and American physical stakes there were substantial also. Wartime expenditures were massive—averaging $6 billion a month between 2003 and late 2006.[69] Yet the steady investments of past years in Japan and Germany still loomed much larger in any asset-based calculation.

This volume focuses on understanding the politics that underlie U.S. military presence in two very different parts of the globe: the advanced industrial nations, including Europe and Northeast Asia, and the developing world, with a special focus on the Islamic countries. It is in the latter "arc of instability" where America's footprint has expanded so rapidly since 9/11. Yet it is in the former nations where America's embedded presence lies, reinforced by long-standing material stakes, alliance commitments,

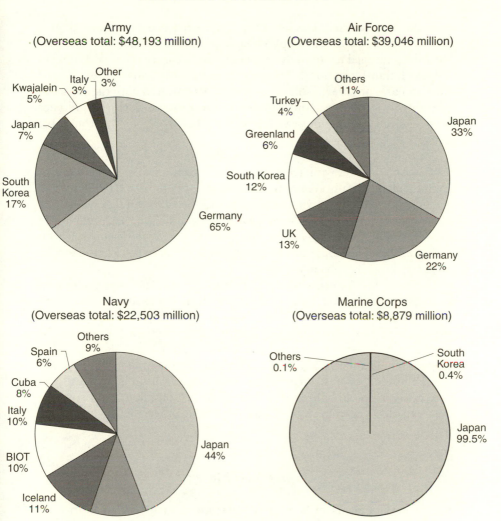

Figure 2.7. America's Heavy Investment in German and Japanese Bases
Source: U.S. Department of Defense, *Base Structure Report*, 2005 edition.

and political-economic linkages that cannot be ignored, either in the era of Iraq involvement or beyond.

EMERGING CHALLENGES FOR AMERICAN POLICY

As we saw in chapter 1, foreign military bases in independent nations are a historically unique phenomenon, with a provenance of less than three-quarters of a century. Despite their brief existence—no more than a human lifetime—overseas deployments are already vulnerable and embattled, challenged profoundly by twenty-first-century political and technological transformations. The vast majority of British, French, and Russian bases on foreign soil have already disappeared with the sunset of their unwieldy empires. And America's own forward-deployed presence is under siege as well—most visibly in Iraq, but more quietly around the globe.

The coming of democracy does not make things easier, even for a democratic America. As we have seen, democratization, like other types of regime shifts, typically creates major uncertainties in base relations, often brings groups to power with bitter past experience of foreign bases, and often leads to foreign-troop withdrawal. In the Philippines, democracy in the late 1980s was followed by disappearance of America's largest air and naval bases abroad, and the prognosis in much of the Islamic world, including Iraq, is problematic also.

The issue for America today is to identify fundamental underlying strategic interests, and then to devise tactical approaches sensitive to emerging political-economic realities so as to maximize the prospect of their realization. Concretely, as following chapters will suggest, the United States needs to retain a global basing presence so as to stabilize the world political economy and to confront terrorism. Yet that presence needs a lower profile, stronger geographic concentration in politically secure areas, more globalized distribution of key functions, and stronger area expertise regarding non-Western nations, especially in the Islamic world.

A Singapore Model?

Recent developments in Southeast Asia present a useful illustration of some key issues involved. Washington has, since the early 1990s, quietly established extensive contingency facilities, and concluded a SOFA with Singapore, that would facilitate rapid and efficient deployments to the heart of the Southeast Asian region. Indeed, a "Singapore model" of base relations—involving legal and logistical infrastructure, intelligence coordination, prepositioned equipment, and even aircraft carrier dry-dock facilities, as well as *strategic but minimal* involvement of U.S. military personnel—has evolved. It may be a future model for bilateral, informal, nonalliance defense cooperation worldwide, not least in the continuing war on terrorism, across the global "arc of instability" that has become so central in U.S. security planning since 2001.[70]

The heart of the Singapore model is first-class infrastructure, prepared to American specifications. In March 2001, Singapore completed, at its own expense, construction of a deep-draft pier at Changi Naval Base capable of servicing and, if necessary, repairing U.S. aircraft carriers, with the USS *Kitty Hawk*, based in Yokosuka, Japan, being the first of many American ships to use the facility. The Singapore government's substantial alterations to accommodate U.S. forces doubled the prior physical size of the preexisting naval base on the same location.

Singapore hosts only a minimal number of U.S. military personnel— 110 sailors (officers and enlisted) together with around 60 Navy civilians and others are the key element.[71] Yet despite the small numbers, the activities of these personnel are critically important to the functioning of the U.S. Pacific Fleet, especially after the U.S. Navy's withdrawal from the Philippines at the end of 1991. Those activities center on logistical support for the fleet.

Commander, Logistics Group, Western Pacific (COMLOG WEST-PAC) was established in Singapore in July 1992. It is the U.S. Seventh Fleet's principal logistics agent and bilateral exercise coordinator for Southeast Asia. As such, it plans the resupply of food, ordnance, fuel, and ship repairs for U.S. Navy ships in an operations area stretching over fifty-one million square miles of the Pacific and the Indian Oceans—from the mid-Pacific to the east coast of Africa. COMLOG WESTPAC also plans and manages funding for ship repairs at U.S. facilities in Yokosuka, Japan, and Guam, as well as at commercial repair facilities in Singapore, Japan, Malaysia, Indonesia, and Australia. COMLOG WESTPAC handles all these activities with only around sixty U.S. military and five civilian personnel.

A final element of the Singapore model is an extensive program of joint exercises and training to assure effective, cooperative action between the United States and local military in an emergency. More than one hundred U.S. Navy ships a year call at Singapore, and U.S. fighter aircraft regularly deploy there. Singapore was a transit point for U.S. ships, troops, and aircraft during the Gulf War, while Singapore's Paya Lebar Air Base supported U.S. airlift operations to Somalia.

For its part, Singapore's military began training with U.S. Army Pacific units in 1981, and has continued to do so ever since. Both its navy and air force regularly carry out combined exercises under the Cooperation Afloat Readiness and Training Program, with a U.S. Navy task force. Singapore Air Force F-16 crews also train at Luke Air Base, Arizona, and then participate systematically in joint exercises with U.S. military counterparts.

American defense cooperation with Singapore is thus intensive and multifaceted, with major positive implications for U.S. national security.

It is also deeply and seamlessly integrated through state-of-the-art communications with key components of the Pentagon's global basing system—in Yokosuka, Diego Garcia, and around the world. The island of Singapore and its bases lie directly on the strategic Straits of Malacca, astride the major sea-lanes from Northeast Asia to the Middle East. U.S. military personnel in Singapore are a major element of this overall equation. Yet their number—less than two hundred personnel in total—is surprisingly small—so small that they do not make standard lists of the major U.S. garrisons abroad.

IN CONCLUSION

The Singapore model is clearly not a panacea for America's embattled garrisons abroad, as will be clear in the coming pages. America's military will never be simply a low profile, back-office operation. It needs the Diego Garcias of the world: nonpoliticized, strategic locations that allow for the confident placement of concentrated firepower. And it needs the Qatars also, with their local expertise and operational, in-theater control centers, to support actual combat. Yet as a vital element of a globalized national-security system, which Pax Americana is steadily becoming, Singapore and the paradigm it represents may be an important reference point for the future.

This chapter has suggested three important challenges for future American national-security policy that flow from the growing vulnerability of foreign military bases. The first, and perhaps most fundamental, is that developing a policy science of base politics is both important and possible: important due to the broad yet unfinished strategic tasks of forward deployment enumerated in chapter 1, and possible due to the systematic regularities observable cross-nationally in base-related interactions. Secondly, this policy science should involve modeling—identifying functional relationships within political systems that make it easier to understand base-politics outcomes more generally. Thirdly, the foregoing pages indicate that understanding subnational forces affecting base politics—local NGO pressure groups, local governments, diverse national bureaucracies, and their organizational permutations—is crucial to understanding policy outcomes.

Beyond prescribing a particular analytical approach, the preceding pages also suggest the need for particular attention to certain still-neglected variables that appear to repeatedly influence base-politics outcomes in nation after nation. Among these variables are regime shifts, technological change, patterns of local government autonomy, and political leadership. Embedded historical experience—particularly with foreign occupations that may have occurred long ago—also plays a crucial role in determining the political viability of foreign bases in host nations. It is to the analytical task of specifying these key variables more precisely, and relating them more systematically to base-politics outcomes around the world, that we now turn.

CHAPTER THREE

BASE POLITICS

A CONCEPTUAL INTRODUCTION

OVERSEAS MILITARY BASES are an old idea that is once again being reexamined, amidst the deepening controversy over American involvement in Iraq. Traditionally a creature of empire, since the late 1930s bases have frequently existed on the soil of independent nations, as we have seen. In this relatively new incarnation, they are severely challenged today by new political and technological trends, including populism and the increasing range of advanced weaponry—not to mention the rising distaste for American unilateralism and the mechanisms that sustain its Pax Americana.

Yet overseas bases persist for five basic reasons. Apart from persisting classical security dangers, such as the possibility of war on the Korean peninsula, geopolitical logic—including the need for a stabilizer and guarantor in volatile, important regions like Northeast Asia and the Middle East—commends the continued existence of bases. The territorial control, reassurance, and strategic deterrence functions of bases, centrally important until the end of the Cold War from Berlin and South Korea, have by no means disappeared.

Technical national-security requirements in such areas as logistics and defense communications are likewise an enduring rationale for some degree of forward deployment, on the part of any nation aspiring to global power. Satellite ground stations, communications facilities, and "listening posts" to monitor nuclear testing, for example, all generally require some foreign presence. In addition to "soft-security" concerns, such as combating drug trafficking in Latin America,[1] resource security, and the antiterrorist struggle also provide important justifications for forward deployment in the twenty-first century.

Even with the Cold War over, for example, supertankers still need to pass unimpeded through the Straits of Hormuz, within sight of the shores of Iran, to energy consumers throughout the world. If anything, global dependence on their safe passage is rising, with America now importing 60 percent of its oil and Japan a full 99 percent.[2] Energy sea-lanes cannot be protected, or terrorists deterred, or definitive strategic intelligence provided, by spy satellites and Predator drones alone.

Beyond the mechanical security functions they perform, overseas bases—particularly those of the United States—also play a *systemic* role in the global political economy that is vital, although often overlooked. Together with the abstract international rules that are so often stressed,[3] bases serve as crucial guarantors against destructive regionalism and balance-of-power rivalry at the heart of the global system, inhibiting the nationalistic, mercantilist forces that proved so subversive of peace and prosperity during the first half of the past century. Indeed, overseas bases have almost imperceptibly become crucial implicit enforcers of transnationalism, and thus catalysts for rising transcontinental trade and investment, in ways that abstract rules alone never could have been.

The geoeconomic and geopolitical logic in world affairs for bases, however, is no guarantee of their political viability within individual national political systems. Indeed, there is powerful cautionary evidence across history to document the subtle, complex, and often decisive *constraints* imposed by host-nation base politics—and by the parallel missteps of basing nations—on foreign military presence. Iraq is only the latest painful manifestation of the mutual management failures that can occur.

The consequences of a broader unraveling beyond Iraq in the current complex, interdependent elements of the global U.S. basing network, however, could be sobering. There are disturbing reasons to believe that if bases become generally infeasible in allied but independent nations—as they were throughout history until the late 1930s—the very stability of the delicate and deeply integrated global economy itself, especially its volatile financial dimension, would be at risk. Our task, in this chapter, is to begin to understand analytically this weighty subject: just *how* host-nation politics influences prospects for maintaining the base facilities in the many parts of the world that will be strategically and economically required to stabilize the global political economy in coming years.

WHAT BASE POLITICS IS AND WHY IT MATTERS

"Base politics" is defined here as the interaction between "basing nations" and "host nations" on matters relating to the status and operation of local military facilities in the host nations, together with related transnational interactions involving nonstate actors.[4] Local military facilities, it is important to note, can include a wide physical variety of sites, including airfields, naval ports, garrisons for ground forces, military communications ground stations, administrative facilities, and logistical depots.[5] Their diversity is clearly rising, and their transparency ironically declining, in the emerging information age. For purposes of simplicity, all will be considered "bases" if there is actual deployment of over one hundred foreign military personnel, and a significant, if not total, degree of basing-nation discretion regarding access and freedom to operate.[6]

To be sure, the character of bases has changed significantly over the years. With changing technology and political-military imperatives, the physically formidable, expensive, yet static fortifications of old are being supplemented by lighter, more flexible, and more individually dispensable facilities for monitoring and communications, as well as military operations. Especially in an age of terrorism, when reaction speed is of the essence, so-called lily pads, distributed widely across the developing world, in proximity to its wild, ungoverned recesses, are becoming an important basing variant, on a scale sometimes even significantly smaller than the bases discussed above. Smaller facilities, broadly distributed across host populations, were also stressed in the U.S. Army's December 2006 counter-insurgency manual.[7] Yet these fragile outposts cannot themselves supplant the central geopolitical role of major bases in key advanced industrial nations.

Whatever the form and location, the strategic importance of forward deployment for a global power like the United States makes it a potential continuing pillar of American national security. And as long as American forces remain posted overseas, base politics will be a continuing concern, no matter how embattled, in varied forms of political-military conflict, those putative guardians of American global interest may be. The associated base politics are necessarily a continuing concern for a global power like the United States, in order to stabilize these embattled garrisons or at least to make their fate easier to predict.

Base politics also has important implications for political analysis in more theoretical terms. It obviously affects the fateful patterns of war and systemic change in international politics that Robert Gilpin and other hegemonic-stability theorists have analyzed.[8] In drawing attention to the importance of subnational and transnational institutions—such as defense ministries, military general staffs, local governments, and NGOs—base politics also highlights the importance of the subnational realm in determining policy-outcomes between the nation-state and the individual.[9] Base politics clearly points to the theoretical difficulty in neatly segmenting comparative and international-political behavior, suggesting the need for new concepts to make sense of this interactive, two-level reality.

In total, U.S. overseas deployments at the onset of the Iraq War in the spring of 2003 were more than triple their scale on the eve of the 9/11 terrorist attacks.[10] American deployments had expanded decisively in the developing world, in a new range of volatile, thinly governed, and largely undemocratic nations, giving the U.S. global presence a sharply different profile from that of Cold War days. Amidst sweeping transformation in the deployment patterns and technological capabilities of U.S. forces overseas, as they move into an increasing number of non-Western and often unstable nations, base politics is assuming new prospective salience in American diplomacy, international security policy, and even electoral calculations. That general salience it seems likely to retain for the foreseeable future, given the looming uncertainties that America's overseas bases face in an ever more volatile, dangerous, and at times antagonistic, world.

Complex Dynamics of Base Politics: The Domestic Dimension

In understanding why overseas bases are so vulnerable, even as their political-economic importance in assuring stable interdependence rises, we briefly consider here both the international and the host-nation domestic dimensions of base politics. Base politics, it is important to note, is a qualitatively distinct variant of politics as a whole, with at least four defining traits:

1. A "*two-level*" character, with interrelated domestic and international dimensions. Many of its general parameters, such as mutual security treaties authorizing the presence of foreign forces, security assistance linked to basing, and status-of-forces agreements (SOFAs) defining mutual rights and duties, are established through *international* agreement. Yet content and implementation, not to mention the profile of response to them, have deep roots in domestic, often profoundly local politics.[11]

2. Sharply divergent *elite* and *mass-political dimensions*, involving intimate, often confidential cooperative diplomatic dealings with foreign counterparts, as well as contentious interaction with domestic groups disinclined to cooperate with foreign militaries.

3. Unique *institutional* features, such as a disjunction of costs, benefits, and administrative responsibility, that breed frustration and irresponsibility— especially among local governments and NGOs with limited stakes in cooperative outcomes.[12] National governments, after all, are typically responsible for national security, and negotiate conditions for the presence and operation of foreign bases, including SOFAs and host-nation support (HNS) arrangements with foreign diplomatic and military counterparts. Yet these details, together with the actual behavior of foreign forces, profoundly affect the environment, prosperity, and public order of local host communities that cannot shape, and have no responsibility for maintaining, the broader national-security relationships themselves.

4. Complex *psychological dimensions*. Since base politics involves foreign military presence, it often simultaneously evokes both nationalist ambivalence and economic dependence in the host-nation's response to foreign bases.

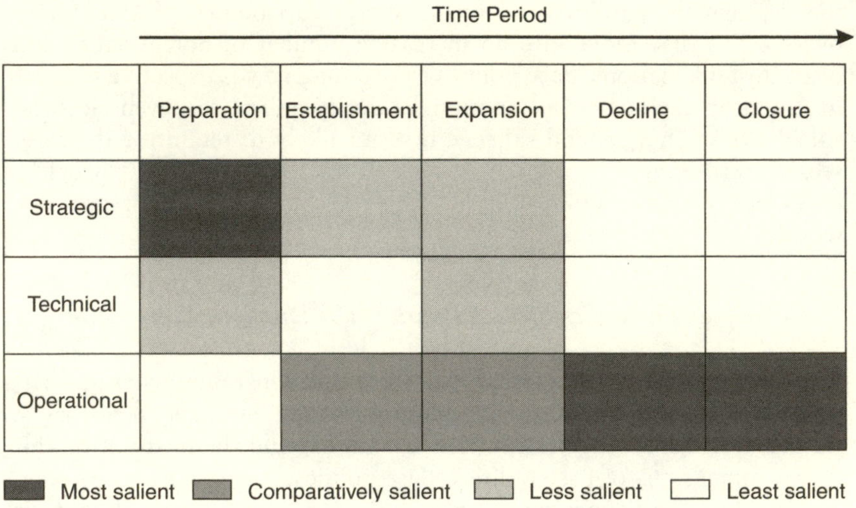

Time Period

	Preparation	Establishment	Expansion	Decline	Closure
Strategic					
Technical					
Operational					

■ Most salient ■ Comparatively salient ☐ Less salient ☐ Least salient

Figure 3.1. The Base Life Cycle

The large compensatory financial flows attached to foreign base rentals, materializing suddenly like windfalls unrelated to personal effort, intensify the psychic ambivalence and complexity surrounding base politics.

There are at least three qualitatively distinct varieties of base politics, each salient at different points in the life cycle of military bases. The fundamental distinctions are laid out in figure 3.1. "Strategic" base politics—the best-known variant, and the stereotype that conventional wisdom often assumes to be the only variant—is salient in the initial planning and establishment of bases. It figured importantly, for example, during the late World War II and early Cold War periods, when America's original global basing network was conceived. It also becomes periodically important in the basing nation, when defense technology changes in major ways, provoking consideration of new basing patterns. The early 1960s, when ICBM technology became operational, and the Pentagon consequently reconsidered SAC bases in the Middle East, as well as the post-9/11 era, when DoD began restructuring Asian and European deployments in response to the revolution in military affairs, and the antiterrorist struggle, were likewise such watershed periods.

The second variant—"technical" base politics—is a relative of the first. It involves the process of bureaucratic planning, consultation, and disputation—both within the basing nation and between it and the host country—associated with the implementation of original strategic plans. Most aspects are consistently low-profile, but some can be contentious cross-nationally: deployment of nuclear-capable aircraft or weaponry, for example. Like "strategic" base politics, the "technical" dimension is typically concentrated at the early stages of the basing life cycle.

The third variant—"operational" base politics—is a very different creature from the other two types of decision-making. It concerns the allocation and disposition of base-related resources: budgets, land, physical assets, and weaponry, for example. It is omnipresent across virtually the entire base life cycle, yet remains remarkably obscure to all but the most veteran observer, except when it dramatically intervenes to terminate, perpetuate, or constrain a faltering base presence. "Operational" base politics, which profoundly affects both the terms on which base presence is offered and renewed by host nations, as well as the propensity of basing nations to perpetuate their presence, critically affects the longevity of bases because it shapes the incentives of domestic host-nation groups—both national and local—to accept foreign military forces on their soil. This operational, frequently distributive-political dimension is the principal (although not the exclusive) subject of this research.

In policy terms, the importance of all three variants of base politics is clear. Put simply, base politics as a whole determines the concrete, on-the-ground profile of a military power's global reach, and the local political viability of its offshore commitments. It establishes the viability of deterrence and gives credibility to alliances. Base politics also shapes the broader political evolution of host nations, as has been so clearly true in South Korea, Turkey, Iraq, Afghanistan, and the Philippines. During the Cold War the geopolitical importance of offshore bases was self-evident to nearly all American defense strategists. With the advent of a global struggle against terrorism, it has become so once again.

Complex Dynamics of Base Politics: International Dimensions

There is a second dimension to the two-level interactions that constitute base politics: the trans-national aspect. Alliance context, and geopolitics more generally, clearly influence host-nation base politics, just as presidents, defense ministers, and local mayors do.[13] Precisely how and why the outside world matters are enormously complex topics at the interface with international relations. The analytical problems involved lie beyond the scope of the fundamentally comparative political analysis presented here. Yet a few generalizations concerning the impact of broad international factors on the base politics of host nations are clearly in order, given the constraints they place on how base politics operate in individual countries.

Analytically speaking, geopolitics is decidedly a *background variable,* influencing the general *contours* of base politics in individual nations, while rarely serving as a direct determinant, or proximate cause, of base-politics outcomes, especially at the subnational level. The most important role of geopolitics, like that of strategy, is in the early stages of the base life cycle, as noted in figure 3.1. Geopolitics helps determine where basing nations decide to situate their forward-deployed facilities.

Yet even then technical and distributive-political forces are also at work. The onset of the Cold War did not, for example, explicitly decree the opening of Kadena Air Base in Okinawa, any more than the fall of the Berlin Wall mandated the closing of the Subic Bay Naval Base in the Philippines. Yet the related geopolitics did shape the priorities of both American and host-nation decision makers on security issues—including those related to the bases. Geostrategic concerns have thus been *moderated* through the actors described in this volume, who have parochial incentives of their own.

The indirect, yet on occasion eminently substantial, impact of geopolitics on basing patterns, and on base politics more generally, clearly varies from country to country, and by historical epoch as well. It was substantial during the Cold War—especially the early Cold War—when deterrence of the Soviet Union, and the inhibition of intra-European rivalries, strongly influenced basing patterns. And the impact of geopolitics is greater in the economically and strategically vital parts of the globe than elsewhere. Basing patterns in Central Europe, the Middle East, and Northeast Asia have felt the imprint of geopolitics somewhat more strongly than have those in other parts of the world.

Geostrategy impacts on host-nation base politics in several ways. First, and perhaps most importantly, it causes basing nations to *prioritize* the base politics of certain host nations in their policy planning, and in the attention given to a particular country's base issues by the basing nation's top leadership. During the Cold War, for example, geostrategy inevitably mandated a central role for German base politics in American policy planning given Germany's position at the heart of the divided and heavily armed European continent. Geostrategy may also cause a basing nation to devote more *resources*, both human and financial, to stabilizing the base politics of some nations than of others.

Geopolitics has, indeed, helped more than is generally appreciated to create and foster some of the most predictable supporters of the global U.S. military presence outside the United States. Its role in the creation and sustenance of Japan's Liberal Democratic Party, Germany's Christian Democrats, and Italy's Christian Democrats, in particular, is notable given the backing that it gave these groups during U.S. occupation periods. These parties, in turn, have supported and helped legitimate the

American base presence in their respective nations, inspiring high levels of HNS for locally based U.S. forces, as will be documented in chapter 8.

Whatever early impact geopolitics may have indirectly had in configuring the structure of base politics in key host nations before 1955, its role has clearly waned over time. Even in countries like Japan and Germany, where the shadow of geopolitics loomed large early in the Cold War, parochial domestic interests have become increasingly salient in determining where, why, when, and under what conditions bases come and go. And in a wide range of developing countries stretching from South Vietnam and Iran to the Philippines, Saudi Arabia, South Korea, and Iraq, domestic base politics have trumped or seriously constrained geopolitics, even in countries of perceived major strategic significance.

A second influence from the international sphere on our comparative base-politics area of emphasis is *alliances*. These security agreements among nations were especially crucial strategically during the Cold War years of bipolar nuclear confrontation for the ways in which they provided nuclear guarantees to non-nuclear nations, and thus discouraged the proliferation of nuclear weaponry.[14] Alliances were thus important to the foreign-policy elites of potential battleground states like West Germany, although the broader populace at times had a more jaundiced view, as will be shown in chapter 4.

It should be noted in passing, however, that bases operating under the terms of formal alliance relationships appear to be generally perceived as more legitimate in host nations than those outside an alliance framework. They clearly tend to be more stable than their "nonalliance" counterparts. Nationalist forces in the Mediterranean and the Middle East, for example, forced the American military out of Wheelus Field in Libya (1969) and Kagnew Station in Ethiopia (1975), just as they made the British military presence untenable in Egypt (1954), Jordan (1957), Iraq (1958), and Aden (1967). In only one of these six Anglo-American cases were basing relationships reinforced by alliance ties.[15] Conversely, where alliance relationships, or strong prospects thereof, have reinforced basing ties, as in Spain, Portugal, Greece, Korea, and Turkey, basing relationships have been able to withstand strong political shocks that they might not have weathered in the absence of such alliances.

Bases operating under multilateral auspices, such as those of NATO or the United Nations, also appear to be generally regarded as more legitimate at the local level than those operated under bilateral arrangements. In Japan, for example, several American bases in controversial locations, such as the Futenma Marine Corps Air Station in the heart of Okinawa's crowded Ginowan City, appear to have enjoyed added legitimacy from their standing as United Nations bases, given the greater popularity of the UN than of the U.S. military in Japanese society, especially during the

1950s and 1960s. The NATO aegis has also helped legitimate the American military presence in other defeated Axis nations, particularly Germany, by neutralizing otherwise politically damaging identification of the United States as a former enemy.

Multilateral frameworks, however, conversely appear less effective in dealing with concrete base-related problems, such as crime and environmental issues, than those under bilateral auspices. Clearly the subject of how alliances relate to base politics is an important topic for future research, especially for Cold War-period strategic studies. It is, however, beyond the analytical ambit of this fundamentally post–Cold War, comparative-politics-oriented assessment.

RELATION TO PREVIOUS RESEARCH

How host nations view bases on their soil—and particularly why those foreign intrusions are so detested—is a favorite subject of journalistic literature in international affairs. There is also periodic polemical work on "blowback" against foreign military presence, particularly in the Islamic world and Latin America.[16] This literature ascribes considerable importance to cultural and popular emotional determinants of human behavior, and often depreciates the legitimacy of conventional national-security calculations typically made by national elites.

Particularly since the March 2003 U.S. intervention in Iraq, there has been a surge of debate about the nature and implications of American empire—as well as the role of foreign deployments in sustaining it.[17] Unlike the "empire debate" of the 1980s,[18] which had a strong political-economic cast, the more recent discussion has focused on technical military capabilities and modes of governance, with some attention to comparison with previous empires.[19] There has been remarkably little consideration of host-nation responses, although some of the comparative literature suggests the virtues of a low imperial profile, and responsiveness to the underlying sensitivities of subject peoples.[20]

There is likewise remarkably little comparative literature on the host-nation politics of forward deployment, despite its manifest theoretical and practical importance. There are, to be sure, descriptive studies on individual base negotiations,[21] as well as the more journalistic works mentioned above. Yet these varied descriptive and polemical studies provide little solid analytical foundation for the academic study of foreign military deployments themselves.

There is a substantial and growing body of scholarly literature that makes inferences about military matters, including host-nation stances toward base politics, based on a normative "constructivist" approach.

Some scholars focus on the systemic-level socialization occurring, which accords states key roles as the source for individual identities. Others, by contrast, direct more attention to domestic-level socialization within particular states in order to understand their institutionalized norms, and the relationship of those norms to international outcomes.

There is, however, remarkably little systematic comparative literature on the actual host-nation politics of forward deployment, especially at the sub-national level, despite its manifest theoretical and practical importance. There are, to be sure, descriptive studies on individual base negotiations, as well as periodic polemical work on host-nation "blowback" against foreign military presence, as noted above. Yet these varied descriptive and polemical studies provide little solid analytical foundation for the academic consideration of foreign military deployments themselves.

There are, to be sure, a few solidly researched studies of the global American military presence, which shed important definitional light on patterns in base politics more generally. Robert Harkavy, for example, draws important distinctions among types of foreign military presence, and objects of bargaining regarding access.[22] Christopher Sandars draws attention to embedded factors in base politics—especially distinctions in the historical origins of U.S. bases—that cannot be ignored.[23]

At the other end of the conceptual spectrum from the macroscopic analyses of empire and global military presence are a few more narrowly focused case studies. Most of these are histories that chronicle the evolution of individual bases in relatively descriptive fashion.[24] A few are broader, more enterprising comparative histories, which utilize multiple case studies to elaborate more ambitious political-economic themes.[25]

There are also a few sociological, anthropological, and sometimes also chronological studies. Most of these consider how military bases influence the communities they occupy, and, to a lesser extent, the reverse.[26] None, however, systematically explores the nature of civil-military relations at individual bases, or in the communities surrounding them, from the disciplinary standpoint of political science.

There is, as well, a growing literature on the politics of military-base closures in North America.[27] While some of this writing draws theoretically useful comparisons between U.S and Canadian domestic policies toward bases closures,[28] it does not consider the central issue for base politics as a whole: how *host* nations deal with *foreign* military bases on their own soil. Apart from the rather technical preoccupation of much of this domestically focused research—considering the pros and cons of closure by commissions as opposed to legislative action, for example—the existing base-closure literature deals with a very different type of political problem than is considered here.[29]

One might ask why there is so little scholarly literature pertaining to base politics, despite the manifest policy importance of the subject and the added conceptual richness that it provides to comparative political analysis as a whole. The answer may well relate to the sociology of knowledge in this area. Most academic students of political-military issues are either current or would-be military professionals whose primary concerns are the prescriptive relationships between basing decisions and strategy, rather than the real-world constraints. Those with refined practical understanding of how politics impacts basing are mostly government officials. And bureaucrats, invariably cautious and circumspect, have little incentive or opportunity to write about often contentious base issues, despite their frequently extensive personal experience in handling such questions.

THE PROBLEM FOR ANALYSIS

Overall, this study will concentrate on developing a *predictive* capacity to anticipate where base politics are leading in any given host country, rather than a *prescriptive* set of normative judgments about where they should or should not go. This volume seeks to determine how host-nation politics shapes the profile of foreign military basing, and what implications can be drawn from an understanding thereof for American public policy. It makes four central presumptions, and does so for the purpose of delimiting the subject, rather than to make normative judgments: (1) the stability of overseas base presence is typically a central policy objective of major world powers; (2) systematic comparative analysis can greatly enrich the study of base politics; (3) given the central current role of the United States in world affairs, particular intellectual attention should be given to how host nations respond to American military bases; and (4) to fully understand and predict base-politics outcomes, one must disaggregate the nation-state, and be sensitive to possible divergence in national and local interests, especially those of communities in the actual vicinity of military bases.

Obviously many technical, nonpolitical factors influence base politics itself. *Changing technology*, mandated by the revolution in military affairs (RMA), is one powerful determinant. Also important are the *type of base* in question (from large, conventional facilities to small, technical listening posts), the *host nation,* the *nature of the agreements* between basing and host nations, and the *alliance context* of the base relationship.

Changing technology can crucially alter the nature of bases themselves. At times such change dictates more low-profile listening posts and ground stations, as well as fewer large deployments of combat troops.

Presumably this configuration makes bases easier to accept, as they become less intrusive and troublesome, with only a *limited* human element. While this analysis centers on the political responses to bases themselves, rather than on the larger technological changes behind their structural transformation, it will consider, in the policy sections of chapter 10, how technological trends can be harnessed to configure basing to minimize potential irritants. Major obstacles to local acceptance nevertheless often remain, especially in non-Western nations, as the recent Iraqi, Turkish, South Korean, and Saudi Arabian cases so dramatically testify.

Such obstacles are likely to remain substantial in future, or increase in magnitude, as conventional interstate conflicts of the Cold War era give way to struggles in unstable developing nations against terrorism, drugs, and other dangers that thrive amidst political chaos. Between 1995 and the end of 2004 the number of countries hosting U.S. bases rose 58 percent to thirty-eight, with 53 percent of the new bases in developing nations, and more than two thirds of those being in the Islamic world.[30] More than two-thirds of the new host nations into which U.S. forces have moved since 9/11 are also nondemocratic, posing significant questions of how U.S. policy should deal with possibly transitional dictatorships. These issues will be considered at length in chapter 5.

METHODS OF ANALYSIS

This volume explores the nature of base politics through eclectic, complementary methods. First, it will outline in chapter 4 the logical structure of the distinctive base-politics contest, identifying typical actors that recur in typical national cases, and the underlying conflicting and cooperative relationships among those actors. Then the book presents a typology of variants identifiable cross-nationally, and tests several falsifiable hypotheses concerning why patterns of base politics have the cross-national distribution that they do.

In chapter 5, the study will consider, in particular, five basic propositions about base politics that are presented, and then tested. They have been selected for their ability to clarify the features of leadership, demography, and institutional heritage that most influence the propensity of host nations to retain foreign bases once they are established on their soil. These prospectively key base-politics precepts include:

1. *The Contact Hypothesis*: "Base-community conflict is a function of how frequently and intensely base inhabitants and the general community interact." Such interaction, which tends to generate civil-military conflict, is in turn postulated to be a function of population density in the areas where

bases are located. Countries with high population densities, such as South Korea, and high local population concentrations, such as the environments of Seoul, Madrid, Athens, and Baghdad, will tend to have relatively contentious patterns of base politics compared to less populated areas.

2. *The Colonization Hypothesis*: "Antibase sentiment and the prospect that bases will be removed from a nation are a function of whether a host nation has been colonized in the past by the basing nation." The more substantial the colonial experience, it is contended, the more likely that bases will be politically rejected by the host nation, and ultimately removed. Although the tendency could be countervailed by other factors, nations like Egypt, Panama, and arguably Iraq can be expected to have a persistent, historically rooted bias against Anglo-American bases.

3. *The Occupation Hypothesis*: "Liberating occupations where a noncolonial power displaces a totalitarian, illegitimate regime lead to stable base politics thereafter." Nonliberating occupations, conversely, can lead to broad popular resentment of the occupiers, especially when the occupiers are identifiably complicit with important elements of the old order prior to the occupation, as was true in South Korea between 1945 and 1948, or fail to provide a comprehensive sense of security and empowerment, as in Iraq from 2003–2004.

4. *The Regime-Shift Hypothesis*: "Host-nation domestic political regime shifts lead to 'basing-nation' military withdrawal."[31] In empirically testing this proposition in later sections of this volume, the research hypothesizes that the prospects of foreign troop withdrawal following regime shifts, such as decolonization, military coups against feudal regimes, or even democratization, is high.[32] One policy-relevant implication of this proposition, if validated, would be that the advent of democracy in transitional nations like Iraq might more likely lead to turbulence rather than stability in base relations.

5. *The Dictatorship Hypothesis*: "The United States tends to support dictators in nations where it enjoys basing facilities, and often condones their creation in such nations." However intensely the American people tend to dislike dictatorship in their own country, and elsewhere in the abstract, in reality their government tends to support dictators in base politics abroad, this proposition argues, despite the perverse longer-term consequences that flow there from.

In sum, this study aims to comprehensively explore how host-nation politics affect the capacity of major powers to succeed in the difficult task of sustaining their overseas forward-deployed presence. It has substantial implications for the basing policy of the United States, as well as that of other major powers. Not least, it has significant relevance for the future of American basing in volatile developing nations, both in Iraq and elsewhere.

This effort has four major analytical dimensions. First, in chapter 1 we explored the embedded institutional elements that are the "heritage of history"—especially Cold War strategic political history—the point of departure, going forward, in the base-politics equation. Second, in chapter 2 we considered the political and technological pressures on base politics—particularly the revolution in military affairs, regime shifts, and the post-9/11 war on terrorism—that make future base politics increasingly uncertain, even as growing global interdependence makes it more consequential to world stability.

The heart of the book, and the third key element of the analysis, examines in depth the generic forces that drive base politics worldwide, and that shape their ability to respond to the manifest need for stability that globalism and interdependence have produced. This analysis will contend, in chapter 4, that base politics in country after country manifests certain vital, remarkably similar structural elements, including the presence of some actors with conservative and yet transnational interests, and others with primarily grassroots concerns that national leaders often neglect. Failure to understand the importance of this provincial second group, and to compensate it adequately for the costs it incurs, can greatly increase the instability of base politics.

In chapter 5, the book will explore some recurring contextual influences on base politics, including local population density, and the historical origins of foreign military presence. It develops the key concept of "liberating occupations" as a predictive tool for understanding prospects of long-term base stability. In chapters 6 and 7, the analysis will present four recurring cross-national variations in base politics, and the reasons for their prevalence. Thereafter, chapter 8 will consider the distinctive, pivotal role of finance in stabilizing base presence, where substantial funds are strategically employed, as well as in fueling pressures for downsizing and withdrawal of bases when such support is lacking or misperceived.

The fourth and final section of the study will examine implications of key findings for policy and for theory, at the crucial intersection of comparative politics and international affairs. Chapter 9 will layout strategic options for the future, including both transforming and downsizing foreign base presence. Chapter 10, by contrast, will elucidate more concretely the challenging implications that disturbing trends on the ground suggest for American policy and for theory.

The basic objective throughout these pages is to elucidate future challenges for American policy regarding forward deployment. Yet great-power comparison is useful in this task, for Britain, France, and Russia have faced problems in downsizing their imperial basing networks that America may also one day confront. The study finds that local regime shifts are a time of perilous transition for a foreign military presence, and offers suggestions as to how the perverse effects of such transitions may be neutralized. Based on a consideration of concrete contemporary cases, it proposes both political-economic countermeasures to sustain U.S. presence in the face of social change within individual countries, and diplomatic steps to dilute the effect of local politics in any one nation on the broader fabric of global security and economic prosperity.

Throughout the ensuing pages, three persistent themes recur. One is that history is a crucial source of raw material for understanding how base politics works, and how its structural rigidities came to be. The second is that powerful political and technological pressures are threatening a worldwide American basing structure that is a vital guarantor for stable global political-economic interdependence. And the third, more optimistic, is that base politics is a deadly, yet rationally comprehensible contest, with finite and multiple, yet systematically recurring, patterns that are amenable to comparative analysis. It is to that final, most fateful topic that we now turn.

CHAPTER FOUR

THE NATURE OF THE CONTEST

To THE EXTENT that casual observers—both popular and scholarly—think much about base politics, they tend to conceive host-nation views of bases in broad cultural terms. "Muslims—or Saudi Arabia or Iraq—are 'anti-base' because they oppose the military presence of infidels on national soil," it is said. Australians, conversely, share a "community of values" with the United States, and tend to be "probase" as a consequence, it is reasoned.

Constructivist approaches to politics and international affairs present these casual arguments more formally. Prevailing norms, they suggest, are not only the determinants of national worldviews, but also the primary source of political interests. For them, changing global normative conceptions are the driving force behind state decisions with respect to national security.[1]

Clearly nations often have broadly held collective norms. Peter Katzenstein and Thomas Berger, for example, have substantiated the existence of broadly held, antimilitarist "institutionalized norms" in Japan, as epitomized in the "no-war" Article 9 of the 1947 Japanese Constitution.[2] Bernard Lewis has suggested a deep aversion in the Islamic world to the sustained local military presence of Christian "nonbelievers."[3]

While not questioning the existence and even the legitimacy of normative sentiments toward bases, or toward military matters more generally, this volume presents the politics of national security—and specifically the host-nation politics toward foreign military bases on which it focuses—in a very different light. It argues that while norms clearly shape perceptions and, by definition, concepts of right and wrong, they can—but do *not necessarily*—determine interests or behavior. Indeed, constructivist efforts to account for individual behavior, especially the actions of key policymakers, are typically underpredictive, and often misleading. Such efforts fail to explain the enormous intranational variation in citizen attitudes or political stances toward bases. They also fail to specify the causal pathways through which collective understandings bring about political action.[4]

Historical-institutional analysis is also deficient for parallel reasons. While identifying the parameters within which individuals must act, it does not identify or adequately conceptualize the incentives to which individuals respond, or the information available to them. Like constructivism, it cannot easily account for intranational variation, or for abrupt behavioral changes over time.[5]

Rather than focusing on norms and institutions as central causal agents, this study instead focuses analytic attention on the level at which actual real-world decisions are made: that of the individual decision maker. It argues, as a first hypothesis, that material incentives for individuals and grassroots organizations, when properly targeted at the microlevel, can override prevailing norms. Such incentives can hence ultimately become the primary operational source of political interests in host nations, transcending the importance of culture and even, in many instances, institutional considerations or national strategy in shaping actual base-politics behavior.

The *level* of analysis is especially consequential in host-nation base politics, as will be clear in the pages to follow, due to the distinctive *bifurcation* of interests that characterizes this issue area. National leaders, especially well-established ones, typically *support* existing foreign bases on diplomatic grounds. Grassroots actors, by contrast, lack these cosmopolitan, transnational incentives, and thus typically *oppose* bases as a result. The more decentralized and democratic a political system, the more complicated base management tends to be. And the bias of base politics around the world increasingly tends in that destabilizing direction.

OUTLINE OF THE CHAPTER

This chapter introduces the generic structure of base politics, highlighting the conflicting national and local incentive structures that lie at its heart, which give rise to its potential volatility. The chapter then proceeds to identify in general the key players, both for and against, who determine base-politics outcomes, as well as their characteristic strategies and incentives. It concludes by describing central issues considered in base politics, and the varied processes by which relevant issues are alternately enflamed and resolved.

Obviously there is considerable cross-national variation—the heritage of history and other particularistic circumstances—in players, institutions, incentives, and processes. This variation will be elaborated in succeeding chapters, with particular emphasis on how those country-specific characteristics contribute to the stability or instability of forward deployment. To grasp general tendencies, and the broad structure of conflict and cooperation involved in base politics as a whole, however, it is useful to view the process more abstractly at the outset, and to build a model, however crude and imperfect, with which to evaluate the cases to follow.

This chapter begins with a survey of actors typically opposing the bases, because they usually set the agenda to which national policymakers, as the established, conservative force, must respond. It then describes the probase forces, a strikingly different and more constrained group. Finally, the chapter contrasts the tactics and strategies adopted by the two sides, showing why probase forces so consistently tend to prefer quiet compensation politics, while their opponents adopt higher-profile, often populist strategies. In emphasizing the disjunction between national and local incentive structures with respect to base politics, it prefigures the emphasis on grassroots dialogue and compensation strategies as a means of enhancing base stability that is developed more concretely in the concluding policy-oriented chapters.

THE IMPORTANCE OF SUBNATIONAL ANALYSIS

To understand outcomes in base politics, and to prescribe policies capable of shaping them, it is thus critical to disaggregate the nation state, and examine the incentives and structural relationships that prevail within individual nations, at the actual level where real-world decisions are made. Opinion and interests in this issue area are naturally polarized, making aggregate national-level analysis often dangerously superficial. In a universe where citizens and their leaders are profoundly divided on the merits of the questions at hand, talking about "national" attitudes, beliefs, or positions can obscure important analytical questions, and fail to accurately predict ultimate national behavior.

To focus on incentives rather than values and institutions is *not*, it must be reiterated, to ignore the indirect causal relevance of these latter factors. Prevailing collective norms can affect the incentives of decision makers by shaping the returns they expect to receive for particular courses of action. Okinawa's intensely antimilitarist political culture,[6] for example, can make it attractive for rational maximizers to use antimilitary appeals to seek material compensation. This behavior can, in turn, further enflame broad popular consciousness, and increase the long-term prospect of foreign-military withdrawal. Yet the impact of values on policy outcomes is critically mediated, it must be emphasized, through the behavior of individual actors, who respond in the main to *incentives* rather than to abstract norms per se.

Similarly, individual compensation-seekers in Okinawa cannot ignore the institutional structure of the U.S.-Japan alliance or the tripartite U.S.-Japan-Okinawa relationship in their calculations. Both of those broad institutional parameters enhance the leverage of individuals in seeking compensation, since the alliance makes bases in Okinawa indispensable, and the above-mentioned tripartite relationship forces the Japanese central government to be sensitive to Okinawan compensation requests in order to smoothly maintain those bases.[7] Yet these parameters are, in the final analysis, only *resources for bargaining*, rather than determinants of action. It is ultimately *individuals*, once again, who decide what behavioral course to pursue, with normative and institutional parameters relevant primarily in biasing their incentive structure.

KEY CONCEPTS

Conceived as a problem of utility-maximization for individual decision makers, the study of base politics becomes a realm in which, this volume suggests, game theory is quite relevant. Highly abstract formulations lose much utility in explaining the complex, nitty-gritty world of host-nation support, foreign military sales, and base-offsets. Yet general concepts differentiating various types of contests, and specifying their general payoff matrices, can be quite relevant, especially when they are sensitive to institutional context.[8]

Three simple notions from game theory, in particular, are useful in clarifying the patterns of base politics to be considered in the following pages. The first, and perhaps the most important, is the concept of incentives to nonagreement.[9] In most mixed conflict-cooperation situations, Thomas Romer and Howard Rosenthal argue, the interests of the parties in question are served by some sort of constructive outcome. Where "incentives to nonagreement" prevail, however, the actors in question have no vested interest in a cooperative outcome. Their incentives, conversely, are in a nonresolution of the issue in question. This situation is, as we will see, a common occurrence in base politics, where grassroots opposition groups frequently lack a stake in cooperative outcomes, such as base-lease extentions, at the national level, and must be compensated, often substantially, to induce such a cooperative outcome. Where the opposition groups are not compensated, chaos or policy-drift can easily occur.

A second game-theoretic notion of considerable relevance in base politics is that of *"iterated games,"*[10] or contests repeated on multiple occasions over time. Iterations, of course affect payoff structure—the more one can reasonably anticipate that a cooperative interaction will be repeated, for example, the more flexible one can become with respect to the outcome on any given occasion. Conversely, the more uncertainty about future repetitions, the higher the stakes of any given interaction, inducing a disposition toward rigidity and unwillingness to take risks in placating an adversary.

The felicitous impact of iteration on payoff structure for all players help make interpersonal networks, which involve ongoing, semi-institutionalized interaction, important in base politics. This iterative effect also makes regime stability in host-nation politics a matter of greater importance than would otherwise be the case. Without the prospect of iteration, misperception and overbidding can easily occur, and chaos can all too easily reign. U.S.-Philippine base negotiations during the late 1980s and early 1990s, in which political regime changes, geopolitical transition, and major volcanic eruption made the continuity of parameters and decision makers uncertain, are a classic case in point.

A final key analytic concept in base politics is that of *two-level games*, or contests in which key decision-makers must interact at dual levels in order to achieve a single interdependent outcome.[11] Base politics, as suggested earlier, is by definition a matter of international political interaction— between the host nation and the basing nation, in particular. It is simultaneously, however, a matter of domestic coordination—among foreign and defense ministries, local landlords, and protest groups, for example. Outcomes in base politics must frequently take account of developments at both levels, with considerations at one level often becoming an absolute constraint on agreement at the other. Thus Okinawan local political objections, for example, stalled implementation of the March 1996 U.S.-Japan summit agreement to close the Futenma Marine Corps Air Station and move its functions to northeastern Okinawa for well over a decade, despite a continuing consensus at the national level to implement the agreement. The concept of two-level games is thus one of considerable importance to understanding outcomes in base politics, especially when they involve drafting or revision of international security treaties and base-leasing agreements, which can easily have sensitive domestic political dimensions.

THE OPPOSITION: ANTIBASE MOVEMENTS IN COMPARATIVE PERSPECTIVE

Foreign military bases on another nation's territory are almost always controversial. Even amidst the Blitz of World War II, with England in danger of invasion, there was extensive murmuring in Britain about their American cousins being "oversexed and over here." Australia, which has fought shoulder to shoulder with the United States in each of its foreign wars since 1917, has never consented to the formal presence of regularly stationed U.S. military forces on its soil since the darkest hours of World War II.

Although foreign bases almost invariably provoke local opposition, the profile of such opposition, and its impact on national policy, varies sharply from country to country, and across time in any given country as well. How are we to understand the varied profile and varied effectiveness of antibase movements?

Previous chapters have considered the extreme cases of antibase opposition—when, for instance, a regime shift leads to a wholesale withdrawal of foreign forces in their entirety due to fundamental policy differences between host and basing nation. Our concern here is more limited. This chapter focuses on the varied profile of protest movements themselves, and their relationship to national policy.

Varieties of Antibase Protest

Seen cross-nationally, one can conceptually distinguish three kinds of antibase protest movements that can be classified in terms of motives. These include: (1) *Ideological* protesters, who oppose bases on philosophical or policy grounds; (2) *Nationalistic* protesters, who oppose bases primarily on cultural grounds, or due to the perceived violence they impose on national sovereignty; and (3) *Pragmatic* protesters, who object to bases due to the way they function—crime and environmental pollution are among their typical concerns, together with inadequate financial compensation, where that is a live policy issue.

Actual protest movements can spring from, or be sustained by, a mixture of motives. Broadly speaking, ideological concerns were especially salient during the Cold War—Marxists opposed U.S. bases as a manifestation of American imperialism, while pluralists opposed Soviet bases on converse grounds. Philosophical opposition to nuclear weapons was also a strong, catalytic force for antibase protest, especially following the deployment of Pershing missiles to Western Europe during the early 1980s.

Nationalist impulses, often mixed with philosophical concerns, have grown especially salient over the past decade. Since the waning of the Cold War in the early 1990s, and the consequent blunting of traditional ideological conflict,[12] the United States has loomed especially large in international affairs. Its unilateralism in this unipolar world has, not surprisingly, been attracting strong nationalist resentment, easily directed at that quintessential symbol of American power—bases overseas. Such nationalist sentiment has been especially strong of late against U.S. bases in the Islamic world, just as it was in the 1950s against British bases, and for forty years (1945–early 1990s) against Soviet bases in Eastern Europe.

Pragmatic opposition to bases, due to the social and environmental disruption they can from time to time produce, for example, is the least dramatic of the three forms of opposition. It is also the form of protest most amenable to policy suasion. Understanding pragmatic protest groups, so as to distill practical means of stabilizing base presence where strategically vital, will hence be the central focus of analysis in this section.

In the case of pragmatic protest, the "low-cost-of-disagreement" factor looms especially large—particularly at the local level in compensation-oriented democratic societies with antiwar traditions. The case of Okinawa, presented in greater detail in chapter 6, is a good case in point. Incentives toward "pragmatic protest" are very strong there, because such protest both reflects local sentiments, thus gaining votes for local politicians, and also induces the central government to heavily compensate an impoverished, relatively remote prefecture.[13] Not surprisingly, Okinawa has an unusually decentralized local government structure, and large numbers of referenda on base-related issues. Despite substantial amounts of protest, and forcefully declared dissatisfaction, the presence of American bases in Okinawa has in reality been remarkably stable for over a half-century.

The Ecology of Pragmatic Protest

To understand the origins of anti-base protest—particularly pragmatic protest—it is important to grasp both the profile of protest itself, and also the causal agents that provoke it. Two of those agents—nationalism and ideology—have origins far transcending the specific circumstances of individual bases and their surrounding environments. But pragmatic protest flows *directly* from local conditions, making it crucially important to understand such elements of base ecology as population density and historical context; such topics will be thoroughly explored in chapter 5.

Why Protest-Intensity Varies Cross-Nationally

Democratic countries where American bases are concentrated in heavily populated areas also tend, as a general matter, to be countries where antibase protest is vigorous. This pattern is especially strong in nations such as South Korea, the most heavily populated major nation in the world apart from the Benelux countries. The pattern was also pronounced in Spain, the Philippines, and Greece during the 1970s and 1980s, where major U.S. bases lay close to the national capital.

Antibase movements conversely tend to be weak in nations such as Britain, Germany, Japan, and Italy, where bases are more broadly distributed across the host nation—even where, as in the latter three erstwhile Axis nations, there is a strong local history of opposition to the United States. Interestingly, they seem to be weak in these nations even when a left-oriented government, to whom militant demonstrations appear as a particular challenge to their professed ability to govern, is in power. The remarkably muted response of the left-oriented D'Alema government, led by members of the former Italian Communist Party, to the tragic 1998 Italian cable-car incident, is a clear case in point.[14]

The Contact Hypothesis, stipulating that, where other factors are held constant, the level of civilian personal contact with bases determines attitudes toward them, will be presented in detail in the next chapter. It appears to hold at the local as well as at the national level. High-density, semiurban jurisdictions are *precisely* the areas where antibase sentiment is strongest, even within countries that generally tend to support the presence of U.S. forces.

In Japan, for example, opposition to U.S. bases is strongest in Kanagawa Prefecture, just south of Tokyo, which is one of Japan's most urban jurisdictions, and in Okinawa, which is also densely populated. It is weakest in Iwate Prefecture (Misawa), in the northeast, and Sasebo in the southwest, even though they are geographically close to North Korea and the Taiwan Straits respectively, and perform sensitive defense functions that could make them easily vulnerable to retaliation by an adversary. Population density clearly appears more important than strategic vulnerability as a determinant of local opposition to U.S. bases in Japan.

The Crucial Role of Catalysts

In its routine form, base politics is generally a quiet, elite-oriented matter, handled discreetly behind closed doors, "in the interest of national security." The general public tends not to be involved, which often facilitates smooth handling of such issues. Elites are more likely to have cosmopolitan, transnational interests than their grassroots counterparts. Lacking such ties and directly confronting the crime and pollution that bases produce, local actors can be said to have "low costs for disagreement," as noted above.[15]

CATALYTIC INCIDENTS. Catalytic incidents, such as crimes and accidents, transform base politics from a matter of shadowy behind-the-scenes deal making into matters of public interest, and in doing so often have a decisive and dramatic impact on policy outcomes. The crash of a U.S. Air Force (USAF) plane near Tachikawa Air Base in the western suburbs of Tokyo in 1964, for example, led to the closure of the base within a year. Another USAF crash in Okinawa in 1968 led to the cessation of bombing activities against North Vietnam from there in 1969. The tragic rape of a twelve-year-old Okinawan girl by U.S. servicemen in 1995 led to massive demonstrations and ultimately the 1996 agreement to relocate the Futenma Marine Corps Air Station to a new venue on that volatile island. The 2002 death of two Korean high school girls in a road-side accident widely publicized on the Internet likewise had a broad impact both on U.S.-Korean political relations, and even on the Korean presidential election a few months later.[16]

Crimes and accidents, in particular, grab media headlines, and attract the attention—and often the resentment—of people who normally would not be conscious of base issues. Almost invariably, these marginal activists, often students or other idealists, are people with few incentives to support presence of a base. And in countries whose culture differs substantially from that of the basing nation, and where embedded historical resentments exist, marginal activists may be strongly hostile to bases, causing the catalysts that mobilize them to create serious problems for base-community relations, and even for the local viability of bases themselves.

HUMAN CATALYSTS. At times the catalyst for protest can be human, as opposed to technological or situational: individual leaders, authoritative personal networks, or institutions with special legitimacy. Particularly important to effective transnational protest are "rooted cosmopolitans"—people and groups "who are rooted in specific national contexts, but who engage in contentious political activities that involve them in transnational networks of contacts and conflicts."[17] The struggle against the deployment of Pershing nuclear-capable missiles to NATO bases in Western Europe during the early 1980s offers good illustrations of such human catalysts at work. They transformed what had been frequent but relatively ineffectual protests against nuclear weapons deployed at U.S. bases in West Germany during the 1950s, 1960s, and 1970s into one of the most substantial domestic political challenges to the NATO alliance in its history.

The issue in the early 1980s was whether five European NATO members (West Germany, Britain, the Netherlands, Belgium, and Italy) were politically capable of deploying Pershing II missiles to U.S.-NATO bases on their territory, in accordance with a December 1979 NATO decision mandating such action. The protests against the proposed deployment were particularly fervent and organized in West Germany, Belgium, and the Netherlands. The strength of the peace movement in those countries clearly stemmed from the strength of the catalysts involved.

Three types of human catalysts were common to the three cases. Most important in agenda setting were clearly the *Gegenexperten* (counterexperts). These relatively knowledgeable intellectuals, many of them university professors or research scientists, provided a critical, neopacifist alternative to NATO contentions regarding nuclear-arms strategy.[18] They played a key role in providing the Green Party, one of the main opponents of the Pershing deployments in Germany, with mainstream political acceptance by intellectually legitimating their radical claims.

A second major catalyst for the anti-Pershing movement of the early 1980s was the church. Protestant groups predominated among protestors in the Nordic countries and Holland, while both Catholics and Protestants were active in Germany and Belgium. The Dutch Interchurch Council was especially active and effective in the peace movement, in contrast to leaders of Anglican churches in Britain and to Roman Catholics in general, who proved more conservative. Overall, the stance of religious groups was crucially important in determining patterns of success and failure, due to the unique legitimating role the church was capable of conferring on opposition groups in Europe.[19]

A third pivotal group was organized labor. In Germany, the support of union leaders for a five-minute peace strike, in which around eight million German workers participated late in 1981, gave substantial momentum to the movement.[20] The relative strength of labor in Germany, the Netherlands, and Scandinavia, and its strong ties to local socialist parties, helped to account for the particular strength of the antinuclear, antibase movement in those countries.

Networks and organization, often growing out of earlier, nonbase-related struggles, have also proved crucial in the notably vigorous antibase protest movements in East Asia. The Philippine base protest movement of the late 1980s, for example, clearly had its origins in the anti-Marcos struggles of 1985–86. The massive Naha protests of December 1995, the largest in Okinawan history, against the aforementioned rape of a twelve-year-old local girl by American GIs were organized by the Okinawan Women against Military Violence, a group of close friends bonded by common participation just two months previously in the Beijing International Women's Conference. Similarly, the huge rallies and Internet publicity protesting the killing of two young Korean female high school students in June 2002 by an American military transport vehicle were organized by activists bonded by common participation in rallies supporting the Korean World Cup semifinalists only two months before.[21] Human catalysts clearly play a key role in energizing antibase protest, with bonding socialization processes and legitimization mechanisms greatly magnifying the efficacy of their protests when those factors prevail.

Technology is Lowering Transnational Borders

Cell phones and the Internet are rapidly changing the nature and potential of antibase protest movements, with potentially fateful implications for the nature of base politics itself. Traditionally, as has been noted, base politics have been largely a policy exercise for the elite, involving largely foreign and defense ministry bureaucrats and businessmen, with powerful vested interests in the status quo. Technology, however, is breaking the "elite-cartel" monopoly on strategic information, endowing protesters with new coordination-capacity for their movements. It thus empowers grassroots groups with little stake in base presence, who previously lacked effective access to the base-politics policy process.

Suddenly students, housewives, and other common citizens have ready access to detailed, often graphic information on how bases function, and on infractions by foreign military personnel, in real time. They also have new means for grassroots organizing over the Internet, and by cell phone, that were not available before. High levels of organization in civil society—and high levels of autonomy for those NGOs—leverage the potential of antibase movements still further.

South Korean antibase protests since 2002 are a striking manifestation of all these forces simultaneously and synergistically in operation. As Pippa Norris points out, South Korea has had one of the highest growth rates of NGO organization in the world over the past fifteen years or so.[22] It has also had one of the world's highest rates of increase in Internet penetration, which by 2002 had reached a higher rate of *usage*, relative to population, than in the United States.[23] The major U.S. bases in Korea are concentrated in rather high-density areas close to, or within, the national capital of Seoul. In this environment, technology can easily leverage crimes or accidents, to create powerful anti-base protest. And it indeed tends to do so, as illustrated in the 2002 high school student tragedy and in other recent incidents.

South Korean NGO reaction to its government's Yongsan Relocation Plan (YRP), through which the U.S. military's Yongsan garrison in the heart of Seoul will move south of the Han River to Pyontaek, is a vivid illustration of the new role of technology in Korean base politics. On July 23, 2004, for example, the SPARK NGO group,[24] strongly opposing the terms of the Yongsan relocation, obtained a copy of the agreement between Germany and the United States on the redeployment of the U.S. air base in Rhein-Main, Germany—a case closely analogous to Yongsan. It received this copy from BUND, the largest environmental NGO in Germany, with a membership of 350,000, with whom SPARK had developed close cooperative relations, courtesy of the Internet.

As a result of intensive Internet and telephone consultations with BUND, SPARK prepared, and uploaded on its website, a detailed comparative analysis of the Rhein-Main and Yongsan base redeployments. This electronically enabled joint research established several inconsistencies unfavorable to the U.S.-South Korea agreement, including: (1) Much greater specificity in the U.S.-German agreement, regarding construction and finance plans, as well as environmental restoration; (2) clear cost ceilings and specification constraints regarding the replacement facility in the German case; and (3) environmental provisions making restoration the responsibility of the U.S. government, and allowing Germans unrestricted base-access rights to investigate environmental degradation.

After uploading the detailed comparison on its website, SPARK on July 29 asked the Korean Foreign Ministry for a formal copy of the agreement on the YRP under the ROK Information Disclosure Act. Upon being refused, SPARK quickly turned to the U.S. Air Force in Europe (USAFE), under the U.S. Freedom of Information Act, and rapidly obtained a formal copy of the U.S.-German agreement. Thanks to new technologies of communication, it thus both developed a strategic working relationship with the German NGO BUND, enabling it to do systematic comparative Germany-Korea research on base-relocation conditions, and also exposed the rigidity and circumspection of the Korean Foreign Ministry, thus fueling the antibase movement in Korea.[25]

Governments, of course, have long had flexible modes of communication with one another, and the ability to rapidly confer and coordinate, much longer than have opponent activists. What is new—with the dawn of the twenty-first century—and consequential for base politics, is how the balance has shifted, and what the new situation demands of more conservative forces. The Establishment, in a word, no longer has the informational upper hand. Critics of bases at the subnational level—including many at the grassroots with incentives to nonagreement—now can exchange information, defuse it to the broader public, and plan protest strategies transnationally much more quickly than has ever been true before. And thanks to intensified personal contact and shared experience, such critics also have the *inclination* to coordinate more closely than before.

Cases presented here and in chapter 7—especially the Vieques antibase movement in Puerto Rico and protest movements in South Korea—testify to the power of new transnational forces operating in base politics. Such forces can help precipitate the actual closure of military facilities, with diffuse echo effects around the world.[26] Yet they can also have more geographically focused implications of great importance, close at hand.

Political Structure Mediates the Impact of Technology

In assessing the impact of antibase groups on policy, it is crucial to understand not only their views, and the underlying motivation for those views, but also the position of such groups in the host-nation political system. Technology is clearly changing their role, as noted above. So, too, are innovations in national administrative structure, which on the surface would appear to bear little relationship to base politics.

In decentralized, relatively pluralistic political systems, with autonomous or supportive mass media, antibase protest can be quite visible, uninhibited or even supported by local political authority, and resonant across the national political system as a whole, due to the autonomy of local leadership. South Korea since the mid-1990s is a striking case in point, due to the rapidly growing autonomy and assertiveness of local governments and NGOs. In more centralized political systems like that of Japan, by contrast, central authorities with transcendent foreign policy interests and leverage with mass media can more easily inhibit, suppress, or ignore an analogous level of grassroots protest, and even the pronouncements of local leaders.

In several countries, including South Korea and Japan, transnational information sharing and advocacy has intensified pressure for change in SOFAs, by revealing cross-national discrepancies perceived to be unfavorable to the host country. In South Korea transnational interactions have greatly complicated the Yongsan Redeployment Plan, as noted above, by exposing the extremely favorable terms, relative to those accorded by Germany, that the ROK government accorded to the United States. Internet cooperation between the Korean SPARK and the German BUND NGOs, as well as SPARK's filings under the U.S. Freedom of Information Act in the summer of 2004 with the U.S. Air Force in Europe, providing information that the Korean Foreign Ministry withheld, were critical to the outcome.[27]

Transnational interaction within Europe fueled resistance to the Pershing deployments of the early 1980s. Parallel dynamics within the Islamic world have clearly complicated base politics in Turkey, Pakistan, and Saudi Arabia, especially since the Afghan War. Clearly the transnational dimension of base politics in the Islamic world—both among Muslim nations and between them and the United States—will loom large in years to come, given the potential of the Internet and other new technological forms for easing cross-border communications.

Over time, a gradual worldwide increase in local autonomy may be broadening the efficacy of local protest—itself energized by new mobile technology. State structure, in concert with technological change, in short, clearly matters. Indeed, it may well be evolving so as to empower protest groups. Yet these environmental considerations, which often tend to enhance grassroots protest and increase its political efficacy, should be clearly distinguished from nationalist, antibase sentiments per se.

PRO-BASE POLITICS

The notion of foreign bases on national soil is, as we have noted from the outset, a historically unusual concept, and one elementally difficult for host nations to accept. Across history, overseas bases have been almost universally the essence, or at least the residue, of empires, either formal or informal. Until after World War II, truly independent nations did not host foreign bases on their soil. Once they arrive, foreign bases almost inevitably cause all sorts of nuisance, even as they enhance national security. Foreign soldiers commit crimes. Their vehicles can be noisy, destructive of nature, accident-prone, and can cause pollution. In almost every country there is a backlash, to some degree, against foreign military presence.

So if there is such a broad historic aversion to, and prejudice against, foreign bases, who, then, actually supports them? Who welcomes new bases, and who works to sustain support for the ones that already exist? How does the interest advocacy of these support groups compare—in tactics, resources, and networks—with that of their opponents? What broad cross-national contrasts can we draw? These are the issues that this section considers, regarding one of the most counter-intuitive topics relating to base politics that we will examine.

The Central Actors

As in the case of antibase protesters, the motives of probase actors include some mix of ideology, nationalism, and pragmatism. The three elements, however, appear to be more tightly fused among base-supporters. The supporters also appear to be a more homogenous group sociologically, relatively upscale, without the sharp income and education gaps among their membership that characterize the protesters.

Among the most important groups of probase actors in almost every host nation are the "conservative internationalists." These are the politicians, businesspeople, expatriates, and occasional idealistic citizens with stakes, often material, in the form of status quo interdependence with the broader world that a base presence generally facilitates. Their transnational orientation contrasts to the stronger grassroots perspective that typically characterizes base opponents.

Unlike their opponents, base supporters lack incentives to nonagreement. They have a converse stake in making often unpopular arrangements work. More likely than not, base backers are pragmatic and nationalistic, but not ideological. Like their opponents, they are more than occasionally duplicitous, since they need to appeal to multiple publics in the complex base-politics decision-making process.

Concretely, the sections of foreign ministries dealing with "basing-nation" allies, together with the top leaderships of these foreign ministries themselves—tend to be backers. So are defense ministries, provided that there are symbiotic relations between the basing-nation military and local defense authorities. This is usually the case, since basing nations like the United States typically provide military aid and sale of desired military equipment as key elements in base-support packages. Indeed, foreign military sales (FMS) have traditionally been a key element in sustaining base relationships in nations with powerful local militaries, such as those of Turkey, and, in previous eras, Spain, Portugal, Greece, and the Philippines.[28]

National political leadership generally tends to be engaged in base support, where continued presence of American bases is a key foreign-policy interest of the nation in question. In Japan, for example, the so-called Yoshida Doctrine, propounded by long-time Prime Minister Yoshida Shigeru (1946–47 and 1948–54), was implemented by diverting a portion of defense expenses toward domestic economic development, while partially compensating for this diversion through generous host-nation support for American bases in Japan.[29] Sometimes, as for Kim Dae-Jung and especially for his successor Roh Moo-Hyun in South Korea after 2002, supporting foreign base presence has meant running into tension or conflict with one's own core political constituencies. Leadership can often be crucial to whether bases are sustained in such situations.

In South Korea, a powerful presidency has historically filled this base-supportive function, despite the inherent political delicacy and contradictions involved. In the Philippines, by contrast, President Corazon Aquino, responding to her grass-roots constituency, betrayed more ambivalence about the U.S. bases there in the late 1980s, thus feeding the antibase movement without supporting it directly. To the extent that the Roh administration in South Korea showed ambivalence about local American troop presence after early 2003, or passivity in defending the presence of those forces, it also helped fuel local expression of latent antibase sentiments, much as Aquino did fifteen years earlier in the Philippines.

Beyond the government ministries and political figures with explicit foreign-policy functions, the breadth of probase support around the world by definition depends on how embedded base politics are in a given nation's local political economy. There is great national variation here, as chapter 8, dealing with host-nation support, suggests. In Japan, for example, base politics are deeply embedded, both in the local communities where bases exist and also at the national level, with a broad range of domestic beneficiaries. Workers on American bases, for example, are paid from host-nation support funds, and much of the land on which bases are built (three-quarters in Okinawa, for example) is leased by the Japanese government at favorable rates. New construction on the bases—all paid by the same Japanese government—is also substantial.

In Korea, by contrast, local groups benefit far less from the presence of bases. In contrast to Japan, there are few lucrative lease payments. Much base land has been requisitioned under eminent domain, and landlords close to bases do not generally find their presence lucrative, since they typically receive no lease payments. Indeed, conflicts over the use of private property arbitrarily dedicated to military use appear to be the largest source of base-related conflict in South Korea.[30] Local contractors providing repair and other services to the U.S. military do, of course, benefit, like distributors and shop owners with a military clientele. Yet their scale is much smaller than in Japan, and contracts are less profitable.

National business communities tend to be supporters of foreign, especially American, base presence, for broader political-economic reasons. U.S. military presence is perceived to imply American political-economic stability guarantees, and often preferential, asymmetric economic benefits, in return for hosting U.S. forces. In early postwar Europe security-related American economic support took the form of massive Marshall Plan aid transfers, while in East Asia it took the form of asymmetrical market-access opportunities.[31] Both tended to be greater, after the Korean War began, in countries that hosted American forces. Throughout the world, the indirect economic dividends of close security ties to the United States clearly attracted the local business world to the concept of hosting U.S. forces.

Big business is thus generally a probase constituency, due to its support for broad "milieu goals" served by base presence. In the case of early post–World War II Europe, this quid pro quo was massive reconstruction aid; in East Asia it was access to American markets, as noted above. More recently, business, together with many host-nation governments, and indeed a broad range of the local public, has been attracted by the political risk-reduction role of American bases especially as that translates into improved terms of access to international financing. This has been particularly true in Eastern European countries such as Poland, Bulgaria, and Romania—all recent hosts to U.S. bases. Local anticommunist or anti-Russian elites may assume that as long as American forces are present, it is less likely that there will be invasions from abroad, or modifications in free-market, democratic systems, thus encouraging foreign investors to focus on favorable economic conditions in such countries rather than on political risk.

Three generations removed from the Korean War, clientelism is, to be realistic, also often a major driving force in probase politics. The presence of bases, after all, typically generates economic benefits for local communities in areas such as Germany and Korea, where bases are large, relatively permanent, and involve substantial numbers of support staff and dependents.

In the Rhineland and Bavarian sections of Germany, in particular, where forces resisting a prospective invasion of Western Europe have been deployed since the 1950s, local stakes in continued U.S. military presence are especially high. Overall, Germany in 2005 hosted an American military community of over 175,000, including almost 120,000 dependents, in addition to more than 58,000 military personnel.[32] The Kaiserslautern Military Community alone consists of five major Air Force installations (including sprawling Ramstein Air Base), and ten major Army installations. The largest American military community outside the United States, it is home to around 44,000 military personnel and their dependents, making up one-fifth of the local population.[33] In cases such as these, where cultural conflict is minimal and local economic stakes are substantial, base relations can be relatively positive, even in heavily populated areas—a matter to which we will return.

Where the concentration of U.S. forces in the local population has been high, and overall base relations have been good, local authorities have indeed frequently become activists in trying to retain bases in the face of Pentagon efforts to downsize them. The mayors of Kaiserslautern and several nearby municipalities in the Rhineland, for example, visited the Pentagon and other U.S. government officials in Washington, D.C., in the spring of 2003 to lobby against downsizing of American forces in their areas, while allies sponsored research studies drawing attention to the importance of continued U.S. presence there. Schweinfurt, Bavaria, has also been deeply concerned.[34] German local governments have also pressured their central government in Berlin to oppose the downsizing of U.S. forces in Germany, thus becoming an important "veto player" in the face of the prospective policy changes implied by the "transformation strategy" of the George W. Bush administration.

Cross-nationally, civic groups have tended to be more antibase than not. There are, however, occasional important exceptions, especially when local civil society has a strong military tradition, or cultural affinities with the basing power. In South Korea, for example, the antibase movement of 2001–2003 provoked periodic probase counterdemonstrations in front of the sprawling Yongsan U.S. Army garrison in downtown Seoul and at Seoul's City Hall.[35] The Christian Council of Korea (CCK), and the General Association of Christian Associations, a major conservative umbrella group, were among the major probase activist groups, supported also by Korean War veterans.

Recently generational differences have often been an important factor in base politics. Just as voters in their twenties and thirties have often been markedly skeptical toward U.S. bases, especially in Korea, older people—particularly those above sixty—have been strongly supportive. Where a nation's history features a critical transforming experience, as Korea's does with the Korean War, this sort of generational split can be especially prominent.[36]

IN CONCLUSION: NATIONAL VS. LOCAL INCENTIVES

Base politics, this chapter has suggested, is a complex, bimodal contest. The most visible and volatile element is an intransigent grassroots opposition—often young and parochial in its political tactics, if diverse and transnational in intellectual provenance and connections. The key weapon of such grassroots opposition is visible protest, and its allies tend to include mass media, the intellectual community, and aggrieved local groups.

Confronting this high-profile, populist, and often vehement opposition is a more conservative group of base supporters. Many are bureaucrats or businesspeople. Most have cosmopolitan interests in international affairs. Powerful in the routine decision processes of their nation, this group tends to prefer settling base issues quietly, and avoiding polarizing confrontation, in which populist opposition appeals disadvantage them.

Whether base issues can indeed be settled quietly or not often depends on the case at hand. Unpredictable catalysts such as crimes and accidents render base-politics outcomes at the grassroots, base-specific level chronically uncertain. Yet resolution also often depends on the historical and demographic context. It is to those environmental factors, so fatefully surrounding the penumbra of decision, to which we now turn.

CHAPTER FIVE

THE BASE-POLITICS ENVIRONMENT

COMPARATIVE PERSPECTIVES

WE HAVE IDENTIFIED the major actors in base politics, as well as the general logic of their interaction. Now it is necessary to consider dynamic external sociopolitical forces, often destabilizing, which drive the process itself, and often determine its outcome. Virtually all of the remarkably small number of base-politics studies undertaken so far focus on individual countries or bases, rather than such dynamic cross-national factors, and are hence a form of static area-studies research.[1] While often well crafted empirically, they focus on individual trees in the base-politics forest, and not on what drives the dialectic of support for and opposition to bases more generally. Understanding that broader, underlying rationale for patterns in base politics is the central analytical concern of this chapter.

A guiding precept throughout this work is that comparative analysis can improve outcomes: that generalizations capable of enhancing base management and base relations can be produced by systematically understanding the similarities and differences among nations. As the following pages will graphically illustrate, host nations do *not* react in *uniform* ways to the presence of foreign forces; neither do individual host nations respond consistently over time. And their varied reactions often fail to correspond closely to generally accepted local norms.

Yet base politics nevertheless has a clearly predictable aspect, especially at the national level. There are remarkably consistent relationships, crossnationally and over time, between historical and demographic variables, on the one hand, and patterns of base politics, on the other. As we will see, basing nations that establish themselves early in a host country as "liberating occupiers" have incomparably stronger prospects of retaining their basing presence than those identified locally as neo-imperialists, for example. Basing nations also invariably have troubled base relations in heavily populated areas.

These uniformities, it is argued, should allow analysts to predict the disposition of particular host nations toward foreign base presence, and to anticipate the prospective behavior of basing nations as well. This chapter explores the general biases that extrapolitical factors create in base politics in an effort to aid assessment of how relations among bases, host governments, and communities will actually evolve in concrete situations. Generally speaking, these environmental factors do not ease the prognosis for foreign bases, but rather point to danger signs for those embattled garrisons that can only be ignored at the basing nation's peril.

HISTORICAL PROVENANCE AND BASE POLITICS

Like earthquakes in the natural world, regime shifts in the political realm can trigger massive transformation. They have sweeping, often unsettling implications for base politics, as also for other aspects of social life. As with earthquakes, there is always a new moment of indeterminacy with regime shifts, when the sheer *possibility* for major transformation, and even chaos, is unusually great, because the players and the policy context in which they act are often new.

Yet exactly what *sort* of transformation occurs in the process of regime shift matters very much for everyday base politics, as the varied consequences of MacArthur's 1945 arrival in Japan, Corazon Aquino's 1986 "People's Power" uprising in the Philippines, and the 2003 fall of Baghdad all suggest. Depending on its configurations, a transition in host-nation governance can force immediate foreign troop withdrawal, stabilize foreign presence for generations to come, or give birth to anguished domestic struggles that leave outcomes painfully in doubt. The consequences of particular types of regime shifts are remarkably predictable. And they offer, like seismology, important insights both for policy, and for future individual action.

There is much in the historical sequencing of base politics that is strikingly indeterminate, leaving considerable scope for leadership to impose its imprint on history. Much has been written lately about the pros and cons of formal and informal empire.[2] What is clear, as the following pages will show, is that *formal* empire, at least, typically leads to volatile host-nation politics in its aftermath, within the ex-colonies. Conversely, postwar occupations can potentially produce the reverse outcome.

If occupations follow tyrannical dictatorships to which the occupying power had no connection, and open positive new alternatives for a nation's citizens, occupations can potentially be seen as liberating and can stabilize base politics for many years thereafter. The crucial imperative, historical experience suggests, is thus for occupiers to be perceived in host nations as liberators, not as imperialists. In much of the Islamic world, where Britain and France have long histories as imperial powers, that is a difficult, but crucial, distinction.

Historical origins, in short, are crucial to understanding the institutional environment in which base politics develops thereafter. The following pages outline the diverse and fateful paths along which the relations of host and basing nations can flow. And they seek to clarify the daunting challenges to stability in base relations that security partners confront when their relationship flows from empire—even when, as in the U.S.-Filipino case, they have been long-standing allies and battle comrades.

THE TRAVAILS OF IMPERIAL SUCCESSION

The Colonization Hypothesis presented in chapter 3 suggested that imperial powers find it difficult to retain their base presence in the aftermath of a host-nation's independence, no matter how strongly they want to do so, and no matter how benevolent the colonial experience has been locally perceived to have been in their erstwhile colonies. As indicated in table 5.1 (pp. 100–101), the evidence appears to substantiate this proposition. Britain, France, and the United States all had trouble maintaining a forward-deployed presence in newly independent nations once their colonial interlude in those nations had ended. So, too, did the Soviet Union in relation to its long-time satellites once the Berlin Wall fell. Indeed, within a decade of the Soviet collapse, the Russians had withdrawn their formal military presence from every one of their former satellites, including Cuba and Vietnam, and from more than half of the constituent republics of the former Soviet Union as well.

The Russian military's tribulations in the "Near Abroad" clearly illustrate the general aversion of host nations to foreign bases as leftover trappings of empire. In two cases (those of Tajikistan and Belarus), the Russians remain as guests of unreconstructed dictators through special deals with the local despot. In two other instances (those of Moldova and Georgia), the Russians remain in portions of the countries, in support of local separatist groups. Only in Armenia and Kyrgyzstan (the latter of which also hosts American forces) have they been tolerated by both leaders and the general populace, for highly case-specific reasons.

The logic of this persistent cross-national aversion to hosting the military of former imperial masters is clear. Establishing true independence stands among the highest priorities of fledgling nations, and the presence of long-established colonial forces naturally stands in the way. Removing such forces can also be a strong catalyst for national unity—an especially useful tool for national elites confronting new and fractious national polities while lacking legitimacy of their own. Appropriating foreign bases can also, like nationalization, provide local nationalist leaders with much needed physical, financial, and/or

TABLE 5.1.
The End of Empire and the End of Base Presence

	Host Nation	Independence	Withdrawal[a]
Great Britain	South Africa	1910	1962
	Iraq	1932	1958
	Jordan	1946	1957
	Ceylon	1947	1956
	India/Pakistan	1947	1947
	Malaysia	1957	1967
	Cyprus	1960	—
	Singapore	1962	1967
	Malta	1964	1979
	Kenya	1964	1964
	Vanuatu	1980	1980
	Belize	1981	1994
	Brunei	1984	—
	Hong Kong	1997	1997
United States	Cuba	1902	—
	Panama[b]	1903	1999
	Philippines	1946	1992
France	Indochina	1954	1954
	Morocco	1956	1956
	Guinea	1958	1959
	Malagasy	1960	1975
	Senegal	1960	—
	Ivory Coast	1960	—
	Chad	1960	—
	Gabon	1960	—
	Central African Rep.	1960	—
	Algeria	1962	1962
	Comoro Islands	1975	No
	Djibouti	1977	No
	Vanuatu	1980	1980
Russia[c]			
Satellites	Cuba	—	2001
	Vietnam	—	2001
	Poland	—	1993
	East Germany	1990 (unification)	1993
	Hungary	—	1991
	Czech	—	1991
"Near Abroad"[d]	Lithuania	1991	1999
	Armenia	1991	—

TABLE 5.1. (*Continued*)

Host Nation	Independence	Withdrawal[a]
Georgia	1991	—
Latvia	1991	1994
Estonia	1991	1994
Azerbaijan	1991	1994
Ukraine	1991	1993
Uzbekistan	1991	1994
Kazakhstan	1991	1994
Kyrgyzstan	1992	—
Belarus	1991	—
Moldova	1991	—
Tajikistan	1991	—
Turkmenistan	1991	1994

Sources: CIA, *World Factbook*, available at http://www.cia.gov/cia/publications/factbook/; *Keesings Contemporary Archives*, London: Keesing's LMD, available at http://keesings.gvpi. net/keesings/lpext.dll?f=templates&fn=main-h.htm&2.0/.

Notes:

a. "Withdrawal" dates denote the departure of imperial powers from their former colonies.

b. In the case of Panama, independence was from Colombia, but the Canal Zone was under U.S. legal jurisdiction until 1999, when it was ceded to Panama under the 1977 Torrijos-Carter Treaty.

c. Russian satellites are included in this calculation as they were under strong Russian/Soviet geopolitical control during the period in question, and thus a de facto component of empire.

d. The "Near Abroad" refers to one-time constituent parts of the Soviet Union, later formally independent after its dissolution at the beginning of 1992.

symbolic resources to help them sustain or reinforce their own domestic political dominance.

Interestingly French bases are the exception that illustrates the political logic behind the broader rule. As indicated in figure 5.1, while British base presence disappeared with independence in all but 14 percent of the Untied Kingdom's former possessions, French bases persisted nearly three times as frequently—in 38 percent of France's ex-colonies. The durability of those French bases appears due to the neocolonialist tendencies often pervading French relations with nominally independent former colonies. Where French forces are not summarily expelled through wars of national liberation, as they were in North Vietnam and Algeria, those forces quite frequently remain under neocolonialist arrangements that are distinctively durable, from a comparative perspective. Certainly this was the classic pattern in Senegal, Ivory Coast, Gabon, and other such neocolonialist extensions of the Parisian Metropole.

Britain, in contrast to France, has smartly withdrawn its forces from former colonies. The only major exception, apart from post-2003 Iraq involvement together with the United States, has been Cyprus.[3] There the Royal Air Force (RAF) continues to maintain a major presence in the Sovereign Base Areas at Akrotiri and Dhekelia in order to defend British energy interests in the Middle East, while also inhibiting the serious local ethnic conflict between local Greeks and Turks that has intensified in the wake of colonial rule.[4] This enduring British presence is legitimated by a supportive clause in the 1960 international treaty establishing the Republic of Cyprus.

Britain has also intermittently maintained a military presence in Oman since the Darfur rebellion of 1964–76, although its deployments there lack the scale and institutionalization of Cyprus.[5] In Kenya (1964), South Yemen (1967), Malta (1979), and Hong Kong (1997), British forces withdrew almost immediately in the wake of colonial rule. Since the Suez debacle of 1956, when the Anglo-French attempt to retake the nationalized Suez Canal was rebuffed by the United States, followed by their withdrawal from Jordan (1957), Kassem's Iraqi coup, and the ensuing evacuation of Habaniyyah Air Base (1958), the British have learned to retire gracefully and avoid the awkward but inevitable trials of imperial succession.

For the post–World War II United States, given its preeminent global role, avoiding the perils of imperial succession has been more difficult. America has not had the luxury of gracefully retiring from erstwhile colonial responsibilities. Yet host-nation resistance to U.S. postimperial presence has been remarkably similar to that confronted by the British and the French. Three major base-politics cases have been involved: those of the Philippines, Panama, and Guantanamo Bay, Cuba. The bilateral politics of Guantanamo have been quite static, due to the frozen state of U.S.-Cuban relations since the revolution of 1959.[6] American interactions with both the Philippines and Panama illustrate clearly, however, the difficulties for even the United States of imperial succession, and the dangers of ethnocentrism and lack of political sophistication that have more recently plagued the U.S. effort in Iraq.[7]

The U.S. presence in both the Philippines and Panama was, to be sure, relatively durable, lasting until 1992 in the former and 1999 in the latter case. Some of the dynamics were different, with Panamanian president Torrijos proactively seeking American withdrawal in Panama, and Aquino more passively reflecting diffuse antibase frustrations in the Philippine case, which Foreign Minister Raul Manglapus nevertheless evocatively described as "parricide." "We must slay the father figure," he passionately argued.[8]

Yet American bases ultimately fell prey in both instances to pressures from populist nationalism, and to the chaos accompanying leadership transition in a turbulent, self-assertive developing nation. Were American relations with Cuba to thaw, Guantanamo would be highly vulnerable also. And the United States made a fateful mistake in appointing an American viceroy with limited Middle East experience, however able, to administer Iraq following the fall of Saddam Hussein.[9] That only helped confirm in Arab eyes America's role as imperialist rather than liberator. As the managers of base politics worldwide have often learned to their chagrin, imperial succession is a perilous path.

THE STABILIZING HERITAGE OF LIBERATING OCCUPATIONS

Over more than a century of active military deployment beyond its shores, the United States has struggled with politically charged base politics in former possessions like the Philippines and the Panama Canal Zone. Indeed, it has ultimately withdrawn from virtually all such areas. The only exceptions are Guantanamo Bay in Cuba, a unique heritage of the Cold War, and Puerto Rico, since 1947 tied to the Stars and Stripes by a commonwealth agreement.

The U.S. has also experienced frequent trouble in informally allied Third World nations previously occupied by European colonial powers, such as Morocco, Ethiopia, Libya, and of course, Iraq. Ultimately it has ended up withdrawing from virtually all such countries. The experience of other imperial powers—Britain, Russia, and even France—has been similar. They simply cannot sustain a long-term basing presence where the historical heritage of Europeans as imperialists is strong.

Base politics in nations that the U.S. has occupied for extended periods of time and then returned to independence, however, are often paradoxically and strikingly different—much more stable and positive, as the Occupation Hypothesis presented in chapter 3 has suggested. As indicated in table 5.2, the United States has occupied four nations for periods of at least three years since the end of World War II—two in Europe, and two in Asia. These nations have diverse political heritages and cultures. Their peoples in several cases conducted bitter struggles in wartime against U.S. forces, with large numbers of local citizens killed and maimed, particularly by U.S. bombing.[10]

Yet none of these nations has ever expelled the American military from its shores. Indeed, these four countries continue to have the most substantial and enduring U.S. military presence anywhere in the world outside the Middle East. Paradoxically the incidence of serious political

TABLE 5.2.
A Paradox—Conflict, Occupation, and Base Stability

Country	When Occupied by the U.S.	Wartime Casualties[a]	Current U.S. Presence[b]
Germany	1945–1955	3,500,000	Continuing/ 58,000
Japan	1945–1952	3,300,000	Continuing/ 34,000
Italy	1943–1947	330,000	Continuing/ 9,000
South Korea	1945–1948	1,312,836[c]	Continuing/ 30,000

Sources: Joseph C. O'Brien, *WWII: The Casualties*, available at http://web.jjay.cuny.edu/jobrien/reference/ob62.html; U.S. Department of Defense, *Worldwide Manpower Distribution by Geographical Area*, 2005 edition.

Notes:

a. "Wartime casualties" denote those incurred in wars in which the United States was a principal opponent of the occupied nation, or intervened in an international conflict.

b. Figures for U.S. troop presence are those for September 2005, rounded to the closest 1,000.

c. All casualties in South Korea were incurred during the Korean War (1950–1953).

backlash against American forces is substantially less than in most places where the American presence is smaller.

Why has the host-nation support for U.S. military presence been so unusually stable and accommodating in these four nations, each of which has bitter memories of wartime confrontation with, and bombardment by, the Americans, not to mention the degrading experiences of occupation? The cases present an interesting and potentially significant study in the impact of political engineering on institutional structure, and ultimately on social outcomes, since they share few common features other than their experience of occupation. In a post-9/11 world in which interventionism and "nation-building" are once again in vogue, the early post–World War II cases may provide insights into what occupations contribute to making a foreign military presence enduring.[11]

Common Institutional Heritage

The four nations long occupied by the United States share a common institutional heritage that appears to account for much of the unusual stability and flexibility in their local base politics. The political-military dimension of this heritage consists of five embedded elements, which contrast to patterns in nonoccupied nations: (1) large, but decentralized troop presence, broadly distributed across the country; (2) declining troop presence in postoccupation years, albeit from high initial occupation-period levels; (3) cooperative transnational diplomatic and military

Political/Policy Trait	Germany	Japan	Italy	South Korea
Decentralized Troop Presence	Yes	Yes	Yes	Yes
Declining Troop Presence	Yes	Yes	Yes	Yes
Cooperative Political-Military Networks	Yes	Yes	Yes	Yes
Antinationalist Purge	Yes	Yes	Yes	No
United States Associated with Local Dictator	No	No	No	Yes

Figure 5.1. Why Occupation Produces Base Stability: Comparative Perspectives

networks, together with grassroots institutions systematically linking local officials with their American counterparts; (4) smooth intra-alliance operating procedures, reinforced by general popular acceptance of a legitimate U.S. occupation purge, which generally eliminated nationalist and communist elements opposed to both democracy and a local American presence; and (5) no U.S. history of close previous association with local dictatorship or a former colonial power. The key political-military elements of the common institutional heritage of American occupation are indicated in figure 5.1

Beyond the foregoing, the "liberating occupations" of the early post–World War II years in Europe and Japan promoted broad social reforms that enhanced their legitimacy as liberators. In Japan, for example, the Allied Occupation broke up cartels and large *zaibatsu*, introduced universal suffrage, legalized labor unions, and promoted land reform. These progressive steps allowed it to credibly claim to be reviving the pre-1931 tradition of Taisho democracy,[12] and hence "liberating" Japan. Germany and Italy also had long-standing liberal traditions to which the post–World War II occupations there could and did appeal.[13]

The Italian Paradox

Seen in comparative perspective, there are intriguing empirical contrasts between the base politics of the above nations as a group, with their common histories of American occupation, and adjacent areas to which these cooperative nations would appear to be culturally and politically similar. This paradox of cultural similarity coupled with base-politics distinctiveness is especially pronounced in the case of Italy, reinforcing our argument that embedded history matters. Italy has been much more supportive of the local U.S. military presence than Mediterranean neighbors such as Spain, Greece, and Turkey, despite its World War II confrontation with the United States and the continuing presence in the Italian National Assembly of one of the most powerful local protocommunist parties in the industrialized world.

Italian military support of the United States began in the early postoccupation period, and continued through a remarkably stalwart involvement with the controversial George W. Bush administration intervention in Iraq.[14] Italy, in contrast to her neighbors, never once tried to renegotiate its base agreements with the United States during the Cold War, or to reduce the U.S. military presence on its territory.[15] In contrast to Spain, Greece, and most emphatically France, it never raised problems regarding nuclear weapons.

To the contrary, Italy has indicated a willingness to accept a wide variety of nuclear weapons on its territory, including Jupiter missiles in the 1960s and ground-launched Pershing cruise missiles during the 1980s. In the late 1980s, Italy also accepted F-16 aircraft withdrawn from Torrejon in Spain, provided that the NATO infrastructure fund would bear the costs.[16] And in the late 1990s, with a former communist, Massimo d'Alema, as prime minister, Italy quietly resolved an egregious incident in which U.S. Marine aviators flying illegally low, in populated areas, clipped a cable-car line, and sent dozens of Italians to their deaths near a major Dolomite ski resort.[17]

To be sure, the United States did have occasional differences with Italy on base-related security issues, especially in the 1970s and 1980s, including particularly the third-country deployment of locally based forces. Like other European members of NATO except Portugal, Italy denied the U.S. overflight rights in connection with its resupply of Israel during the 1973 Yom Kippur War. It also protested American actions following the 1985 hijacking of the cruise ship *Achille Lauro*, and in the wake of Ronald Reagan's 1986 air strike on Libya. Yet overall, Italian support for the United States on base-related issues for more than a half-century since the occupation has been consistently positive, to a remarkable degree that provides strong support for the "liberating occupation" argument, as we shall see.

Korean Exceptionalism?

While the various extended U.S. occupations left a distinct institutional heritage in host nations, especially relevant to local elite political-military decision making, they also bequeathed, in most cases, a distinct *popular legitimacy* to host-nation governments. In contrast to predecessor regimes, the new governments were not implicated with local dictatorship or colonization.

They were, instead, the outgrowth of "liberating occupations." This autonomy from an ignoble past likewise facilitated smoother base relations with the United States than would otherwise have been the case. Korea, as suggested in figure 5.1, was a partial exception to the foregoing Liberating Occupation Hypothesis that demonstrates the logic of the more general rule.

In Germany, Japan, and Italy, the early post–World War II United States was clearly established in the general public mind as a liberator, clearly distinct from the discredited local wartime authorities. In Korea that was not so true. American occupation forces, appearing suddenly at the end of World War II in a country regarding which they had little real knowledge, relied heavily on the hated local Japanese occupation-era power structure, thus alienating much of Korean public opinion.[18] During the late 1940s, U.S.-occupied South Korea was beset by demonstrations, diffuse political unrest, and incipient insurgency. This local disenchantment was partially disillusionment with an occupation authority that appeared colonialist by association.

The occupation of South Korea formally ended in August 1948, with Koreans remaining distinctly ambivalent about the U.S. role.[19] The United States recovered its local legitimacy there only through the Korean War. To be sure, Korean civilian as well as military casualties were horrendous, with over two million people, North and South, perishing in the conflict. Yet North Korea initiated the war, and savagery from the North was unforgettable. The United States honored its commitments to the South in blood, losing 37,000 of its own troops and contributing generously to Korean reconstruction once the conflict was over.

The U.S. presence in South Korea thus enjoyed for many years an alternate legitimacy as liberator—flowing not so much from Occupation as from cooperation in the Korean War. Yet the complex, suppressed memories of early post–World War II occupation were far from fully positive, due particularly to the informal American tolerance for Japanese collaborators. As generational change dulled memories of the bitter Korean War itself, and as democratic transformation after 1987 stirred resentments of U.S. support for the military dictatorship that had preceded it, the American presence in Korea grew more controversial at the mass-popular level than in the other formerly occupied nations. This controversy persisted even as the elite-level institutions inherited from the Occupation continued to perform the harmonizing functions for base politics in Korea that they played in Germany, Italy, and Japan.

Empire versus Liberating Occupation: Manifestations in the Islamic World

Every army of liberation has a half-life.
—*General David Petraeus, FDCH*
Congressional testimony, January 23, 2007

Since the end of the Cold War, and especially since 9/11, the locus of American overseas deployments has shifted from Europe and East Asia to the Islamic world—an area of special historical and cultural sensitivity for Western military forces. The dual symbolism of the Crusades and early twentieth-century Anglo-Saxon imperialism no doubt leaves American and European forces with special political handicaps and vulnerability in the Middle East, far beyond Iraq. The embedded heritage of past imperialism, plus the traumas of regime shift, forced British troops out of Egypt (1954), Jordan (1957), Iraq (1958), and South Yemen (1967), while making long-term American military presence similarly untenable in Morocco (1962), Saudi Arabia (1962), and Libya (1969).

The continuing—indeed, arguably intensifying—general ambivalence in the Islamic world about Western political-military intervention is well-known.[20] Yet there appears to simultaneously be substantial admiration in some quarters for Western political-economic models, and considerable cross-national variation within the region in the intensity of local sentiment regarding America and its political role, with some groups, such as Moroccans and Lebanese Christians, even overtly positive about the United States.[21] Given these nuances, and the policy importance of the question, it is worth asking whether the concept of "liberating occupations," seemingly relevant to base politics in Europe and East Asia, might be usefully applied in the Middle East.

Three recent and ongoing cases in the Islamic world—seen against the backdrop of "liberation occupations" of the past elsewhere in the world—cast special light on the viability of longer-term American basing presence there, in support of the global struggle against terrorism. These crucial cases are Bosnia, Afghanistan, and Iraq. While the first two cases offer some reason to hope for a stable American presence there, should regional security imperatives dictate, the latter is clearly more problematic. The positive implications for certain types of Western security presence

	Afghanistan	Bosnia	Japan	Italy	Germany	Iraq
Pre-existing Regime (Dictatorial)	Yes Radical Fundamentalist (Taliban)	Yes Dictator (Milošević)	Yes Dictator (Tojo)	Yes Dictator (Mussolini)	Yes Dictator (Hitler)	Yes Dictator (Saddam)
Occupier Ties to Previous Colonial Power	No	Limited	No	No	No	Significant
Multilateral Dimension	Yes (ISAF)	Yes (IFOR)	Some	Yes	Yes	Little
Foreign Occupation Administrator	No	No	Yes	Not Long	Yes	Yes
Local Leader	Yes (Karzai)	Yes (Izgebovitch)	Yes (Yoshida)	Yes (de Gaspari)	Yes (Adenauer)	No (Bremer)
Legitimating Procedures	Yes (Loya Jirga)	Yes (Elections)	Yes (Elections)	Yes (Elections)	Yes (Elections)	Limited Elections Initially Denied
Occupation Troops (6 months to 1 year after Occupation)	7,500	32,000	190,000	NA	340,000	146,400

Figure 5.2. Preconditions for Liberating Occupation

Sources: http://gdb.u-shimane.ac.jp/neardb/nenpyo/1946.html; and IFOR website, at http://www.nato.int/ifor/ifor.htm.

Note: Italy presents a special situation for which the "occupation troops" category is inappropriate. Italy concluded an armistice with the Allied Powers in September 1943, and declared itself a co-belligerent, but World War II continued on its territory until the spring of 1945.

in Afghanistan, together with the disturbing preliminary implications for Iraq, are elaborated in chapter 10.

Bosnia, Afghanistan, and Iraq—like Japan, Italy, and Germany before them—are all cases where the United States itself at the outset had clear aspirations to achieve a "liberating occupation." America arguably intended its forces to occupy briefly, transform local politics in Wilsonian fashion, and then depart. Broadly speaking, Bosnia and to a lesser degree Afghanistan have been markedly more successful in their transformation efforts than Iraq, albeit not on the decisive Japanese and German patterns.

Significantly, as noted in figure 5.2, the Bosnian and Afghan cases share important features with one another that they do not fully share with Iraq. Most importantly, the military interventions in both Afghanistan (after the very early stages) and Bosnia were deeply multilateral: in both cases a broad multilateral agreement, setting parameters for domestic political as well as international cooperation, came within two months of the onset of American-initiated military intervention. The Intervention Force (IFOR) in Bosnia and the International Security Assistance Force(ISAF) in Afghanistan were primarily responsible for local security from early on, thus diluting the dominant, unilateralist presence of the United States.[22] Similarly, the United Nations Mission in Afghanistan (UNAMA), established in March, 2002, assisted domestic administration in Afghanistan, in place of direct occupation, while NATO, OSCE, the IMF, and the United Nations were all involved in Bosnia. In Iraq, by contrast with these other cases, the United States was more unilaterally dominant, although not entirely alone.[23]

Afghanistan and Bosnia, as shown in figure 5.2, also rapidly established local post-transition leadership, amplifying the image of liberation. Hamid Karzai parachuted into the Kandahar area with guerilla forces in early October 2001, while Bosnia declared independence from Serbian Yugoslavia. Iraq, by contrast, was ruled by the U.S.-dominated Coalitional Provisional Authority (CPA) for fourteen months after the fall of Baghdad. The CPA administrator himself, Paul Bremer, was the consummate generalist—an efficient, poised, but indelibly American diplomat, formerly ambassador to the Netherlands, whose combination of elite Washington background, suspicion of democracy, lack of Middle East language skills or cultural background, and personal distance from the turbulent, parochial Iraqi political process made it difficult for him to help build the institutions and political infrastructure requisite for healthy base relations, not to mention pluralist democracy.[24]

To intensify the imperial cast of the American presence still further, CPA Administrator Bremer countermanded initial occupation promises of early elections, admittedly against the advice of the UN's local Special Representative, Sergio de Mello.[25] In contrast to this pattern, legitimating procedures for local authority were undertaken in Bosnia and Afghanistan early on. Bosnia, for example, held general elections in September 1996—only nine months after the Dayton Peace Accords[26] while Afghanistan held a traditional *loya jirga* (grand council) to ratify Karzai's accession to national leadership in June 2002, and held a general election to elect him as the first president in October 2004.

The Japanese and German cases, to be sure, involved considerably more arbitrary American sociopolitical engineering than prevailed in Bosnia and Afghanistan. The parallels in this respect between the American approach to Iraq and to the former Axis powers were indeed strong. Yet the decisive difference, as Paul Bremer himself pointed out in his memoirs, was that Japan and Germany were decisively defeated, and hence more willing to accept a fundamental redefinition of their national parameters than was Iraq.[27] Additionally, as Bremer noted, the United States had far fewer troops on hand, relative to population,[28] and had far less time to plan the occupation itself.[29]

Given America's more precarious political position in Iraq, relative to the early post–World War II Japanese and German situations, it was all the more incumbent on U.S. forces to respond sensitively to underlying host-nation domestic political dynamics, and to do so in a timely fashion. This they were manifestly unable to do so. By late 2003, six months after the invasion, the insurgency was beginning to gain traction. There are clearly groups in pluralist Iraq, including Kurds and certain Sunnis, with incentives of their own, based on fear of Shiite dominance, to desire an extended American military presence there.[30] Yet their latent support, some of it no doubt persisting, was increasingly overwhelmed by the backlash against a CPA presence increasingly seen as imperial and insensitive to Iraq's underlying problems.

Yet any future U.S. presence in Iraq, as we shall see in later chapters, must come to terms with history, and with the stark, exclusive alternate roles of "imperialist" and "occupying liberator," which Iraq's political tradition offers to foreign interventionists. These categories do not, of course, necessarily conform to more universal and less historically rooted notions like freedom and democracy that Americans hold dear. American policymakers, not surprisingly, failed to grasp initially either the potential or the danger that they faced in being forced unwittingly into one of these roles.

Shortly after Baghdad fell, according to an early Iraqi poll, 43 percent of Iraqis viewed Americans as liberators. By the fall of 2003, just six months into the occupation, this ratio had fallen to 15 percent due to errors such as suspension of elections, autocratic rule by an American administrator, aggressive search and destroy missions, and failure to clothe the American presence in more multilateral, "Arab-friendly" symbolic garb.[31] Despite a gradual learning process, involving increasingly refined counterinsurgency strategies,[32] America has failed to effectively utilize in Iraq the considerable potential symbolic power of its own democratic origins, and its most powerful rhetorical contribution to global affairs: its role as a "liberating occupier."[33]

Past occupations, in sum, have been much more conducive than imperial successions to stable long-term U.S. forward-deployed presence overseas, despite the heritage of wartime destruction and bitterness from which those occupations arose. The differences between occupations and imperial successions have two specific origins: (1) the greater *legitimacy* that occupations have enjoyed, due to their association in the popular mind with liberation, rather than with colonial rule; and (2) the *institutional reforms*, including the purge of noncooperative elites, that occupations have typically undertaken with substantially more vigor than imperial successors have done.

Korea is the partial exception that demonstrates the broader rules, and that thus counterintuitively provides important lessons for current U.S. Middle East strategy in connection with the ongoing antiterrorist struggle. Korea was clearly a *less* successful occupation than counterparts in Germany, Italy, and Japan for reasons that prefigure the problems the United States has recently experienced in Iraq. America did *not* establish itself so clearly as a "liberating occupier" in Korea as elsewhere, though this failing was temporarily mitigated by U.S. intervention to repel aggression from the North during the Korean War. We will return to the important subject of the *policy implications* of the successful Liberating Occupation model of base politics in the conclusion of the book, relating it to contemporary policy problems confronting the United States in the Middle East today.

COPING WITH THE FLOODWATERS: REGIME SHIFTS AND BASE POLITICS

The historical heritage of base politics naturally includes two dimensions: (1) the residue of the basing nation's presence, be it imperial or liberating; and (2) the transformations wrought in the host nation itself by a shift in external political-economic parameters such as alliance relationships. The foregoing pages have considered the first aspect. Now we move to the second.

Regime shifts, particularly transitions to democracy, have classically been recognized as having profound implications for national security, weighing heavily on prospects for war and peace.[34] The notion that regime change to democracy leads toward peace—a basic intellectual justification for the American intervention in Iraq—has venerable roots, dating back to Immanuel Kant and Woodrow Wilson. Yet this proposition is all too rarely tested in concrete cases.

The notion of regime change, so central to current debates in international affairs, need clearer empirical specification. There are two aspects of this latter fateful transformation within the host nation: (1) the initial indeterminacy, and even chaos, wrought by a regime shift heralding the end of foreign dominance, such as democratization in Eastern Europe; and (2) the regime type that ultimately follows in its wake. This successor regime type could be dictatorship, democracy, or some permutation in between. We will consider first how regime shifts intensify uncertainty, and hence potential turbulence in base relations. Then we will look at how dictatorship and certain variants of democracy can alternatively stabilize and complicate the political-economic environment with which base politics must contend. As we will see, there is no straightforward relationship between democracy and America's global basing relationships—if anything regime changes to democracy make base politics more difficult, rather than easier, for the United States, at least in the short run.

Regime shifts can significantly complicate key aspects of host-nation base politics: (1) the coherence of host-nation elite networks that negotiate and ratify base agreements; (2) public sentiment toward foreign forces, especially those which have been closely identified with previous dictatorial regimes; and (3) the profile and base-related incentives of key host-nation political actors, such as the military, mass media, civilian bureaucrats, and NGOs. These political earthquakes also reveal latent popular resistance to foreign bases, often seething at the grassroots, and flowing from anti-imperial resentments, or from the concentration of foreign military forces in highly populated areas.

Regime shifts, in short, sharply reconfigure the chessboard of host-nation domestic base politics, releasing latent, often unsuspected pressures, and introducing chronic domestic uncertainty. Such uncertainty also often constrains prospects for international agreements, including intra-alliance transactions, at the international level as well.[35] In the post–Cold War world, as geostrategic constraints on base politics decline, regime shifts may grow more important as a determinant of basing patterns in host nations. And as bases in unstable Central Asian, Middle Eastern, Latin American, and African nations proliferate in connection with the global antiterrorist struggle, the chances also rise that regime shifts in the aggregate will become a more important American policy concern, and a rising constraint on future basing.

Implications of Regime Shifts

In addition to their apparently powerful role in provoking foreign military withdrawal, democratic transitions also appear to provoke five more limited, but nevertheless unsettling types of change in host-nation base politics:

1. *Intensified pressures to downsize foreign military presence*, with an emphasis on closings of high-profile bases in urban areas. In Spain, for example, Socialist Workers Party Prime Minister Felipe Gonzalez demanded closure of the U.S. Torrejon Air Base outside Madrid in 1988, and the transfer from Spain of its 401st Tactical Fighter Wing.[36] Ultimately, the base was downsized, and then closed in 1996. In Greece, left-oriented Prime Minister Andreas Papandreou similarly demanded closure of the U.S. Hellenikon Air Base in the outskirts of Athens in 1988, following major defections

from his coalition to more radical groups in national municipal elections.[37] In Korea, there has similarly been long-standing political pressure for closure of the Yongsan Garrison American headquarters in the center of Seoul, and a formal 1991 U.S.-Korea agreement to do so, with the final movement of American forces scheduled to occur close to two decades later. In Iraq, analogous downsizing pressures from host-nation politics were also persistently discernable during 2004–2007, despite the heavy local reliance on U.S. forces.

2. *Rising emphasis on antinuclear issues.* Both Spain's Gonzalez and Greece's Papandreou, for example, strongly pursued this theme, as have NGOs throughout the world, recently in increasing coordination with one another via the Internet.

3. *Intensified pressure for large increases in base rentals.* This pattern has been virtually universal in transitional democracies. Russia, Britain, and France have been economically unwilling or unable to respond, making lease-payment issues a principal reason for their departure from nations as varied as Mongolia, Malagasy, and Vietnam. The United States has similarly faced a massive escalation of demands from new democracies, as noted above. In Kyrgyzstan, for example, President Bakiyev demanded a 100-fold increase in rent on U.S. bases, from $2 million annually to $200 million, after his 2005 democratic election victory, and ultimately settled for $150 million in July 2006.[38] Except in the Philippines, the United States has reluctantly acceded. Unlike other basing nations, America has thus far had the resources to honor its increasing financial commitments, although future patterns remain unclear. The financial dimension of base politics is considered more comprehensively in chapter 8.

4. *Pressure for change in command structure.* In South Korea, for example, a U.S.–South Korean Combined Forces Command (CFC) has existed since 1979; it has traditionally been headed by an American four-star general responsible directly to the Pentagon. With democratization in 1988, the South Korean side first pressed for, and then achieved, peacetime command responsibility for the CFC, followed by populist pressures during 2005, supported by President Roh Moo Hyun, for ROK wartime command responsibility as well.

5. *Pressure for operational constraints on the use of foreign bases.* Most conspicuously, the Turkish National Assembly refused transit rights for using local bases as a staging area for 165,000 U.S. ground troops prior to the initiation of the 2003 Iraq War, and limited use of American air bases in Turkey for operations against Iraq.[39] Similarly, Greece and Spain limited use of local U.S. bases for Middle East operations during the Yom Kippur War of 1973. Iraq under the democratic al-Maliki government frequently imposed operating constraints on American forces during 2006–2007.[40]

DICTATORSHIP, BASE POLITICS, AND AMERICAN POLICY

Dictatorship, of course, is a superficially stabilizing refuge in the face of the uncertainties of regime change in a nation with significant foreign bases. Previous research has frequently noted in passing that the United States does indeed tend to support dictators in developing nations.[41] U.S. backing for the Somozas in Nicaragua, Mobutu in Zaire, Park Chung Hee in Korea, Papadopoulos in Greece, Franco in Spain, Marcos in the Philippines, and Karimov in Uzbekistan, to cite only a few examples, has been often remarked upon. Early support for democratic transitions seems to be much more limited, especially where the United States has an established military presence, although Congress tends to be more supportive of democratic oppositions than the White House.[42]

There is little systematic research on how this traditional American support for strongmen relates to base politics. In a tentative attempt at exploring this relationship, the Dictatorship Hypothesis presented in chapter 3 suggested that Washington tends to support dictators in nations where it enjoys basing facilities, and often condones their creation in such nations. This section provides some additional evidence bearing on this question. The casual assumption in existing literature is that maintaining a stable base presence is a principal reason for support of dictators, and that the United States uncritically supports dictators that back a U.S. military presence.[43] If this received wisdom is true, it suggests an interesting and important empirical paradox: Why do U.S. administrations *support* dictators in the *short run*, if doing so *harms* the *long-run* strategic interests of the United States, while also contradicting deeply held national values?

It should be noted at the outset that American policy does not universally support dictators, even where they host important American military facilities. President Jimmy Carter, in particular, was personally averse to such support, and often expressed it vocally. Indeed, Park Chung Hee's dictatorial rule was a principal impetus behind Carter's 1977–79 attempt to remove U.S. ground forces from South Korea, as Don Oberdorfer clearly points out.[44] Yet Carter was nevertheless circumspect in dealing with Philippine dictator Ferdinand Marcos in the 1979 base-lease renewal negotiations.[45]

The George W. Bush administration has also made support for democratic governments a cornerstone of its foreign policy, especially under Secretary of State Condoleeza Rice. This sort of conservative Wilsonianism at times came in conflict with basing policies. The Bush administration, for example, sharply condemned the Karimov regime in Uzbekistan following the 2005 Andijian massacre, leading the Uzbek government to force American withdrawal from its strategic Khanabad base, which had been important to the antiterrorist struggle in Afghanistan after 9/11.[46]

Sometimes American leaders may actually back the removal of such dictators from office, even when the country in question hosts important bases. Ronald Reagan, for example, acquiesced early in 1986 to strong pressures exerted within the U.S. government by Senate Foreign Relations Committee Chairman Richard Lugar, Secretary of State George Shultz, diplomatic trouble-shooter Philip Habib, and others, to press Ferdinand Marcos to resign from office, despite the presence of strategic U.S. bases in the Philippines.[47] At a lower level and in an earlier era, U.S. Ambassador to South Korea Walter McConaughy played a key role in the removal of President Syngmun Rhee in the face of massive student demonstrations against Rhee's autocratic rule in 1960.[48]

Yet the general pattern suggested in the Dictatorship Hypothesis does prevail. American policy *does* frequently back dictators. And the tendency to back dictators—and to refrain from demanding their removal—appears to be *greater* where bases are involved, America's democratic ideals, and the uncertain long-term prospects of such despots, notwithstanding.

The propensity of U.S. forces to locate in nations with authoritarian regimes has clearly, if perhaps unavoidably, intensified since 9/11, making this issue of even greater significance for American policy than previously. The sixteen nations with which Washington had well-institutionalized base relationships in 2000 were mainly democracies, with an average Freedom House score of 1.875.[49] The eighteen nations, many in the Islamic world, with which the United States established new base agreements between 9/11 and the end of 2002, however, had an average Freedom House score of 3.94, significantly more authoritarian on a one to seven scale.[50]

Why U.S. Policy Backs Dictators' Hosting Bases

To understand why American policy tends to back dictators in nations hosting U.S. bases, it is useful to return to the basic political dilemmas of base politics in developing nations outlined in chapter 4. Whatever personal stakes and cosmopolitan understanding national political elites in host nations may possess, the mass public and local governments in such countries often have incentives to nonagreement. For them, bases mean crime, noise, and pollution. To make things more difficult, the people experiencing these irritations most directly often lack broader, countervailing national security concerns.

Due to its underlying interest structure, base politics thus tends to operate most smoothly when the mass public is *not* involved, and when elites face few incentives to compete in stirring nationalist fervor. These conditions by definition tend to be well satisfied under a stable dictatorship. Thus, it is not surprising that American policy tends to back dictatorship when bases are involved, all things being equal, and when stable popular support in host nations for American bases is not available.

Concrete comparative empirical examination allows us to deepen our insights. Franco's Spain and Park Chung Hee's Korea, for example, are clearly useful and appropriate comparative cases. Both leaders were former generals, with experience in counterinsurgency operations, with common divide-and-rule leadership styles. They both confronted a divided opposition in a Cold War environment. Comparative analysis of base politics during their respective periods of domestic political dominance permits the following generalizations of broader relevance to base politics under dictatorship:

1. *U.S. Defense Department working-level concerns tend to be highly pragmatic in nature—what facilities can be provided, at what cost, and how efficiently.* The 1951 Joint Chiefs of Staff survey team that prepared the basis for establishment of U.S. bases in Spain, for example, was typical: its overriding concerns were military efficiency and the specific operational requirements of each service branch.[51]

2. *Working-level State Department concerns are with regional diplomatic considerations*: in Spain, for example, the impact of bases there on overall relations with Western Europe and Latin America. Those areas had opposed Franco's fascist takeover in the 1930s.[52]

3. *The Cold War powerfully shaped American policies toward dictators, as those were formulated at the strategic level.* The U.S. National Security Council, for example, rationalized guarded support for the stability of the Franco regime after the landmark 1953 Pact of Madrid, which established U.S. bases in Spain, precisely on this basis. The NSC actually listed the stability of the Franco regime, and prevention of any communist or procommunist regime in Spain, as major objects of American policy toward Spain.[53] This rapprochement with Spain occurred, of course, less than fifteen years after Franco's victory in the Spanish Civil War, which he had achieved with Hitler and Mussolini's enthusiastic and explicit backing.

4. *Dictators recognized the leverage that the Cold War gave them.* And they consciously manipulated that leverage in their dealings with the democratic West, from the Cold War's very early days.[54]

5. *The United States tends to support a particular* type *of dictator, rather, of course, than dictators in general.* It does not typically back highly ideological dictators, or, with a few exceptions, those that are revisionist in international affairs.

6. *The dictators that the United States supports, however, are typically rather pragmatic, nonideological individuals.*[55] They tend to be involved in complex internal coalition building,[56] for which the U.S. base presence tends to provide important domestic political support.

7. *The domestic political meaning for dictators of American bases typically comes in two areas: legitimacy and financial support for their client groups.* The most important clients of such dictators are typically the military and business elites, so foreign military sales (FMS) and trade access to the American market become for them especially attractive quid pro quos in return for base access.

8. *Dictators that the United States supports tend to claim that their regimes are transitional to a state of affairs permitting democracy compatible with American values.* Thus, Franco stressed the anticommunist struggle and Christian values implicit in his continued authoritarian rule. Park Chung Hee similarly emphasized that his Yushin extraconstitutional order, after 1972, would continue only until a national political emergency, created by the confrontation with North Korea, and the Asian regional uncertainties created by American retrenchment policies in Vietnam and the Taiwan Straits were clarified.[57]

9. *Due to the unusual domestic political significance of bases under dictatorial regimes, the location of those bases often assumes distinctive patterns, which may be different from those in democracies.* Franco, for example, wanted American bases to be highly *visible*. As a consequence, the major U.S. bases established in Spain during his era were located near large cities—a highly distinctive pattern internationally, and a source of major base-politics friction within Spain once Franco was gone. The largest facility, Torrejon, with the longest runway in Europe, and strategic nuclear functions that made it highly vulnerable to Soviet retaliation, was built very close to Spain's capital of Madrid in 1953, with Franco's strong support. The United States, in return, became the first great power to recognize Franco's Spain, providing the dictator with external as well as domestic legitimacy.

10. *U.S. resistance to dictators has typically been a "passive distancing" policy,* like that pursued by U.S. Ambassador Philip Habib toward President Park Chung Hee in Korea after the declaration of martial law there in the early 1970s.[58] While not overtly pressing for the strongman's ouster, the United States typically limits diplomatic contact—a nuance visible to local elites, but often to few others. The overall popular impression, as a result, is American backing for tyrants that the general public does not support.

Dictatorships typically create injustice and domestic mass resentment, while inhibiting development of healthy political institutions conducive to long-term stability. While strongmen have often been broadly supportive of U.S. global strategic goals, they have also at times been obdurately nationalistic and uncooperative, especially in their later years, as the cases of Park in Korea, Marcos in the Philippines, and Franco in Spain all show. Most importantly, dictatorships are fragile politically, and breed a strong backlash, both against their leadership and their foreign allies, when they ultimately come to an end. Repressive regimes contribute dangerously, in a word, to the long-term vulnerability in host-nation politics of America's embattled garrisons—a vulnerability enhanced by the rapid recent advance of democracy, and accompanying political uncertainty, throughout the world.

GEOGRAPHY'S POWERFUL ROLE

Apart from history, geography, in its relationship to demography, also significantly shapes the environment of base politics, and makes its permutations increasingly uncertain. Indeed, the spatial distribution of bases within a nation profoundly affects public reactions to bases, and ultimately the political stability of basing presence more generally. In particular, substantial base presence in or near heavily populated areas can be destabilizing to long-term basing prospects, as we will see.

This section of the research, a partial test of the Contact Hypothesis presented in chapter 3, considers spatial distribution patterns for U.S. military bases in four nations: Japan, South Korea, Germany, and Turkey. These are countries that together host more than three-quarters of the American troops permanently deployed outside the United States, and have done so for a sufficient period (more than five years) to permit realistic evaluation of how location affects local response to the bases.[59] They are from three distinct culture areas, and host the three largest deployments of U.S. forces in the world outside the Middle East. Yet inferences can be made from the past cases presented that should be relevant to the new group of post-9/11 bases as well.

Opposition to the bases, as expressed in demonstrations against them, is the most consequential potential indicator of local response. Opposition has thus been selected as the dependent variable in testing the Contact Hypothesis. The proposition to be tested regarding the causes of popular opposition is as follows: the more *contacts* that U.S. bases and their residents have with local citizens, the more likely it is that frictions will occur. More simply, this hypothesis can be expressed as:

The actual magnitude of personal contact between American soldiers and host communities in any given context is of course difficult to verify. As a proxy for such contact, this analysis therefore uses the population density of local-government units (provincial or prefectural). The operating assumption is that soldiers and their dependents will interact more intensively with local citizens when large numbers of those citizens surround them, and that military-civilian contact will thus vary directly with such population density. Broadly speaking, frictions will be greater in urban than in rural areas, and will be intensified by urbanization.

The a priori rationale for this hypothesis is twofold. First, American soldiers tend to be young, active, and often culturally insensitive, making it likely that personal contact with local citizenry will lead to conflict. Secondly, the existence of the bases themselves will be more offensive in more densely populated environments, due to the greater prospect of crime and various forms of environmental disruption, ranging from irritating noise to air and water pollution. The mere existence of the bases may also, in some environments, put downward pressure on the price of real estate around those bases, thus irritating local landowners.

Cross-national evidence, presented in table 5.3, appears to broadly support the Contact Hypothesis. Antibase activities and sentiment do seem to vary with the population density of the countries in which bases are located. Thus, South Korea, the most densely populated nation in our sample, has the highest level of antibase sentiment. Germany, one of the least densely populated, appears conversely to be the least antagonistic to the local American military presence of the four nations studied.

TABLE 5.3.
Base Frictions Higher in Crowded Areas:
Cross-National Comparisons

Country	Base tensions	Military Density[a]	National Average Density
South Korea	High	1,215	1,284
Japan	Moderate	2,013	888
Turkey	Fairly High	464	228
Germany	Low	525	598

Sources: U.S. Department of Defense, *Base Structure Report*, 2006 edition; for Germany, Federal Statistical Office and Statistical Offices of the Länder and the Federal Statistical Office website, at http://www.statistik-portal.de/Statistik-Portal/en/en_jb01_jahrtab1.asp (as of 2004); for Japan, *Japan Statistical Yearbook 2006* (as of 2005); for South Korea, National Statistical Office website, at http://www.nso.go.kr/eng/index.html (as of 2004); CIA, *The World Factbook* website, at https://www.cia.gov/cia/publications/factbook/geos/ks.html#People (as of 2006); and for Turkey, Statistical Yearbook of Turkey, 2005 edition (as of 2000).

Notes: Statistical data are for the 2000–2006 period, as noted above. Assessments of base tensions are for the 2000–2003 period, as documented in press reports.

a. "Military density" denotes average number of people per square mile in the three provinces/prefectures of a given nation that host the largest number of U.S. military personnel.

The comparison of "military densities" with general population densities in Korea and Japan do suggest an interesting anomaly: that Korean base frictions are somewhat higher, and Japanese frictions lower, than population densities in the local jurisdictions where most bases are located would suggest. This indicates to us that other factors are also at work. As we shall see, center-periphery relations and differences in the configuration of civil society also appear to influence the profile of base frictions in nations hosting military bases.

The Contact Hypothesis appears to hold *within* nations as well as between them. Thus, within Japan base relations are more delicate in Kanagawa prefecture near Tokyo, with a high population density of 3,639 per square kilometer, and major bases at Yokusuka and Yokota,[60] than they are in Okinawa Prefecture, with three-fourths of total USFJ stations, and Aomori Prefecture, where Misawa Air base is located, with population densities of only 598 and 150 per square kilometer, respectively. Similarly, in Korea, antibase sentiment in Seoul, with a population density of 16,994 per square kilometer, where the large Yongsan U.S. garrison hosts more than 4,000 U.S. troops, is much stronger than it is in Kyonggi-doe (Camp Casey and Osan Air base) and Cholla buk-doe (Kunsan Air Base), with population densities of only 1,049 and 238 per square kilometer, respectively, as suggested by table 5.4.

There are of course outliers from the broad proposition presented in the Contact Hypothesis as we have suggested. Japan as a whole, for example, appears to have lower levels of antibase sentiment than its overall population density, or the population density of its prefectures hosting bases, would otherwise dictate. Turkey, conversely, has higher levels of antibase sentiment. Here is where base countermeasure policies (in the case of Japan) and Islamic cultural resistance (in the case of Turkey) appear to come in, to bias antibase resistance up or down.

Population density, and the related civil-military contact that it implicitly represents, thus provide a provocative, if clearly still tentative, first-cut explanation for base-related, antibase frictions. Yet the Contact Hypothesis has greater problems accounting for *change* in such sentiment. Base structure in all of the nations examined has been relatively constant for the past 30 to 40 years. Increasingly pervasive urbanization can account for a sustained secular increase in base frictions. Yet there is also a cyclical dimension that is harder to explain. Why do frictions rise and fall, as they so clearly have in Korea and Okinawa, in particular?

Factors beyond geography alone are thus clearly at work in shaping the overall patterns of antibase sentiment and activism. As has been suggested earlier in this chapter, such case-specific factors include political regime shifts, the embedded heritage of occupation and colonial rule, political leadership, mass media impact, and the influence of culture. Yet

TABLE 5.4.
Demonstrating the "Contact Hypothesis":
Evidence from within Key Nations

Base Locations[a]	Level of Tension[b]	Density[c]	Base Personnel
Japan			
Kanagawa	High	3.639	16,511
Okinawa	High	0.598	16,253
Aomori	Low	0.150	4,102
Nagasaki	Moderate	0.361	3,203
Yamaguchi	Low	0.244	2,742
South Korea			
Kyonggi-doe	High	1.049	25,579
(North of Seoul)			
Seoul	High	16.994	4,615
Cholla buk-doe	Moderate	0.238	2,766
Daegu	Low	2.868	1,531
Kyongsangbuk-doe	Moderate	0.142	1,354
Kangwon-doe	Moderate	0.092	1,043
Busan	High	4.827	377

Sources: U.S. Department of Defense, Base Structure Report, 2005 edition; Japan Statistical Yearbook 2006; and Korean National Statistical Office website, at http://www.nso.go.kr/eng/index.html.

Notes:

a. "Base locations" denote prefecture/province rather than city.

b. "Level of tension" is defined in terms of relative number of incidents and demonstrations.

c. "Density" figures are for population density of individual prefectures/provinces, expressed in terms of thousands of residents per square kilometer.

population-density, as indicated here, also appears to be a powerful, if latent and largely unnoticed, determinant of American military presence overseas. Its potential impact becomes clearly evident when democratization and other sociocultural forces, as well as Internet and mobile communications technology, make mass popular opinion increasingly relevant to policy processes. As both urbanization and democratization advance worldwide, they generate intensified grassroots pressures against foreign bases, which tend to be much stronger in urban and urbanizing regions than in more predominantly rural areas, as we have noted.

How Institutions Quietly Mediate Demographic Impact

Demographic pressures do not exist in a sociopolitical vacuum. They obviously operate through existing institutions. How does political structure, to take one especially important intervening variable, mediate the impact

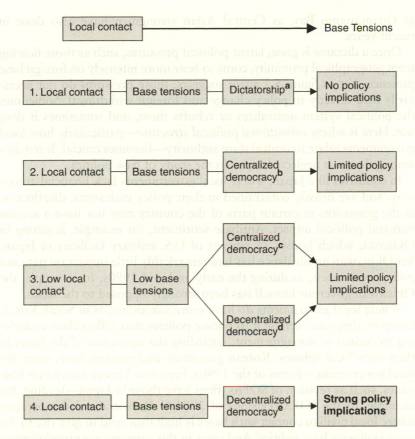

Figure 5.3. The Contact Hypothesis and Four Scenarios

Examples:

(a) Franco's Spain and Park's Korea;
(b) Okinawa (Japan);
(c) Turkey (countryside);
(d) Germany and Italy (low population density);
(e) Seoul (Korea).

of demographic factors such as local contact on base politics? And what are the consequences for policy? Figure 5.3 suggests the implications.

As figure 5.3 indicates, the pressures of the Contact Hypothesis on base relations operate in a wide variety of political systems. But they are inhibited by strong men in dictatorships; Park Chung Hee, Francisco Franco, and, for many years, Ferdinand Marcos, among others, were attractive to American leaders for the stability that they assured for the American military around the periphery of their bases. Ironically, Fidel Castro also performs an analogous service for the U.S. military at Guantanamo Bay, as Central Asian strongmen have also done in recent years.

Once a dictator is gone, latent political pressures, such as those flowing from geographical proximity, come to bear more intensely on foreign base presence. Yet as figure 5.3 again suggests, those pressures do not necessarily lead directly to policy change and foreign withdrawal. Sometimes the political system neutralizes or rebuffs them, and sometimes it does not. Here is where *subnational political structure*—particularly how local governments relate to central state authority—becomes crucial. It remains among the most neglected topics in the study of base politics.

In countries like Japan, where local governments lack financial autonomy, and are heavily constrained in their policy endeavors, disaffection at the grassroots in certain parts of the country may not have a serious national political impact. Antibase sentiment, for example, is strong in Okinawa, which houses 75 percent of U.S. military facilities in Japan. Yet Okinawan ambivalence has had remarkably little impact on national policy, even when, as during the early and mid-1990s, for example, the Okinawan governor himself has been strongly opposed to the bases.

Where local governments *do* have more autonomy, as in South Korea, however, they can exercise it to pursue policies that reflect their underlying incentives to nonagreement, regarding the operation of the bases in their own local spheres. Korean governors and mayors have, since the local government reforms of the 1990s, been *much* more activist on base issues, such as revision of SOFAs, than have those in Japan—leading, for example, to the SOFA revisions of 2001.[61] Decentralized democracies where local civilian contact with bases is high thus tend to give rise to the most explosive base politics. And cases in this category are growing more and more common, intensifying the challenge worldwide to America's embattled garrisons.

The policy implications of the Contact Hypothesis for some of the most strategic U.S. basing relationships are thus substantial, and intuitively obvious, although rarely perceived. Antibase sentiments, for example, translate much more easily into pressures for policy change in Korea than in Japan, given the volatile combination of higher population density and stronger local autonomy in the former case. Administrative decentralization and local self-government—prima facie, solely domestic decisions—can thus have significantly destabilizing foreign policy consequences: a sobering reality not adequately perceived. And to neutralize these destabilizing consequences of congestion and grassroots democracy, keeping military bases away from densely populated areas makes eminent political sense, especially in decentralized, democratic political systems.[62]

We have seen, in the past two chapters, that base politics is indeed a contest, replete with incentives and operating rules, as well as a broadly comprehensible transnational logic. Yet base politics is simultaneously an interaction profoundly shaped by historical-institutional parameters, and by demography as well, in ways that create a variety of distinct patterns. Outcomes in base relations are to some extent predictable—once, that is, the inputs are understood. Yet it is crucial to understand the nature of the subnational political game being played, and the often unsettling results that emerge. It is to this crucial problem of categorization—understanding what trees inhabit the base-politics forest—that we now turn.

CHAPTER SIX

BASE POLITICS DECONSTRUCTED

FOUR PARADIGMS

BASE POLITICS, we have argued here, is best understood, despite its highly symbolic and controversial nature, as a matter of personal, rational decision. The ultimate players in the base-politics contest are *individuals*; ranging from NGO activists to national leaders, they respond to particular information and incentives unique to themselves.

These players, of course, often have deeply held values and cultural biases. Sometimes, as in the Middle East, cultural and ethnic consciousness significantly shape policy outcomes, in part through their impact on concepts of order and rationality.[1] Yet those values are far less determining than often assumed, as specific cases presented later in this volume clearly suggest.

Although it is ultimately individuals that really *act*, in both domestic and international politics, they act in *institutional contexts*. Such contexts, as Douglass North and others have pointed out, profoundly constrain human interaction. They also critically set the parameters within which people make choices, and ultimately shape socioeconomic performance. Institutions, in short, are a crucial intermediate variable linking incentives and individual decision with social performance.[2] And institutions, although they have multiple origins in the interplay of economic, political, and social forces, tend to be profoundly shaped by national historical-political circumstances.[3]

This rational-actor focus aids greatly in comparative analysis and policy prescription. To the extent that we can legitimately assume rational individual response to given policy parameters, understanding those parameters, together with the demographic environment and intervening sociopolitical institutions, should enable us to approximately predict base-politics outcomes. That ability, in turn, should provide a useful asset in configuring appropriate policy.

The clear importance of national experience in structuring, and ultimately embedding, political-economic "rules of the game" can be seen in the sharp cross-national contrasts evident in the varied national approaches to market capitalism.[4] As Alexander Gerschenkron pointed out, for example, a country's experience as an "early developer" or "late developer" critically shapes its underlying national institutions and exercises an impact on economic outcomes often more substantial than short-term market signals themselves. Similarly, historical position in the process of global development and standing in the global political-economic order can also profoundly shape the security policies and institutions of nations through the impact of such position on domestic state structure and interest-group configuration.[5]

RATIONALE FOR CLASSIFICATION

The central analytical concerns of this volume, of course, are contemporary and political rather than historical. We are interested in the details, and the specific decision rules, of the distinctive contests in which base-politics participants engage, rather than in how those contests themselves came to be. Yet historical context is certainly material to our interests in that it can profoundly shape institutional rules, which tend to persist for extended periods of time. And the historical context that shapes those rules, in most instances, is decidedly both national and political.

This chapter outlines four distinctive paradigms of base politics: "compensation" politics; "fiat" politics; "bazaar" politics; and "affective" politics. Each variant—an ideal type, rather than a precise representation of any specific empirical reality—has distinctive rules, with characteristic processes and outcomes. Each of these patterns is broadly distributed across the world, and exists in more than one country. To demonstrate this reality, we purposely illustrate each pattern with cases drawn from multiple culture areas.

As noted earlier, our particular research concern, among multiple potential approaches to base politics, is in how host-nation leaders manage base relations once bases have already been established. This needs to be the focus, due to the very real prospect—fraught with strategic implications—of their downsizing or disappearance. Within that universe of issues, we direct special attention here to the two alternative policy tools that leaders typically employ domestically in dealing with base issues—coercion and material compensation. Given the contrasting incentive structures of national and grassroots interests in most nations, as discussed in chapter 4, some mix of these two tools is generally necessary to maintain stability in base relations.

It is, of course, entirely possible that host-nation leaders may *not* want to maintain stability in base relations. This is clearly a crucial issue for basing powers like the United States that must deal with host countries, but can be addressed within the framework presented here. If host-nation

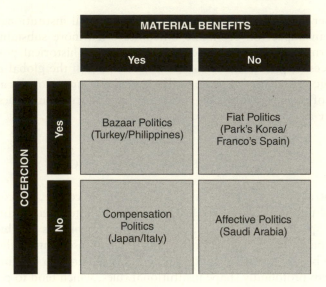

Figure 6.1. Paradigms of Base Politics

leaders elect to bargain with the basing power, even at the expense of stability, their behavior falls within the bazaar-politics paradigm. If they are rejectionist, it becomes a variant of affective politics.

Individual base-politics patterns themselves are deeply tied to national political features and historical experiences, however, so they tend to be concentrated in particular regions of the world, and in particular nations. In this chapter we present each paradigm in a specific national context where it is especially salient before generalizing briefly about its broader comparative relevance. One must keep in mind, however, that these patterns are ideal types—abstract models of policymaking not fully present in their entirety in any specific national context at any given point in time.

The broad relationships of these four paradigms of base politics to one another is presented in figure 6.1. Each involves a different mix of coercion and material benefits in the maintenance of stability in base relations. As is clear from the typology, compensation politics, practiced heavily in Japan, involves provision of material benefits to supporters without forcefully coercing antagonists. It is antithetical to the fiat politics long practiced in South Korea, which often involved substantial coercion of dissenters, especially prior to the democratic transition of the late 1980s. Conversely, bazaar politics, typically practiced in Turkey, which involves extensive, case-specific bargaining and military coercion of various social groups, and affective politics, characteristic of Saudi

Arabia, which implies more emphasis on base-relations regulation through generalized societal norms, and less direct coercion, are also contrasting ideal types.

None of the four varieties of base politics, it should be emphasized, is unique to any one particular country, to any one historical epoch, or to any one geographical region. Indeed, compensation politics is practiced in Italian and Azorean villages as well as Japanese base towns, while U.S.-Philippine interaction in the late 1980s often manifested a bazaar character remarkably similar to that between the United States and Turkey fifteen years later. And affective politics—the substitution of norms and national sentiment for explicit coercion and compensation as a vehicle for creating and reinforcing mutual expectations—has implicitly governed important parts of Anglo-Saxon base relations, as it has the presence of U.S. forces in Saudi Arabia, albeit to very different ends in the Anglo-Saxon and the Islamic cases.

Although the varieties of base politics are widely distributed geographically speaking, there are definite trends over time in their relative prevalence and strategic importance. With the waning of feudalism across the developing world in the 1950s and 1960s, followed by a relative decline of full-fledged dictatorship worldwide during the 1980s and 1990s, fiat politics and affective politics have been growing less common. Conversely, the variants providing material benefits, bazaar politics and compensation politics, have grown more salient, and more crucial in sustaining the presence of America's embattled garrisons abroad. Given the scale of resource-transfers involved in compensation politics, and the deteriorating fiscal circumstances of industrialized nations as they grow older, that variant of base politics seems more and more fiscally difficult to sustain, leaving chaotic bazaar politics as a principal, yet profoundly unappetizing, residual variant.

The prospect is that volatile bazaar politics will become especially salient in America's base-politics dealings with immature democracies and dictatorships in developing nations. That is precisely where a rising share of base facilities are being located in the post-9/11 world. This emerging reality has important implications for U.S. basing strategy, to which we will return in chapter 10.

COMPENSATION POLITICS

Repression and coercion represent a common approach to base politics in much of the world. When dissidents resist governmental policies toward foreign bases, including forcible acquisitions of private land, the government simply crushes their protests. Sometimes host-nation governments supplement coercion with a "carrot-and-stick" approach toward prospective dissenters, although that is far from always true.

Compensation politics is a distinct pattern of base relations involving little or no such coercion, but substantial material payment. Such payment flows typically from the host-nation government to various interests in the host nation that are adversely affected by foreign base activity. Through such payments, states aim to neutralize antibase sentiment and to stabilize foreign base presence.

Compensation politics tends in reality to be the most stable of the four base-politics paradigms, as long as funding to support compensation is substantial, predictable, and internally generated, rather than flowing more unpredictably from the basing nation. The Japanese pattern of compensation-politics resource-flows exhibited all of these characteristics from the 1980s into the first decade of the twenty-first century, although whether it can continue to do so in the future, given intensifying resource constraints, is problematic. The details of compensation-politics decision-making processes are illustrated in figure 6.2.

The compensation-politics paradigm of base relations is potentially a stable one, as suggested in figure 6.2, provided that high resource-flows toward key participants are smoothly maintained. Yet those flows need to be sensitive to, and ultimately to satisfy, the base-related demands of relevant interests, both in government and in civil society. Compensation politics, because it concerns attempts by individuals to maximize their own utility, can thus create a substantive tension between the sentiments and the material interests of actors in base politics. To resolve this tension, sensitive subnational mediating bodies are often required.

Espousing antimilitarism can be a very real sentiment, as it clearly has been in Okinawa since World War II. Yet under the compensation-politics paradigm, expressing such sentiment can paradoxically elicit compensation, as long as the bases themselves, against which so much antipathy is generated, are not withdrawn. The paradigm thus often gives rise to secrecy and complex, multilevel bargaining, coordinated by politicians and specialized mediating institutions, that makes the underlying stability of its interactions often appear to be more volatile than they are in reality. *Compensation politics requires legitimating processes*—paralleling financial compensation itself—that render the funding of protest groups more than simple payoffs in their eyes, and in the critical estimation of their home societies.

Japan and American Bases: The Underlying Paradox

Japan, whose recent base relations illustrate the compensation-politics paradigm very clearly, had never hosted foreign forces on its soil prior

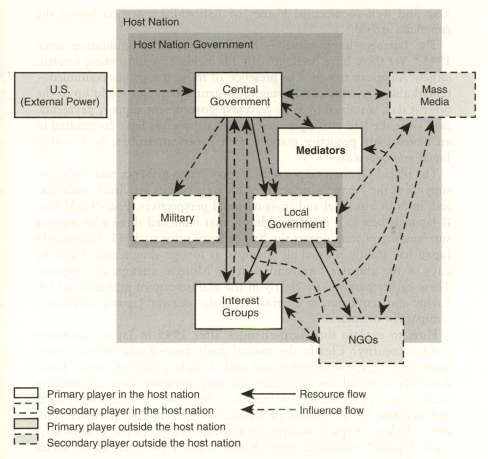

Primary player in the host nation — Resource flow
Secondary player in the host nation —— Influence flow
Primary player outside the host nation
Secondary player outside the host nation

Figure 6.2. The Compensation Politics Paradigm

to World War II. Its government does, however, have a long history of crushing dissidents and protest. Ōmotokyō, Nichiren Buddhism, and other religious groups contesting State Shintō in the 1930s, for example, often felt the harsh hand of the Kempeitai repressing their protest activities.[6]

Since 1945 Japan has continuously hosted one of the largest contingents of foreign forces on its soil of any nation in the world, currently totaling around 40,000 American troops. Those forces arrived as occupiers in late 1945, after a bitter, brutal war in which 3.3 million Japanese, as well as several hundred thousand Americans, died.[7] The U.S. occupiers were culturally and racially alien to Japan in almost all respects, and generally spoke little Japanese. The Japanese people themselves had had a long and well-documented history of nationalist assertion before the American arrival.[8]

The Japanese have ostensibly had a culture of antimilitarism since 1945.[9] Yet there have been virtually no incidents against these foreign, largely American troops. The presence of those troops has continued—remarkably smoothly considering the wartime heritage—right up to the present day, sustained by large Japanese government support payments. And since the late 1990s Japanese forces themselves have cooperated in an increasingly proactive manner with American troops, both within Japan and overseas.

The placid Japanese response to foreign-troop presence and the active support of the Japanese government for its activities are clearly paradoxical, in both historical and cross-national perspectives. Post–World War II Japan is heir to a martial tradition that launched three wars against surrounding powers during the half-century prior to 1945. Historically Japan has stoutly resisted all attempts at foreign domination from the days of the abortive fourteenth-century Mongol attempt at conquest. These earlier patterns are clearly in the mainstream of international behavior and sentiment, in contrast to early postwar Japan's distinctive, semipacifist orientation.

How to explain the sharp changes after 1945 in Japan's attitudes toward security? Clearly the radical early post–World War II transformation in Japanese institutions and thought processes, which paradoxically changed the American military presence into a liberating occupation, is part of the explanation.[10] Yet how can such an explanation account for the smooth persistence of U.S. military presence from the turbulent, atypical occupation era right down to the present day, when Japanese economic strength and military potential are so much greater?

Since the end of the Allied occupation in 1952, this volume maintains, a vital additional element in the Japanese government's relatively successful management of base relations has been compensation politics. "Compensation politics" is defined here as "politics directed primarily toward advertising and satisfying demands for material satisfaction between grantors and supporters, as opposed to those politics oriented toward attaining nonmaterial goals."[11] The networks of regular participants in this form of resource-allocation, through which members assume reciprocal benefits and obligations, can be termed "circles of compensation."[12]

Compensation politics is ubiquitous in Japan generally, and highly salient in Japanese base politics specifically, as will be established in coming chapters. As will be shown in chapter 8, Japan provides more than $4 billion annually in host-nation support for U.S. military forces in Japan, and has consistently headed the list of host-nation contributors for more than two decades.[13] Even more importantly, from the perspective of base politics, the vast majority of this funding goes to compensate local-level domestic interest groups that provide varied base services. Beneficiaries include construction companies, base-worker labor unions, electric-power firms, and landlords renting facilities to the U.S. military.

More than Money—Mediating Institutions Crucial

Those disadvantaged or injured by the bases, through accidents, noise pollution, or criminal activity, for example—are also provided for, under the compensation-politics paradigm, through timely, case-specific allocations, such as semiautomatic sound-insulation for all residences in the vicinity of air bases. This process has, in Japan, an important, and distinctive, institutional element: the Defense Facilities Administration Agency (DFAA, or Bōei Shisetsu Chō in Japanese), which serves as the principal subnational mediator in domestic base politics. Its primary responsibility has been nothing other than claims adjustment—particularly adjustment of claims against the USFJ, which the Japanese government is bound to process at its expense under the U.S.-Japan SOFA.[14]

Given the delicacy of resolving citizen claims against a military body, especially in places like Okinawa, with a strong antimilitarist tradition, a mediator with strong grassroots sensitivity is clearly needed. An autonomous subsidiary of the Japanese Ministry of Defense, the DFAA also has handled other politically sensitive, compensation-oriented tasks, apart from claims adjustment, such as negotiating rentals of land for base facilities, employing staff for U.S. bases, handling labor relations on bases, and settling terms of real-estate dispositions when bases are withdrawn.[15] It has eight nationwide branch offices, including local representation in nearly every community hosting a major U.S. or JSDF base, giving it unique ability to respond rapidly and generously to any problems in base relations that might occur.

In fiscal 2006, the DFAA budget was nearly ¥525 billion (almost $5 billion), or 11 percent of Japan's entire defense budget.[16] The DFAA spent more than a quarter of that sum to alleviate base-related noise through soundproofing for schools, homes, and other local buildings. It also spent extensively to improve the living environments in host communities by building parks, community centers, and other amenities.

DFAA has been by far the largest defense-compensation agency currently operating on behalf of U.S. forces anywhere in the world. As we have seen, its operations play a substantial role in stabilizing the presence of U.S. forces in Japan. DFAA's role is especially strategic due to its per-suasiveness with local groups incurring injury or inconvenience at the hands of the military, that would otherwise hold strong incentives to disagreement with the presence of the bases themselves.

The DFAA, and indeed most of the compensation aspects of Japanese base politics, have their roots in the early postwar U.S. Occupation (1945–52). Indeed, the DFAA itself is the direct, lineal descendent of the Special Procurement Agency (Tokubetsu Chotatsu Cho), which was established in 1947 to deal comprehensively and strategically, at varied levels of the Japanese government, with procurement, management of facilities, and other "duties" (*ekimu*) the Occupation forces required. In 1949 it was attached directly to the Prime Minister's Office (Sorifu) as a special external bureau, and continued in that privileged status until 1958. Until 1962, this Special Procurement Agency was tasked solely with addressing the needs of U.S. forces and the communities surrounding them, although its functions were merged with those of a parallel body handling SDF base construction in that year, to become the DFAA.

The DFAA's distinctive historical evolution endowed it with unique structures, networks, and organizational goals conducive to politically ef-ficient compensation politics. Perhaps most importantly, it was well con-nected at the highest levels of the Japanese government, allowing it to cut through bureaucratic and lower-level political resistance that might other-wise have complicated its operation. In addition, it was tasked specifi-cally, narrowly, and unambiguously with facilitating smooth U.S. base management and preventing it from being immobilized by conflicting goals. Thirdly, DFAA had enough institutional autonomy to prioritize its own parochial objectives, centering on base stability, over the more nar-rowly military, and less political, concerns of its parent Ministry of De-fense.[17] Japan's postwar pattern contrasts sharply to those of Korea, the United States, and most major military powers, where base relations are institutionally more integrated with general military operations.

Significantly, the Special Procurement Agency, and its successor, the DFAA, preserved the established, positive networks of relations with local communities, based on as many as thirty-six local offices nation-wide, each equipped with an advisory board, that grassroots occupation commanders and civil-military relations personnel had created.

The decentralized, locally oriented, yet politically connected DFAA has turned out to be quite effective in its tasks, although this effectiveness has been marred by occasional incidents of bid-rigging and related corrup-tion.[18] The DFAA's relative success demonstrates, in microcosm, how the institutional residue of an extended, thoughtfully conceived occupation of liberal intent can have stabilizing implications for base politics that

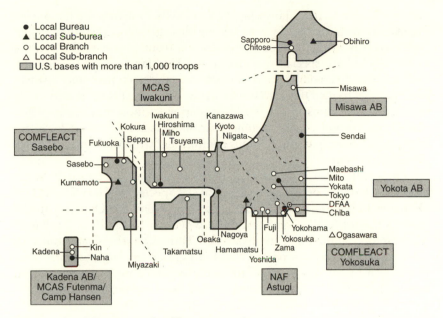

- ● Local Bureau
- ▲ Local Sub-burea
- ○ Local Branch
- △ Local Sub-branch
- ▨ U.S. bases with more than 1,000 troops

Figure 6.3. DFAA Local Office Network

Sources: DFAA Website: *http://www.dfaa.go.jp/en/profile/location.html*; and U.S. Department of Defense, *Base Structure Report*, 2005 edition.

Notes: AB denotes "air base"; NAF denotes "Naval Air Force"; MCAS denotes "Marine Corps Air Station"; and COMFLEACT denotes: "Commander Fleet Activities."

transcend the resources that actually change hands, and that persist long after such an occupation has ended.

The relative success of Japanese-style compensation politics is thus *not* simply a matter of the money involved. Indeed, the secret seems to lie in a combination of four things: (1) the *financial* element; (2) a legitimating *nonmonetary* dimension; (3) the existence of *local networks* between communities and the DFAA that allow for negotiation of delicate details; and (4) *institutional autonomy* for the base-relations mediator, who stands *between* defense authorities and the public. The DFAA's semiautonomous compensation functions and structure are thus synergistic with those of the Joint Committee on U.S.-Japan Security Relations, a broader bilateral coordinating body that brings together key officials of the U.S. Embassy in Japan, the MOD, and the Japanese Foreign Ministry, but is detached from any specific government agency per se.

The Joint Committee, which handles day-to-day matters falling under the Mutual Security Treaty, serves as a useful working-level arena for both protest and representation. It is a strategic "slice of the onion," as one participant put it, that allows Japanese officials to defuse the nationalist impulses of local citizens by representing their grievances without raising such concerns to the level of diplomatic confrontation with the nation's major ally. Many specialists consider the U.S.-Japan Joint Committee, with a distinctive combination of institutional detachment and involvement parallel to the DFAA, to be one of the most successful security coordination mechanisms in the world—superior to those operating within NATO, for example. And the compensation tools at its command are said to be, together with its autonomous institutional structure, a major source of this effectiveness.

Compensation, in both the Committee's material and its symbolic dimensions, has also been a central tool of the Special Advisory Council on Okinawa (SACO), set up to handle base problems on Okinawa in the wake of the tragic 1995 rape case there. SACO has recently had well over $200 million annually at its disposal.[19] Ultimately the strategic use of these funds, in a fashion related closely to grassroots requirements, combined with the provision of an arena for symbolic protest, were central reasons for SACO's relative success, as will be elaborated in chapter 8.

The Roots of Compensation Politics

Although compensation politics is by no means unique to Japan,[20] it appears to be quite prominent in base politics there. What accounts for this unusual salience? Why is Japan so seemingly distinctive in this aspect of its base politics, at least in comparative perspective?

The liberal heritage of Allied Occupation has clearly played a positive role. U.S. forces, as noted earlier, established the predecessor of the DFAA, which inaugurated the practice of ad hoc, grassroots payments to offset the cost and inconvenience imposed by U.S. military activities. SCAP also established a tradition of periodic base-commander liaison with local communities where bases are located—a pattern that has continued to this day.

Compensation politics remains salient in Japan, building on preexisting institutions, for two reasons: (1) because resources available to the government for allocation have been substantial; and (2) because alternative means of conflict-resolution have been blocked. Rapid economic growth, low levels of general military spending, and historically low entitlement levels explain relatively clearly why distributive resources available to government for allocation have been so high. Why coercion and other methods of social stabilization have not been more important in post–Japan, however, requires a more complex and subtle recounting.

There was, to be sure, a tradition of compensation in prewar Japanese politics, stressed by Hara Kei and a range of Seiyukai political associates intermittently for the first thirty years of the twentieth century.[21] But much more often the conservative response to political challenge during that period was repression. A principal reason that compensation politics was more salient in the postwar era than previously was simply that repression, given the lack of a powerful, legitimate military, had become much less feasible and legitimate.

The postwar Japanese government has had substantial powers of public-employee dismissal, but few other coercive resources at its disposal. In contrast to the German case, Japan's constitution does not provide a ready judicial vehicle for curbing radical groups.[22] The national police forces, not to mention the military, were disbanded soon after World War II, and have never been fully reconstituted and legitimated.

The conservatives' lack of coercive tools for maintaining stability was by no means due to a lack of interest in them. In early 1951 the Ordinance Review Committee proposed establishment of a Public Security Ministry, just before the end of the Allied occupation.[23] Prime Minister Yoshida announced plans to consolidate the various autonomous police forces in Japan, and actually considered establishing a Japanese version of the U.S. House of Representatives Un-American Activities Committee to investigate domestic subversion.[24] Yet only the consolidation of the various police forces was ever achieved. And that followed three long years of bitter domestic struggle, ultimately compelling the conservatives to summon police into the Diet building to forcibly clear Socialist obstruction.

In late 1958 Prime Minister Kishi Nobusuke proposed a major increase in national police powers, in preparation for the envisioned U.S.-Japan Security Treaty revision.[25] A storm of criticism from the Left forced him to retract his proposed police bill (Keishoku Hōan). This unexpected political setback both limited the range of tools subsequently available to Japanese conservative leaders in the face of dissent, and fueled further protests aimed at curbing the expansion of state coercive power.

Allied forces were effectively constrained from active intervention in Japanese political affairs during the early postwar period by fears of prospective domestic political backlash.[26] By the fall of 1951, with the Allied occupation drawing to a close, Japanese policymakers saw that they had to face the prospect of phased American withdrawal from Japan. Forceful suppression of labor unrest and political protest demonstrations had, of course, been commonplace during the prewar period, and the postwar conservatives were tempted to revive some of the old tactics in suitably adjusted form. Yet they faced sustained and spirited Diet opposition, forcing them to shelve most proposals. Intermittent criticism from the International Labor Organization (ILO), often coordinated with opposition party protests, also inhibited LDP efforts to curb labor, especially in the controversial area of public-sector union activities.[27]

The Japanese conservatives did periodically try other means of stabilizing their rule and enhancing their coercive capabilities. Revising the electoral system, strengthening the police, and reconstituting the powers of the prewar Home Ministry were among the options they actively explored.[28] Yet these efforts yielded remarkably little.

Every government, to be sure, employs what it considers to be a judicious combination of "the carrot and the stick." The distinctive feature of the Japanese case is a fateful combination: the extent to which both the "stick" is missing, and the pressures to provide the "carrot"—so widely available as a dividend of high growth in a low-military-budget economy—are overwhelming. Compensation politics clearly has a general political-economic logic for Japan, rooted in the stability imperative mandated by highly leveraged economic growth. Compensation also has an overlapping political-military logic in the base-politics arena, for both Japan, and for the United States as well. For Japan, compensation politics stabilizes the presence on Japanese soil of vital American power-projection capabilities traditionally proscribed under its "no-war" constitution. For the United States, such Japanese payments defuse opposition to a strategically vital complex of bases that could cost at least $40 billion to replace.

Japan's defense-budget allocation decisions have been roundly and routinely attacked over the years, especially in the United States, for undermining Pacific security, due to an alleged free-riding character. As chapter 8 will make clear, Japan has in fact contributed to the common defense quite extensively in the host-nation support (HNS) area. Indeed, it has provided more bilateral HNS to back up the U.S. military than any other nation in the world.

Comparative Dimensions

Seen comparatively, Japanese HNS appears to be not only large in quantitative terms, but also distinctively effective in building acceptance of the U.S. military presence in Japan, due to the broad grassroots-support coalitions that it fosters. In addition, the defense-dividend funds diverted to civilian purposes such as public-works spending have been used over the years to stabilize conservative political dominance in Japan. They did so by providing an extraordinary degree of material compensation to swing constituencies such as small business and remote local areas disadvantaged by the growth process, that otherwise would likely have supported more radical political forces.[29]

The regionally targeted nature of the compensation process in Japan, centering on Okinawa, and its configuration towards local needs, appears to bare some broad similarities to patterns in Italy and Portugal. Neither of Japan's southern European counterparts has a close equivalent to the DFAA or SACO, which have helped to fine-tune and accelerate Japanese central government responsiveness to local base problems. The unusual importance of local governments in base management, for different historical reasons in the two European cases, does, however, result in a functionally similar adaptation of base-relations policy to local needs.[30]

There is no inherent reason, other than cost, why compensation politics could not be a recipe for stabilizing the U.S. base presence outside Japan, as well as within it, if strategic and political rationales were available and institutions to efficiently broker compensation could be created. Many elements of the compensation-politics pattern, such as decentralized, case-by-case mediation of local citizen grievances, including fishing and environmental problems, appear to be practiced in Italy.[31] Portugal also long provided extensive base-related community support in the Azores, facilitated by substantial American economic assistance in return for access to the strategically important Lajes Air Base.[32] The Japanese practice of rapid, low-profile, and substantial grassroots-oriented financial support to allay local frustrations over pollution, crime, and other negative base externalities through decentralized organizations like the DFAA could in principle also be relevant in Central Asia, the Middle East, Eastern Europe, and other prospectively volatile areas in which the U.S. military has become active since 9/11.[33]

As we noted in chapter 4, the incentives to non-agreement problem at the local level is one of the most pervasive and fundamental difficulties that foreign forces encounter anywhere. Efforts to respond to grassroots discomfort, involving "symbolic" compensation as well as money, are especially important for the way they create local stakes in foreign base presence. Such efforts address this endemic incentives to non-agreement problem that lies at the heart of foreign base difficulties worldwide. They may thus be a partial recipe for stabilizing the American presence in many of the volatile nations to which it has expanded in connection with the global struggle against terrorism. Yet the availability of funds, as well as host-nation inability to create effective mediating structures like Japan's DFAA, create important obstacles to use of compensation politics widely as a base-politics stabilization tool, despite its clear effectiveness in postwar Japan, and in much of Mediterranean Europe.

BAZAAR POLITICS

Another paradigmatic pattern of base relations that might grow increasingly prominent in future is bazaar politics. This two-level process includes both domestic and international dimensions and involves complex and unstable iterative bargaining, in which national leaders serve as brokers. It is similar in certain respects to traditional Middle Eastern commercial negotiation—hence its name.

The concept is clearly relevant in volatile Islamic societies where local elites are dependent on foreign security guarantees, vulnerable domestically, and reliant on interests both at home and abroad for their prosperity and even for their survival. The notion is also relevant, however, in the Philippines, contemporary South Korea, and other areas far from the souks of the Middle East. Like compensation politics, fiat politics, or affective politics, bazaar politics is an ideal type, not necessarily found, in its pure form, within any given nation but with broad applicability throughout the world. Bazaar politics tends to appear in host nations where strong local demands, unstable national politics, and a reliance on outside powers for resources ultimately used for domestic allocation stir a particularly complex, interactive, and unpredictable political contest.

"Bazaar politics," as used here, has six defining characteristics, mainly imposed by the unusual structure of the political interactions and the resource flows involved. Collectively, they produce an environment of indeterminacy and bargaining, leading to bazaar-style haggling, and often indeterminate outcomes. Such dynamics are not salient when outcomes are more predictable, as under the compensation-politics paradigm.

Among the most distinctive structural features of bazaar politics is the complex interdependence between domestic and international determinants of base policy, corresponding to the "two-level games" paradigm. In instances of bazaar politics, ranging from Kyrgyzstan (2005) and Turkey (2003) to the Philippines (1991) and Greece (1970s), the resources needed to sustain domestic interest groups typically flow from outside the national system itself, typically in the form of base-rental payments, foreign military sales, trade access, or overseas development assistance, with all the complex psychological and political baggage that such forms of host-nation receivership can imply. It contrasts to the general configuration of the compensation-politics paradigm, under which resources for allocation are typically generated internally, as in postwar Japan. Leaders of the host nation must bargain aggressively under the bazaar-politics paradigm—even haggle and play aggressive dual games—to achieve optimal outcomes, often duplicitously provoking nationalist sentiment at home, in order to strengthen their bargaining hand with foreign allies.

Needless to say, the delicate nature of this complex transnational interaction leads to volatile, uncertain outcomes rather different from the more stable patterns of compensation politics, where resource-allocation patterns are not transnational in nature.

Bazaar politics also involves, secondly, some degree of compensation to domestic interest groups, albeit of uncertain magnitude, for their cooperation with national-government policies toward locally deployed foreign-military forces. The most important compensated constituency is typically the domestic military. Turkey, for example, is in the midst of a major, twenty-year, $100 billion military modernization program. Its armed forces are continually interested in high-performance weaponry from the United States, unconstrained by what they consider onerous political conditions.[34] They are perennially uncertain, however, as to just what sort of hardware they may be able to procure.

Thirdly, the bazaar-politics paradigm involves considerable uncertainty regarding the scale of resource flows, since resources for domestic allocation flow from abroad, in interaction with volatile domestic political processes. This endemic uncertainty intensifies the complex, duplicitous bargaining behavior, both at the domestic and the international levels, that is typical of the bazaar-politics paradigm, presented in figure 6.4.

Fourthly, the bazaar-politics paradigm is characterized by a pattern of persistent, pressing, and simultaneously complex domestic constituent demands. In the countries where this pattern is salient, frequently in the Islamic world, foreign bases are distinctly unpopular. Groups impacted by these foreign encroachments are strongly insistent on a quid pro quo for accepting their presence. Where the bazaar-politics pattern prevails, host nations are typically engulfed by social transition, with urbanization proceeding rapidly, and large populations of educated yet underemployed intellectuals restively and critically monitoring all visible dimensions of their nation's foreign-policy behavior. Local political institutions, characteristically, are underdeveloped, exacerbating the natural uncertainties of base negotiations that involve ratification procedures.

Developing countries, with their imbalance between rising political participation and halting political institutionalization, are classic candidates for domestic political instability.[35] Yet in the post-9/11 world, such volatile nations are also often of considerable and increasing political-military significance, especially in the Islamic world. This dualism sets up a situation where the basing nation may be willing to pay a significant price for basing or transit rights, especially in crisis situations where the host nation has geopolitical leverage.

Such fees are typically not as high today as during the last days of the Cold War, due to waning Great Power rivalry. Yet they can still be very

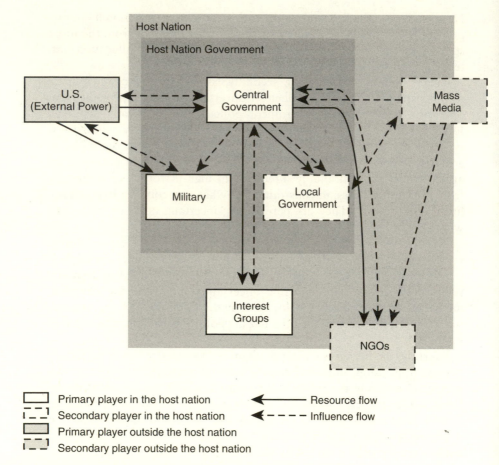

Figure 6.4 The Bazaar Politics Paradigm
Note: Too many games of negotiation to hammer out stable policies.

substantial. U.S. aid to strategic Central Asian nations close to the northern borders of Afghanistan—like Uzbekistan, for example—more than tripled in the year after 9/11.[36] And American assistance to Kyrgyzstan rose seventy-five-fold—to $150 million in 2006—the year after Uzbekistan expelled U.S. forces next door.[37]

Prima facie, bazaar politics should be a distinctively stable base-politics pattern. It involves, after all, compensation, which is stabilizing under the compensation-politics paradigm. Bazaar politics also involves a fifth characteristic, coercion, as noted in figure 6.2. Student protestors are often the object of such coercion. Precisely because this form of base politics tends to be so volatile and uncertain, often taking place in unstable developing nations, governments are tempted to stabilize the domestic social parameters surrounding it by cracking down harshly on dissent. Turkey and the Central Asian states have shown this pattern clearly, as the Philippines also did at times during the 1980s.

Bazaar politics, however, also involves iterative policy decision making, a sixth key characteristic. In the complex, manipulative concerts, often transnational in character, which bazaar politics often involves, the same issue can be visited many times with only marginally different results, provoking mass frustration. Such repetitive yet unstructured patterns make systematic grassroots compensation difficult. They also often render coercion against undisciplined students, workers, and other mass social forces painfully and persistently necessary, as long as the paradigm prevails in a particular national context.

Bazaar Politics in Turkey

A clear example of bazaar politics at work is Turkey's bargaining with the United States between mid-2002 and early 2003 concerning terms of access for American forces on the eve of the Iraq War.[38] The haggling began with former U.S. Deputy Secretary of Defense Paul Wolfowitz's July 2002 visit to Ankara, during which he expressed the American hope to launch anti-Saddam ground attacks into Iraq from bases on Turkish territory. During his December 2002 visit, Wolfowitz reportedly asked to base 80,000 or more U.S. troops in Turkey, so as to facilitate a second-front northern offensive in a prospective conflict, complementing a parallel thrust up from Kuwait in the south.[39] Pentagon estimates at the time reportedly indicated that inability to open such a second front in the north could cost the United States an additional one thousand casualties.[40]

Turkey's pragmatic, if insensitive, response was to bargain, with American lives prospectively at stake. Ankara linked Wolfowitz's urgent request for basing access to matters of priority concern to Ankara: (1) Economic compensation; (2) terms of access; and (3) access for the Turkish military itself to northern Iraq. Turkey's AKP Islamic government also slowed and segmented its response, attempting to maximize leverage against a Bush administration conversely intent on moving against Saddam Hussein as rapidly as possible.

Delay seems to have been a major tactical weapon. Turkish Prime Minister Tayyip Erdogan did not forget, for example, to segment decisions, and to repeatedly haggle with the United States for added concessions before asking his parliament to approve incremental usage of Turkish airspace by the American military, despite urgent demands from Washington for decisive action.[41]

Coercion was continually a factor in the background of the decision-making process. The Turkish military—guardians of the Kemalist secular tradition—was clearly anti-Islamist. On three occasions in the recent past—1960, 1971, and 1980—it had staged veto coups to forestall Islamist tendencies in incumbent governments. And in 1997 it had indirectly deposed the Erbakan Islamist government as well.[42]

It was not until early January 2003, after weeks of procrastination, and less than three months before the projected invasion of Iraq, that the Turks even allowed American technicians into Turkey to assess the suitability and condition of prospective bases. And then it was not until February 6—by which time the United States had hoped that Turkey would already have granted permission for American access—that parliament even agreed to let a *token* 4,000 U.S. personnel into Turkey to upgrade facilities. The Turkish government demanded an exorbitant access fee of $300 million for doing so. And it insisted, furthermore, that this authorization did not imply approval for the subsequent entry of American combat troops. It thus further segmented and complicated the approval process, simultaneously frustrating the United States.

Despite an increase from $4 billion to $6 billion in the U.S. offer of grants in cash, or a proposed $24–30 billion in loan guarantees with favorable payback periods and rates,[43] Ankara continued to haggle for a better deal. Turkish negotiators insisted that duties on Turkish textile exports to the United States should be reduced. They further demanded a written guarantee of their attractive package, to safeguard it in the face of prospective congressional opposition. The Turkish leaders, their substantial demands notwithstanding, refused to put the access issue to the required parliamentary vote in their own National Assembly. Meanwhile, around five U.S. ships carrying tanks and other heavy equipment for the Fourth Infantry Division were floating helplessly off the Turkish coast; another thirty of similar intent were streaming rapidly in the same direction.

On February 26, the government introduced a measure into Parliament permitting 62,000 additional U.S. troops, 255 jet aircraft, and 65 helicopters into Turkey for a period of six months. On March 1, in the wake of a Turkish National Security Council meeting at which the powerful Turkish General Staff (TGS) remained silent on any prospective pact, Parliament narrowly rejected the measure, by a margin of just three votes. Three weeks later, on March 20, hours after the Iraq War commenced, the Turkish parliament reversed itself and endorsed a fall-back agreement. This was to allow overflight rights permitting resupply so as to facilitate a lighter and smaller U.S. airborne attack against northern Iraq that was to come later.

Yet this second-best outcome did not allow American assault troops onto Turkish territory. Indeed, it left the U.S. Fourth Infantry Division's heavy equipment floating off the Turkish coast for weeks before it was belatedly redirected to Kuwait. Ultimately that equipment proved virtually useless to the overall campaign against Saddam Hussein.

As a consequence of Turkey's failure to allow a real second front in the north of Iraq, Mosul and Kirkuk, not to mention Saddam Hussein's birthplace of Tikrit and much of the Sunni Triangle, remained unconquered—even as coalition forces entered Baghdad and Basra. This hiatus, of course, gave militants more opportunity to organize and stockpile for the savage guerilla war that was ultimately to ensue than they otherwise would have enjoyed. U.S. Secretary of Defense Donald Rumsfeld later argued that this failure to gain access through Turkey contributed greatly to the strength of the insurgency in the "Sunni Triangle" that was soon to emerge, although clearly many other factors were also at work.[44]

The duplicitous bazaar politics between the United States and Turkey involved in the run-up to the Iraq war clearly resulted in major miscalculation between the two sides. Both the Turkish government and its military thought that Washington had little choice but to give Ankara whatever it asked for, and to wait until the Turks were ready to deal. By failing to recognize that American policymakers had other viable, albeit less palatable, options, both the military and the civilian leaders in Ankara overplayed their hand. Conversely, the United States, particularly the Pentagon, assumed that Turkey, as a treaty ally, would be much more cooperative than it proved to be, factoring it into war plans in ways that turned out to be domestically infeasible in Ankara.

It is useful to step back and ask both why the Iraq transit decision was such a clear case of bazaar politics, and what it implies for policy and theory. It is, after all, somewhat counterintuitive that the United States and Turkey should be haggling with one another over matters of life and death, given their long history of stable, cooperative relations. Bazaar politics had *not* arisen previously in this bilateral relationship with such intensity—why, then, at this juncture? And what can one learn from this case regarding the sorts of circumstances in which bazaar politics is likely to arise in future, both in Turkey and elsewhere?

The fragmented power structure and competing interests in Turkish domestic politics during 2002 appear in retrospect to have been the central reason that American transit negotiations with Ankara took on such a contradictory, manipulative "bazaar" character. Both the two key Turkish institutional actors in the case—the TGS and the ruling, moderate Islamist Justice and Development Party (JDP) wanted a stable, cooperative outcome with the United States. Yet neither wanted to take ultimate political responsibility for the approval of an unpopular American transit request, which was being sharply condemned in both continental Europe and the Islamic world.

The TGS and the JDP, after all, were long-standing rivals, with the TGS having forced a predecessor Islamist group from power in 1997. JDP rule was not well institutionalized, the party having just come to power in November 2002 on a 34.3 percent share of the vote. Indeed, its leader, Tayyip Erdogan, was not even a formal member of Parliament. The TGS may well have calculated that a major foreign-policy setback, especially in relations with such a key ally as the United States, might destabilize the JDP government, giving the TGS either more leverage or more congenial national leadership with which to deal.[45]

The fluid nature of the overall political situation also contributed to the bazaar-politics character of the decision making. No political leader, after all, was firmly in power, and no cohesive elite cartel was capable of both coordinating national bargaining with the United States and enforcing the terms of an agreement domestically. Turkish leaders, as was dramatically clear from the March 1 vote, could not implement domestically a bargain they had solemnly agreed to internationally, even one that was highly lucrative for the key domestic protagonists. Clearly the rising influence of grassroots democratic forces, with their attendant incentives to nonagreement, were an important factor at work.

For policy, the clear implication of this case is that foreign interests must deal with bazaar politics by disaggregating the host-nation state. They need to see for *themselves* who the key subnational actors are, and to consider the incentives of those subnational actors (such as the military, political parties, students, and local business groups) quite directly. For theory, the implication is that more analytical attention must be accorded to: (1) the catalytic forces producing overlapping domestic and international win-sets; (2) the incentive structure of subnational actors; and (3) the impact of democratization and regime shifts on subnational incentives and policy-coordination processes.

Bazaar politics, as noted above, is an abstract, ideal-typical paradigm, as are the other three patterns (compensation politics, fiat politics, and affective politics) that are presented here, with manifestations in a broad variety of national and regional contexts. It applies very well in the 2002–2003 Turkish case. It may also be quite relevant, as just noted, in many other instances of negotiation with transitional democracies in strategic developing nations where the United States pays base rental, rather than relying on HNS payments from its allies, and where domestic pressures for interest-group compensation on base-related issues are also strong. Such cases have grown ever more numerous in the post–Cold War, post-9/11 world.

Bazaar Politics in the Philippines

The Philippine base negotiations of 1990–91, and analogous cases in Greece and Spain, bear striking similarities to the Turkish variant of the bazaar-politics paradigm. In each case, host-nations' expectations were strong for major payments from the United States due to the strategic importance of the bases in question. The host-nation government in each case was both internally disunited, and subject to strong cross-pressures from the turbulent civil society of its own emerging democracy.

All the key players in these base negotiations had strong incentives to bargain hard, and to be both mercenary and duplicitous in their dealings with the United States. Cold War superpower rivalries between the United States and the Soviet Union intensified these host-nation impulses. Yet the central players also had strong incentives to see a concrete transaction emerge—to see a sale made in the end, regardless of the haggling involved along the way.

The Philippine base negotiations (1987–91) provide an excellent illustration, as noted above, of bazaar politics at work. Manila entered the negotiations of the late 1980s witnessing the lucrative fruit of negotiations elsewhere in the world.[46] It also knew clearly that the United States considered facilities like Clark Field and Subic Bay to be highly strategic, especially following the fall of Saigon and the Soviet naval buildup of the 1980s in Vietnam.[47]

Following the downfall of Ferdinand Marcos in 1986, the new reformist Aquino administration, although quite conscious of the economic and strategic value of strong ties to the United States, deeply resented previous U.S. backing for Marcos. The deposed dictator had, after all, been responsible for the murder of Aquino's late husband, as well as a broad range of injuries and insults to other members of the new administration. To make matters more difficult, Aquino's government was heavily cross-pressured by activist, antibase NGOs and populist politicians who had been its principal backers in the anti-Marcos struggle.

There were also institutional constraints. The new Philippine Constitution, for example, prescribed a tortuous process for base-agreement ratification, which rendered negotiations highly vulnerable to populist pressures—increasing the bias toward volatile bazaar politics. Specifically, the Constitution requires that a treaty with basing nations be "concurred in" by the Philippine Senate and, if the Congress so requires, additionally by a majority of voters participating in a national referendum called for that purpose.[48]

At a minimum, Filipino negotiators, and most of the Filipino populace as a whole, wanted a lucrative, precedent-setting new agreement. The

Filipinos had few incentives to limit or coordinate their lavish expectations, since the prospective resources to be allocated, as in the Turkish case, came exclusively from abroad. The nature of this issue richly encouraged duplicity and manipulation.

On the American side, many wondered if, in the post–Cold War world then dawning, the exorbitant sums and restricted operating conditions demanded by the Filipinos were worth the benefits offered. Ambivalence in Washington, as in Manila, was substantial, intensifying the uncertainty of both bargaining and of outcomes. In the end, of course, U.S. and Filipino negotiators laboriously patched together a complex, exorbitant agreement that nevertheless failed in the Philippine Senate, leading to U.S. withdrawal from some of America's oldest and largest bases outside the United States.

Virtually every case of bazaar politics, concentrated in strategic emerging democracies of the developing world, has similarly involved volatile, contradictory interest-group pressures and policy consequences. In each instance, elite dominance of policy processes could potentially help generate positive-sum outcomes, but was not always politically feasible. In those limited instances where mutually satisfactory results were actually achieved, political brokers—playing conciliatory international and domestic roles like that of Turgut Ozal in Turkey during the 1990–91 Gulf War—were crucial to positive outcomes—just as in a bazaar. Yet whether such brokers will emerge when needed is always in question, compounding the uncertainty of bazaar politics.

FIAT POLITICS

This paradigm, the converse of the compensation-politics pattern characteristic of postwar Japan, is particularly common when the host nation is a dictatorship. Policymakers rely on coercion rather than compensation to enforce popular adherence to security policies generally, and to host-nation policies toward foreign bases in particular. In its dealings with the private sector, the government typically requisitions; it does not appease. Land for foreign bases, or for military training grounds, for example, is typically *taken* from the private sector at nominal rentals, to the extent that rentals are provided at all, through direct appendages of the host-nation military.[49]

The fiat-politics paradigm of base relations, in short, is highly command-oriented. It accords power resources, domestic legitimacy, and external support to a centralized national-security apparatus, typically the military, that is prone to use those resources to assure base-politics stability. The basic pattern, relying on very different tools than compensation politics, is presented graphically in figure 6.5.

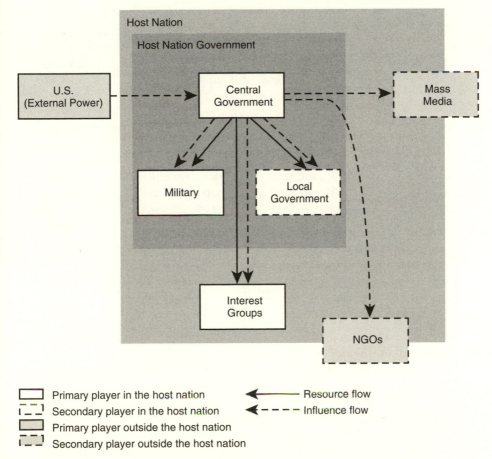

Figures 6.5. The Fiat Politics Paradigm

The Coercive Dimension

Under the paradigm of fiat politics toward foreign bases, most closely approximated in cases like Park Chung-Hee's South Korea (1961–79) and Franco's Spain (1953–75), the host-nation government behaves in a highly authoritative fashion toward both local interest groups and allied foreign governments. It is relatively straightforward in its dealings with both domestic and international constituencies. It is likewise predictable both in presenting options, and in honoring commitments once made. This straightforward approach contrasts to the complex, devious dualism (nominal antimilitarism combined with covert compliance) that is more characteristic of compensation politics, or often of bazaar politics.

Coercion and stiff penalties for dissent are hallmarks of fiat politics. The Korean approach under Park Chung-Hee, with roots dating back to the anticommunist struggles of the early postwar period, was typical. The cornerstone of state policy toward dissent and dissenters was the National Security Law. That law, still on the books, defines "antinational" groups, subject to sanctions under the law, as "any domestic or foreign association or group of people, which intends . . . to disturb the nation."[50] The law mandates death sentences and stiff prison terms for a wide range of vague offenses, including "praising or promoting" anti-national groups (Article 7); meeting or communicating with members of such groups (Article 8); and failure to inform law-enforcement or intelligence services of the broad range of infractions defined as crimes under the law (Article 10).

This straightforward, authoritative approach, a hallmark of fiat politics, has both domestic and international origins. Domestically, successful practitioners of fiat politics tend to be military strongmen, in nations of two varieties: (1) where civil society is either traditionally weak, as in Korea or Central Asia; or (2) where it is incorporated and allied with the state, as in Spain and much of Latin America. Internationally, fiat politics tends to be salient where the host nation has substantial leverage on its hegemonic alliance partner because the host nation provides scarce and strategically valuable resources to the common alliance.[51]

Thus, the American involvement in Vietnam, and the famed Korean Blue Tiger Division's engagement there, strengthened Park in his base-politics dealings with the United States. So did Korea's substantial early host-nation support in kind for U.S. Forces in Korea (USFK), such as the 1974 storage and maintenance of war stockpiles (WRS) program.[52] Similarly, the deepening Cold War competition with the Soviet Union, and the rising strategic importance of SAC bases in that context, immeasurably strengthened Franco in negotiations on the landmark 1953 Treaty of Madrid. This brought U.S. bases—and a bilateral security arrangement highly controversial within NATO—to a Phalangist regime whose famed Blue Division had fought alongside Adolph Hitler's Wehrmacht at Stalingrad little more than a decade earlier.[53]

Fiat politics, in short, has highly salutary implications for base relations as long as dictatorship persists. The host nation is clear in its goals, and capable of honoring its commitments. When substantial protests occur, they are signals of real intent to expel or substantially modify the mandate of foreign forces, not a duplicitous bargaining strategy is as so common under other paradigms.

In a democratic environment, conversely, fiat politics can be a highly destabilizing mode of conducting base relations. Under this paradigm, there are no malleable networks or institutions for two-way communication.

In addition, there is no tradition, as under the compensation paradigm, of using government resources actively to coopt private-sector interest groups.

Fiat Politics in South Korea

Under the Park, Chyun, and Roh Dae Woo military regimes (1961–93), South Korea provided a classic case of fiat politics successfully at work in base relations. Yet the ROK has given birth, over the generation of democratization since then, to highly unstable patterns of base relations—precisely because the fiat-politics tradition prevented Korea from developing the infrastructure of communication, compromise, and compensation that become so important to stable base relations in a democratic society. The contrast to Japan, with its sophisticated social-mediation institutions, born of occupation, and bred in a semipacifist democracy, is striking.

The workings and impact of South Korea's National Security Law, outlined above, provide a graphic illustration of the perverse, embedded consequences that the fiat-politics tradition, flowing from decades of military rule and North-South confrontation, has bequeathed to a democratic South Korea. The broad application and draconian penalties provided under the law have criminalized a wide range of protest activities. They have sanctioned, in particular, much university-student activism that would be much more lightly punished, if at all, in Japan, Europe, or the United States.

As a consequence, many Korean student activists of the 1970s, 1980s, and 1990s incurred criminal records, and often prison terms, that prevented their returning to mainstream society once they were released. These activists, who moved heavily to careers in the mass media, NGOs, labor unions, and the academic world, began to form an institutionalized "protest subculture" with a strong bias toward social and political radicalism. Their movements gained increasing momentum under the progressive Kim Dae Jung and Roh Moo Hyun administrations (1998–2008).

This South Korean pattern of activist recruitment contrasts strongly, as do patterns of institutional mediation, to the sociology of protest in Japan, as noted above. There, radicals unburdened by criminal records, due to Japan's more liberal treatment of exdissidents, and its lack of a Korean–style National Security Law, have typically become moderate in later years. And they have returned to mainstream society after the activism of their youth.[54]

Korean politics, like those of Japan but in converse fashion, thus provide clear evidence of the enduring importance of institutions in configuring host-nation approaches to military bases on their territory. Flowing from the stark heritage of the Korean War, extended military rule, and a half-century of bitter North-South confrontation, the institutional framework for South Korea's base politics is thus command-oriented. Compared to Japan, it makes strikingly little provision for systematically accommodating the interests and views of civic groups.

Within the national government, South Korea, to be sure, has a Military Installations Bureau technically analogous to Japan's DFAA. But this Korean base-relations entity is integrated firmly within the Ministry of National Defense (MND) itself, as one of nine bureau-level offices. It lacks the autonomy to pursue the base-relations mandate that Japan's semiautonomous DFAA enjoys, the grassroots network provided by the DFAA's extensive system of regional branch offices, and the substantial budgetary resources available to the DFAA. South Korea's fiat politics, in short, have created a very different institutional heritage from that of compensation politics, with major consequences for host-nation base management that persist to this day.

Demographic and sociological complexities have further compounded base relations in South Korea.[55] Simply put, the "386" generation of people in their thirties, educated in the 1980s and born in the 1960s, is anti-alliance, due to: (1) lack of the strong bonding experiences with the United States that the parents of such people had during the Korean War; (2) their own strong generational cohesion, born of the powerful 2002 World Cup experience of supporting the Korean team as it fought to the global semifinals; and (3) the catalytic effect of the protest subculture embraced by many within their ranks. And the 386 generation—the complex descendent of fiat politics, which had no way of accommodating diversity within the national mainstream—is growing steadily more important within Korean politics as a whole.

Special Perils of Regime Transition

Spanish base politics under democratic rule since the death of Franco bear striking similarities, as might be expected, to those of Korea. Flowing from a similar authoritarian heritage, institutions for mediating grassroots base problems are weak, while the protest subculture is strong. In both cases, the heritage of fiat politics, once the dictator sustaining such patterns has departed, has been unstable base relations, where the institutions to accommodate rising participation are lacking. This unstable heritage of fiat politics appears likely to prevail in much of the developing world,[56] and suggests the dangers for American policy of investing heavily in basing relationships with most dictatorial regimes.

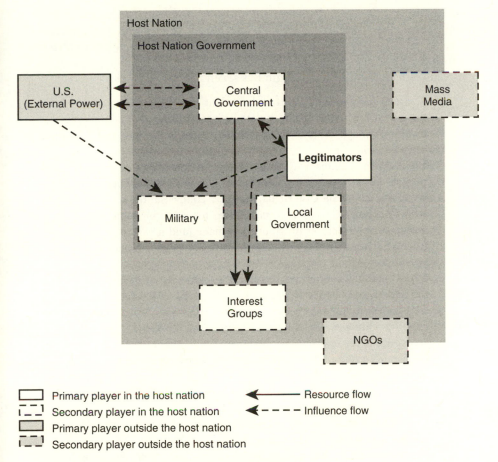

Figure 6.6. The Affective Politics Paradigm

AFFECTIVE POLITICS

As a general matter, this volume emphasizes the importance of predictable incentives in the base-politics process, and the surprisingly marginal role of values in determining host-nation behavior in base-related
issues. To argue that general proposition, however, is not to deny that
culture and affective sentiments can play an important legitimating role
in some limited set of cases, especially where political structure facilitates
such an outcome. The affective-politics paradigm, presented graphically
in figure 6.6, strives to identify the general features of that distinctive set
of cases, with an eclectic emphasis on institutions specifically created to
amplify the impact of values and communal sentiments on base politics

as a whole. It is especially prevalent in traditional feudal societies, as can be seen in Saudi Arabia, although the notion arguably has some relevance also to postindustrial cases where transcendent institutionalized norms prevail, as in Australia and Canada.

The affective-politics paradigm has seven central features:

1. The national government is not dependent on official resource-flows from the outside. It is thus able to isolate its internal decision-making processes from its foreign policy, giving enhanced scope for parochial domestic considerations.
2. Government legitimacy is provided by institutionally propagated, supported, and enforced core values rather than by material allocations. Consequently, as in the case of fiat politics, compensation does not receive strong formal emphasis as a mechanism for achieving state objectives in base politics. Whatever distribution is made (and it can often be substantial, as in Saudi Arabia) is done for other, nominally nondefense-related purposes.
3. Major national institutions reinforce the legitimacy of core values, including underlying concepts of national security.
4. The state typically relies on values-related legitimacy rather than direct coercion to induce conformity with base-relations policies.
5. Base-politics relationships are governed by tacit understandings, often embedded in culture, rather than by codified, transparent rules.
6. Where host-nation culture is different from that of basing-nation troops, the latter are rigorously isolated from host-nation citizenry, and forced to observe distinctive local norms in public places.
7. Cultural norms profoundly shape the operational constraints under which foreign forces operate, the degree of local visibility they are allowed; and the willingness of the host government to allow their stationing at all. Where host-nation and basing-nation cultures are largely different, these constraints can be extreme under the affective-politics paradigm.

Affective Politics in the Islamic World

For more than 1,300 years, since Muslim armies crossed the Pillars of Hercules and entered Christian Spain in the seventh century, the West has stood in delicate political-military relationship with the world of Islam. An important dimension of that complex relationship, especially since the early days of World War II, has been the presence of Western military bases on Arab soil. The American presence dates from wartime bases in North Africa and Saudi Arabia,[57] while that of the British and French dates even further back, to colonial origins.[58] Western political-military interaction with the Islamic world has been intensified recently, of course, by both the war on terrorism, and the world's deepening dependence on Middle Eastern oil and gas.

Given the sharply Manichean Islamic world view, coupled with the Muslim insistence on political supremacy over nonbelievers in Islamic states and the heritage of the Crusades,[59] it is not surprising that value conflicts should intrude deeply into Middle Eastern base politics. The case of Saudi Arabia presents numerous graphic, if extreme, illustrations of how cultural norms can affect base politics in the Islamic world. Due to the continuing importance of fundamentalist Wahhabi Islam as a basis of legitimacy for the Saudi regime, cultural norms have been, not surprisingly, continuously central in U.S.-Saudi base politics for well over a half-century.

The agreement to build an American military air field at Dhahran, next to Aramco's headquarters, and amidst the growing oil fields of Saudi Arabia's Eastern Province, came in August 1945; the U.S. War Department badly wanted shorter and cheaper air routes between North Africa and the still-continuing conflict in the Pacific. King Abdel Aziz was initially concerned about the prospect of a base on his soil, fearing that it would be a first step toward American imperial intervention—a concern that persisted among Saudi royalty throughout the history of the base. Accordingly, in the final agreement, the Dhahran facility was referred to as an "air field" rather than an "air base." Saudi Arabia was also assured that full ownership would revert to the Saudis within three years of the end of World War II.

The Dhahran air field was finally completed in 1946, and the war had already been over for nearly a year by then. By the time the base agreement came up for renewal in 1948, concern about the Soviets compelled both the United States and the Saudis to support renewal. To ensure Saudi control, the king approved only year-to-year agreements, rather than longer-term ones.[60]

Until 1963, Dhahran functioned as an important SAC nuclear base, from which retaliatory strikes could prospectively be launched against the Soviet Union. Its strategic importance did wane with the advent of ICBMs during the early 1960s, even as the winds of Arab nationalism made the Saudis more reluctant to host American forces, and the Kennedy administration's dialogue with Arab reformers compounded problems with the conservative Saudis still further. The facility was closed in 1963.[61]

U.S. troops deployed again to Saudi Arabia following Saddam Hussein's invasion of Kuwait in August 1990, and once again the issue proved controversial in Saudi elite politics.[62] Crown Prince Abdullah, in particular, apparently felt that such a momentous decision as initiating a major foreign-troop presence should be broadly vetted among traditional leaders before being undertaken. King Fahd, however, was more decisive in his support for the U.S. deployment and approved it. The royal family sought and received a fatwa from the Grand Mufti bin Baz, sanctioning the deployment, but opposing fatwas were also issued arguing that the deployment ran counter to Islam.[63]

American troops remained in the Saudi Kingdom until mid-2003, with a small maintenance team remaining still longer at the sprawling Prince Sultan Air Base.[64] But U.S. troops encountered serious problems of legitimacy in that conservative Islamic nation throughout their stay. As the host government could not easily invoke coercion in support of its valued, but in some ways unwelcome, guests and their bases, it was compelled to rely on an affective-politics approach that invoked cultural symbolism to both obscure the foreign presence and affirm its conformity with local values.

Culturally related operational constraints on the day-to-day lives of American personnel have been one important way that affective politics have affected foreign military personnel in Saudi Arabia. Female U.S. soldiers, for example, like all Saudi women, have been forbidden to drive, and were for some time required to wear an *abaja* (total body covering that Saudi women wear in public) while off-base.[65]

Affective politics also seems to have inspired the Saudi government to obscure the visibility of U.S. forces in Saudi Arabia to an unusual degree, especially during the 1990s. Following the Iraqi invasion of Kuwait, for example, the United States deployed over 600,000 troops to Saudi Arabia, and the Saudis built massive, state-of-the-art facilities at Prince Sultan Air Base to accommodate them, going so far as to fully equip the operational headquarters of the entire Middle East Command. Prince Sultan Air Base coordinated air operations in Afghanistan against the Taliban and al-Qaeda during late 2001, while simultaneously enforcing the no-fly zone against Iraq.

Yet Saudi Arabia never formally recognized the basing of American forces, or published a SOFA with the United States. It built its largest facilities for U.S. forces 70 miles southeast of Riyadh on an unmarked road in the open desert, at al-Kharj, in a sprawling, 230-square-mile compound the size of metropolitan Chicago, yet not marked on any map.[66] It tried, in short, to obscure the presence of American troops to the maximum extent possible, even forbidding pictures at Prince Sultan Air Base showing U.S. military vehicles with Saudi license plates.

Affective politics also constrained the very presence of foreign forces to the absolute minimum level that regional strategic exigencies would allow. Saudi Arabia has never permitted sustained base presence by non-American foreign forces, and only allowed the U.S. Air Force to the extent that national-defense imperatives required. Between 1952 and 1963, the justification for Dhahran was nuclear strategy against the Soviet Union; from 1990 to 2003 it was Desert Shield, Desert Storm, and then the enforcement of the no-fly zone over Iraq. Once Saddam Hussein was ousted in 2003, the U.S. military was largely out of Saudi Arabia within a matter of months. By 2005 only 400–500 troops remained to handle such routine liaison tasks as training and military sales.

Why are cultural norms so apparently salient in Saudi base politics—in configuring operational constraints, limiting the American presence, and obscuring even such limited presence as exists? The reasons are deeply embedded in history, and go back to the very foundations of the Saudi Arabian state. Simply put, the Saudi regime's fidelity to and defense of Wahhabi fundamentalist Islamic norms provides its own basic source of political legitimacy, and those norms are often xenophobic at their core. They require, if a foreign presence is allowed at all, that it not be seen in any way as contravening core Islamic behavioral codes.

To the extent that the Saudi regime is perceived domestically as unfaithful to highly exacting Wahhabi norms, or as permitting nonbelievers to wantonly flout them, its own self-proclaimed standing as defender of the Faith, and hence its license to rule, is compromised. To reduce the tension between its contrasting domestic and international requirements for survival, the Saudi regime has had to either obscure the presence of foreign forces or expel them, and to enforce its norms on those forces when their presence could not be obscured. The heart of affective politics, after all, is the enforcement of basic values and communal sentiments. That has been the preoccupation of the Saudi government vis-à-vis the United States.

Saudi Arabia's distinctive approach to base politics is not entirely lacking in coercive or compensatory elements. It is thus somewhat divergent from any one ideal type, although closer to affective politics than to any other. The origins of the Saudi state clearly involved coercion on a massive scale—the al-Saud family's successful campaign in the 1920s to unify the Arabian Peninsula, for example, involved the public execution of 40,000 people and 350,000 amputations—out of a population of four million.[67] Since the first Oil Shock in 1973, the Saudi government has also periodically funded both domestic and foreign dissidents, from Saudi Arabia's bulging petroleum reserves. Yet the governing principle of Saudi base politics has been neither coercion nor compensation, but rather the cultural imperatives of Wahhabi Islam, with their crucial functional utility in assuring the regime's survival.

Embedded History and Saudi Affective Politics

Why have cultural norms—rather than compensation or coercion per se—seemingly been so central in determining Saudi Arabia's approach to base politics? Powerful historical-institutional forces are clearly at work. They have embedded exacting rules of behavior, and expectations that conformity to those rules should be the basis of legitimacy for the Saudi regime itself. Those rules can only be overtly contravened at the cost of endangering that legitimacy—and thus threatening the very survival of the regime.

Affective politics—the instrumental use of cultural symbols and communal sentiments to provide legitimacy, and thus stability—assumed importance in Saudi Arabia through the historic bargain that created the Saudi monarchy itself. In 1745 a provincial emir, Muhammed ibn Saud, and a puritan reformer, Muhammed ibn Abd al-Wahhab, formed a solemn alliance to eliminate the "superstitions," in their view, that had adulterated Islam's original purity.[68] They jointly vowed to return Islam to its fundamentals, and to implement strictly all of its injunctions and prohibitions in the legal, moral, and private spheres.[69]

The al-Saud family's alliance with Wahhabism, consolidated through intermarriage and an agreement that power would be shared over the generations, elevated that family in time from its original status as a minor provincial outlaw group to dominance across the whole of Saudi Arabia. As Stephen Schwartz notes in *The Two Faces of Islam*, it was "a unique fashion of religious and political control, a system in which faith and statecraft would be run as a family business."[70] As Defender of the Faith, however, the Saud family incurred massive new obligations—and important vulnerabilities—that gave birth to the Saudi version of affective politics.

In keeping with the political imperative of sustaining legitimacy by promoting and defending Islam, King Saud first made the hajj more accessible to pilgrims throughout the world, increasing the number of pilgrims visiting Mecca from 90,000 in 1926 to two million by 1979.[71] In 1962 the Saudis founded the Muslim World League to support dawa, or the "call to Islam." The Saudis have also built over 1,500 mosques worldwide over the past fifty years (including over six hundred in the United States),[72] and distributed millions of Korans free of charge.

The key point, in relation to base politics, is that the Saudis committed themselves so heavily to the pious defense of Islam—and enforcement of the strict Wahhabi moral code—that any perceived deviations from that path would undermine their political as well as religious legitimacy. Diverging from the narrow, culturally determined path, in short, made them appear hypocritical. To forestall religious challenge, King Faisal "incorporated" the *ulema*s, or religious authorities, by making them state employees.[73] He and other Saudi leaders also bestowed largesse on al-Azar University of Cairo and other esteemed theological centers throughout the Muslim world.

The Iraqi invasion of Kuwait, and the ensuing Gulf War, did much to undermine the Saudis' religious legitimacy, and thereby to encourage them to be more proactive in affective politics toward the bases.[74] Islamic principles decry, in the view of many fundamentalists, the presence of foreign, "infidel" forces on Muslim lands. Yet Saudi Arabia allowed 600,000 such soldier-infidels on its soil, for leverage in a conflict with another Muslim state.

Following the American intervention, the Saudi leaders found themselves under domestic fire from both left and right. They also confronted rising criticism from Saudi intellectuals abroad.[75] In the end Muslim extremists like Osama bin-Laden also joined the chorus of criticism, encouraging the Saudis on culturalist grounds to obscure and ultimately eliminate the U.S. base presence. Ultimately the culturalist argument triumphed, as national-security imperatives waned with the defeat of Saddam Hussein and American forces largely withdrew in August 2003.

Anglo-Saxon Affective Politics?

Although culture operates in the Islamic world to complicate and constrain the operations of U.S. forces, partly for embedded institutional reasons, in the Anglo-Saxon world it arguably operates in the converse fashion. Britain and Australia, in particular, have become staunch allies of the United States, flexibly accommodating U.S. facilities of major strategic importance with few financial offset arrangements. Britain, for example, has served since the early 1950s as a major base for both the SAC and the U.S. nuclear early-warning system, as noted earlier. It has also been flexibly providing America's most important single base for Middle East and South Asian operations, at Diego Garcia in the Indian Ocean, receiving only some minor arms-purchase offset arrangements in return.[76] As in the case of Saudi Arabia, the Anglo-American "special relationship" has often been based more on tacit understandings than formalized rules.

Australia has shown similar fidelity, demanding minimal explicit compensation in return for often very major commitments, and providing multiple varieties of informal and tacit cooperation in not fully transparent ways. Apart from fighting shoulder to shoulder in every war of the past century in which the United States has participated, the Aussies have also proven willing to station sensitive joint U.S.-Australian facilities on their soil. They have also given the U.S. de facto leeway in running them, while never agreeing to provide bases under formal American control.[77]

Australia has several advantages for C4ISR facilities that make it in the nuclear age among the most strategic, and hence potentially exposed, locations in the world for globally oriented U.S. forces.[78] Australia lies on the far side of the world from the United States, offering satellite coverage of areas not easily reached from other American bases, including parts of Russia, China, and Southeast Asia. In addition, it is not easy for other nations to monitor secret transmissions from locations in Australia's large, lightly populated interior.[79]

At Nurrangar, Australia has long provided a ground station for the early-warning satellites of the Defense Support Program (DSP), one of three in the entire world. Using infrared sensors, these satellites can track Russian missile launches from Central Asia and are capable of providing some of the earliest land-based evidence of such launches on earth. Nurrangar has hence long been a priority target for Russian nuclear weapons.[80]

At Pine Gap, Australia has similarly provided a long-secret satellite ground station largely underground—that is informally run by American intelligence, and, like Nurrangar, highly vulnerable to enemy retaliation.[81] At Northwest Cape, U.S. forces communicate with ballistic missile–carrying submarines, and could potentially send targeting and firing orders to Trident submarines in the event of nuclear war.[82] Australia also engages in close interpersonal coordination with defense-related U.S. government agencies, much of it informal and not fully transparent.

No other American ally in the Pacific, in short, has taken on such delicate and strategic tasks, often with little fanfare. Yet the decisions to establish and sustain such sensitive, essentially American facilities have been remarkably noncontroversial in Australian domestic politics. Only a limited segment of the Australian left has questioned them, together with more visibly conventional U.S. actions, such as the systematic use of Darwin, Australia, as a transit point for B-52s en route to and from Diego Garcia and the Persian Gulf. As in the case of Saudi Arabia, one reason for the remarkably low degree of public controversy in U.S.-Australian base politics is no doubt that so much of the bilateral interaction is informal and uncodified. Yet only between countries that share deep affective sentiments borne of a common heritage would that be possible.

Canada, a more clearly bicultural society, and America's northern neighbor, has had more complex dealings on base-political matters with the United States. It has, to be sure, provided major defense-communication stations on the DEW nuclear early-warning line, defending against Russian nuclear attacks across the Arctic. Yet, perhaps reflecting greater cultural complexity, base-politics relations have not been as seamless as those among the United States, Britain, and Australia. Canada, for example, has not supported U.S. operations in the Middle East, including Iraq, as categorically as have the other Anglo-Saxon powers.

New Zealand appears to be a special case, where underlying security imperatives are not compelling, and where catalytic international experience drove local opinion to a distinctive posture. In July 1984, New Zealand's new Labour government made a commitment to ban all nuclear-armed ships from its waters, and in January 1985 rejected a port-call request from a U.S. warship that refused to confirm a non-nuclear status. Following an escalation of the dispute, the United States in August 1986 officially suspended military obligations to New Zealand under ANZUS.[83] U.S. and French nuclear testing in the South Pacific during the 1960s and 1970s, combined with lack of perceived security threat, seems to have driven a narrow majority of New Zealand opinion to challenge the alliance with Washington on the nuclear issue.

What is generally common among the Anglo-Saxon powers is a willingness to collapse the operational constraints limiting cooperation on base issues with most of America's other allies, in the interest of a broad, intimate, culturally specific alliance, and to declare solidarity publicly to the world. This is the exact opposite of the Saudi pattern of secrecy and rigidity, for a common reason. In both the Anglo-Saxon and the Saudi cases, base relations tend to be governed by the affective-politics paradigm, under which ethnic affinity and national values, rather than compensation or coercion, become the lodestar of base relations.

Yet the fundamental domestic structural conflicts implicit in the base-politics game elaborated in chapter 4 nevertheless remain. In Saudi Arabia it requires an "elite cartel" protected by secrecy to exclude the substantial, insistent, and fundamentalist host-nation groups with incentives to nonagreement. In the Anglo-Saxon world, due to host-nation cultural affinity with the basing power, convincing the grassroots is easier, but nevertheless a continuing challenge. Sustaining a foreign presence is never automatic for America's embattled garrisons.

IN CONCLUSION

We have presented four paradigms of base relations, elucidating, with examples, the distinctive traits of each. How generally does each of these paradigms prevail in the broader world? What do these ideal types tell us about the future course of base politics in real life?

Stabilizing the presence of forward-deployed forces is not, it must be stressed, simply a matter of throwing money at basing problems. In almost any case, it involves some sensitivity to community opinion. The most successful applications of an interactive approach, as in Japan, also feature sophisticated mechanisms for interfacing with local communities hosting bases. These institutions have the delicate charge of identifying the needs of those communities, while also responding rapidly, and in discreet, face-saving fashion, to their requirements.

Clearly the most stable pattern, as noted above, is compensation politics—a variant of base politics that, since it is typically funded domestically by the host nation, imposes minimal demands on basing nations. Its only equal as an attractive pattern for supporting forward deployment is affective politics, where the host nation sometimes has strong bonds of culture and communal sentiment with basing nations such as the United States.

Sadly, the supportive affective-politics variant has by definition only limited applicability in the broader world. Only Britain and Australia have been consistent, categorical American allies over the past century. And even their loyalty has been nuanced by the constraints of domestic politics from time to time. Even New Zealand and Canada, with their Anglo-Saxon cores, have had major base-related problems with the United States, such as New Zealand's "non-nuclear" policy.

Fiat politics was highly common a generation or two ago across the developing world on account of the prevalence of military dictatorships and feudal regimes, in regions ranging from Latin America and East Asia to the Middle East. It proved stable in a static Cold War environment of passive domestic politics that prevailed in client supporters of the superpowers. Yet social mobilization has given birth to more dynamic and volatile civil societies in most of the emerging nations, undermining the relevance of this paradigm outside less economically developed parts of the world, such as Africa and Central Asia.

In all likelihood fiat politics will become even less common and less successful in future. Many host nations may thus confront the serious transitional dilemmas, and consequent need for institutional changes in base relations, that South Korea and Spain have recently faced. Nations with a fiat-politics institutional heritage confront difficult problems in base relations going forward that will require major institution-building as well as financial support to assure stable resolution.

The increasingly salient and policy-relevant paradigm, unfortunately, is bazaar politics. Confronted by the war on terrorism, the United States is being forced increasingly into forward-deployed presence in volatile nations where both domestic politics and foreign relations are fluid. As manifest in both the Turkish case (2003) and that of the Philippines (1990–91), the United States has yet to master the delicate art of dealing effectively with changeable, often manipulative non-Western political systems on base issues, especially where the sensitive application of financial suasion is at issue, as it often is in such cases.

The compensation-politics paradigm may not travel well, and it is costly. Yet due to distinctive stability, its central features—including nonfinancial dimensions—should be more carefully studied for the lessons they can provide regarding how to stabilize such forward-deployed U.S. presence in non-Western nations as is deemed strategically necessary. Such institutional features as Japan's DFAA, Okinawa's SACO, and the U.S.-Japan Joint Committee on Security Cooperation, for example, need to be understood internationally in more detail. They could be studied for clues as to how to respond sensitively to grassroots incentive structures, and how to minimize incentives to nonagreement that otherwise so frequently plague base politics. To these prescriptive questions, gleaned from reflecting on the four paradigms presented here, and to the distinctive strengths and weaknesses of the models presented, we will return in the chapters to come.

CHAPTER SEVEN

BASE-POLITICS MANAGEMENT

THE SUBNATIONAL DIMENSION

SINCE THE VERY dawn of strategic theory itself, nation-states have been the central analytical concern of both theorists and practitioners. It is nation-states, they maintain, that act upon the global stage and that decide issues of war and peace with one another. We have reviewed, in preceding chapters, the base-political strategies of nations, and concede that individual countries *do* have their distinctive national approaches to dealing with foreign forces in their midst.

Yet nation-states, in the final analysis, are not the ultimate units of real-world action in international affairs. It is *people*—not nations—that ultimately act. It is *people*—not nations—that perceive, feel, and decide. Any meaningful analysis of national behavior, or prescriptions for strategy, must thus be mediated through an assessment of how real people, in real institutional settings, actually behave. It must, in a word, have an appreciation for the "micro." It is the micro, after all, that simulates more closely than any other level of analysis the patterns of cognition, and the dynamics of decision, that actually prevail in the real world.

Related to the analytical concerns of base politics, that means disaggregating the nation-state. The preceding two chapters have taken us some distance in that direction. They have detailed the variety of subnational constraints—institutional, environmental, and even cultural—that shape the operation of base politics, and that give rise to its striking and yet systematic cross-national variation.

Now we return, with a deepened sense of the parameters shaping base-politics decision making, to the focus of chapter 4: the real-world actors themselves, and the choices they make. This means considering local governments, mass media, and NGOs, and their interests, when attempting to understand outcomes and when making prescriptions. As is suggested in the following pages, "thinking local" provides a much richer interpretation of outcomes—especially of discontinuous or heterogeneous patterns in those outcomes—than conventional strategic approaches can provide.

Such an orientation also aids considerably in predicting real-world outcomes, since it provides a way to systematically include sub-national interests and institutions in accounts of causality. Case studies generated thereby likewise provide useful tools for judging and improving policy. In short, turning our attention to the trees in the forest—to how they are systematically related, and to their concrete profiles—gives us a detailed appreciation of the nuances concerning why bases stay, and why bases go, that we can get in no other way.

"Thinking local" does, to be sure, raise more unsettling questions about the future of base politics than one routinely hears from generals, diplomats, and businessmen from multinationals. Small-town mayors, students, teachers, and workers, after all, have fewer perceived stakes in global interdependence, and in what pass for national-security imperatives. Yet the information revolution and personal experiences are bringing grassroots actors closer to the concrete costs of national security, especially in time of war. To the extent that base politics becomes a mass political phenomenon, it tends to become more volatile and confrontational than would otherwise be true.

To demonstrate the importance of the grassroots dimension in shaping base-politics outcomes, this chapter presents three substantively important and analytically interesting cases full of empirical puzzles, whose resolution is not wholly intelligible in terms of strategic theory or nation-state, rational-actor analysis alone. It begins with the story of Okinawan bases, which *stay* despite the pervasive antimilitarist culture of that island. It continues with a discussion of the Vieques naval gunnery range, which *goes*, in the face of transnational antibase protest, despite a history of patron-client ties and pro-military sentiment in the American Caribbean, and on the small, tortured island of Vieques itself. Although the Commonwealth of Puerto Rico, of which Vieques is a part, is technically American territory, strong cultural, geographic, and political detachment from the mainland make the Vieques case both analytically and substantively relevant to our central overall concerns with bases beyond America's shores.

The chapter concludes with an instructive yet sobering discussion of how nation-state actors—the United States and Britain in this case—can engineer the micropolitical structure of a base-politics situation on the small but strategic Indian Ocean island of Diego Garcia, in a region where their local presence is limited and largely unwanted. They do so by finessing those micropolitical constraints and maintaining the coherence of national strategy, despite the constraints that base politics might be expected to impose. By coming to terms with micropolitics, this chapter thus aims to extract lessons with concrete relevance for the practitioners of base politics, both pro and con, in an era of momentous global transition.

BASES THAT STAY

Bases throughout the world, these pages have argued, are becoming embattled garrisons—defenders of respected values, crucial to global stability in an era of fragile interdependence, yet beset by hostile forces of nationalism and grassroots civilian resentment. Many have disappeared since the waning of the Cold War. Yet there are some that stay, counter to more general expectations. Empirical puzzles, of course, are the most attractive cases for theory building, because they best clarify causality. In bases that remain in the post–Cold War world, we thus find some stimulating catalysts for a deeper understanding not only of national sentiment, but also, more importantly, of the incentives that really drive base politics.

Okinawa: Antimilitarist Island Brimming with Bases

In all the universe of contemporary base politics, there are few more puzzling and contradictory cases than that of Okinawa. That tiny island of 454 square miles, almost exactly the size of Los Angeles, and smaller than the island of Kauai in the Hawaiian island chain,[1] was the site of the bloodiest battle of the Pacific War: a desperate, existential killing ground on which one-third of the entire Okinawan population of 450,000 people lost their lives, many at the hands of a Japanese military nominally defending them.[2] As many died in the battle of Okinawa as in the atomic bombings of Hiroshima and Nagasaki combined.[3]

Following the war, the U.S. military occupied the island for nearly three decades, expropriating large amounts of Okinawan land to build bases.[4] Naturally, the predominant share of that land has since been returned. Yet American bases continue to occupy roughly 20 percent of Okinawa's entire territory, much of it in the heart of the island's most populous and economically important urban centers.

Apart from aircraft noise and environmental problems, periodic accidents and crimes also plague fragile Okinawan cohabitation with the bases. In September 1995, a brutal gang-rape of a twelve-year-old Okinawan schoolgirl led to a massive protest of 85,000 demonstrators—the largest in the island's history; 27,000 protestors also converged on Kadena Air Base on the eve of the 2000 Okinawa G-7 Summit.

As the heritage of its bitter history, Okinawa has a clear collective norm of antimilitarism, often emotionally expressed. It also features a broad range of entrenched interests actively working to undermine support for the bases. Citizens' groups and labor unions are unusually strong and militant in Okinawa, compared with the situation on the Japanese mainland, with many NGOs working actively against the base presence.

One prominent group, which organized the massive protest demonstrations following the 1995 rape incident, is the Okinawa Women Act against Military Violence coalition, whose broad international contacts are enhanced both by the ease of international travel and by the Internet. Its members have demonstrated at the United Nations, lobbied in Washington, and joined hands with antibase movements around the world, including those agitating against the U.S. Navy gunnery range on Vieques Island off Puerto Rico. Another major protest group is the Okinawa Peace Network, which promotes antibase awareness and organizes rallies and demonstrations, such as the confrontation against the 2000 Okinawa G-7 Summit.

The Okinawan mass media is also deeply involved in antibase protest. The major Japanese dailies do not circulate extensively in Okinawa, and national television, except for the national public NHK network, does not broadcast there. This leaves the *Ryūkyū Shimpō* and the *Okinawa Times*, together with their television affiliates—a veritable information cartel—holding more than 80 percent of the overall local media market.[5] Both publications are stridently opposed to the bases. So are the local Okinawa High School Teachers' Union, the mainstream faculty and students at Ryūkyū University, and the "1-tsubo (approximately four square yards)" small-scale landowners. They buy tiny plots of land inside the bases to establish their legitimacy as antibase protestors.

The major Okinawan political and administrative institutions also voice virtually unanimous antibase sentiment. Long-time Governor Keiichi Inamine (1998–2006), for example, was nominally affiliated with both the conservative LDP, and its coalition partner Kōmeitō. Yet he stridently criticized the bases, insisting that a prospective new replacement facility at Henoko should supplant the current Marine Corps Air Station at Futenma and be built with a fifteen-year limit on U.S. military presence, which the Pentagon adamantly refused to accept. The local Okinawan assembly likewise persistently features an LDP majority, yet frequently calls for a reduction in the American military presence, especially that of the U.S. Marine Corps.

Despite this clear Okinawan collective identity of antimilitarism, a strong antibase bias in the Okinawan media and local government, and a continuing string of incidents relating to the massive concentration of U.S. bases on the island, there is remarkably little transformation in the basing structure, even when political leaders agree to undertake it. In 1996, for example, a decision was made, through the SACO process, to relocate the 835th U.S. Army Transportation Battalion from Naha Port, in the heart of Okinawa's capital, to a much less crowded coastal area near Urasoe City further north. Both mayors supported the move. Yet, more than a decade later, it had not been made.

An even more striking case is the proposed relocation of the Futenma Marine Air Station to a heliport off the coast of the northern Okinawan town of Nago.[6] This move would close a dangerous air field—next to an elementary school in the heavily populated town of Ginowan in central Okinawa—and move it to a sparsely populated seaside location. Such a move would presumably benefit both the Okinawans and the U.S. military. U.S. President Bill Clinton and Japanese Prime Minister Ryūtarō Hashimoto solemnly agreed at their 1996 summit conference to have this relocation completed within five to seven years. Yet the two countries had not even *started* to implement the proposal by the time, nine years later that it was scheduled to be completed. Indeed, the Bush administration in July 2004 proposed to scrap the entire Henoko/Nago base-construction project, and to move the Futenma facilities to a different location entirely.[7]

In October 2005, at a high-level meeting involving top foreign and defense-policy officials of both nations,[8] the U.S. and Japanese central governments jointly unveiled a concrete new plan to relocate Futenma replacement facilities to "shoreline areas of Camp Schwab [in Nago] and adjacent water areas of Oura Bay." KC-130s previously based at Futenma were to be relocated to the SDF's Kanoya base near Kagoshima, in southern Kyūshū.[9] Following the agreement, senior Japanese officials visited prospective sites for the new deployments all over Japan, including Okinawa, to explain the new relocation plans and alleviate the concerns of local residents. Domestically, the "2+2" agreement was explained as an "interim report," scheduled to be finalized in March 2006.

The local communities showed decidedly mixed reactions, as might be expected, reflecting their parochial views. Okinawa Governor Inamine instantly opposed the relocation scheme, as it proposed to leave most of the functions Futenma had been performing, however important in security terms, in his home Okinawan constituency. Other local communities rebelled as well. In February 2006, Kanoya residents in Kyūshū elected a mayor opposing the proposed relocation of functions from Futenma,[10] and a major antitransformation conference at Urasoe City, Okinawa attracted three hundred participants.[11] Clearly, local incentives in Okinawa and Kyūshū diverged from those of their national counterparts.

In January 2006, however, Nago residents in the target relocation area elected a new mayor backed by Japan's ruling parties, amenable to pragmatic discussion with the central government.[12] He showed some willingness to discuss relocation to Henoko, provided that the original 1996 plan for an offshore facility were revived. This concept, however, ran counter to American ideas supporting a mixed onshore-offshore facility, embodied in the October 2005 "2+2" agreement, ultimately forcing adoption of a hybrid plan.[13]

Three major micropolitical factors, no less politically real for being in tension with national strategy, have complicated the actual Futenma relocation, so confidently resolved at the macrolevel well over a decade ago. These grassroots considerations have forced the U.S. and the Japanese national governments into successive revisions of their own proposals. This pattern, of course, inverts the conventional picture of how base politics operate, but the military's grassroots concessions on programmatic details, combined with strategic compensation, have been crucial in assuring that some agreement on Futenma relocation could actually be reached.

First, there are clearly environmental problems at issue. The area off Henoko, to which the Futenma facility was to be moved, is home to the dugong, or sea cow. This sea mammal is found commonly in Southeast Asian coastal waters, but is relatively rare in Japan, necessitating time-consuming environmental impact studies. Even after the dugong issue was surmounted, there was controversy over the prospective physical profile of the proposed Henoko facility, and over the means of construction. These complications slowed the Futenma relocation project still further.

Secondly, there have been sharp differences of corporate interest and opinion regarding the three proposed options (an offshore floating base, a facility sunk into steel piers, and a landfill facility). Ishikawajima Harima (IHI) and other Japanese shipbuilding companies, together with major members of the Hashimoto faction of the ruling LDP, and, reportedly, the U.S. contractor Halliburton as well, preferred the floating offshore facility, which was the original SACO (intergovernmental) choice. Yet the prospective cost was exorbitant—reportedly one hundred times more per year, amortized over its prospective life, than the annual rental on Futenma.[14]

Corporate lobbying was relatively subdued for nearly a decade following the 1996 summit agreement in the face of residential opposition to the project as a whole, which virtually stalled its implementation. Yet the corporate interest in various options naturally did not totally disappear. This continuing corporate concern was reflected in the decision of the U.S. and Japanese governments in September 2005 to restudy the possible construction of an offshore heliport facility close to Camp Schwab.[15] The mainland Japanese defense and construction industries were engaged in this issue, but divided in their support for one of two potential options: the American Henoko shallow-waters plan, backed by Washington; and the Camp Schwab plan, which Tokyo supported.[16]

The offshore-facility concept provided few concrete benefits for Okinawan firms. Ultimately it was dropped in favor of the landfill—the third and final option—due to the prospective dividends for Okinawan

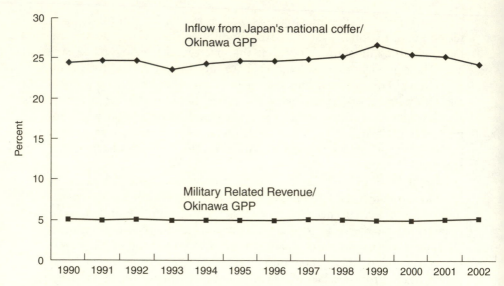

Figure 7.1. The Embedded Heritage of Compensation Politics: Okinawa's Economy, Japan's Central Government, and America's Bases

Source: Okinawa Prefecture Military Base Affairs Office. *U.S. Military Bases in Okinawa*, 2005 edition, at: http://www3.pref.okinawa.jp/site/contents/attach/7520/statistics2005.pdf.

construction firms of the latter approach. Yet Governor Inamine's insistence on a fifteen-year limit for U.S. basing rights at the facility continued to delay construction, despite the prospective benefits to local interests. So the aging, Korean War–era Futenma Air Station, dangerous and outmoded, continued to operate, more than a decade after a summit agreement to close it, despite new plans for the relocation agreed at the May 2006 "2+2" meetings. It remained a striking monument to the sometimes perverse stability bias of Japanese compensation politics.

THE MICROPOLITICAL ROOTS OF OKINAWAN POLICY CONSERVATISM. Beyond the Futenma-specific factors enumerated above, what accounts for this profound conservatism of real-world Okinawan base politics—so sharply at odds with the collective antimilitarist norms of the Okinawan people, as eloquently demonstrated by the results of mayoral elections at Nago and Kanoya City? Several key factors related to the local incentive structure, including rental fees on base land, and Japanese central government compensation for Okinawa, appear to be at work.

Compensation politics, after all, is a deeply embedded pattern in Japanese base relations, as noted in chapter 6. As shown in figure 7.1, total military-related income in Okinawa has constituted roughly 5 percent of the Okinawan Gross Prefectural Product (GPP) since 1987.[17] The military is the third-largest income source in the prefecture, following government aid—itself related to base presence—and tourism.[18] In FY2005, Japan's central government earmarked more than Y7.5 billion (over $600 million) for development in northern Okinawa. And in December 2005, with Okinawa continuing to be reluctant about the Futenma relocation plans, Tokyo decided to add another 10 percent to that figure, bringing it to ¥8.2 billion in fiscal year 2006.

The Okinawan prefectural government (OPG) has routinely criticized the bases, under both progressive and nominally conservative administrations. It has consistently demanded time limits on American military leases for the proposed Henoko replacement facility. Yet the OPG simultaneously benefits from the presence of the existing bases, and from increases in base land leases provided by the Japanese central government, due to the impact of rising base land values on the local tax base within the prefecture. Communities adjacent to the bases also benefit from "burden-easing funds," disbursed liberally by the DFAA, as discussed in chapter 6. That multifaceted agency has also traditionally made substantial compensation payments to individuals for noise, pollution, violation of fishing rights in traditional waters, and environmental counter-measures, which help to stabilize the grudging local tolerance of the existing bases.

Since 1991, lease-land rentals have been the largest base-related expenditure in Okinawa.[19] The rental payments are attractive, as suggested in figure 7.2b, and have grown increasingly so in recent years, amidst the general stagnation in real estate markets across Japan. In contrast to the situation on the Japanese mainland, where less than 10 percent of base land is rented from private individuals, in Okinawa a full 67 percent of the land used for military facilities is privately owned.[20] More than 32,000 "contract" landowners received over ¥76.4 billion ($562 million) in rental income for their properties during 2003.[21] For many, their land was their sole source of income. Apart from conventional base rentals, many Okinawan landowners also profited from a peculiar local institution called "tacit farming." Under this arrangement the American military allows a landowner to continue to farm his plot of land inside a base in order to gain income in addition to the rent. Even when land is returned to the owners, due to the downsizing of bases, the Japanese government additionally continues to pay rent to landowners for up to five years after return of the land, thus giving them a substantial grace period to seek alternate tenants.

As indicated in figure 7.2, the lease payments for land rented to the U.S. bases consistently account for about 2 percent of Okinawan GPP, and that share has been steadily rising since around 1990. Military lease payments in Okinawa have increased in monetary terms every year since 1988, while

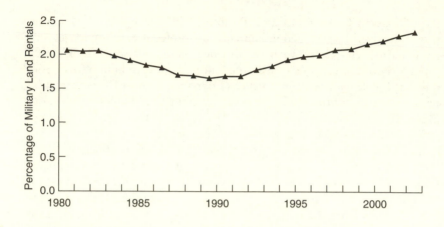

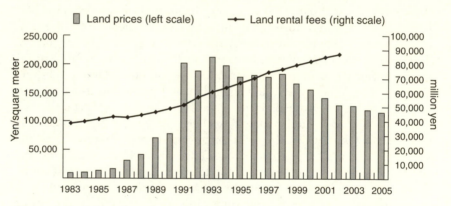

Figure 7.2. The Changing Political Economy of Okinawan Military Land Leases

a. Rising dependency of Okinawan GPP on military land rental fees

b. Decreasing commercial prices for land

Sources: Okinawa Prefecture Military Base Affairs Office. *U.S. Military Bases in Okinawa*, 2005 edition, at http://www3.pref.okinawa.jp/site/contents/attach/7520/statistics2005.pdf, and *Ministry of Land Infrastructure and Transport, Todō Fuken Chika Chōsa* (Investigation of Land Prices) 2005, at: http://tochi.mlit.go.jp/.

Note: While the commercial price of land has been dropping since 1998, base rental fees are steadily rising, making leasing land to the U.S. military increasingly attractive.

commercial land rentals have been stagnant or declining, especially since the outbreak of the 1997–98 Asian financial crisis.[22] Increasing Okinawan base-rental fees, which are far above market-equilibrium prices, clearly give local landowners, many of whom would have few alternative uses for their property, deepening stakes in the continued presence of existing bases.

Thus, there is little wonder that Okinawan base landowners collectively constitute a powerful, insistent interest group—formidably, if discreetly, organized at the grassroots—in Japanese compensation politics. Local landowner associations are represented at the prefectural and national levels by the Okinawa Federation of Landowners of Land Used for Military Purposes, which lobbies the prefectural and central governments on rent-related issues.[23] The federation's powerful veto-player role was evident in the 1996 base-reduction referendum, when it worked strongly against change.[24]

Many Okinawans leasing land to the bases are encouraged by the compensation-politics equation to continue doing so, whatever their personal feelings regarding the bases or the military may be. At least seven particular types of groups in Okinawa benefit economically from the base presence. Together, they create a formidable community for stability in existing base configurations, contrasting sharply and incongruously to the clear antimilitarist tradition of the island as a whole.

Local base workers, together with their unions, also have positive stakes in the U.S. military presence in Okinawa, although those interests are clearly declining in importance relative to those of the base landlords. Yet the bases still employ over 8,300 workers, and base-worker salaries—totally paid by the Japanese central government—come to well over $500 million.

Zenchūrō, the All Japan Security Forces Labor Union, has traditionally been a strong political supporter nationwide of the Japan Socialist Party, and has participated actively in campaigns against the basing presence.[25] It has more than 6,300 members in Okinawa. Yet it nevertheless has symbiotic, interdependent interests with the bases, and indeed with the ruling LDP itself.[26] Since base-worker salaries are paid by the Japanese central government, Zenchūrō needs to make accommodation with the government in order to secure improved treatment for its members.[27] Thus, there have been natural limits—albeit subtle and subterranean ones—as to how far the opposition, especially the Socialists, are willing to push the LDP on base-management issues.

Japanese private firms also have vested interests in the bases. The U.S. military spends $500 million annually on base-related contracts with Okinawan vendors,[28] and local construction companies receive over 80 percent of the total military-construction contracts granted in Okinawa, which amounted to about ¥14 billion in fiscal year 2005.[29] In 2003, the construction sector accounted for a full eight percent of Okinawan GPP,[30] or a significantly larger portion than the 6.8 percent that construction comprised in Japan's GDP as a whole.[31]

Public works expanded massively in connection with preparations for the Okinawa Summit of 2000. And they would presumably benefit further from the huge Futenma relocation project now impending. When it finally gets off the ground, Futenma could take more than five years to complete, and provide thousands of new jobs in an Okinawa with an unemployment rate far above Japan's national average.[32]

Small-scale shopowners are politically pivotal in Okinawa because they are a primary constituency of the Kōmeitō Party, the LDP's principal coalition partner since 1998 at both the national and the local levels. They have recently been important supporters of conservative governors Keiichi Inamine and Hirokazu Nakaimao. U.S. personnel and their dependents spend at least $5 million annually on rental payments for off-base housing, as well as consumer goods and services. This stimulus is obviously important to the fragile local economy of the prefecture, whose nonmilitary prospects remain bleak.

WHEN STABLE BECOMES *TOO* STABLE. The unspoken self-interest of multiple Okinawan constituencies in the stability of the bases—a natural product of compensation politics—becomes clear when attempts are made to move those bases. Whatever strategic benefits military transformation may have in the abstract, it has distinct, and very concrete, political drawbacks in a nation engaged in compensation politics like Japan. Even when the transformation effort also enhances local safety, and eases citizen inconvenience, it can be remarkably difficult to achieve, as the Futenma case so graphically illustrates.

Three factors, in sum, have made Okinawa base politics so stable that base relocations amply justified on prudential or strategic grounds are *politically* difficult to make, even with the tacit support of the American military, as manifest in the cases of Futenma and the Naha Port. First, as noted above, there have been environmental issues, in which the environmental studies paradoxically require quite a long period of status quo maintenance.

Secondly, conflicting, fractionated interests regarding policy options have contributed to gridlock. The most intense interests—those of the landlords—are strongly attached to the status quo. So, too, in a perverse, paradoxical way, are those of many key opposition groups, which have financial incentives to keep the base issues boiling. As long as Okinawan base politics are troubled, the central government, in their estimation—and confirmed by past experience—will continue to compensate them for refraining from even more confrontational behavior. The final factor promoting a paradoxical stability in Okinawan base relations is the nature of the Japanese and U.S.-Japan policy processes. The consent of myriad groups—local communities, the Okinawan prefectural government, the Japanese national government, Japanese public opinion, the American military, and the U.S. federal government among them—is needed to realize a proactive outcome. This conversely affords multiple opportunities for veto-players to obstruct such a positive result.

It is important to distinguish, in the politics of Okinawan basing, between support for the status quo basing structure and support for American basing policy. Insofar as U.S. policy is oriented toward the status quo, there is no issue. Yet the ambitious, transformation-oriented policies of former U.S. Defense Secretary Donald Rumsfeld inspired new ambivalence in the Okinawan political-economic world about Washington, and a complex new divergence of interests, that the more static policies of the past did not generate.

Given the conflicting incentive structures of those desiring change, and the strong, if quiet, preference of landlords for the status quo, the outcome in Okinawa has been, and may well continue to be, policy drift. This surprising stability is tacitly accepted by local players, but could be corrosive of broader national-alliance credibility, and subversive of ambitious American defense strategies in the long run. Such a stability bias is manifest dramatically in both Japanese ambivalence regarding 2004 and 2005 Bush administration transformation proposals to ease basing burdens on Okinawa, and also in the domestic political difficulties of implementing the October 2005 "2+2" agreement. This stability bias of Okinawan base relations—the clear fruit of compensation politics—clearly bodes ill for the rapid implementation of such seemingly dynamic and sensible proposals, whatever their broader strategic logic in the currency of military transformation may ultimately be.

BASES THAT GO

The elemental equations of base politics are all too often obscured in abstract discussions of strategy and national interest. It is crucial, as we have noted, to take a more microscopic view. We need to understand more clearly the incentive structure of those actually making working-level base-politics decisions.

The most fundamental distinction, when the state is deconstructed, is that elite and mass interests often do not coincide. Elites, tending to be more cosmopolitan, more economically interdependent with foreign nations, and more insulated personally from the day-to-day inconveniences related to the presence of foreign bases, are more prone to support that presence. The general public is in normal circumstances more reluctant to do so.

Local opinion and interest can thus often be pivotal in base politics, especially in relatively pluralistic political systems, as noted in chapter 4. The cases of Okinawa, and of Japan more generally, both suggest that base politics can be stable, even where local cultures of antimilitarism are pervasive, as long as local interests are to some degree well satisfied. But what happens when those interests are more deeply injured by the bases, and local sentiments are mobilized against them?

Vieques: Transnational Networks, Media Symbolism, and Protest

Latin America and the Caribbean lack Okinawa's bitter experience with war and militarism. To the contrary, military leaders have traditionally played a major role in national governance, and the military is generally well respected as a profession in this "macho" part of the world. The cultural bias, if any, is the reverse of Okinawa's.

Yet the local politics of military basing in the Caribbean, and their impact on actual policy outcomes, are in many ways remarkably similar to what they are in Okinawa. As we will see, interests, rather than cultural predisposition, have been determinant in Vieques, as they are also in Okinawa. And local interests have been surprisingly potent, even when questions of national strategy and symbolism are involved.

Vieques is a paradoxical story, both in base politics and in American politics more generally, as suggested earlier.[33] The story takes place in Puerto Rico, where the U.S. Navy has strong local influence as a major employer: the nearby Roosevelt Roads Naval Station is one of the largest U.S. Navy bases in the world. The American military owns around 12 percent of the land in Puerto Rico as a whole, and is culturally respected there, as noted above. Indeed, large numbers of Puerto Ricans are serving voluntarily, often in elite, dangerous units like the Marines and the 82nd Airborne Division, in U.S. military operations worldwide.

To compound the paradox, Vieques itself is a small island next to Puerto Rico, over 1,500 miles across the Caribbean from Washington, D.C. Its citizens lack the right to vote Stateside. They are generally only poorly educated, are economically vulnerable, and do not have a tradition of political activism. That their interests would prevail in conflict with those of the American military is far from an intuitively obvious proposition.

Nearly three generations ago, in 1938, the U.S. Navy began acquiring land on Vieques by expropriation. Its objective: to build a major firing range on a small island eight miles off the eastern coast of Puerto Rico. Vieques was only twenty miles long and four miles wide, which made it perfect for naval gunnery practice. By the end of World War II, the navy had bought three-quarters of the 33,000 acres of land on the island for use in maneuvers and for bomb storage.

Unfortunately Vieques, unlike Kahoolawe in Hawaii or most other American naval gunnery ranges, was populated. When the firing ranges were originally set up on the island's western and eastern coasts, many of the population of 12,000 were relocated, some on only a single day's notice, to the center of the island. There they were at least mildly distanced from the gunnery range, although shells routinely flew over their heads to intended targets. By 2000 the total local population had fallen to 9,300. Yet the population *density* remained six hundred per square mile on the tiny island—thirty times the average of twenty per square mile for the United States as a whole.

Lacking a tradition of sustained protest, for well over fifty years the Viequenos suffered bombardment of their island, and a range of unusual ills, without the redress that occurred much earlier at most gunnery and firing ranges used by the U.S. military elsewhere.[34] During the year 2000, for example, around 2.9 million pounds of ordnance were dropped on Vieques—almost half of all that used for military target practice in the entire United States. Of twelve U.S. gunnery ranges, Vieques was the only one, except the uninhabited San Clemente Island offshore California, involving ship-to-shore shelling. Analogous ranges in Massachusetts and Delaware were closed long ago. All ranges involving air-to-ground shelling were in the American South, deep inside military bases. Yet all the ordnance in the U.S. military inventory, except missiles, was used on Vieques—a populated island with nearly 10,000 inhabitants.

The health and environmental consequences of American military activity on Vieques over the years have also been serious. Periodically there have been casualties from the shelling. In April 1989, for example, there was an accident on board the USS *Iowa*, in its operations offshore Vieques, in which an explosion killed 47 men. In 1996 bombs fell perilously close to a local fisherman. And on April 19, 1999, one shot, in a volley of two thousand bombs launched from the USS *Hornet*, hit an observation post on the island and killed a local security guard, David Sanes Rodriguez.

Apart from the direct casualties, the broader health and environmental consequences of the navy's presence on Vieques, as indicated, have also been serious. Infant mortality on the island is 50 percent higher than that for Puerto Rico as a whole, while the incidence of cancer is 27 percent higher. Recent environmental assessments have shown high levels of heavy metals in the local soil, toxics in the water supply, and coral reefs damaged by navy bombs. In August 1999 the U.S. Environmental Protection Agency itself noted that the navy had committed numerous violations of the Clean Water Act and other statutes on Vieques.[35]

The empirical paradox for base politics in the Vieques case is thus *not* the injustice that is so often stressed by residents and movement activists: it is the strange combination of protracted inaction, followed by sudden policy activism that is characteristics of this case. Why did it take so long for the injustices implicit in the Vieques situation to be dealt with? And then why, given this long heritage of inaction, did change occur so suddenly? Only subnational and transnational analysis can provide the answers.[36]

WHY POLICY CHANGE TOOK SO LONG. Many of the factors creating stability in the Vieques situation were parallel to those in Okinawa. The U.S. military was sensitive to the inconveniences of the local situation, and provided some compensation, although it simultaneously stressed its desire to remain on the island. Before the sustained protest movements of the 1990s began on Vieques, for example, the navy built an undersea pipeline from the main island of Puerto Rico to supply previously unavailable fresh water to the island. Periodic payments have also been made to island dwellers to compensate for inconvenience. Beneficiaries of the U.S. military presence at one point went to Washington with a petition signed by 2,500 people, on an island of 9,000, asking the navy to stay on.[37]

It also took time for the infrastructure of later protest to develop. Vieques is, as noted, an isolated island, populated by largely uneducated fishermen and laborers. It needed networks to the broader world in order to give effective political expression to its latent local frustrations. One critical development in this regard was the establishment of proactive NGOs, such as the Committee for the Rescue and Development of Vieques, founded in 1993.[38]

Another important background factor was the U.S. Navy's 1994 decision to locate a $9 million "Relocatable Over-the-Horizon Radar" (ROTHR) on Vieques. The island has historically had a high rate of cancer mortality, and many residents felt that a ROTHR facility would make the problem worse by intensifying carcinogenic microwave stimuli. A three-year struggle to prevent construction of the ROTHR facility ultimately proved futile, but laid the basis for later, more successful activism.[39]

It was catalytic events, ultimately, that dramatized the Vieques problem, brought it to the attention of a wider public, and fused the transnational networks that ultimately proved crucial to substantial policy action on the issue. Most important was the aforementioned death of David Sanes Rodriguez, the civilian security guard, in military shelling of the island during April 1999. This was followed two days later by a gathering of fifteen local boats at the site of the shelling; the establishment of local disobedience camps by the Puerto Rico Independence Party and other such groups; the invasion by one thousand Marines of these disobedience camps, followed by massive arrests; and a subsequent escalation of the protests following the initial violence.

After Sanes's death, the navy never again used live ammunition on Vieques. It always limited itself to inert bombs—dummy ordnance not containing explosives.[40] It returned, near the end of the Clinton administration, nearly one-third of the land it held on the island to civilian control. Yet none of the navy's compromises broke the momentum of the protest movement. To the contrary, that movement escalated its protests, broadened its network, and ultimately forced the total withdrawal of the navy from Vieques as a whole.

WHY CHANGE FINALLY OCCURRED SO SUDDENLY. The second important question for base politics regarding Vieques, as suggested earlier, is why policy change, once begun, proceeded so rapidly. Virtually no change occurred in the miserable circumstances on Vieques from 1938, when the navy first arrived, until April 1999, when Sanes was killed. Yet by June 2001, little more than two years later, President George W. Bush had announced the total cessation of military testing operations on Vieques. What catalytic forces were at work to propel this rapid transformation— at the national as well as local levels?

Four critical forces for change were eroding the U.S. military presence on Vieques. The first was the increasing activism of the local commonwealth government in Puerto Rico. In June 1999 then governor Dr. Pedro Rossello appointed a Special Commission on Vieques, composed of members from the three major local political parties, the Catholic Church, a representative of Vieques fishermen, and the then mayor of Vieques. The commission submitted a report supporting the position of the local community: immediate termination of bombing, total demilitarization and decontamination, return of all lands to the people, and sustainable development of Vieques. This commission was pivotal in legitimating the antimilitary movement, and in enlisting the involvement of key groups, such as the church, the women's movement, and environmentalists, that were central to its broader ultimate success within Puerto Rico.

The local commonwealth government alone, however, had clear limitations, especially in linking the Vieques struggle to broader U.S. national political processes. Even the governor of Puerto Rico was never able to meet with the president or other key White House staffers to discuss Vieques. Official Washington contacts were limited exclusively to the navy and, in the Bush administration, to then Secretary of Defense Donald Rumsfeld.

The limitations of the local Puerto Rican government's efforts were clear in January 2000, when Governor Rossello announced an agreement with the Clinton administration to allow the continuation of bombing in return for $90 million in U.S. grants and the mere promise of a referendum. This agreement was overwhelmingly rejected in Puerto

Rico itself. The NGOs then turned to direct confrontation with Washington and the American military, spurning the governor's self-declared achievements at mediation.

In this deepening confrontation, the NGOs made special efforts to broaden their networks on the U.S. mainland. Between May 2000 and late 2001, close to 1,500 peaceful demonstrators were arrested, and hundreds were sent to prison. Among those incarcerated: U.S. Congressman Luis Gutierrez of Chicago; Jacqueline Jackson; the Reverend Al Sharpton; environmental lawyer Robert Kennedy, Jr.; and actor Edward James Olmos. In New York a well-known Puerto Rican environmentalist was arrested for climbing the Statue of Liberty in protest over Vieques, and others were arrested for civil disobedience actions in New York, Washington, D.C., Connecticut, and elsewhere.

The arrests, and the attendant national publicity stateside, were important catalytic elements in the process of policy change through the consciousness raising that they provoked, particularly on the U.S. mainland. The arrests built on, and ultimately helped consolidate, the emerging transnational dimension of the protest movement. The NGOs capitalized on and solidified these links across the Caribbean by establishing a local stateside office—in Hudson County, New Jersey; by extensively using the Internet; and by traveling extensively—to Okinawa, Guam, Cuba, and elsewhere—to publicize their movement. In turn, activists from Okinawa, Washington, D.C., and elsewhere around the world also came to visit them in Vieques.

A second crucial catalyst to resolving the Vieques struggle was legitimation. The broad Puerto Rican public, and ultimately a substantial segment of the American national political elite as well, had to come to believe that the Viequenos had a just cause. Following the Puerto Rican commission just mentioned, a broad range of epistemic groups, particularly environmentalists, went to Vieques, in the latter half of 1999 and thereafter, to do multiple technical studies documenting the military-related health and environmental damage that local residents had claimed. The Catholic Church also became involved with the issue, as did some decorated Vietnam veterans and retired senior U.S. military officers, lending the Viequenos further credibility.[41]

Thirdly, the crucial key to resolution, in the final analysis, was ultimately transnational networks, including trans-Caribbean ties between San Juan and Washington, D.C. As the Vieques issue broadened internationally through the interaction between Vieques activists and those in Okinawa, South Korea, Guam, and Cuba, much of it via the Internet, defense policymakers in the Pentagon became concerned about possible spillover effects for base politics in other parts of the world that might flow from the increasingly enflamed Vieques confrontation. This became particularly consequential for policy in the Bush administration, due to then Defense Secretary Donald Rumsfeld's general belief in the intrinsic value of transformation away from old-style basing and military operations—irrespective of the details of Vieques itself. He appears to have grasped clearly both the political liabilities involved, and the long-term strategic irrelevance of the Vieques gunnery range itself.

Finally, elite networks, coupled with rising public consciousness of the Vieques issue, also created another, ironically potent constituency for change: high-level Republican politicians. Following the extended post-election Florida recount in late 2000, during which the presidency hung in the balance for a full month, Republicans were highly conscious of the Hispanic vote on the U.S. mainland and realized the salience that the Vieques issue was gaining among Hispanics. Governor George Pataki, facing an uncertain reelection battle in 2002, following the million-vote Gore New York state plurality in 2000, was especially concerned about the disquiet among Hispanics, and made these concerns clear at the new Bush White House.[42]

Some congressional Republicans, such as Senator James Inhofe of Oklahoma, pointed critically to the perverse national-security implications of suspending military-training activities for political reasons. Yet these concerns were over-ridden at the White House. Following a conclave among senior White House officials, including Karl Rove, President Bush's top political advisor, who had voiced concerns that growing opposition to the bombings was costing Bush critical support among Hispanic voters, and a visit to the White House personally by George Pataki, President Bush himself announced the suspension of military operations on Vieques by 2003.[43]

Ultimately the basing implications of the Vieques case greatly transcended Vieques itself. On May 1, 2003, the navy fully vacated the Vieques gunnery range, although the property remained in federal hands. That navy withdrawal was followed in March 2004 by the closing of the massive Roosevelt Roads Naval Station in Puerto Rico, one of the largest American naval facilities in the Caribbean.[44] The navy did continue to operate an offshore range of nearly 200,000 square miles to practice high-tech naval maneuvers, an underwater tracking range for submarines, and an electronic-warfare range in waters near Vieques. The army also kept access to a large National Guard firing range—Camp Santiago, in Salinas, Puerto Rico.

Yet the political reverberations of the Vieques base-politics struggle were loud and continuing, apart from the major retrenchments noted above. The U.S. military also transferred regional headquarters out of

Puerto Rico to Texas and Florida. At the same time, it also relocated the Southcom Joint Command headquarters out of Latin America entirely, moving it northward across the Caribbean to Miami, Florida.

The Vieques case, like that of Okinawa, has its counterintuitive elements, which underline once more the importance of the micropolitical dimension, and the fallacy of cultural determinism in base politics. Although set in a "macho" culture that values the American military and volunteers substantial numbers of its citizens for the most elite and dangerous units, this cultural regard did not lead to a promilitary outcome. To the contrary, the navy was ultimately expelled in 2003 from an island firing range it had occupied for more than half a century, through the efforts of a broad, grassroots movement with transoceanic aspects that captured the symbolic attention of both the Puerto Rican people and many Hispanics throughout the mainland United States.

The striking discontinuities of the case—the abruptness with which the sustained anti-base movement of the late 1990s initially arose, as well as the suddenness with which it ultimately succeeded—are further testimony to the salience of shifting political interests and calculations in determining policy outcomes, as opposed to the more limited and immutable role of culture. Especially striking are the pragmatic calculation of interest, and flexible reaction, of conservative groups in the process, despite an often assumed tendency to dogmatically side with the military. Both Donald Rumsfeld's Pentagon and the Bush-Rove White House, not to mention Republican New York Governor George Pataki, proved to be highly pragmatic on the Vieques issue. Indeed, their tacit support for the demonstrators, once the political potency of their grievances was clear, turned out to be a key element in the protest movement's success.

To fully understand the success of the antibase movement in Vieques, however, one must go beyond the paradoxical pragmatism of its normally promilitary supporters to an important emerging technological and political-economic reality: the growing power of transnational forces in base politics. The apparent contest of a small, unsophisticated island people against the might of the U.S. military was far more than that. Indeed, it was linked in, through television and the Internet, to the global antibase movement, and to Hispanic ethnic politics on the U.S. mainland itself. The formal commonwealth links between San Juan and Washington were only a relatively minor factor enhancing the impact of Vieques developments on American basing policy.

It was precisely those new linkages to the global village—forged through an astute campaign strategy by the movement's organizers—that alarmed conservative forces, and rendered them so pragmatic in the end. Clearly, the Vieques struggle points, for military supporters, to an ominous conclusion. In the information age, when local interests are harmed by bases, countervailing local interests supportive of base presence are nonengaged, and the mass media publicizes the costs of basing to the broader world, there can easily be bases—indeed, literally embattled garrisons—that go.

FINESSING BASE POLITICS

As we have seen, the risks of host-nation base politics are often substantial. Regime shifts can depose allies, bring antagonistic new groups to power, and introduce major new volatility and uncertainty into negotiating processes. Broad, long-term populist trends can make empathetic host-nation elites ever harder to find, and increasingly unpredictable and rigid in their behavior even when they do appear. Culture conflict and symbolic politics can muddy prediction and negotiation as well.

Base politics almost everywhere in the world is growing more volatile—even in Japan and Italy, two rare, long-standing exceptions. At the same time, the advanced nations are being forced, by the war on terrorism, to deploy their troops into an unsavory range of failed states and otherwise stagnant political economies in the Middle East, Africa, and Central Asia, into which they rarely ventured in the past. In these volatile locales (one can hardly call them states), base politics is almost by definition unstable.

For major basing nations like America, it would clearly be nice if base politics could be avoided altogether. Unhappily that is not possible. Yet in coping with this situation, one of the greatest imperatives is clearly finessing base politics wherever it can be done, especially when the construction of major, strategically important facilities is involved. Happily, given the increasingly long-range capabilities of modern strike aircraft, that at least is becoming ever more possible.

Diego Garcia: Answer to South Asian and Middle Eastern Uncertainties?

Virtually in the middle of the vast Indian Ocean, and roughly 3,000 miles due south of the Persian Gulf, lies the tiny island of Diego Garcia. This horseshoe-shaped coral atoll is only fourteen miles long, from tip to tip, with a lagoon four miles across in the middle. It became a British possession, seized from France along with Mauritius, during the Napoleonic Wars, remaining a quiet backwater until after World War II. Over the past quarter-century it has moved from obscurity to become one of the most strategically important military bases on earth, and yet one conspicuously and uniquely removed from the vagaries of base politics. Its emergence and expansion are testimony to the possibility of finding a way around the pitfalls that base politics so often otherwise imposes on military operations.

American military interest in Diego was originally animated by communications difficulties in the vast expanses of the Indian Ocean—one of the few parts of the globe where the United States in the early 1950s did not already have a basing presence. On one occasion the nuclear carrier USS *Enterprise* and two nuclear cruisers suffered a total communications blackout for 8–12 hours while transiting the Indian Ocean.[45] Such failures were fairly common, and inspired the U.S. Navy to dispatch study teams to inspect the island's potential for future use in a global network designed to obviate such problems. In the summer of 1957, the navy's commander of the Atlantic Fleet himself, Admiral Jerauld Wright, visited the island on such an inspection tour.[46]

In 1959 a study for the Joint Chiefs of Staff on the "strategic-island concept" suggested Diego to be one of six islands worldwide of greatest significance for the U.S. Navy.[47] As the British steadily withdrew from East Africa, Mauritius, the Arabian Peninsula, and the Persian Gulf in the 1960s, heading toward Harold Wilson's 1968 announcement of a full British pullout "East of Suez,"[48] this American interest in Diego Garcia began to intensify. Someone had to fill the Indian Ocean strategic vacuum.

Paul Nitze played a central, far-sighted role in catalyzing support for a major American base on Diego Garcia, as he did on many long-term strategic issues of his day. Shortly after the Pentagon's strategic-island study was completed in 1961, Admiral Thomas Moorer, director of the Long-Range Objectives Group, took the concept of an American Diego Garcia base to the Joint Chiefs of Staff and got their approval of the navy-oriented plan, over initial air force reluctance.[49] Thereafter he went to Paul Nitze, then assistant secretary of defense for international security affairs, who initiated formal diplomatic discussions, through his liaison officer in the State Department, on creation of a British Indian Ocean Territory that would allow stable American basing rights. Later, as secretary of the navy, Nitze continued to strongly back the idea of filling the "power vacuum" in the Indian Ocean with a base on Diego Garcia.

One of the central prospective complications was base politics. Diego Garcia was, after all, not an American possession, nor was it situated in a region where the United States was either well-liked or held political sway. India, to the north, was the most influential nation in the area, and adamantly opposed to American regional military involvement, due to its efforts within the nonaligned movement to have the Indian Ocean designated as a "Zone of Peace."[50] Nearby Mauritius was similarly suspicious of American intentions. Diego Garcia, although small, had native inhabitants who were ambivalent. And there were questions about this typically abrupt American intrusion in the House of Commons as well.[51]

Still, the British Government was cooperative. In 1965 Britain, responding to Nitze's earlier quiet initiative, created an autonomous British Indian Ocean Territory (BIOT), splitting off Diego Garcia from Mauritius, an island that was later to become independent, and to grow relatively radical in foreign affairs. Together with Diego Garcia in the BIOT were three other small islands—Aldabra, Farquhar, and Des Roches. The United States was particularly interested in Aldabra as a potential base. Yet it abandoned this idea in the face of a strident campaign by a single British M.P., Tom Dalyell, irate at the potential ecological damage of building a major base on that tiny islet.[52]

Finessing this first exotic encounter with Indian Ocean base politics by shifting their attentions to the less controversial Diego Garcia, the British and U.S. governments, in December 1966, signed a framework agreement that formalized their commitment to the island's strategic development. This pact was to run for a period of fifty years until 2016, in the absence of decisions by either government to terminate it. The territory was to remain under British sovereignty, with facilities available to the United States without charge.[53] Two years later, in 1968, the United States sought formal permission from Britain to build a modest communications facility and associated air field on the island itself.

Then congressional politics began to intervene. Although the House of Representatives Appropriations Committee in November 1969 approved funding for the project, its Senate counterpart refused. Senate Majority Leader Mike Mansfield, a Democrat who was to be a persistent opponent of an Indian Ocean base throughout his remaining Senate career (until 1977), objected that new facilities in new parts of the world were inconsistent with the military downsizing implicit in Richard Nixon's declared Vietnamization policy.

Britain took the next fateful step in finessing base politics on Diego Garcia, side-stepping the deepening divisions in the U.S. Congress. In December 1970, it moved to resettle the 1,200 contract workers living on the island to gather copra on the nearby island of Mauritius.[54] A payment of £650,000 was made to Mauritius to help with the resettlement, and was increased during the 1980s when the endemic poverty of the islanders was revealed. The last contract workers left Diego Garcia in 1971, with Britain quietly adopting an immigration ordinance the same year that deprived these and other traditional Ilois tribal inhabitants of an exercisable right of return.[55] The construction of an air field by U.S. Seabees began soon thereafter. By 1973 both a naval communications station and a major twelve-thousand-feet runway had been completed.

Base politics on Diego Garcia itself had been temporarily neutralized by the resettlement of its inhabitants on Mauritius, and the political separation of Diego Garcia from Mauritius. Yet American politics then began to intervene once again, as the Ford administration, in the wake of the 1973 Yom Kippur War and expanding Soviet operations in Somalia and Mauritius, sought funds for a major buildup in the Indian Ocean. In May 1975, Senate Majority Leader Mansfield once again proposed, less than a month after the fall of Saigon, that the expansion of U.S. military facilities on Diego Garcia be disapproved.[56] His Senate Resolution 160 was formally debated in the Senate for five hours on July 28, 1975, with the scale and implications of the emerging Soviet presence in the Indian Ocean being the major subject of contention.[57]

In September 1975 Senators John Culver (D-Iowa) and Edward Kennedy (D-Mass) requested, in an amendment to the 1976 Military Appropriations Bill, that Republican President Gerald Ford report on the history of U.S. government agreements regarding Diego, and provide a judgment concerning U.S. obligations to those people and previous efforts to assist them.[58] The 1979 Iranian Revolution, and the almost simultaneous Soviet intervention in Afghanistan, however, made Congress appreciate the strategic importance of Diego Garcia—the one major American land base within striking range of both Tehran and Kabul. Just as importantly, major opponents of the base at Diego, such as Majority Leader Mansfield, had left the Congress.[59] The congressional dimension of Diego Garcia base politics thereafter largely disappeared.

Driven by the new strategic situation, the United States and Britain agreed in 1980 to further expand their facilities at Diego Garcia. By 1981 the 12,000 foot runway on the tiny island could handle B-52 bombers as well as PC-3 Orion marine-surveillance aircraft capable of locating submarines. When construction was finally completed in 1986, at a cost of over $500 million, the neighboring lagoon could accommodate a full aircraft carrier battle group, with the naval and aviation fuel-oil storage capacity to support such a massive task force for a full month.

During all of America's subsequent wars—in the Gulf, in Afghanistan, and in Iraq—Diego Garcia has played significant roles. Indeed, B-52s based on the island flew incessant strikes into the heart of the Middle East in each conflict, supported by KC-10 and KC-135 refueling tankers. In the course of the 1991 Gulf War, for example, over six hundred B-52 missions were carried out from the island, while aircraft based in Diego dropped more ordnance on Afghanistan in 2001 than from any other location in the world.[60]

Although base politics were largely finessed in Diego Garcia, it took them a long time to fully disappear. The islanders sued the British Foreign Office for their uncompensated eviction from their homes, and in 2000 the High Court ruled that removal of the islanders was an "abject legal failure." It thereby overturned a 1971 ban by Britain that had prevented the islanders from returning to the island, and set up the prospect of renewed, legally driven political controversy.[61]

In response to this ruling, the British government immediately introduced a new restrictive ordinance, establishing a right to return for all the islands except Diego Garcia—where the vast majority of islanders had lived before their eviction. The islanders in turn again filed suit at the London High Court during 2003, but were once again, in October 2003, denied both the right to return to their home islands and to compensation.[62] The British government in June 2004 finally passed Orders in Council prohibiting access to all the Chagos Islands, overriding the 2000 High Court decision.[63]

Although some legal uncertainties remain, Uncle Sam, in collaboration with his old partner John Bull, appears to have successfully finessed base politics on Diego Garcia to a remarkable degree, on a strategically important problem. It is important to note, however, that the Diego circumstances are rather distinctive ones—not broadly analogous to the problems of embattled garrisons elsewhere. Diego became a virtually unpopulated island, and has never been self-governing. Much as it might like to do so, the U.S. military cannot rely on "Rent-a-Rocks" like Diego Garcia alone as its platforms for global power-projection.

As we have seen in the foregoing pages, it pays to look at the trees in the base-politics forest, not just at the woods as a whole. It is individuals, interacting in subnational groups, that ultimately move nations, often in directions at variance from what either national strategy or intuition might suggest. If subnational base politics cannot be finessed, it must be understood and appealed to. That brings our analysis to the financial dimension—so critical, and so often misunderstood.

CHAPTER EIGHT

THE FINANCIAL EQUATIONS

LOCAL EQUITIES, BASE STABILITY, AND BURDEN SHARING

BASE POLITICS, as we have seen in the past three chapters, is a complex contest, with varied national manifestations. Sometimes it is played well, with clear implications for stability or withdrawal, and sometimes badly, with volatile, prospectively uncertain outcomes, as under the bazaar-politics paradigm. Yet regardless of the dynamic in any particular case, base politics is not just a series of idiosyncratic stories. It has broad patterns that repeat, to a remarkable degree, across cultures, value systems, and types of political regimes, responding systematically to prevailing host-nation incentive structures and institutions.

WHY FINANCE MATTERS

Indeed, as democratization and social change erode the viability of coercion, funding support—for both host-nation interests and often those of the U.S. military as well—becomes increasingly critical to the embattled profile of American forward deployment. When bases need to be moved, as in the impending redeployment of eight thousand U.S. Marines from Okinawa to Guam, money is also the key to smooth resolution.[1] One commonality across nations and cultures in base politics is thus the importance of finance.

As we shall see, who funds the operation of foreign bases, the magnitude and consistency of such support, and which institutions administer it all crucially affect the durability of foreign presence. When money is not forthcoming in expected amounts, or when local demands exceed the willingness of the basing nation to pay—as in the Philippines during the early 1990s—bases fail. When funds are available, overseas bases are more likely to succeed.

The composition of base-support funding—especially how broadly it is distributed to key actors in a host nation's political system—also affects the durability and longevity of that embattled presence. Key political actors need to be compensated to keep the system stable. For both host and basing nations, as well as for key subnational actors within each of them, who gets what, when, where, and how are crucial questions of base politics, as they are of politics more generally.[2]

Finance, it can be argued, may potentially compromise the future of the American military presence in key nations such as Japan, South Korea, and Germany, where host-nation support—and the consequent local burden—is high. Finance holds the key to agreement between alliance partners and the United States as to what the distribution of key costs and benefits flowing from the U.S. forward-deployed presence will look like. The heavy American Navy and Marine presence in Japan, for example, which involves local deployment of both an aircraft carrier and one of three Marine Expeditionary Forces operating worldwide, clearly benefits from the high level of Japanese host-nation support, as will be seen. If that financial support were not available in the current massive amounts—and there are rising pressures in key host nations to reduce it—the U.S. presence itself would likely be much smaller, and more contested.

Some analysts suggest that "if the U.S. ever leaves Japan, it will be because Japan 'turns out the lights'"—cuts support payments rather than directly requests withdrawal—and there is potential truth in this statement. And Japan's incentives to turn out the lights would increase if Japanese strategy were to change—and the current strategic fit between America and Japan, cemented by a lack of budget pressure for defense expansion, were to unravel as a consequence—as Japan acquired more extensive (and expensive) offshore commitments of its own. In that circumstance U.S. forces in Japan (USFJ) and the Japanese Self-Defense Forces (SDF) would be rivals for funds—a most basic and deadly sort of rivalry, often missed by realist scholars focusing on more abstract, geopolitical considerations at the national and international levels.

Finance, it must be noted, does not necessarily stabilize base politics by itself. There have been many instances—of which South Vietnam in the 1970s, the Philippines in the 1980s, and Turkey in 2003 were only some of the most conspicuous—where the United States brandished large sums of money in pursuit of a geostrategic outcome, and nevertheless failed to achieve its policy aims. Political context, including host-nation domestic political structure, is a crucial intermediate variable, as chapter 6 suggested. It generally takes both major financial support (domestic or foreign) *and* mediating institutions that effectively distribute that support to politically key claimant interests to stabilize base politics.

When funds and mediators are lacking in a host nation—which is often—base vulnerability, however, is greatly increased. As was made clear in the previous chapter, rising popular consciousness of base issues throughout the world has compounded this underlying problem. The increasing concentration of American bases in Islamic and other developing nations where they are unpopular has intensified it. As a result, finance has become an increasingly vital, stabilizing link in an otherwise bleak and contentious base-politics equation.

Broadly speaking, from a financial standpoint there are two basic patterns of base politics. In a limited but important range of countries—mainly affluent but once-occupied nations with a tradition of bearing American burdens—the host nation pays the United States to defray major elements of local costs: Japan, Germany, and South Korea head this list. In other instances, as in Turkey, Eastern Europe, and Central Asia, the United States conversely pays the host nation.[3] In a small range of instances, American allies provide financial aid to host nations in de facto support of U.S. basing activities in those countries. Japan, with the largest foreign-aid program in the world apart from the United States, has been especially important in this regard.[4]

THE HOST-NATION SUPPORT DIMENSION

Nowhere, it should be emphasized, does a host nation pay the *salaries* of American forces overseas. And rarely does it pay their operational costs.[5] Yet host-nation support (HNS) can nevertheless be important to sustained forward-deployed presence. Especially in nations where locally provided HNS is large, and the basing relationship to post-9/11 U.S. antiterrorist priorities is somewhat indirect—as in Japan, South Korea, and Germany today—turning off the lights through financial cutbacks could potentially be almost as grave a threat to American presence as revolution.

HNS is, as table 8.1 suggests, a geographically and economically bounded phenomenon. It is relatively common in Western Europe, where it is augmented by NATO. And it is important in Northeast Asia. HNS is also provided by certain affluent nations in the Middle East, including Qatar, Kuwait, Oman, and, until 2003, Saudi Arabia. Yet HNS, which naturally tends to be a function of national affluence, is unusual in Eastern Europe, Africa, Latin America, and the poorer Islamic nations, including Afghanistan and Central Asia. Those, however, are the countries where the bulk of the post-9/11 American overseas presence has come to be.

Bilateral support for U.S. forces reveals deeper patterns of base politics, providing excellent grist for social science theory and comparative analysis.[6] Among the most important dimensions are the following:

1. THE ABSOLUTE VALUE OF THE HNS THAT VARIOUS NATIONS HAVE PLEDGED IN RECENT YEARS TO THE UNITED STATES. Prior to the Iraq War, Germany had, as indicated, the largest contingent of locally deployed

TABLE 8.1.

U.S. Bilateral HNS Costs-Sharing (in $ Billions) Received from Sharing with Selected Allies (1995–2002)

		1995	1996	1997	1998	1999	2000	2001	2002
Japan	U.S. Personnel	47,000	42,962	47,000	40,589	40,244	40,025	39,691	41,626
	HNS Total	4.05	4.58	3.73	4.01	5.18	5.00	4.61	4.41
Germany	U.S. Personnel	73,280	48,878	60,053	68,820	68,196	70,126	71,434	72,005
	HNS Total	1.13	1.30	1.22	0.96	1.38	1.21	0.86	1.56
South Korea	U.S. Personnel	36,016	36,539	35,663	36,956	36,130	36,171	37,972	38,725
	HNS Total	1.72	0.31	0.74	0.75	0.72	0.80	0.85	0.84
Italy	U.S. Personnel	12,007	12,401	11,677	10,508	11,668	11,348	11,854	13,127
	HNS Total	0.52	0.53	1.09	1.11	0.53	0.36	0.32	0.37
Kuwait	U.S. Personnel	771	5,531	1,640	5,274	3,582	4,527	4,300	3,096
	HNS Total	0.67	0.07	0.08	0.18	0.18	0.25	0.25	0.25
United Kingdom	U.S. Personnel	12,131	11,662	11,379	11,166	11,299	11,170	11,361	11,351
	HNS Total	—a	—a	0.09	0.13	0.09	0.13	0.13	0.24

Source: US Department of Defense. *Report on Allied Contributions to the Common Defense,* various editions, 1997–2004.
Note: a. Data unavailable.

U.S. forces. Yet it was only second in aggregate HNS to Japan, which hosted little more than half the number of troops. In the year 2002, Japan's aggregate support for U.S. forces came to more than $4.6 billion—over 60 percent of the entire bilateral HNS that the United States received worldwide. And its per capita support for U.S. troops deployed in Japan was nearly five times the comparable levels in Germany.

2. THE SHARE OF TOTAL AMERICAN STATIONING COSTS THAT ALLIED GOVERNMENTS PROVIDE. Throughout the last half of the 1990s, and into the twenty-first century, as indicated in table 8.2, the Japanese

TABLE 8.2.
Percentage Share of U.S. Overseas Stationing Costs Paid by HNS, 1995–2002

1995	1996	1997	1998	1999	2000	2001	2002
Japan	Japan	Saudi Arabia	Japan	Japan	Saudi Arabia	Oman	Japan
(76)	(78)	(88)	(76)	(79)	(80)	(79)	(75)
South Korea	Italy	Japan	Qatar	Saudi Arabia	Japan	Japan	Saudi Arabia
(64)	(49)	(76)	(65)	(68)	(79)	(75)	(65)
Italy	Spain	Italy	Norway	Kuwait	Kuwait	Spain	Qatar
(50)	(47)	(76)	(60)	(50)	(47)	(55)	(61)
Spain	Saudi Arabia	Spain	Italy	Qatar	Qatar	Saudi Arabia	Luxembourg
(42)	(37)	(47)	(60)	(43)	(47)	(54)	(60)
Turkey	Greece	South Korea[a]	Saudi Arabia	Italy	South Korea	Kuwait	Kuwait
(31)	(33)	(40)	(58)	(37)	(42)	(51)	(58)
Greece	Germany	Greece	Spain	South Korea	Oman	Qatar	Spain
(28)	(25)	(34)	(45)	(27)	(40)	(41)	(58)
Germany	Norway	Norway	Greece	Germany	Italy	South Korea	Turkey
(24)	(25)	(30)	(42)	(27)	(37)	(39)	(54)
—[a]	South Korea	Germany	South Korea	—[a]	Germany	Italy	Italy
	(24)	(26)	(41)		(21)	(34)	(41)

Sources: U.S. Department of Defense, *Report on Allied Contributions,* 1997–2004 editions; the 2004 *Report on Allied Contributions* contains the figures for 2002.
Note:
a. Indicates shares accounting for less than 20 percent of total stationing costs. U.S. Department of Defense does not provide figures for such relatively minor shares.

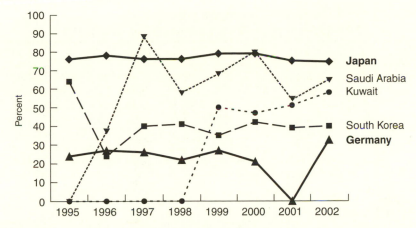

Figure 8.1: Volatility in American Host-Nation Support from Selected Allies

Source: Department of Defense. *Report on Allied Contributions to the Common Defense*, 1997–2004 editions.

Note: The 2004 *Report on Allied Contributions to the Common Defense* contains figures for 2002.

government covered between 75 and 79 percent of total local U.S. stationing costs. In four of the eight years in question (1995–96 and 1998–99), this share was the highest of any ally in the world. Recently Spain, Italy, and several of the Persian Gulf states—all local allies at the time of the United States—have also been among the top contributors, relative to the local expenses of the U.S. forces they host. When administrations change, this support may be endangered, as was true when Spain elected a socialist government in March 2004 and then promptly withdrew Spanish troops from Iraq.

Other nations at times cover an even higher share of U.S. costs than does Japan; Saudi Arabia did so in 1997 and 2000, for example, as table 8.2 suggests, while Oman did so in 2001. Some nations, such as Germany, are nearly as consistent as Japan in financial backing for the U.S. military, albeit at a much lower level of support. Yet no one is both as consistent and as generally supportive of American strategic purposes as is Japan. Indeed, most are significantly more volatile and unpredictable in their backing, as is indicated in figure 8.1.

Whether Japan can continue such substantial and consistent HNS support for U.S. forces on its soil—as the country's crisis of governmental finance deepens, with the graying of its society, and as its rising security commitments abroad multiply—is an open question.[7] Amidst a protracted Japanese economic recession, and expanding international

TABLE 8.3.
HNS Direct-Support Profile Patterns of Selected U.S. Allies

	1995	1996	1997	1998	1999	2000	2001	2002
Kuwait	98.7	93.2	94.2	97.2	97.2	100	96.5	100
Japan	80.4	78.7	79.0	71.8	76.4	77.5	74.9	73.2
South Korea	17.1	100	47.5	46.5	45.0	54.4	54.8	57.7
United Kingdom	—a	—a	3.6	1.0	5.3	3.9	4.7	11.5
Germany	5.3	4.3	1.4	2.4	2.4	7.3	0.9	1.8
Italy	—a	—a	—a	—a	—a	2.3	0.9	0.8

Source: U.S. Department of Defense, *Report on Allied Contributions*, 1997–2004 editions.
Note:
a. Data unavailable or negligible.

security commitments of its own, Tokyo has gradually reduced its HNS budget since 2000. Indeed, during fiscal 2005 the HNS budget was nearly 14 percent lower than at its peak level in 1999.[8]

3. THE RATIO OF DIRECT SUPPORT FOR U.S. FORCES TO TOTAL OVER- ALL SUPPORT FOR THOSE FORCES[9]. As noted in table 8.3, Kuwait was the highest in the world in this category. Around three-quarters of Japan's massive support for U.S. forces in Japan in 2002, however, fell into the di- rect-support category. This is a much higher ratio of direct to indirect backing than in any nation where U.S. forces are forward deployed; South Korea was third.

Nations with high HNS for U.S. forces are generally cases, such as Kuwait and South Korea, where the United States has both fought along- side the nations in question in a recent war, and where that nation continues to face a direct and imminent security threat; neither of these conditions prevails in the Japanese case. The more common allied pattern is for host-nation support to take indirect forms, particularly local tax abatements on bases, training areas, and other land used by U.S. forces. This is the pattern that prevails in Germany and Britain, for example.

4. THE VARIETY IN THE MANIFESTATIONS OF DIRECT SUPPORT. Direct support for base rentals has been miniscule in five of the six large national providers of bilateral HNS support to U.S. forces, as figure 8.2 indicates. The Japanese government, however, pays the rental fees on pri- vate land requisitioned as sites for foreign military bases—an especially strategic function in Okinawa, and one that is unusual in cross-national perspective. In Okinawa, commercial real estate rentals have declined 30 percent between 1998 and 2004, even as base rentals rose at a steady 3 percent rate, unaffected by broader economic trends.

	United Kingdom	Italy	Germany	South Korea	Japan
Base Rentals				(minor)	Yes
Labor Support				Yes	Yes
Utility Costs			Yes (minor)	Yes	Yes
New Facilities Construction	Yes (minor)		Yes (minor)	Yes	Yes

Figure 8.2. Cross-National Variation in HNS Burden-Sharing Profiles
Source: U.S. Department of Defense. *Report on Allied Contributions*, 2004 edition.
Note: Data as of 2002.

Comparative Perspectives: A Northeast Asian Model?

HNS in Japan for locally deployed U.S. forces shows some striking similarities to that in South Korea, both in magnitude and programmatic breadth of support, which, taken together, contrast significantly to patterns elsewhere in the world. Most importantly, as indicated in table 8.1 and table 8.3, the *level* of local support for American forces in both countries has been extremely high. In absolute terms, Japan provides more HNS financial support on behalf of U.S. forces than any other nation in the world, while Korea rivals Germany for the second spot, even though there are twice as many U.S. troops in Germany as in Korea. Korean support for U.S. forces per American soldier is nearly twice that in Germany. And Korean support is also higher than German as a share of U.S. local basing costs. It has risen significantly over the past decade— the period of the Asian financial crisis excepted—even though Korea also contributes heavily to its bilateral alliance with the United States in ground-troop strength, and along many other dimensions as well.

The Japanese and Korean HNS patterns are also broadly similar to one another (and different from other major bilateral patterns of allied support) in that they are more structurally differentiated than elsewhere. There are, in other words, more concrete, differentiated support programs, targeted to address particular challenges that locally deployed U.S. forces confront. Korea, for example, has specific labor, logistics, and

TABLE 8.4.
A Northeast Asian Burden-Sharing Model?

	Japan	Korea	Other Major Allies[a]
Local HNS/U.S. Total Costs	74.5%	40%	39.7%
Direct Support/Total Support	73.2%	57.7%	28.5%
Absolute Value of Total HNS for U.S. Forces	#1	#3	
Variety of Direct Support Categories[b]	4	3	0.5
Labor Costs	Yes	Yes	
Logistical Costs	Yes	Yes	
New Facility Costs	Yes	Yes	
Utility Costs	Yes	No	
Land Rental Costs	Substantial	Limited	

Source:U.S. Department of Defense, *Report on Allied Contributions to the Common Defense*, 2004 edition.

Notes: All data for 2002.

a. Average figures for this group as a whole. Major allies are defined by the volume of total HNS to the United States. Besides Japan and South Korea, the four largest contributors to common defense are Germany, Italy, the United Kingdom, and Kuwait respectively.

b. Direct support categories include: (a) labor costs, (b) base rental expenditures, (c) utility costs, and (d) new facilities costs.

new-facilities support programs, just as Japan has,[10] although it lacks a Japanese-style utilities-support program, or much support for local real estate interests.[11]

The Korean government has, however, agreed to pay the entire cost of relocating USFK headquarters from Yongsan Garrison in the center of Seoul to Pyeongtaek and Osan, south of the capital, by 2013.[12] It had acquired approximately 11.5 million square meters of land for the new site, at an estimated cost of over $5 billion in 2005. In the vicinity of the prospective base Korea's central government is spending $1.1 billion to develop Pyeongtaek economically, even designating it as an "international town" so as to stimulate foreign business investment.[13] As in Okinawa over the past decade, the Korean government has also begun allocating substantial amounts of money to placate local Pyeongtaek landowners in a bid to defuse sharply rising antibase sentiment.[14] This new strategy represents an important departure from older patterns of traditional Korean fiat politics, in which coercion rather than compensation was typically used to acquire base-related land, in favor of a more conciliatory approach that has proven quite successful—if expensive—in Japan.[15]

Korea also broadly resembles Japan in providing primarily direct rather than indirect support for U.S. forces. In 2002, as indicated in table 8.3, nearly 75 percent of such support in Japan, and nearly 58 percent in South Korea, was direct, in the form of payments and subsidies from the host-nation government, rather than tax abatements of various kinds. This ratio rose steadily over the course of the 1990s in Korea, as the Korean government progressively expanded its direct financial commitments to USFK in the face of a deepening North Korean nuclear, chemical, and biological threat.

The process of HNS policy development in Korea so far also appears to broadly, although not perfectly, resemble that of Japan. As in Japan, policy innovations in Korea have typically emerged suddenly and discontinuously, at critical junctures, in response to tensions in the bilateral alliance with the United States.

Although confronting a truculent North Korea throughout the 1960s and 1970s, South Korea experienced the Guam Doctrine (1969), Vietnamization (1969–73), sudden American rapprochement with mainland China (1971–72), and ultimately the mid- and late 1970s—involving the fall of Saigon (1975). Following that period of historic transition in American policy, the Carter Korean withdrawal proposals (1977–79) were a major catalyst for HNS policy change in Korea as they were in Japan. During 1974, for example, the Korean government began providing USFK with logistical support to defray the cost of storage and maintenance of war stockpiles (WRS), as well as assistance with new construction (CDIP).[16] In 1986 the latter evolved into cash support payments. During fiscal 1977 the South Korean government also began supporting the operational costs of American troops in the country.

Likewise, in FY1978 the Japanese government inaugurated its "sympathy budget" (omoiyari yosan), nominally to express empathy with the difficulties of American servicemen confronting a rising yen. The major programmatic innovation, however, in FY1978 was labor subsidies to defray the burden of salary payments to Japanese workers threatened with layoffs due to yen revaluation. Further, Tokyo inaugurated HNS support for construction of new base facilities in FY1979. This included both aid for USFJ housing and recreational facilities, as well as more narrowly defined military construction.

During the 1980s, HNS support in Japan—and, to a lesser extent, in Korea—was magnified by the rapid pace of local economic growth and fiscal expansion. Strategy was not absent: expanding alliance security requirements during the Reagan years, of course, also played a role. Especially notable were the reopening and expansion of U.S. Air Force facilities at Misawa in northern Japan after 1982. Those facilities were particularly crucial at the time, in two respects: (1) for monitoring North

Korean and Soviet communications; and (2) for projecting credible U.S. operational capabilities against both the important Soviet strategic presence in the Sea of Okhotsk and the submarine-launched ballistic missile (SLBM) base at Petropavlovsk. Those expansions were funded generously by the HNS construction programs generated during the "Korean withdrawal" critical juncture noted above.

During the 1990s, although Japanese and Korean HNS patterns show strong similarities, flowing especially from their common origins in the "Korean withdrawal" critical juncture of the 1970s, those patterns also have important differences. The differences arguably stem from the differential path of economic growth in the two countries, and from the differing critical junctures that they have individually confronted in their political-economic relationships with the United States since 1990. The major developments biasing their HNS patterns in subtly different directions over the past fifteen years have been the following:

1. **THE GULF WAR OF 1991.** This precipitated the introduction into Japan in FY1991 of utility subsidies to defray the rising cost of electric power to U.S. forces, also benefiting Japanese power companies. It has no analogy in Korea, or indeed elsewhere in the world.

2. **THE KOREAN NUCLEAR CRISIS OF 1994.**[17] This provoked extended U.S.-ROK HNS negotiations over the 1994–97 period. Those talks produced, inter alia, the November, 1995 U.S.-ROK Special Measures Agreement. This understanding provoked, according to Korean calculation, an annual increase of Korean HNS contributions during 1994–97 of 32.3 percent annually, compared to a Japanese increase of 5.4 percent, contrasting to a German *decrease* of 57.3 percent for the same period.[18]

3. **THE OKINAWAN CRISIS OF 1995–96.** Precipitated by the tragic rape of a twelve-year-old Okinawan girl by American GIs in late 1995, massive demonstrations in Naha prompted a reexamination of U.S. facilities and procedures in Okinawa, leading to a new "facilities-movement" subsidy by the Japanese national government, introduced in FY1996.[19]

4. **THE ASIAN FINANCIAL CRISIS OF 1997–98.** This financial cataclysm savagely impacted the Korean political economy, leading to an inevitable decline in HNS support levels, but had much less impact in Japan. This differential impact (combined with the major increases in Korean HNS during 1995–97 under the 1995 Special Measures Agreement) accounts for the greater volatility of Korean, as opposed to Japanese, HNS spending, as calculated in U.S. dollars.

In the profile of Japanese and Korean HNS outcomes, one can discern important patterns that are shared, to a limited degree, in the other nations that give bilateral HNS support to the United States. These common traits—more pronounced in the Japanese/Korean cases, but only by a matter of degree, appear to include the following: (1) major physical U.S. base presence; (2) host-nation perception of American bases as having major strategic and economic importance to them; (3) host-nation affluence; and (4) historical experience of tension in the basing relationship, during which Washington was widely perceived to consider downsizing and/or withdrawal. The major increases in HNS contributions seem to occur during and just after these periods of tension in base relations, and then to be sustained in subsequent basing agreements.

Shaping HNS Policy Outcomes: The Key Role of Critical Junctures

"Critical junctures" during which discontinuous changes occur in base-support financial arrangements appear to have three distinctive traits: (1) a crisis character, which calls the legitimacy of existing arrangements into serious question; (2) stimulus for change, flowing from the crisis character of the juncture; and (3) time pressure on the parties involved, due to clear deadlines for policy resolution.[20] The distinctive nature of the pressures operating during such intervals—mutual and asymmetric anxiety about preserving the bilateral security relationship—explains the substantial host-nation HNS contributions, it is argued.

Such a general formulation also accounts for not only Northeast Asian cases, as previously indicated, but also for Germany's relatively high and long-standing HNS contributions. Those date from the 1960s, when the perceived American financial burden was both substantial and exacerbated by the growing exigencies of dollar defense. In the late 1960s, crisis in the basing relationship was precipitated by congressional efforts, led by Senate Majority Leader Mike Mansfield, during the Vietnam War to force downsizing in U.S. deployments in Europe under the so-called Mansfield Amendment. West German support for American forces in that country shot up, and stayed at promised levels for many years, before slowly declining.[21] It increased once again, ironically enough, in 2002, in the wake of bilateral disagreements over American intervention in Iraq, and Pentagon threats in the wake of 9/11 to shift forces from "Old Europe" to "New Europe."[22]

HNS support for U.S. forces in the Middle East followed a similar general pattern, with the Gulf War of 1991 as the catalyst. Prior to that conflict, American military presence in the region was limited and grudging. Thereafter, major facilities emerged, especially in Saudi Arabia, Kuwait, Oman, and Qatar, with substantial HNS levels to match.

Overall, the comparative picture of HNS support for U.S. forces abroad is a clear, if somewhat counterintuitive, one. U.S. allies, to be sure, tend to get a free ride as they become more affluent. Yet when the American presence in their nation or region comes into question, or when major exchange-rate shifts substantially intensify the economic burden on the United States to any great extent, they contribute in order to preserve that presence. Host nations, in an extremity, have put their money where their mouth is, taking clear financial steps to perpetuate U.S. presence. Whether they will continue to do so, should their finances deteriorate and their alternative global commitments broaden, is an open question, contributing to the increasingly fragile and embattled character of America's forward presence across the world as a whole.

WHERE UNCLE SAM PAYS

The HNS providers to American forces worldwide are particularly important, of course—both for the economic contribution they make and for the political backing that such support implies. Yet they make up only a small and declining share of the nations that host American bases worldwide. Far more common are the cases where the United States *pays* nations to host bases, rather than getting paid for doing so.

Such cases of American funding were the universal norm until the 1960s. As American troops become more heavily involved in developing nations in connection with the post-9/11 war on terrorism, they are becoming more prevalent once again. And an increasing share of America's financial transactions relating to bases are assuming the volatile, uncertain form of bazaar politics outlined in chapter 6.

How much, then, does the United States actually pay others for hosting its bases? How and why do such payments vary over time? How do they shape national patterns of base politics? These questions are all centrally important to a comprehensive understanding of base politics, and will be the focus of analysis here.

The first question—how much basing nations actually pay for the facilities that they occupy abroad—is surprisingly difficult to answer. There are published figures, of course, on foreign military sales (FMS), as well as on foreign aid (both economic and military) that host nations receive. One can also calculate the foreign aid that American allies provide, and how that varies with the presence and absence of foreign bases. Yet the overall packages that host nations receive, and their relationship to the details of basing arrangements themselves, generally remain both classified and largely insulated from public scrutiny.

Despite the analytical difficulties, four concrete generalizations are possible:

1. MOST OBVIOUSLY THE UNITED STATES GENERALLY PAYS A LOT OF MONEY FOR ITS FOREIGN BASES. Willingness to host American bases is clearly not the only criterion that Washington uses in decisions to grant military aid and official development assistance. The affluence of host nations is obviously also a consideration, as in the case of host nations like Saudi Arabia. It is, however, possible to see relationships between willingness to host American military bases and receipt of military aid, as suggested in tables 8.5 and 8.6.

2. FORMER HOST NATIONS THAT HAVE REJECTED AMERICAN BASES RECEIVE EITHER NO AID OR MEASURABLY LESS THEN WHEN THEY WERE HOSTING U.S. BASES. As is evident in table 8.5a, the severity of such declines obviously varies with the conditions under which U.S. troops depart, with South Vietnam and Taiwan being the polar cases, both during the mid-1970s. Economic assistance does not decline as rapidly with bases closures as does military aid, as table 8.5b indicates.

TABLE 8.5a.
New Host Nations and American Aid (in $Millions):
Military Assistance[a]

Country	Year Base Opened	Y − 2	Y − 1	Y[b]	Y + 1	Y + 2
Hungary[c]	1995	7.9	0.7	0.8	4.2	11.1
Poland[c]	1995	0.7	0.7	1.7	17.5	13.6
Bulgaria	2001	10.4	6.0	17.1	9.7	20.3
Ecuador	2001	5.6	0.5	0.6	3.6	1.6
Kyrgyzstan	2001	1.9	1.4	2.2	11.6	5.0
Uzbekistan	2001	2.2	2.3	2.9	37.1	9.7
Average increase rate (%)			−41	74	570	11.0

Source: U.S. Agency for International Development, *U.S. Overseas Loans and Grants* (Green Book), 2004 edition.

Notes:

a. "Military assistance" includes foreign military sales financing grants; funds for international military education and training; support for peacekeeping operations; and funding for bilateral military-assistance programs.

b. "Y" refers to the year U.S. military bases are established, while "plus" and "minus" figures denote years before or after the year of establishment.

c. Poland and Hungary joined NATO in March 1999.

TABLE 8.5b.
New Host Nations and American Aid (in $Millions): Economic Assistance[a]

Country	Year Base Opened	Y−2	Y−1	Y[b]	Y+1	Y+2
Hungary[c]	1995	11.7	3.3	27.1	23.9	12.8
Poland[c]	1995	33.1	4.8	87.1	73.7	46.2
Bulgaria	2001	39.5	48.8	61.6	59.7	57.8
Ecuador	2001	39.7	76.0	63.4	86.4	88.9
Kyrgyzstan	2001	53.0	47.3	37.2	77.6	56.9
Uzbekistan	2001	39.4	34.0	62.3	167.3	75.0
Average Increase Rate (%)			−11	418	47	28

Source: U.S. Agency for International Development. *U.S. Overseas Loans and Grants* (Green Book), 2004 edition.

Notes:

a. "Economic assistance" includes development assistance; food aid; refugee support; migration impact assistance; narcotics-control funding; child-survival, and pediatric-health support; non-proliferation funding; and antiterrorism program support.

b. "Y" refers to the year U.S. military bases are established, while "plus" and "minus" figures denote years before or after the year of establishment.

c. Poland and Hungary joined NATO in March, 1999.

3. NEW HOST NATIONS ARE TYPICALLY REWARDED GENEROUSLY. This pattern became well-established during the Cold War and has continued in its wake. During the two years following their first acceptance of an American base, new host countries tend to receive substantially more military assistance on average than they were previously granted, as indicated in table 8.5.

This American tendency to reward new host nations was especially striking in Uzbekistan following 9/11. U.S. military aid there skyrocketed more than 12-fold, from $1.7 million in 1995 to $17.5 million in 1996, and it grew rapidly for similar reasons in Hungary and Bulgaria as well. In Ecuador military support soared 6-fold, following the establishment of a U.S. base at Mantas, from $0.6 million in 1995 to $3.6 million in 1996.

4. AMERICAN BASE-RELATED PAYMENTS INCREASE WHEN HOST-NATION REGIME CHANGES OCCUR AND THE U.S. BASES SURVIVE. This pattern is clearly illustrated in all countries following democratization that fall in the category of "successful accommodation" in table 2.1. The only partial exception is South Korea. It received no military aid from the United States between 1994 and its clear regime change in 1998, when longtime dissident President Kim Dae-jung was inaugurated. The data is presented in table 8.6.

TABLE 8.6a.

American Aid to Ex-Host Nations That Have Closed American
Bases (in $Millions): Military Assistance[a]

Country	Year Base Closed	Y − 2	Y − 1	Y[b]	Y + 1	Y + 2
Morocco	1963	7.6	7.3	5.1	2.4	12.7
France	1966	0.6	0	0	0	0
Libya	1969	1.9	1.2	0.3	0.1	0
Taiwan	1973	125.9	140.4	148	92.8	82.7
South Vietnam	1975	3,321.6	778.8	576.8	0	0
Ethiopia	1977	38.0	7.0	2.7	0	0
Philippines	1992	155.3	205.4	37.7	17.5	0.9
Average Increase Rate (%)		−36	−38	−59	−32	

Source: U.S. Agency for International Development. *U.S. Overseas Loans and Grants*
(Green Book), 2004 edition.

Notes:

a. "Military assistance" includes foreign military sales financing grants; funds for international military education and training; support for peacekeeping operations; and
funding for bilateral military-assistance programs.

b. "Y" refers to the year U.S. military bases are established, while "plus" and "minus"
figures denote years before or after the year of establishment.

TABLE 8.6b.

American Aid to Ex-Host Nations That Have Closed American
Bases (in $Millions): Economic Assistance[a]

Country	Year Base Closed	Y − 2	Y − 1	Y[b]	Y + 1	Y + 2
Morocco	1963	103.6	56.0	72.2	41.0	46.3
France	1966	0.7	0	0	0	0
Libya	1969	3.0	2.9	2.5	0.5	0
Taiwan	1973	145.1	140.4	148.0	92.8	82.7
South Vietnam	1975	3,823.3	1,433.1	817.7	2.5	0
Ethiopia	1977	61.8	19.7	9.7	10.3	15.8
Philippines	1992	506.4	563.6	288.3	141.6	77.4
Average Increase Rate (%)		−39	−18	−44	−21	

Source: U.S. Agency for International Development, *U.S. Overseas Loans and Grants*
(Green Book), 2004 edition.

Notes:

a. "Economic assistance" includes development assistance; food aid; refugee support;
migration impact assistance; narcotics-control funding; child-survival and pediatric-
health support; nonproliferation funding; and antiterrorism program support.

b. "Y" refers to the year U.S. military bases are established, while "plus" and "minus"
figures denote years before or after the year of establishment.

TABLE 8.7a.

U.S. ODA (in $Millions) to Strategic Host Nations Following Regime Shifts: Military Assistance[a]

Country	Year Regime Changed	Y−1	Y[b]	Y+1	Y+2	Y+3
Portugal	1974	1.0	0.8	3.2	0.5	33.5
Greece	1975	67.5	86.0	224.7	156.0	175.0
Spain	1975[c]	25.3	2.8	0.7	137.0	137.0
Turkey	1982	252.8	403.0	402.8	718.3	703.6
Average Increase Rate (%)			−6	97	4,859	1,653

Source: U.S. Agency for International Development, *U.S. Overseas Loans and Grants* (Green Book), 2004 edition.

Notes: In all the cases indicated, American forces remained in the host nation.

a. "Military assistance" includes foreign military sales financing grants; funds for international military education and training; support for peace-keeping operations; and funding for bilateral military-assistance programs.

b. "Y" refers to the year U.S. military bases were established, while "plus" and "minus" figures denote years before or after the year of establishment.

c. Due to the change of fiscal year calculation in 1976, with the start of the fiscal year changed from July 1 to October 1, statistics for 1976 include both figures indicated as 1976 and 1976 TQ figures, as presented in *U.S. Overseas Loans and Grants* (Green Book), 2004 edition. The three-month transition period in 1976 (July 1 to September 30) was treated as a distinct reporting period.

Spain began its path from fascism to democracy in 1975, with the death of Francisco Franco. Assistance to Spain, whose bases had proved important to U.S. forces re-supplying Israel in the 1973 Yom Kippur War, soared during the transition to democracy of the late 1970s, and especially following the advent of a Socialist government in 1982. A similar pattern is clearly discernable in Portugal following the leftist coup of 1974, against the authoritarian Caetano regime, as indicated in table 8.7. At stake was U.S. Air Force access to strategic Lajes air base in the Azores, also critical to the resupply of Israel throughout the 1970s.[23]

U.S. ODA to Turkey similarly increased within two years of its democratic transition in 1982, as also shown in table 8.7. Aid continued at high levels throughout the 1980s and 1990s, as a democratic Turkey became arguably America's most important Islamic ally. American aid to Kyrgyzstan, host to the highly strategic Manas Air Base, also rose sharply following the local 2005 democratic revolution, and the near-simultaneous expulsion of American forces from neighboring Uzbekistan.[24]

Lags between democratization and increases in U.S. aid payments appear to flow from the fact that base agreements are normally negotiated only every three to five years. Major increases thus come at the time

TABLE 8.7b.

U.S. ODA (in $Millions) to Strategic Host Nations Following Regime Shifts:
Economic Assistance[a]

Country	Year Regime Change	$Y-1$	Y[b]	$Y+1$	$Y+2$	$Y+3$
Portugal	1974	1.0	0.8	15.5	82.1	165.0
Greece	1975	67.5	86	289.7	156.0	175.0
Spain	1975[c]	28.3	5.8	0.7	147.0	144.0
Turkey	1982	453.8	704.1	688.8	857.8	879.5
Average Increase Rate (%)			−4	496	5,327	28

Source: U.S. Agency for International Development, *U.S. Overseas Loans and Grants* (Green Book), 2004 edition.

Notes: In all the cases indicated, American forces remained in the host nation.

a. "Economic assistance" includes development assistance; food aid; refugee support; migration impact assistance; narcotics-control funding; child-survival and pediatric-health support; nonproliferation funding; and antiterrorism program support.

b. "Y" refers to the year U.S. military bases are established, while "plus" and "minus" figures denote years before or after the year of establishment.

c. Due to the change of fiscal year calculation in 1976, with the start of the fiscal year changed from July 1 to October 1, statistics for 1976 include both figures indicated as 1976 and 1976 TQ figures, as presented in *U.S. Overseas Loans and Grants (Green Book)*, 2004 edition. The three-month transition period in 1976 (July 1 to September 30) was treated as a distinct reporting period.

of renegotiation. Whatever the timing, these increases during the democratization process constitute a major financial burden on American deployments in developing nations. And they do not always stabilize the American basing presence, as the case of the Philippines in the early 1990s so graphically demonstrates.

Despite variations by country, the overall pattern is clear. The United States rewards nations that host its bases in less affluent parts of the world, such as Central Asia, Eastern Europe, and Latin America, as some of its allies, such as Japan, also appear to do.[25] Washington likewise tends to reduce its aid to those that reject its military presence, compounding the increased political-economic risk premium that the absence of such presence appears to independently instill. In a globalizing, democratizing world, in which local institutions ever more sensitively reflect rising popular disenchantment with foreign forces, finance is an important, if often controversial, countervailing weapon for America's embattled garrisons, in maintaining their global presence.

Base politics are, it should be noted, only one relatively minor consideration, however, in determining American foreign-aid allocations. In fiscal 2002, the United States did, to be sure, provide $494 million in gross

ODA to Pakistan, and $188 million to Afghanistan. Both nations, of course, hosted U.S. bases, and had begun to play major roles in the struggle with terrorism.[26] Yet they only ranked fourth and tenth, respectively, on the overall list of American aid recipients, behind nations like Egypt, Russia, and Israel, which did not host bases.

IN CONCLUSION

As is clear from the foregoing pages, there is considerable variation in the financial arrangements that the United States makes with the nations that host its bases. Most affluent nations—stable parts of the world's "functioning core"—share a significant portion of the costs that the United States would otherwise incur through its presence on their shores, apart from the salaries of American troops, which the Pentagon always bears. This allied support undoubtedly allows Washington to finesse the "dangers of overextension" so often stressed by Paul Kennedy and others.[27]

In developing nations, the financial pattern is reversed, however, and the United States generally pays. To be sure, the financial cost to the Pentagon of its massive overseas base presence is not spiraling the way it did during the climactic Cold War years, apart from the costly commitment in Iraq. Yet the increasing concentration of American bases in the developing world, and the rapid spread of base-political concerns to a range of volatile, impoverished nations in the "nonintegrating gap" there,[28] creates new long-term political challenges and financial burdens. These remain largely unexplored, and deserve a clear place on the future American policy agenda.

Before turning explicitly to implications for policy, let us first review our findings regarding the impact of finance on base politics. Perhaps most importantly, we have found that high levels of locally provided host-nation support correlate broadly—although not universally—with stable forward deployment. Some host nations, conspicuously including Japan, appear to be stabilizing foreign base presence by directing large amounts of money in support of it in ways that also generously compensate domestic interests. This proactive host-nation compensation politics naturally also deepens basing-nation interest in committing troops overseas. The U.S. Marines, for example, have been significantly more interested in keeping the III MEF in Okinawa under generous HNS arrangements than they would be were those support mechanisms not to exist. And they are conversely more inclined to redeploy to the United States as HNS support levels decline.

There are, however, exceptions to this apparently felicitous pattern—that money will produce stability in base relationships—even in Japan.

The May 2006 U.S.-Japan base-transformation package, which projected over $6 billion in expenditures by Japan to the year 2014 in order to move eight thousand U.S. Marines to Guam, and achieve other strategically rational adjustments in American basing within Japan,[29] stirred a firestorm of domestic protest there. It appears that special expenditures to support the movement of foreign forces out of Japan and to aid construction of military construction elsewhere are especially controversial with Japanese voters—particularly when they are part of a large, conspicuous policy package.

Saudi Arabia, in another illustration of the limits to the stabilizing role of finance, paid a larger share of American HNS costs in 1997 and 2000 than any other nation in the world, as table 8.2 points out. The Saudi government built the state-of-the-art, multibillion-dollar Prince Sultan Air Base for U.S. forces, with state of the art command and control systems, which coordinated air operations in the 2001 Afghan War.[30] Yet two years later, American forces were gone from Saudi Arabia. And their presence in South Korea, another big HNS contributor, was deeply troubled. Causal forces deeper than the financial were clearly at work in all these instances.

Cases where the U.S. pays point to the same conclusion: money is generally important, but its utility depends upon how expectations are managed. In the Philippines, for example, American base payments in the mid-1980s were second highest in the world, next to those to Turkey. Yet five years later, the U.S.-Philippine basing relationship had ruptured, and American forces were evacuating some of their largest overseas bases, following the Philippine Senate's rejection of a pact that the country's own diplomats had negotiated. The Filipino government did not oppose hosting U.S. bases, but demanded much more money than the United States was prepared to pay. The Filipino government apparently did not feel it needed the American bases badly, and assumed that Washington had the determination to stay at still higher rental fees.

The distinctions made in chapter 6 suggest that the way in which financial patterns are linked to domestic political processes is critical in determining base-political stability. When the relationship between funding and host-nation cooperation fails to be structural and systematic, as under the bazaar-politics paradigm prevalent in the Philippines of the late 1980s, or when financial support of U.S. forces undermines government cultural legitimacy, as in Saudi Arabia, large HNS payments do not satisfy local interests. When those payments are routinized, systematic, and sensitively targeted to key political constituencies, as under the compensation-politics paradigm of postwar Japan, those payments can, however, be temporarily stabilizing—so long as generous HNS funding continues, and the scale of the funding is not so large and conspicuous as to attract the wrath of host-nation voters.

The key issue is thus whether finance—either that of the basing or of the host nation—creates "local equities" that link host-nation domestic politics positively and systematically with the presence of foreign forces. Given the nature of the base-politics contest, as discussed in chapter 4, such a linkage is often crucial to stabilizing base politics. Grassroots interests in host nations often have incentives to nonagreement that make them unsupportive of foreign bases, unless systematic and substantial grassroots compensation takes place.

Over the past five chapters, we have outlined the underlying structure of base politics and examined its variations. We have pointed continually to the commonalities across nations, and to the possibilities of prediction that flow from understanding them. Above all, we have continually seen the fragile, embattled standing of America's troops abroad in the domestic politics of most host nations, and their deepening reliance on money—America's own or that of allies—to stabilize their presence. In the concluding chapters to follow, we first outline options for basing policy, and then offer thoughts on how America should choose among the complex and often disturbing options still at its command.

CHAPTER NINE

BASES AND AMERICAN STRATEGY

EMERGING OPTIONS

A STRONG BIAS toward forward deployment is clearly embedded in twenty-first-century America's political-military institutions, and in much of our traditional psychology. As we saw in chapter 1, these investments are the heritage of a century's conflicts and geopolitical expansion by the United States, dating back to the Spanish-American War and even before. Today we are a global power, with the concrete assets and prerogatives, which that standing implies. Beyond the global influence sacrificed through an end to forward deployment, it would cost the United States well over $100 billion to replace its bases overseas, including many of the largest and most elaborate logistical facilities and fuel depots in the world—if, that is, it could start tomorrow, and if its current foreign allies would permit.[1]

They might well not do so. In many ways, these American bases are the embedded consequence of past imperial victories, unlikely ever to be repeated. Strategic American outposts at Diego Garcia and Ascension, for example, are islands that Britain won two centuries ago through the Napoleonic Wars. America has also built on its occupations of Axis powers Germany, Japan, and Italy, where it continues to maintain some of its most important bases, well over half a century after World War II. There is an American aircraft carrier, to be concrete, deployed at the entrance to Tokyo Bay, in Yokosuka, birthplace of the Japanese Imperial Navy. For half a century there was an American air base at Rhein Main in Frankfurt—Germany's busiest commercial airport. Local nationalist sentiments simply would not permit a reoccupation of such facilities in today's world, no matter how global we all consider ourselves to be.

There are manifest costs, both political and financial, involved in any actual reconfiguration of the American global basing presence Yet there is still clear analytical value in rethinking that presence from the ground up, given the human costs involved in sustaining it, and the enduring fragility of America's embattled garrisons as it has been outlined in this volume. The basing structure, after all, needs to be related to emerging national priorities. Even the $100 billion plus in existing base-asset value pales in comparison with the massive price tag—half a trillion and counting—for the Iraq War alone.[2]

Outlining the options for the future of American overseas bases, and assessing their prospective cost in blood and treasure, are the delicate task of this chapter. Beginning with a vision of "Fortress America," which proposes harnessing advances in technology to permit a strategic return from foreign overinvolvement to our native shores, the chapter also outlines "Defense Transformation," the George W. Bush administration's new variation on the forward-deployment paradigm. It then contrasts both "Fortress America" and "Defense Transformation" to the "Classic Pax Americana" that found favor during the latter half of the 1990s. In each case, the analysis strives to identify the political as well as intellectual parameters of the emerging debate over what America's foreign basing profile should ultimately be. Such an exercise is useful in identifying the options for consideration regarding the future of overseas bases, including the value of transformation policies currently underway, which will be discussed at the end of this chapter.

"FORTRESS AMERICA": A WORLD BEYOND BASES?

"What we should want in these circumstances," George Kennan noted not long after the collapse of the Soviet Union in 1991 "is the minimum, not the maximum, external involvement."[3] Technology, economic trends, and geopolitical developments are now conspiring, in the view of some grand strategists, to make that minimal American overseas political-military involvement both possible and necessary.[4] The United States, they firmly contend, will ultimately be much more secure if it withdraws from major foreign bases, reinforces robust nuclear, naval, and long-range aerospace capabilities, and leverages its global influence through a detached, balance-of-power oriented "offshore-balancing" strategy.[5]

The "Fortress America" approach thus rests on a distinct set of assumptions about what determines stability in the global political economy as a whole. The proponents of this notion assert, contrary to the assumptions of realist theory, that stability can be maintained by cooperative self-interest—*without* the necessity of direct foreign military presence. William E. Odom and Robert Dujarric argue, for example, that the United States is a new type of imperial power, "wealth-generating and voluntary"—in other words, a cooperative empire where the clients benefit as much as the metropole.[6] This situation, in their view, creates incentives for states to align with the United States but also to voluntarily reform their own domestic political and economic institutions along liberal lines to qualify for membership in the U.S.-orchestrated Western-alliance system. America, in short, *need not* reach out to transform others, as those nations have strong incentives to prepare *themselves* for active involvement in a liberal system congenial to American interests.[7]

Odom and Dujarric maintain that this benign American empire is sustainable over the long run unless the United States itself takes the wrong steps, including aggressive political-military moves that erode the foundations of its empire by provoking international distrust. The real threat comes from unilateral U.S. actions, including controversial foreign military deployments, that prevent the American empire from being "wealth-generating and voluntary." Here, they suggest that the post-2003 U.S. military involvement in Iraq, which has of course extracted a high political and economic cost already, will continue to weaken the foundations of an American imperial system that otherwise is fundamentally strong.

Jim Garrison argues that the United States stands in a position to completely transcend imperial politics by using the absence of serious competitors in the world to lay alternative foundations for effective global governance. In discussing the rise and fall of previous empires, he maintains that imperial governance itself is not sustainable in the long term. Yet the United States can use its preeminent power to oversee a peaceful transition to a new global political order, and do so *without* a coercive, forward-deployed basing structure, he argues.[8]

With or without a configuration of global geopolitical forces that sustains American preeminence without forward deployment, technological advance clearly is giving the United States ever-stronger capacity to strike its adversaries, including foreign terrorists, from afar. At the onset of the Kosovo, Afghan, and Iraqi military campaigns, for example, the U.S. Air Force attacked enemy radar sites, telecommunications facilities, and other sensitive targets directly from the continental United States. Using B-2 stealth bombers based at Whiteman Air Base in Missouri, operating on forty-four-hour round-trip missions from their American homeland, the air force in the October 2001 Afghan campaign, for example, destroyed Taliban air capacity, as well as communications systems, in the very first moments of the war, without using any bases in the vicinity of Afghanistan at all.[9]

At a more tactical level, the United States eliminated Muhammad Atef, al Qaeda's military chief, with a Predator drone in Afghanistan in October 2001,[10] and did the same to suspects in the bombing of the USS *Cole*, as they were traveling a rural road in Yemen fourteen months later.[11] A Predator was used once again during January 2006 in an attempt to kill Osama bin Laden's principal lieutenant, Ayman al-Zawahiri, in the lawless tribal regions of northern Pakistan, where even Special Forces could not easily penetrate.[12]

B-2s devastated enemy air defenses in Afghanistan, as also in Kosovo and Iraq, from a transcontinental distance. Thanks to long-range strike aircraft and stand-off weapons, such as the Joint Direct Attack Munition (JDAM), U.S. forces of the early twenty-first century have returned smoothly from what were in previous wars highly dangerous commando missions. And they have done so with no casualties whatsoever—in any of the three potentially perilous cases noted above.

The U.S. Air Force also extensively used long-range strike aircraft, operating from distant facilities, for more routine target-degradation in both Afghanistan and Iraq. In doing so, it hoped to minimize the political backlash in the Islamic world against its air campaigns that might flow from using bases in the Muslim world itself. In the Afghan campaign, for example, over two-thirds of all the munitions expended during the war, by volume, were dropped by B-52s, whose stark white exhaust trails in the blue autumn sky were an indelible hallmark of that struggle. The Air Force based eighteen heavy bombers, including eight B-1Bs and ten B-52Hs, at Diego Garcia, from which they carried out daily and nightly runs over Afghanistan, more than 3,000 miles away.[13]

Innovative new Wind-Corrected Munition Dispensers, also recently used for the first time in combat; as well as precision JDAM munitions; "Power Scene" simulators of target areas that allowed pilots to preview prospective target areas in great detail from their home bases; and coordination through a Combined Air Operations Center in Saudi Arabia permitting in-flight target refinements all allowed long-range bomber pilots to achieve extraordinary precision in all sorts of weather. That precision particularly unnerved Taliban and al-Qaeda veterans of the earlier anti-Soviet campaign of the 1980s. Indeed, they had expected airpower to be applied much more indiscriminately and imprecisely than was the American practice in the fall of 2001.

As a result of DoD procurement decisions of the 1980s, intended to develop a credible capacity for long-range nuclear strikes from Stateside bases into the deep interior of the Soviet Union, the United States has developed and deployed a formidable manned long-range bomber capacity. By 2005, the U.S. Air Force had 82 B-52 H, 88 B-lB, and 21 B-2A (stealth) aircraft in its operational inventory,[14] each capable of delivering nonrefueled payloads between 6,900 and 8,800 miles.[15] The Cold War functions of this strike capacity, of course, largely disappeared with the collapse of the Soviet Union. Yet the nuclear bomber fleet has been reconfigured, with the addition of new precision weapons, augmented by sophisticated new information technology, into a formidable new conventional capability as well.

There were unprecedented uses of Unmanned Aerial Vehicles (UAVs), including the Global Hawk and the Predator, in the Afghan War—the first time that such drones had ever been used in combat. Both the Predator and the Global Hawk, originally developed to undertake unmanned Cold War missions in dangerous nuclear- or biological-conflict environments, are being adapted for more contemporary counterinsurgency struggles. Although the Predator is slow, and has a relatively short range, it is designed to be rolled into a C-130 aircraft, so it can be readily and rapidly deployed to distant locations.[16] The Global Hawk, however, has formidable independent long-range capabilities that the Predator does not possess.

The Global Hawk first showed its long-range strike potential in Linked Seas 00. In that May 2000 trans-Atlantic NATO exercise, the Hawk provided direct, unmanned support for amphibious operations in Portugal from its station at Eglin Air Base in Florida.[17] A year later, in April 2001, the Hawk flew 7,500 miles nonstop across the Pacific to Australia, setting a new world record for UAV endurance. A half-year later, following 9/11, it was deployed to Afghanistan in support of Operation Enduring Freedom. There it seems to have performed well also, especially in an experimental battlefield-reconnaissance role. The Global Hawk's cloud-penetrating electro-optical and infrared sensors can survey an area the size of Illinois in just twenty-four hours, relaying the imagery received in near real-time to battlefield commanders.

With more than half its components made of lightweight, high-strength composite materials, the Global Hawk is able to fly both far and for long periods of time. It has a range of close to 12,000 nautical miles, at an altitude of 65,000 feet, and is capable of flying at sustained speeds of up to 400 miles per hour for as long as thirty-five hours. Clearly the Hawk could ultimately be a mainstay of Fortress America capabilities, should the United States elect a more limited, less forward-deployed global role.

And there are more sophisticated post–Cold War long-range strike aircraft, potentially unmanned, still coming. So-called stealthy UCAVs (Unmanned Combat Aerial Vehicles) are even more admirably suited than the Predator for precision operations like the antiterrorist strike in Yemen. They could also ultimately buttress such a detached Fortress America role, although these UCAVs are not scheduled to reach combat units generally until around 2010.[18] Lockheed Martin in mid-2004 also announced a major new research contract with the Pentagon to develop expendable supersonic vehicles, under the Defense Department's RAT-TLRS program.[19] These unmanned warplanes will be able to fly at Mach 4 speeds to distant parts of the world for precision strikes against American adversaries, with little need for land bases along the way.

Making UCAVs a mainstay of the American military requires not only producing many more of them, but also developing high-tech communication systems to link the aircraft with one another and with the command centers. The Pentagon's Future Combat Systems megaproject is working to fill this gap. It is currently developing eighteen kinds of sensor-loaded combat vehicles and advanced communications technologies to link soldiers with vehicles, planes, robots, and one another.[20]

The U.S. Navy is also developing flexible deployment concepts, anchored in emerging technology, that reduce its prospective overseas basing requirements. These center on its "Sea Basing" strategic concept.[21] That idea involves a combination of expanded naval deployments, more prepositioned supply ships, and "lily pad" access to foreign ports, to allow the United States to operate more or less independently around the world.

Many enthusiasts of the so-called Revolution in Military Affairs (RMA) argue that with the United States able physically to strike at potential enemies anywhere in the world, overseas military bases and deployments are basically unnecessary. Former RAND analyst and U.S. Air Force official Christopher Bowie, for example, writes that high-tech weaponry such as the B-2 bomber, equipped with advanced munitions, "would not need bases in theater . . . raising the possibility of conducting paralyzing and disarming blows from the United States."[22] The National Defense Panel, mandated by Congress, similarly envisions U.S.-based forces that could "project significant power . . . within hours or days, rather than months."[23] Indeed, virtually all of the "vision" statements of the individual military services and the Joint Chiefs of Staff expect to see a more agile, rapidly deployable, automated, precise, and long-range strike force in the United States by 2010 or 2020.

The costs of maintaining forces abroad is also high—another potential argument for returning them to a Fortress America Stateside. Even when those forward-deployed forces had been reduced by over 50 percent from Cold War levels, as during the late 1990s, they still accounted for around 250,000 personnel out of a total active-duty strength of 1.4 million.[24] And the cost of equipping, training, and paying those troops represented roughly one-fifth of America's massive annual defense spending total.[25]

The costs of forward deployment must be balanced, of course, against the very real costs of long-range precision-strike capabilities. B-2 (stealth) bombers, for example, have effective global strike capabilities well demonstrated in America's recent wars, but they cost $730 million each.[26] And each JDAM, which the United States used at a peak rate of 3,000 a month in Afghanistan, costs $14,000.[27]

In a world of terrorism, where the missile-accuracy and other technological capabilities of America's conventional adversaries are also growing stronger, the danger to U.S. troops deployed abroad is also growing, making long-range precision weaponry attractive from a force-preservation perspective. The terrorist threat has been clearly manifest, not only in Iraq, but also before that in the attack on the USS *Cole* in Aden harbor, and on U.S. Embassies in Nairobi and Dar es-Salaam. As Paul Bracken points out, North Korea, China, and Iran, among others, also now have intermediate-range ballistic missile capabilities, including China's SS-9s and North Korea's mobile Nodong, capable of endangering U.S. bases in Japan and the Middle East. This problem, as Bracken argues, will only grow more serious in future.[28]

Apart from the exposure to increased danger that it presents to American troops, forward deployment also has other important negatives in human terms, it is argued.[29] Troops in Korea and Bosnia, most marines in Okinawa, air force pilots in the Middle East, and navy sailors and marines at sea face months at a time away from their families.[30] Large deployments abroad often complicate relations between the United States and its allies, as frictions on Okinawa, for example, clearly demonstrate.

Perhaps the most telling argument against forward deployment, in the view of critics, is that in the final analysis it does not serve America's most fundamental interests in a post–Cold War world—or indeed, in important respects, even those of the key allies that American troops are protecting. In contrast to Cold War days, when the U.S. forward-deployed presence was larger and the Soviet threat was clear, overseas bases today do not provide substantial extended deterrence to American allies, especially when those bases are threatened militarily by the increasingly accurate precision weapons of adversaries.[31] To the contrary, American bases may subject the host country to unwelcome "blow-back," it is alleged.[32] Such bases are generally costly, despite substantial burden-sharing support from some allies. And those bases are potentially difficult to use operationally to show resolve in some strategically important cases. In contingencies ranging from the Ukraine and the Baltic to the Taiwan Straits, implicit host-nation restrictions on sensitive third-country deployment reduce the strategic value of many overseas bases to the U.S. military.[33]

Given America's formidable long-range technological capabilities, coupled with the costs, dangers, and constrained utility of deploying American forces abroad, the prudent course of action—even in a realist strategic calculus—is to base U.S. forces at home until they are really needed in a conflict, Fortress America proponents contend. Then, when necessary, those forces could lash out rapidly, across oceans and continents, with space-power, long-range air power, and other elements of what might be called a "reconnaissance-strike complex." In this way, it is argued, they could both defend U.S. interests from America's homeland, and also avoid the distinct negatives of forward deployment.

Fortress America perspectives are bolstered politically by their clear attractiveness to a broad spectrum of domestic interests within the United States. Important elements of the Congress, public opinion, the defense-industrial complex, and the defense-analytical community clearly see the merits of the arguments just presented, especially given the protracted, costly struggle in Iraq. Fortress America, after all, promises substantial spending on advanced, domestically produced aerospace technology, combined with the prospect of reduced domestic base closings, not to mention lessened foreign battle casualties.

Many traditional internationalists in the State Department, multinational corporations, and elsewhere do not, of course, favor this option. They cite, among other arguments, the difficulty of defending energy sea-lanes from afar, not to mention concrete host-country political-economic concerns that the United States holds abroad. Internationalists also cite the continuing inaccuracy of even the most advanced precision weapons and intelligence. Technology, they argue, is simply not mature enough to replace all foreign bases, considering the difficulties that computer systems inevitably have in taking over the countless decisions that pilots need to make, and the inevitable danger of frequent breakdowns in communication links.[34]

Critics of Fortress America also cite the political backlash that long-range military strikes inevitably engender in the developing world. For example, the Predator strike in Pakistan during January 2006 directed against al-Zawahri, the number 2 leader of al-Qaeda, failed, due to incorrect intelligence, to hit its target. Instead, it killed seventeen innocent civilians, prompting condemnation even from the conservative local Pakistani government.[35]

Despite the steady progress of precision technology, military success continues to depend heavily on accurate intelligence as well. To secure such intelligence, the United States needs listening posts in parts of the world where it has difficulty gathering accurate information. Inside the Sensitive Compartmentalized Information Facility (SCIF), at Camp Lemonier in Djibouti, for example, civilian and military intelligence analysts collect diverse kinds of information, including the personalized local knowledge that comes only from establishing a concrete physical presence in forward locations. "You can't hear unless you're here," as Major Mike Poehlitz, head of the army civil-affairs unit based in Djibouti, noted ruefully.[36]

Yet whether, in the face of persistently high financial and human costs, the long-term political influence of these internationalist naysayers is sufficient to defeat the simple popular appeal of Fortress America is open to question. The notion's latent attractiveness for a nation burdened by protracted, costly conflict in distant lands may well make it an increasingly popular option in years to come.

CLASSIC PAX AMERICANA

Contrasting sharply to the Fortress America option is the traditional pattern of American basing policy since the Korean War—what might be best called "Classic Pax Americana." The basic elements of this strategy include: (1) creation and maintenance of a U.S.-led world order based on preeminent American political, military, and economic power, and on American values; (2) maximization of U.S. control over the international system by preventing the emergence of rival powers in Europe and Asia; and (3) maintenance of economic interdependence as an American security interest.[37] Forward deployment in Western Europe, Northeast Asia, and the Middle East has been fundamental to this strategy, in order to check potential hegemonic rivals and to assure adequate energy supplies.

The logic of Classic Pax Americana was relatively simple. Interdependence among allies of the industrialized world was crucial to global prosperity and well being, including that of the United States; instability caused by Soviet threats and communist domestic inroads was the central threat to that interdependence; and extended deterrence was the means through which U.S. strategy should counter that threat. America's post–World War II strategy, as Wolfram Hanrieder points out, thus involved *dual containment*—both of the Soviet Union *and* Germany/Japan.[38] U.S. forward deployment in Germany, Japan, and their environs was central to this broad neutralization of both potential challenges to American power and of regional balance-of-power rivalries.

Forward deployment was crucial under the Cold War variant of Classic Pax Americana for several reasons. First, it helped provide extended nuclear deterrence in support of European and East Asian allies,[39] since the presence of American forces was tangible evidence of U.S. commitment to them.[40] Such commitment was especially important in a Cold War system that was both nuclear and bipolar, by signaling that the allies in question were under American protection and thus did not need their own nuclear weaponry.

U.S. troop presence had two other important roles under Classic Pax Americana. First, it performed conventional as well as nuclear-security reassurance functions for U.S. allies, reducing the incentives of nations like Japan and Germany to pursue nationalist policies of independent rearmament that might complicate regional balance-of-power equations. U.S. presence also helped, especially in presumptively unstable nations like early postwar Italy and Japan, to assure *domestic* political stability. This was an especially prized commodity for conservatives that could otherwise no doubt more easily have been dislodged from power. Significantly, *all* of the major G-7 allied governments of the early post–World

War II period, when major trans-Pacific and trans-Atlantic security frameworks were consolidated, were in conservative hands. Most of them, as in Italy, France, and Japan, were only precariously so, and confronted serious left-of-center opposition that made them grateful for American political, military, and economic support.

Beyond its narrow political-military functions, the American global footprint has also leveraged U.S. foreign policy in a broader sense. It has literally become "a bellwether of U.S. attitudes and approaches to foreign policy." As such, stable troop presence has both signaled broad support for allies and deterrence of potential antagonists, even where troops have not been optimally deployed, from the perspective of military operations.

Classic Pax Americana, however, also had important costs for the United States. As Robert Gilpin, Paul Kennedy, and others have noted, it was economically costly in an era when American economic strength was declining relative to that of major allies.[41] As Christopher Layne points out, it also compelled the United States to advocate and represent a set of interests in which its own intrinsic stakes were markedly less than those of allies.[42] Over time, the distortions grew greater and greater, resulting in increased frustration and pressures for change. They were especially great within American domestic politics in time of war—especially when war was perceived as particularly costly in human terms, as in Vietnam, and increasingly in Iraq.

THE ARGUMENT FOR INCREMENTAL CHANGE

A third, more eclectic school of strategic thinking is both convinced of the need for modification of America's global role and skeptical that radical transformation is either feasible or desirable.[43] Michael O'Hanlon argues, for example, that numerous stubborn technical realities, ranging from the limitations of sensors to the modest rate of advances in most types of engines, make it difficult for the U.S. military to achieve its strategic purposes without extensive foreign bases.[44] Conceding many of the human negatives of extensive forward deployment, he and others of the "incrementalist" school argue for a more limited reduction in U.S. military deployments and overseas bases, as new technologies and moderations in the geopolitical landscape begin to permit such developments.[45]

The incrementalist school presents four main strategic reasons for a continued offshore basing presence, beyond the controversies of the American Iraq presence. First, the need to maintain air superiority requires offshore bases. Even in a world where long-range U.S. bombers such as the B-2 can strike targets far distant from America's homeland, as they did in Kosovo, Afghanistan, and Iraq, aircraft with shorter ranges are needed to patrol the skies around them, as well as to refuel them. Those aircraft need foreign bases.

A second reason for foreign bases relates to the need for ground forces abroad. These forces would be crucial in the event that friendly countries might be attacked and defeated before U.S. forces could respond, making it necessary to evict an aggressor. They could also be necessary for various kinds of reconnaissance and/or counterterrorist activities. Ground units may well get lighter and more mobile over time, but they will inevitably continue to be large, heavy, and quite unwieldy to deploy.[46] This reality will necessitate an offshore supply presence—either bases or prepositioned equipment—to allow such forces to respond to contingencies in a timely manner.

A third reason for at least some offshore bases—even if scaled down and isolated to minimize expense and conflict with local societies—is the need for safe ports and friendly harbors, it is argued. These could, for example, be important to assuring secure passage in the energy sea-lanes from the Persian Gulf to consumers in the United States, Europe, and East Asia. The only way to move heavy ground forces and their equipment is, and prospectively will remain, by sea. If ports are required, it is much better to control them in advance. Thus the need is crucial for naval bases, or at least access agreements in potentially strategic areas.

A final rationale for a foreign base presence is strategic: the value of a "tripwire" that links a nation's formal security commitments tangibly to its intercontinental geostrategic capabilities, and thus enhances deterrence. In the case of the United States, this logic can be formidable: with by far the most substantial, diverse, and accurate military arsenal on earth, including nuclear weapons and state-of-the art delivery systems, the United States is in a position to retaliate at any conceivable level to attacks where its forces are engaged. Deterrence is strongest when a potential aggressor realizes that U.S. forces would suffer casualties in any attack that it might attempt, so could credibly be expected to retaliate.

A base presence can thus be of value not only in narrow military terms, but also in ensuring the credibility of a broader security alliance, such as that between the United States and South Korea with respect to the North, so the argument goes.[47] Such alliances can have utility not only in military, but also in political-economic terms, by reducing the "risk premium" of deepened interdependence. This argument, and the broader incremental modifications of Classic Pax Americana outlined above, have found favor with many classical internationalists—at the State Department, on Capitol Hill, in the academic world, and with centrist elements of both political parties. As will be made clear in the following section, this classic logic of the Cold War is being increasingly questioned by a new strategic logic, oriented toward exploiting massive, asymmetrical U.S. military capacities that have emerged especially clearly in the post–Cold War era to counter new asymmetric terrorist threats of the twenty-first century.

To argue for overseas bases generally, of course, is not to argue for bases in any one specific location. Incrementalists converge generally on the utility of large, power-projection oriented bases in politically stable locales such as Diego Garcia, but differ sharply on appropriate configurations within the Middle East, in particular. A large military presence there has been a cornerstone of American policy since the 1991 Persian Gulf War, but some incrementalists, joining forces with Fortress America advocates, argue that such a presence undermines American interest more than it protects them. [48] Apart from providing a focal point for jihadists, facilitating their recruitment, such a U.S. presence also destabilizes important American regional allies such as Jordan, Saudi Arabia, and multiple Persian Gulf states, it is argued. A strong air and naval presence on Diego Garcia in the Indian Ocean and around the Persian Gulf should be able to assure America's core security interests—contingency support for Israel and assurance of continuing oil supplies—it is maintained.[49]

DEFENSE TRANSFORMATION

With the collapse of the Soviet Union in the early 1990s, followed by 9/11 a decade later, America's security environment has radically changed. Gone, at least for the moment, is the specter of superpower nuclear confrontation. Ominously emerging are more fluid threats—no less deadly for their subnational character, as the 9/11 attacks so dramatically demonstrated.

This changing environment, in the view of a dominant stream in the early twenty-first-century defense debate, mandates "defense transformation." "For most of the last century," President George W. Bush argued at the 2002 West Point graduation, "America's defense relied on the Cold War doctrines of deterrence and containment. In some cases, those strategies still apply. But new threats also require new thinking. Deterrence—the promise of massive retaliation against nations—means nothing against shadowy terrorist networks with no nation or citizens to defend. Containment is not possible when unbalanced dictators with weapons of mass destruction can deliver those weapons on missiles, or secretly provide them to terrorist allies."[50]

Although the imperatives of change may be driven by the revolution in military affairs, they are given particular force in the twenty-first century, proponents contend, by the global struggle against terrorism.[51] President Bush argued in 2002 at West Point, for example, that "the gravest danger to freedom lies at the perilous crossroads of radicalism and technology. When the spread of chemical and biological and nuclear weapons, along with ballistic missile technology—when that occurs, even weak states and small groups could attain a catastrophic power to strike great nations. Our enemies have declared this very intention, and have been caught seeking these terrible weapons. They want the capability to blackmail us, or to harm us, or to harm our friends."[52]

Defense transformation, in the mind of its advocates, amounts to nothing less than innovation on a grand scale—on a par with the comprehensive technological and organizational revolutions that created the Patton tank strategy of late 1944, or the U.S. Navy carrier task forces and Marine Corps amphibious warfare capability of World War II.[53] Driven by the exigencies of ongoing conflict in Iraq and elsewhere, these advocates see it as a crucially important matter for national security: Paul Wolfowitz notes the precedent of the battle tank—deployed first by the British and French during World War I, but used decisively as a weapon against them during the German blitzkrieg of 1940, when they failed to grasp its potential as rapidly as their adversary.[54]

Broadly speaking, defense transformation is seen as pursuing three key imperatives, compelled by the global struggle against terrorism and its potential linkages to weapons of mass destruction. Those perceived imperatives are: *speed, intelligence,* and *precision.*[55] Changes in technology, including military hardware, are one element of the response, emphasized by many defense contractors and many Pentagon officials as well. Yet technology is *not,* in the Wolfowitz vision, at least, the sole—or even the most central—aspect of defense transformation. Resource shifts and organizational change are also in his conception highly important and synergistic with technological change.[56]

Transformation began, in the view of many defense analysts, during the Clinton administration, or even before. General Eric Shinseki, U.S. Army Chief of Staff during 1999–2003, in the view of some, "began transforming the Army as soon as he came in."[57] Elements of the army, such as the Third Mechanized Division, reportedly organized to meet modern threats well before then Secretary of Defense Donald Rumsfeld took office.

During the first George W. Bush administration, transformation meant cancellation of several major Cold War weapons systems, such as the Army Crusader artillery system, the Navy's DD-21 future surface combatant program, and the Army's Comanche stealth helicopter program, and the redirection of resources toward more mobile "smart ordnance," such as the Excalibur artillery round, capable of ten-meter accuracy.[58] It also meant a reinforced emphasis on joint, interservice operations, given new momentum by the progress of digital technology. As Wolfowitz noted, it led to such incongruous but effective combinations, employed in the Afghan War of 2001, as Special Forces troops, mounted nineteenth-century style on horseback for mobility in the rugged Afghan terrain, calling in air strikes from fifty-year-old Air Force B-52s, using advanced twenty-first-century communications.[59]

Defense transformation clearly implies, to its advocates, major shifts in U.S. global-basing patterns, to enhance mobility and to adapt to the political-military implications of technological change. Both *security* and *strategy* clearly mandate such an approach, they argue. As Paul Wolfowitz pointed out in 2002, "U.S. forces depend on vulnerable foreign bases to operate—creating incentives for adversaries to develop 'access denial' capabilities to keep us out of their neighborhoods. We must, therefore, reduce our dependence on predictable and vulnerable base structure."[60] This security element of the base equation means both missile defense and enhanced conventional security for existing bases, and possible redeployment of U.S. forces, as in South Korea, away from "tripwire" roles into areas where they are more secure and effective.

General James Jones, post-9/11 commander of U.S. forces in Europe, also stressed the strategic implications of defense transformation for basing. During the spring and summer of 2003, in particular, he talked frequently of rotating troops from "Old Europe," particularly Germany, to light, temporary camps, or lily pads, in countries of the "New Europe," such as Bulgaria, Romania, and Poland, as well as African nations like Djibouti and Central Asian countries such as Kyrgyzstan.[61] The strategic rationale was to be close to the often ungoverned areas of developing, predominantly Islamic, regions where terrorists were thought to dwell. In 2004, as the U.S.-German frictions over the Iraq War dissipated, and as German lobbying in Washington, D.C., intensified, the political momentum for major redeployment away from "Old Europe" began to wane. Whatever the local political constraints in individual host nations, however, defense transformation for the Pentagon does continue to mean substantial down-sizing of the massive "Malls-of-America" fixed bases of the Cold War period—many of them located in Germany—and a redeployment of forces to multiple lily-pad facilities scattered across the Middle East, Africa, and Central Asia.[62]

WEIGHING THE ALTERNATIVES FOR AMERICA

It is not easy to judge the alternative approaches outlined above. Each presents a critical dimension of the new national-security realities that this nation urgently confronts in the twenty-first century. Yet a coherent approach to the policy prescriptions outlined in the next chapter requires that we make our standpoint clear.

In choosing among the alternatives presented here, three decision-criteria seem central. First, an ideal approach must take full account of the historic revolution in military affairs now underway, and maximize its prospective benefits for national security, subject to reasonable political constraints. Second, this approach should be sensitive to the delicate global political-economic context in which bases are embedded—particularly the implications of global security interdependence for financial-system stability and alliance credibility. Finally, in considering bilateral relations, the ideal strategy needs to be mindful of both national and local interests and concerns.

The Fortress America and the Defense Transformation approaches have the particular strength of sensitivity to the historic changes in defense technology now underway. Yet both largely ignore the important diplomatic and host-nation political contexts within which base politics are also inevitably embedded, as well as the substantial economic costs of redeployment.[63] The dangers of such political and diplomatic insensitivity are clearly apparent in recent base-politics frictions with a variety of established allies, including South Korea, Germany, and Japan—not to mention Iraq.

When diplomacy, host-nation politics, and international economic stability are factored in, there is much to be said, beyond the turbulence of the conflict in Iraq, for an updated, appropriately downsized version of Classic Pax Americana as an ultimate substantive goal. A substantial basing presence in the three corners of the trilateral world, after all, continues to help stabilize both Europe and Asia, as it has since the Korean War, by inhibiting conflict among large regional powers, such as Germany, Russia, Japan, and China. Large basing complexes in nations like Japan, Italy, and Germany, drawing on the considerable investments America has already made there, can also support action in more unstable parts of the world, such as the Middle East.

The critical outstanding issue is clearly "how to get from here to there." In that area incrementalism, which counsels deliberation, careful preparation, and marginal change, together with a cool-headed understanding of national interest, has much to recommend it. The driving force is not timidity, but a sober realization of the delicacy of the international financial system, and the complexities of global political-economic interdependence. America may need to downsize its global presence, and act less audaciously, but the need for its global leadership is enduring.

The uncomfortable realities of terrorism and deepening global resource-interdependence create strong arguments for some residual basing presence in the "arc of instability" across the developing world—albeit often small-scale, highly mobile, and temporary—that a Fortress America approach cannot provide. How this presence should be configured, how change in preferred directions should be managed, and how American military deployments in the industrialized nations should be stabilized are the primary prescriptive concerns of chapter 10. In that next, concluding chapter, we present our conclusions for policy, based on the evidence and the alternatives suggested in these pages.

CHAPTER TEN

IMPLICATIONS FOR POLICY AND THEORY

We HAVE ARGUED strongly throughout this study that base politics around the world shares, across cultures and political systems, certain core characteristics that make it possible to meaningfully compare on a cross-national basis. American bases everywhere are in the post-Iraq era now in prospect to some degree embattled garrisons. Yet their relative vulnerability to host-nation pressures varies considerably across the globe.

In chapter 3 we presented five hypotheses about base politics in general, to explore across the broad universe of more than ninety host nations where UN P-5 military forces have been based in substantial numbers for extended periods since the outbreak of the Korean War. At last it is time to return to them, and to summarize what we have learned. Then we must draw implications both for theory and for policy in the turbulent and trying times that the concept of forward deployment now confronts around the world.

EMPIRICAL FINDINGS: A BRIEF REVIEW

The first of our propositions, the Contact Hypothesis, was a demographically and geographically rooted contention: "Base-community conflict is a function of how frequently and intensely base inhabitants and the general host-nation community interact." We have found, in the world of cold, everyday life, that civil-military contact indeed predictably generates grassroots pressures that threaten to enflame base relations. Popular discontent with the negative, everyday externalities of bases—noise, crime, and broader environmental pollution, just to cite the most basic—clearly appears to be greater in crowded countries like Korea than in less populated nations like Germany and Italy. And the same proposition also tends to hold within host nations also—frictions are predictably greater around bases in crowded Seoul and in suburban Kyonggi province surrounding Seoul than they are in rural areas of Korea.

Our investigation did, however, also reveal that mitigating, intervening variables help shape the actual impact that social contact has on base politics. When bases develop strong, integral relations with local communities, and culture conflict is minimal, the destabilizing impact of contact in crowded areas appears to be reduced. These positive conditions clearly seem to have pertained in West German base towns such as Wiesbaden during the 1950s, for example.[1]

The nature of the contact stimulus also makes a difference. Routine accidents and criminal incidents do not appear to stimulate as sharp a backlash in areas of low population density as in high-density areas. Major changes in basing parameters—such as the 2006 proposals for redeployment of carrier aircraft to Iwakuni, Japan—can, however, stir fierce opposition, even in a low-density area.

National administrative centralization also makes a big difference. Where national governments have strong control over subunits, such as provinces and municipalities, as in Japan, base politics tends to be more stable, given constant demographic parameters. This is true even when chronically dissatisfied local areas—such as Okinawa—exist.

National governments, after all, tend to be dominated by cosmopolitan actors with clear stakes in international relations, and incentives to overrule grassroots interests when necessary. In decentralized systems, such as recent-day South Korea, by contrast, where more local-government autonomy prevails, base politics tend to be more confrontational and chaotic. Local leaders and interest groups, with stronger incentives to nonagreement, have more influence, and more freedom to express their parochial views in uninhibited fashion, than in more centralized political systems.

An important related issue, generally neglected in conventional analyses of base politics, is thus how political structure is trending. The clear pattern across both the advanced and developing worlds is toward decentralization and pluralism, as has occurred in South Korea since 1987, and as is beginning to happen even in Japan as well. *This decentralization will likely have a destabilizing impact on base politics* that as yet is not widely perceived, or whose links to changes in political structure are not well appreciated.

An extreme and much more visible form of this tendency for pluralism to complicate base politics can be seen in failing states of the developing world. Iraq, of course, is a dramatic case in point. The erosion of its central governing authority has made local base politics highly complex, and entrapped U.S. forces in a cross-fire of domestic ethnic conflict. It is crucial, beyond Iraq, that American forces avoid failing states where they do not credibly establish themselves as liberators, on all but a very short-term basis.

Our second proposition, the Colonization Hypothesis, that "colonial experience substantially reduces the prospect of stable foreign base tenure in a host country," was strongly confirmed by our data. Indeed, we found that in almost every instance where a U.S., British, French, or

Russian base was established through colonial succession, that base has now disappeared. The only exceptions are in Guantanamo Bay, Cuba, where the United States and Cuba lack operating diplomatic relations; in Cyprus and Brunei, where special British political understandings, embedded in independence arrangements, continue to prevail; and in a few former French colonies, where Paris maintains ongoing neocolonial ties. Although the decolonization process is now largely completed, it has long-term negative implications for the stability of base politics wherever its heritage exists.

Our third contention, the Occupation Hypothesis that liberating occupations by a noncolonial power lead to stable base politics," was also largely confirmed by our study. Italy, Germany, and Japan, continents apart, appear to have the most stable patterns in the world of host-nation support for American forces, despite the once-bitter struggle they conducted against the United States during World War II. South Korea, however, which was also occupied from 1945–48, provides an intriguing partial exception to this hopeful pattern that reveals the causal dynamics behind the broader rule.

In the former three cases of occupation—Italy, Germany, and Japan—Americans were unambiguously received as liberators. They clearly opposed the preexisting dictatorial regime, were locally perceived as rejecting imperialist pretensions, and fostered positive, noncollaborationist elements in local civil society. In Korea, by contrast, occupation forces were *not* so well accepted, due to their aloof and collaborationist bias, leading to initially troubled base relations, expunged only by the Korean War. The problem of Korea's early postwar American occupiers was simple: lack of a clear "liberation strategy" led to their falling unwittingly into the company of collaborationists, generating the attendant host-nation resistance to colonial-master surrogates alluded to above.

The Occupation Hypothesis also appears to be intriguingly relevant in the contemporary Islamic world, as was noted in chapter 5, with major implications for U.S. policy. In the Balkans (1990s), and to some extent in Afghanistan (2001–present), Western troops established themselves as liberators. Their presence was broadly accepted, making the longer-term prognosis for stability relatively bright, although problems remain. In Iraq, this crucial recognition did not occur, despite broad popular distaste for the prior dictatorship of Saddam Hussein, and the prognosis for stability—on domestic political grounds, at least, is correspondingly darker.

The problem of American occupiers in Iraq, in being unwittingly typecast as imperialists rather than liberators, has some parallels to the pre-1950 Korean case, or to those of the Philippines, Panama, and Cuba, albeit with more serious economic, political, and strategic implications in the volatile yet energy-rich Middle East. Unilateralism, a failure to designate local leaders early, vacillation on the issue of popular elections, early failure to provide elemental public services, including security, and a sweeping, arbitrary purge of government officials, all helped convert a promising potential liberation into a deepening, *avoidable* quagmire. So did hesitation in recreating local security forces, search-and-destroy operations insensitive to local conditions, and a lack of occupation forces sufficient to maintain order outside massive secure facilities like Baghdad's Green Zone, as the early legitimacy of the Coalition Provisional Authority steadily eroded.

The Regime-Shift Hypothesis, that "host-nation political regime shifts lead to basing-nation withdrawal," another pessimistic proposition, was also strongly, although not perfectly, confirmed by our data. Over the past half-century, basing nations have withdrawn in about 80 percent of the historical cases where "regime shifts" have occurred in nations hosting foreign military bases. And basing nations rarely withdraw otherwise. The major exception to this pattern is Britain, which has pursued the most realistic basing policy of any major power: strategic withdrawal. The British have been generally rewarded with better relations to erstwhile host nations as a consequence, where they have followed this policy, and have avoided the dangers of overextension more effectively than the French or the Russians. Strategic withdrawal unfortunately has only limited applicability for the United States, however, given the strategic and political-economic imperatives of its global role.

The Dictatorship Hypothesis, that "the United States tends to support dictators in nations where it enjoys basing facilities and often condones their creation in such nations," also sadly appears to be borne out in our analysis, albeit with some interesting nuance. U.S. governments *do* generally appear to have supported dictators in nations hosting American bases, and to a degree greater than in American foreign policy more generally. The second George W. Bush administration is an intriguing exception, at least insofar as its 2005 repudiation of Uzbek dictator Islam Karimov, following the Andijian massacre, even at the cost of its strategic Khanabad air base, is concerned.[2]

Congress, it should be noted, is often more skeptical of dictators, as well as generally more sensitive to human-rights violations, than is the White House. And U.S. presidents do often disengage from dictators they had previously supported when dictatorship leads, through the catalyst of a transparently flawed election, conducted by a politically vulnerable dictator, to major anti-regime unrest. Belated yet decisive repudiation of Marcos in the Philippines (1986), or Rhee in Korea (1960), are important examples of this phenomenon.

IMPLICATIONS FOR POLICY

Beyond the details of the specific arguments that we have considered here, this research suggests, in the aggregate, a powerful cautionary note to base-politics managers in the United States and other basing nations of the post-9/11 world. America's overseas bases are now, and will likely remain, in the world beyond Iraq—a key cornerstone of both global political-economic stability and U.S. national security. Yet bases are also profoundly—and increasingly—embedded in their local political-economic contexts. As the scope of American forward deployment unavoidably broadens to more nations, and especially to a larger number of *unstable* developing nations, in the continuing global struggle against terrorism, host-nation base politics will become central to U.S. national security. Yet they will also grow more problematic. Coping with base politics abroad, under a variant of the "incrementalist" orientation outlined above, will require a much more comprehensive policy approach than has been apparent in Washington thus far, with manifestations at three levels: grand strategy, host-nation strategy, and host-nation tactics.

Grand Strategy

This research suggests a number of maxims, directed toward the distinctive strategic and tactical challenges for America's embattled garrisons that now loom on the horizon. In the area of grand strategy—this country's overall global approach to the problem of forward deployment—we conclude the following.

1. **BEWARE OF OVEREXTENSION.** The problem has been most starkly and dramatically illustrated by the decline of the once-proud British Empire, which since the mid-1970s has retained bases outside its possessions only in Brunei, Germany, Cyprus, and—recently—in Iraq. The difficult political-economic circumstances that caused Britain to sharply downsize its basing network over the past two generations are obviously somewhat different from those which the United States confronts today. To be sure, the United States looms much larger in the global political-economic system, with both greater capabilities, and larger ongoing responsibilities than did even Imperial Britain. In 2005, for example, America's national defense budget amounted to $423 billion, or more than double the total of all other major powers combined, and more than eight times that of current British defense spending.[3]

Greater global capital mobility clearly allows the contemporary United States to sustain larger financial imbalances today than could the

United Kingdom a generation ago.[4] Yet rising American deficits and a weakening U.S. dollar suggest that some significant political-economic constraints on American power may well exist. The British experience in managing constraints, establishing basing priorities, smoothly downsizing, and maintaining influence—despite limited military and financial resources—are therefore of more relevance to American policy than is often appreciated. Britain's earlier imperial experience also provides useful benchmarks in global political coordination for the world's current sole superpower.

Among the concrete lessons for America regarding overextension, flowing from past British base politics experience, are the following.

1. Nations benefit from being realistic about their economic capacity to sustain large militaries. Britain realized its limits early—especially when led by Labour governments. Clement Attlee saw the dangers of overextension in Greece, Turkey, and India during 1946–47; Harold Wilson did so similarly with respect to Southeast Asia in the mid-1970s.

2. Retrenching powers must be alert to the geopolitical implications of their cutbacks, and take steps to offset them. Britain eased the strategic impact of its withdrawal "East of Suez" of the 1960s and 1970s, for example, by aiding the United States in establishing the joint Diego Garcia air and naval facilities in the Indian Ocean. For the last two decades, Diego Garcia has allowed the United States, in cooperation with Britain, to exercise enormous political-military leverage in the Persian Gulf and South Asia, even when it has lacked substantial direct territorial presence there.

3. Basing nations need to be eclectic in their mixture of unilateral and multilateral orientations. The British, for example, accepted some limited involvement by both France and Turkey in their strategic Egyptian protectorate before World War I.[5]

4. Basing nations can benefit politically by professing their desire to downsize and withdraw, even while being slow to implement such plans. Britain, for example, combined sixty-six formal promises to withdraw its troops from Egypt with seventy-two sustained years of occupation.[6]

French base politics, while demonstrating the "virtues," for the basing nation, of neocolonial elite cooptation, also illustrates the political costs of overextension. In a pattern unique among the great powers, the French military presence has been expelled every time there has been a regime shift in a nation hosting French troops over the past half-century—*without exception*. French politicians, bureaucrats, and military personnel typically grow so close to the incumbent regime, in the nations like Ivory Coast, Gabon, and Senegal that host French troops for extended periods, that when the regime changes abruptly, its successor has strong incentives to throw French forces out. And the French, unlike the British, never strategically withdraw, preferring to extract the rising economic costs of sustaining overseas military presence from the host countries themselves, in neocolonialist fashion.

2. MAKE POLITICAL RISK REDUCTION A PRIORITY. Precisely due to the potential perversity of host-nation base politics, it needs to be avoided and neutralized where realistically possible. Concretely, this means, first of all, locating large, strategically important bases involving substantial capital investment—for which permanence is obviously important—in politically invulnerable areas. Diego Garcia in the nonself-governing British Indian Ocean Territory (BIOT), roughly 3,000 miles southeast of the Persian Gulf, is one such ideal location. Guam, although a self-governing Commonwealth, features a nearly comparable strategic environment,[7] being located deep in the western Pacific within range of Asia, in stable political association with the United States.[8]

American strategy, of course, cannot ignore the stark reality that many emerging national-security challenges loom in unstable developing nations, especially in or near energy-rich Islamic countries where political risk is inherently high. The United States can best deal with this grim reality by basing in small, politically stable nations on the periphery of troubled areas that have strong geopolitical reasons to ally with America, and under any circumstances far from major cities. Energy-rich Qatar, on the Persian Gulf, which houses CENTCOM's Middle East operations center at the sprawling al-Udeid Air Base, is an illustration of the sort of basing that the United States should seek in the Islamic world.

There are other things America can do to reduce the inherent risks of base politics, apart from seeking depoliticized basing locations or considering how to reduce the necessity of overseas bases in general. For example, giving some priority to rapid-deployment forces, including Special Forces that are deployable quickly from the United States itself, or the territory of close allies, is one constructive option.[9] *Diversifying deployments* to multiple redundant locations, in areas where at least some facilities are imperative, also reduces the political risk of dependence on any one. So does the recent disposition among American forces in the developing world toward smaller bases—forward-operating locations (FOLs), or "lily pads"—that involve more limited costs, and hence lower political-economic risk. In counterinsurgency situations, operating bases, ideally small, need to be in reasonable proximity to the population, to facilitate protecting them, without disrupting their daily lives.[10]

3. "DEAL WITH DEMOCRACIES" IS TOO SIMPLE A MAXIM. It has recently been fashionable to argue that "democracies invariably turn out to be more reliable hosts in the end."[11] This admonition coincides with inclinations broadly shared by many Americans, both liberal and neo-conservative. Yet it has, we have found, only limited utility as a practical guide to policy.

Some mature democracies, such as Britain, Japan, and Italy, we have found, have indeed proven to be politically stable sites for U.S. basing over the past several decades. Shared values most closely approximates a sufficient explanation in the British case, but our subnational analysis of the non-Anglo-Saxon nations uncovered multiple alternative economic and structural factors there, such as high levels of compensation, sophisticated mediating institutions, and decentralized mechanisms for capturing grassroots opinion that also played important stabilizing roles. That "shared democratic values" alone are not even a sufficient condition for base-politics stability—even in mature democracies—is clearly apparent in the French case, where American forces were asked to leave that clearly democratic nation in the mid-1960s.

In transitional democracies, which comprise the largest group of nations into with U.S. forces have deployed since 9/11, the challenge of base politics is clearly often very severe. Iraq is only one of several vexing cases in point. In emerging democracies from Korea to Kyrgyzstan—also including the Philippines, Spain, Greece, and Turkey—problems of base-politics management have often been more challenging for the United States than under autocratic rule.

This difficult transitional reality is not sufficient reason to prefer dealing with dictators, or to inhibit political transition, as U.S. administrations typically, although not universally, did until the mid-1980s. Clearly democratic successors—in Spain, Portugal, Greece, and the Philippines, to name a few—have resented friendly U.S. government dealings with their dictatorial predecessors, suggesting, in hindsight, the value of an arms-length approach. Yet this vague, general maxim does not provide an adequate guide for policy in a world where strategic, operational, and country-specific institutional considerations must also figure into the policy equation. More refined parameters, flowing from history and subnational structural context, are clearly needed.

4. **LIBERATING OCCUPIERS ARE ACCEPTABLE, BUT COLONIZERS ARE NOT.** Douglas MacArthur's seemingly imperial approach worked in devastated postwar Japan, as did that of Lucius Clay in Germany. But that was because the United States provided a credible prospect of personal liberation through universal suffrage, land reform, and economic liberalization, in addition to public order, while avoiding neocolonial designs. It helped that America had no previous record of imperial involvement with these nations. The U.S. presence in the Balkans and Afghanistan has

shown elements of the same positive, early postwar pattern, the Islamic background of local hosts in both of the latter cases notwithstanding.

Other great powers have had on occasion similar positive experiences as liberating occupiers. The French in Central Europe, Italy, and the Balkans during the Napoleonic Wars; the Russians in Bulgaria for a century after the Crimean War; and the British in Ethiopia after liberation from Mussolini are all cases in point. It is possible for foreign troops of powerful nations to be welcomed abroad when they are clearly seen as the agents of national liberation.

Base relations have been much poorer, however, in postcolonial situations where the basing nation was the former colonial power. In such cases, of which the Philippines was one and Panama another, foreign bases have invariably been removed, as they were in most former British and French colonies after independence. Soviet troops were widely detested in Eastern Europe after World War II, with Bulgaria a partial exception, and were forced by host-nation domestic political pressures to withdraw soon after the fall of the Berlin Wall. This fateful contrast between "liberating occupation," on the one hand, and "colonization," on the other, has major implications for American policy now, and will continue to matter in future years.

Clearly the local backlash produced by an explicit occupation during 2003–2004, coupled with the brutality of search-and-destroy missions, concentration of forces in large operating bases, and the sordid legacy of Abu-Ghraib, have caused the United States major subsequent base-politics difficulties in Iraq. To understand the apparent contradictions in the often hostile host-nation response to American deployments there, and acceptance expressed in former Axis nations like Japan and Germany, it is well to remember the distinctive historical heritage of Mesopotamia, Iraq's early twentieth-century precursor.

Mesopotamia, now Iraq, experienced years of British imperial rule during the 1920s,[12] as it suffered the unfortunate missteps of Anglo-American intervention nearly eighty years later. That latter intervention toppled a brutal Saddam Hussein dictatorship in 2003. Yet it so badly mishandled the aftermath that it failed to earn credit for the liberation, and triggered a sharp, understandable, but arguably unmerited, "anti-imperialist" counterreaction. To be sure, the underlying, historically embedded obstacles to success in Iraq were substantial, albeit difficult in many cases to perceive, in advance of the 2003 toppling of Saddam's regime.[13] Yet the conclusion that the prospects for allied success were sharply, critically, and probably unnecessarily reduced by an unprepared and culturally naïve occupation seems inescapable.

The Iraq debacle has involved a multitude of occupation-period missteps that arguably did not need to happen. Apart from Anglo-American bilateral dominance of the Coalition Provisional Authority, its clear-cut occupation character, abrupt dissolution of the military, purge of even minor Baathist functionaries, and appointment for more than a year of an American resident administrator who, although able, had virtually no area or language expertise, all contributed to later difficulties. Vacillation with respect to democratic reforms, failure to rapidly reconstitute an Iraqi security force, and insufficient on-the-ground allied troop strength also contributed to the burgeoning insurgency.[14] America *could* have been a liberating occupier. But that, sadly, was not how its troubled involvement came to be perceived by the Iraqi people in the CPA's critical early days.[15]

The political challenges to foreign military presence so evident in Iraq need to be neutralized in the post-Iraq world by a comprehensive base-politics program that systematically recognizes and learns from the Iraqi experience. Use of flexible, rotating deployments through a dispersed network of bases; frequent joint exercises; enhanced prepositioning under more flexible American legislation; and private, local security guards to relieve troops of routine security functions could all be helpful.[16] The United States, to be sure, has extensively used highly expensive American private contractors to support the military in Iraq, but it has delegated them so much discretion that their financial-incentive structure, rather than broader national purposes such as political conciliation, have dominated America's on-the-ground presence, with often perverse consequences.[17]

Some successful innovations during the Iraq years deserve to be retained and built upon—particularly those that have reinforced the latitude for local commanders to reach out to local communities. The Commander's Emergency Response Program, which provides money to local U.S. officers to put civilians to work as a way of reducing resistance to American presence in individual neighborhoods, is a case in point. Provincial Reconstruction Teams (PRTs), consisting of State Department officers embedded with combat brigades, to coordinate local reconstruction efforts, mainly by hiring Iraqi companies, have also proven useful, although their scale of operation has been less than in some previous counterinsurgency conflicts.[18] The key overall functional requirement is to respond flexibly and in a timely fashion to local socioeconomic needs and incentive structures.

On the political side, the difficult yet crucial imperative is for Americans to be perceived and accepted as liberators rather than as imperialists. Multilateral military sponsorship, regionalization of security responsibilities, rapid transition to local independent leadership, and reliance where possible on the informal local power structure are some concrete maxims for achieving these fundamentally political goals.[19] American actions in Afghanistan, where the United States rapidly installed a national leader who had spent much of his adult life in the United States, gave

Hamid Karzai special legitimacy by first parachuting him into the country to fight with anti-Taliban resistance forces and then cooperating with European allies to convene a *loya jirga* legitimating his rule within months of victory. These successful initial steps suggest that politically sensitive legitimation strategies initiated by the United States can be fruitful even in the Islamic world.[20] Such strategies can, as early local support for Karzai showed, both dispel perceptions of Americans as imperialists, and also enhance the image of the United States as liberator.

The British experience with base politics and liberal empire provides both positive and negative lessons for future American policies. The British experience with counterinsurgency in Malaya, to be sure, provided the U.S. military with important, positive lessons for their operations in Vietnam and Iraq.[21] Yet British behavior in the Suez crisis is a powerful illustration of the more negative pattern.[22] The British responded petulantly and aggressively to Nasser's populist baiting, blundering into a misguided collaborative attack on Egypt that was oblivious both to the transnational power of Arab nationalism and the misgivings of their American allies. Britain's ill-fated conspiracy with the French and Israelis cost them basing presence and political-military standing not only in Egypt, but also in Jordan, Aden, and elsewhere across the Arab world. Indeed, the uncharacteristic jingoism of Whitehall's Suez fiasco, with its single-minded focus on a military solution without regard to political context, greatly accelerated the decline of a British global standing that had previously been sustained well beyond the U.K's long-term economic capabilities by its generally adroit, sensitive diplomacy.

5. VIEW BASING IMPERATIVES IN A GLOBAL SYSTEMIC CONTEXT. It is crucial, in an era of increasing potential mobility, to look beyond the bricks and mortar of specific facilities to their underlying global strategic rationale. Logistical imperatives, to be sure, create an understandable status-quo bias within the uniformed military for maintaining existing facilities around the world. America's military has, for example, made huge investments in fuel depots, warehouse facilities, ammunition dumps, hospitals, and communications facilities in Germany, Okinawa, and Diego Garcia that give them an enduring logic as base locations, if only for financial reasons. Indeed, it would cost nearly $6 billion to replace Kadena Air Base in Okinawa, together with its nearby ammunition-storage annex, and at least $3.5 billion to recreate the sprawling Ramstein Air Base in Germany.[23] Bureaucratic inertia and local politics tend to intensify this conservative bias held by the U.S. military, which was for many years also reinforced by the static security imperatives of the Cold War.

Strategy in the post–Cold War world, however, imposes very different demands. With the end of bipolar confrontation against the Soviet Union, both the military need for large, fixed forward land bases in Central Europe and their strategic utility in providing extended deterrence have waned. A parallel pattern is also evolving more slowly in Northeast Asia.

Conversely, rising lift capacity and better communications, including a sophisticated global satellite infrastructure, are making it easier and easier to move both equipment and people rapidly around the world. As we have noted, the U.S. military moved more troops and equipment in the first three weeks of the Gulf War than it did in the first three months of the Korean War. And the military's flexibility has risen substantially since then. The military is also prepositioning large and increasing amounts of equipment at strategic locations worldwide. Indeed, the number of prepositioned supply ships the U.S. military has stationed around the world has risen from twenty-five to more than forty over the past decade.[24]

There is also a new strategic imperative for flexibility and speed in U.S. deployments, reinforced by post-9/11 developments. Just as logistical and communications constraints are being relaxed, the need for access is rising, especially in parts of the developing world that were never the site of major Western bases during the Cold War. That is especially true with respect to remote, ungoverned areas in Africa, Central Asia, and the Middle East, where terrorists can easily hide, train, and conspire. The consequence of these post-9/11 imperatives is new demand for lightly prepared facilities—even prepositioned equipment coupled with SOFAs and other legal understandings that permit flexible access—into which U.S. forces can flexibly and rapidly move at short notice, when military conditions require.

The bottom line is that basing imperatives need to be seen in a *systemic* context. The system as a whole is global, and individual bases play varying functional roles within it. They may well thus be increasingly distinct in their responsibilities.

One partial paradigm for the future in this regard is what might be called the "Singapore Model," as we noted in chapter 2. Strategically deployed American forces are central to the overall political-military equation in Singapore, but small in number and low in profile. Military infrastructure, including ports, air fields, repair facilities, hospitals, and communications, is first-rate. There are also major caches of prepositioned equipment in place.

Quiet contingency arrangements for how a major troop influx would be handled have been systematically made. In the event of a regional contingency, a smooth, rapid buildup would be easy to achieve. And under normal peacetime circumstances, the U.S. presence can efficiently serve major logistical functions, from cutting paychecks to coordinating tsunami relief by American forces across Southeast Asia and the Indian Ocean.

Singapore-type operations are a powerful complement, as part of America's global-security system, to more narrowly military facilities like Guam or Diego Garcia, which provide power projection. Singapore-style technical functions could reasonably be located in several diverse parts of the world. Small island or peninsular states such as Qatar or Bahrain could play analogous roles in the Middle East, and in fact already do so to some degree. And the "Singapore model" of low-profile militar-support facilities and highly operational contingency arrangements could also potentially be applied in Latin America, or even Africa, although Singapore-style operational efficiency would be hard to match anywhere.

6. OPPOSITION GROUPS ARE GOING GLOBAL, SO POLICYMAKERS NEED TO DO SO ALSO. One of the key findings of this volume, graphically demonstrated in the Vieques, Okinawa, and South Korean cases, for example, is that many opposition groups have detailed knowledge of parallel activities elsewhere in the world. And such groups are increasingly coordinating transnationally, particularly via the Internet, often linked by "rooted cosmopolitans" that are influential in multiple societies.[25] Both dissidents and most host-nation governments negotiating with the United States are also acutely aware of inconsistencies in U.S. policy from country to country, and exchange information on such matters also, as the Korean, German, and Okinawan cases presented above make graphically clear.

Host-nation governments, like dissident groups, also increasingly look abroad for benchmarks elsewhere in the world by which to establish positive policy parameters. When they negotiate SOFAs or lease payments, in particular, they are often keenly aware of precedents in other countries, as well as their own unique strategic positions. The bazaar-politics paradigm, epitomized in the Philippine, Turkish, and Kyrgyzstani cases presented in chapter 6, shows this global-consciousness pattern and its policy implications especially well.

It is a natural impulse for American policymakers, faced with the growing cosmopolitanism of both their antagonists and their ostensible allies, to embrace standardization. Doing so supposedly helps to minimize cross-pressures from different nations, and from varied interest groups within them, not to mention criticism from the U.S. Congress. As suggested below, policymakers need to resist this tendency to homogenize political approaches, even as they consolidate standards, except where they have strong strategic or political-military reasons for uniformity.[26] At the same time, however, decision makers clearly need a practical means of becoming systematically conscious, in a world of information overload, of just what transnational cross-pressures they confront.

Host-Nation Strategy

American basing policy needs to consider not only broad questions of global location, and general issues of political risk, but also how to respond to specific countries. As we have found, nations vary sharply, depending on culture, history, and institutional context, in their response to foreign militaries on their soil. Yet many of these striking differences are predictable, and U.S. policy must take them more systematically into account.

This volume suggests three important ways that American policy can better relate to the varied national base-politics environments that it confronts.

1. BE ALERT TO THE DANGERS OF POLITICAL TRANSITION. Recent Washington political rhetoric has acclaimed the virtues of political change—especially the coming of democracy—for America's national security. This volume suggests a more cautious stance. While welcoming democracy on philosophical grounds, policy must be alert to the complications it generally poses for base politics. The foregoing analysis has shown that the likelihood of foreign military forces ultimately withdrawing in the wake of a domestic political regime shift in a nation hosting them has been 80 percent for the UN P-5 nations over the past half-century, with most of the regime shifts democratic, and most of the withdrawals involuntary. Russia lost every one of its bases in Eastern Europe, Mongolia, and ultimately even Vietnam and Cuba with the fall of the Berlin Wall, and only retained bases in seven of the fifteen former Soviet republics.[27] Britain and France similarly lost most of their overseas bases in the wake of decolonization and democratization, as noted in table 2.1.

Even in the case of American bases the likelihood of withdrawal following regime shifts—of which Iraq's democratization represents one— has been 67 percent. And the prospect of regime shifts in other Middle East, Central Asian, and African nations into which the United States has recently begun to pour its troops is on the historical record substantial.

Where regime shifts do not compel American forces to withdraw, historical experience shows that such developments still provoke thorny, often unexpected problems in base relations, with which local U.S. military-liaison personnel, and even local American embassies, prove ill-equipped to deal. Democratization in Spain, Portugal, Greece, Turkey, South Korea, and even Kyrgyzstan, for example, all provoked major host-nation escalation in base-rental financial demands. Democratization has also often led to new agitation for revision of SOFAs, thorough environmental clean-ups, restrictions on third-country deployment of U.S. troops, and attempts to impose constraints on the deployment of American nuclear-capable forces. Democratization has also, not surprisingly, led in Iraq to escalating criticism of American troop behavior, demands for local trials of crimes committed by U.S. servicemen, insistent requests for operational constraints on the deployment of American forces there, and ultimately popular demands, however rhetorical, for American withdrawal.

In their extreme form, regime shifts can ultimately lead toward political chaos and the emergence of failed states, as occurred in Somalia in the 1980s and 1990s, Afghanistan in the 1990s, and as threatened to occur in Iraq during 2006–2007. To the extent that the antiterrorist struggle and geopolitics require a U.S. presence in failed states, the logic of this study suggests a pattern of "soft basing"—flexible, mobile, geographically remote from major population centers, and, ideally, detached from domestic ethnic conflicts. More substantial deployment in stable nations nearby is another complementary possibility.

2. NETWORKS COUNT: FOCUS ON BUILDING INCLUSIVE HOST-NATION POLITICAL NETWORKS, INCLUDING MEMBERS OF THE OPPOSITION. In an ideal political-military world, America's bases would all be insulated from local politics—either through location in secluded areas far from urban centers, or at apolitical sites such as Diego Garcia. Unfortunately such a configuration is unrealistic in many cases. Thus, policy must inevitably grapple with the hard problem of how to contend with host-nation political systems, including both national leadership and opposition.

Process tracing in concrete cases like the Philippines and Turkey suggests that inability to communicate and distorted mutual expectations are the problems that most typically cause host-nation regime shifts and usually lead to worsening base relations, that ultimately provoke foreign military withdrawals. And the lack of face-to-face listening intensifies the absence of trust that in turn produces communications failures.[28]

Consciously fostering local base-politics networks, including participants from opposition groups, in dealing with base issues can be a means of avoiding these problems, with informal policy-study groups involving local American diplomatic personnel and visiting academics being one option. Integrated, far-sighted teamwork between local embassies and U.S. civil-military liaison personnel is also crucial in stabilizing expectations and mutual understanding among key host-nation domestic political groups themselves. Such mediation can be especially important in multi-ethnic host nations, like Iraq, where stable, cooperative elite networks potentially can play a crucial role in inhibiting mass ethnic conflict. It is crucially important, however, for the spadework to begin before ethnic tensions escalate, as the Iraqi case so tragically shows.

3. STUDY BEST-PRACTICE INSTITUTIONS EVERYWHERE, AND SHARE THE UNDERSTANDING OF CROSS-NATIONAL EXPERIENCE. The quality of base relations varies sharply around the world, this study has found. Part of this variation no doubt reflects varying local perceptions of American forces themselves. Yet another part of the variation is clearly *institutional*. Institutions, like history, matter greatly to base politics, this study has found, and can make a substantial difference to how smoothly functional policy outcomes are achieved. In both Spain and Korea, for example, an authoritarian institutional heritage of fiat politics, the product of long-time military rule, greatly complicated base relations with the United States once democracy came. The experience of one was clearly relevant to the other in important respects, although the cross-regional connections were rarely made, and potential lessons may have gone unlearned. Similarly, the counterintuitive stability of base politics in Italy and Portugal, as compared with their relative volatility in neighboring Spain and Greece, may suggest lessons also relevant elsewhere in the world.

Where inconsistencies or inequities exist in the treatment of host nations, those are increasingly apparent and toxic in the digitally globalized Internet age now dawning. Opposition groups can easily unveil and advertise cross-national inconsistencies in SOFAs, HNS agreements, and local handling of individual base problems. The U.S. government needs to stay ahead of the competition, and address inequities where it can.

Conversely, best practices in base relations should be broadly known and disseminated. Developing, centralizing, and sharing a cross-national understanding of base-politics experience, and acting on the implications, could measurably improve base relations in individual cases. It could also reduce the hypocrisy and naïveté regarding cross-national comparisons that in turn undermines the credibility of the officers handling those relationships.

The U.S.-Japan and the U.S.-Italian bilateral security relationships, in particular, appear to have developed institutions for managing base relations that are especially effective and that bear further analysis, oriented toward adapting them more broadly. In Italy, the practice of decentralizing base negotiations, thus allowing localities to customize their own specific accommodations with individual bases in their locality, deserves further study. Italy, interestingly, is the only NATO nation with which the United States never signed a bilateral SOFA, leading to a patchwork of localized frameworks for base relations, which has, surprisingly, turned out quite well.

Japanese institutions for handling base relations, and the American willingness to adapt to them, have likewise proven quite functional. Concretely, the Japanese Defense Facilities Administration Agency (DFAA) appears to have helped significantly in stabilizing base relations by rapidly and flexibly compensating aggrieved parties at the grassroots. It has also served effectively as a monitoring mechanism for local feedback regarding American bases.

As noted earlier, local communities with bases in their vicinity are typically a pivotal constituency in Japanese base politics. And their orientation toward the local base presence turns critically on the quality of communication with, and support from, higher authority that they receive. The DFAA, together with the U.S.-Japan Joint Committee on Security Relations, and region-specific, targeted institutions like the Special Action Committee on Okinawa (SACO), help to address this classic base-politics problem of local-national interface in ways that may be of relevance elsewhere in the world.

Community-liaison mechanisms with American forces in Germany have also been successful, as noted earlier, and many bear emulation. U.S.-German Friendship Weeks involving the U.S. military and military participation in German festivals have worked well in cementing base relations since the 1950s.[29] At a more operational level, in February 2003 the city of Kaiserslautern in the Rheinland opened a German-American Community Office as a drop-in point for both American and German citizens, to help local American military and their dependents with German administrative matters, while also providing general information on the city and its surrounding region.[30]

Half a world away, USFJ also encourages social interaction with local Okinawan communities in order to deepen mutual understanding and foster friendship. Henoko City, Okinawa, which hosts the marines' Camp Schwab, holds an annual "Henoko Sport Day," inaugurated in 1973. Kadena Air Base similarly has organized a "Kadena Special Olympics" annually since 2000. This now involves 5,000 people, including 1,500 American volunteers drawn from a wide range of other bases as well as Kadena.[31] In order to consider more systematic steps to improve communication in Okinawa, beyond these ad hoc, base-specific initiatives, a Tripartite Liaison Committee consisting of representatives from USFJ, the Japanese central government, and Okinawa Prefecture also meets periodically to discuss such questions.[32]

General Tony Zinni has pointed to the serious U.S. governmental problem of "stovepiping," or lack of sufficient horizontal communication. He cites the communications lapses between the state and defense departments, which compounded the political naïveté of the early occupation of Iraq, right after the fall of Baghdad, as a typical and important case in point. Zinni suggests establishing a National Monitoring and Planning Center (NMPC), with counterpart bodies at the operational and tactical levels, as a concrete first step toward resolving such difficulties.[33] Such a body could also be a useful clearinghouse for the sort of cross-national data on base relations that this study suggests is badly needed. An NMPC could also work through the policy implications of such cross-national comparison, and then disseminate, as appropriate, to counterparts in foreign governments.

Host Nation Tactics

Strategy, be it global or national, is not all there is to base politics, and base policy-making. Decision makers also need to think concretely about how to *realize* their key objectives. A few simple findings flowing from this research, centering on the crucial importance of political sensitivity in the implementation process, are also of relevance to that challenge as well.

1. **CONTACT MATTERS.** We have seen a strong, cross-national correlation between high population density and base frictions at the local level. Such a correlation also prevails to a remarkable degree, both cross-nationally and within individual host nations also. Limiting human interface between U.S. forces and local populations—where locations involving minimal contact are strategically feasible—may help to reduce political risk. Clearly contact matters. The policy implications, however, vary with the political-military context.

In a war-time situation, some forms of contact, such as patrolling, oriented toward increasing tactical intelligence and stabilizing the surrounding local socioeconomic environment, may well be a positive thing. The concentration of the American military in large, isolated forward operation bases, with huge logistical requirements, that make extensive land transportation over vulnerable road arteries necessary, has been cited as one major reason for their early failures in Iraq, for example.[34] The imperatives of counterinsurgency may imply a decentralized national presence and interactive relationships with local communities, as the December 2006 U.S. Army counterinsurgency manual suggests.[35]

In a peacetime situation, however, where the imperative of understanding and responding rapidly to mass popular sentiment is less immediate, limiting human interface between U.S. forces and local populations—where locations involving minimal contact is strategically feasible—may help to reduce the political risk.[36] There is value in mediating institutions like Japan's DFAA, as noted earlier, but broader, unstructured contact may be counterproductive, especially where wide cultural gaps prevail.[37]

The U.S. government should therefore seek to configure its basing, where militarily feasible, so as to be sensitive to the broader sociopolitical environment. Reliance on geographically remote bases, substitution of technical facilities like monitoring stations for conventional bases where possible, and prepositioning of equipment so as to reduce the need for continuously manned bases can all help to defuse prospects for unwanted conflict between U.S. forces and local civilians. In the Iraqi case, this means a "political Plan B" involving ultimate redeployment to congenial peripheral areas, once the overall political situation stabilizes, as was done in Saudi Arabia after the Khobar Barracks bombings of 1995, if American bases are to be maintained at all. One post-conflict alternative could be concentrated deployment in less-populated sections of relatively hospitable regions such as Kurdistan with additional contingency reserves, including Special Forces units, in Kuwait and possibly Jordan.[38]

In some cases, of course, strategy or operational realities may make it difficult or counterproductive to situate bases in remote locations—especially in highly populated nations like South Korea, Japan, or Germany. In counterinsurgency situations, close proximity to the populace, without disrupting daily lives, may be positive as has been noted.[39] Where urban or suburban locations are unavoidable or actually desirable, military public affairs strategies become especially important. The appearance of transparency and openness to contact—to the extent that it is consistent with operational realities—can significantly improve base relations. German-American "friendship weeks" and Okinawan base-community festivals are clear cases in point.[40]

2. BUILD COMMON EQUITIES, ESPECIALLY AT THE GRASSROOTS LEVEL. One of the central problems of base politics around the world, as we have seen, is that for local governments, NGOs, and individual citizens at the grassroots, the balance of costs and benefits relating to foreign bases is very strongly negative. Bases generate crime, noise, pollution, and other ills, while producing little perceived as positive. Their benefits, so typically obvious to leaders in a national capital, appear, at the grassroots, to accrue either to foreign contractors or to a very limited and exclusive community of local elites.

British experience with base politics, in the context of empire, is instructive for America now. The British consciously tried to give local groups *personal* stakes in their empire through symbiotic mechanisms such as indirect rule. The United States unfortunately was more direct, intrusive, and oblivious of local interests in the early stages of its Iraq involvement, as when its occupation abruptly and categorically abolished the Iraqi police and military, although Washington has fortunately revised this approach somewhat since the summer of 2004. Several other errors of commission and omission also seem to have been committed early on, including the failure to send sufficient troops to secure public order, the heavy reliance on American private contractors, excessively long, direct occupation rule by the CPA, and the paucity of experts on Iraq or Islam in American governmental institutions dealing extensively with Iraq. Even at the end of 2006 only thirty-three of one thousand U.S. embassy personnel in Baghdad spoke passable Arabic, with only six of them seriously fluent, which was far too few.[41]

Effective nation building clearly requires substantial in-country military manpower. In Germany, Japan, the Balkans, and Afghanistan, twenty troops per thousand local residents was the accepted norm. In postwar Iraq, however, the United States deployed only one-third of that ratio.[42] In stark contrast with the insufficient number of American troops in Iraq, the British, for example, had substantial military manpower in both Egypt and India, where their nation-building efforts were most successful. During their days of liberal empire in the 1880s, less than one-third of Britain's armed forces was stationed at home in the United Kingdom. This compares to more than four-fifths of the American military that has recently been deployed stateside in peacetime.[43]

Consciously limiting its deployment of uniformed forces to Iraq, the U.S. government instead relied heavily in the early days of occupation on private contractors. Halliburton and similar firms, however, had much more limited incentives to be sensitive to the local Iraqi sociopolitical context than either earlier British colonial administrators, or even their contemporary American government counterparts. In fact, sensitivity to Islamic culture and efforts to earn trust from local people were a decisive difference between the American and British forces operating in Iraq since the fall of Saddam Hussein in 2003. Seven-thousand-odd British did away with helmets and combat body gear soon after the fall of Saddam's regime—but before the Sunni insurgency gained force—and patrolled the cities in berets, their guns lowered in an attempt to foster trust. American troops, by contrast, were required by their rules of engagement to wear helmets and body armor in the war zone at all times, and to respond actively to any gunfire. While these rules were in both cases no doubt driven by a realistic assessment of local conditions, they also indicate a more pervasive operational mindset.

The British similarly put more trust in locally hired policemen in their zone of responsibility in southern Iraq than did the Americans further north, where Paul Bremer's CPA headquarters had been responsible for abolishing the national police force. The British troops were also briefed more thoroughly and comprehensively on Arab cultural differences.[44] Although ethnic configurations have no doubt made stabilization in Basra, with its lack of a substantial Sunni population, easier than in Baghdad, it is also true that the British seem to have been more effective in maintaining peaceable relations with local groups than American forces generally were, controlling for the ethnic factor, in the 2003–2004 period before the insurgency gained significant momentum.[45]

Again, Britain's experience in India suggests a healthy caution about heavy reliance on private contractors in the political-military realm that the United States did not heed in the early post-invasion days in Iraq.[46] The Sepoy mutiny of 1857–58—in which native Indian soldiers of the private British East India Company rebelled at perceived maltreatment and disrespect to their religion by that firm, thus igniting broader violence against British interests in India—was a case in point.[47] Thereafter, the British left determination of politically sensitive economic matters, together with broader imperial administration, to mixed political and civilian bureaucratic hands, and explicitly avoided devolving sensitive governmental tasks to private contractors.[48]

Indirect application of power, in short, through experienced administrators and long-term local allies, tends to be far superior to direct, overt imperial rule.[49] Britain ruled four hundred million Indians largely through the less than a thousand elite members of its Indian Civil Service, backed by the substantial yet discreetly deployed veteran military personnel alluded to above. This pattern of administration proved highly stable for nearly a century, in part because it was perceived locally to be, on the whole, just and equitable.

A perceived lack of common equities, however, can dangerously erode the host-nation legitimacy of foreign basing presence. Indeed, the deepening local perception in Iraq during 2003–2004 that the U.S.-led occupation, while enriching foreign contractors, was not improving everyday living standards, or giving common people a stake in the status quo, helped fuel the budding Sunni insurgency.

The early failure in Iraq to effectively build common equities between the CPA and the Iraqi people contrasted sharply to the systematic efforts that the British typically made in their empire to create common equities, under the system of indirect rule.[50] Intensified efforts to understand the subtleties of local cultures, and to win the trust of local people, could also help stabilize relations with host nations, as the American and British experiences in Iraq since 2003 suggest. If the position of U.S. bases overseas is to be stabilized, that balance of equities has to be brought into equilibrium, so that bases are tolerated, if not welcomed, by local residents in host nations.

Japan, where base relations with U.S. forces are remarkably stable despite a bitter historical heritage, illustrates two important aspects of a resolution to this problem: *government institutions* for building common local equities, and *broadly distributed local economic opportunities*. Japan's DFAA works at building positive community relations with U.S. as well as domestic military bases, and provides flexible "burden payments" to negatively impacted communities and individuals. The U.S.-Japan Joint Committee on Security Relations and SACO in Okinawa provide efficient bodies for rapid redress of base-related problems.

Economic benefits from the bases are also distributed to a broad range of local groups, helping to build common equities that stabilize the domestic political position of bases in the host-nation political economy. The bases themselves are largely located on private land, giving landlords a stake in base persistence, especially since landowners receive significantly above-market rental rates. Farmers benefit from the base presence by being allowed, at least in Okinawa, to undertake "tacit farming" inside the bases, which allows them to harvest crops on the fringes of runways and other peripheral land, even while renting such property to the military. The Japanese central government, through the DFAA, also provides well-appointed public facilities, including well-designed cultural and recreation centers, swimming pools, and other useful facilities, such as garbage-processing plants. Local companies also provide on-base construction and other contractual services, such as interpreters, civil affairs liaison officers, and secretaries.

There are important caveats and corollaries to compensation politics, it should be noted. This form of base stabilization works well only when two conditions pertain: (1) resources keep flowing continuously to targeted base communities; and (2) no ambitious efforts are made to move existing bases. Compensation politics creates strong vested interests that can be at once supportive of existing bases and resistant to moving them, as the Japanese case shows very clearly. The most politically effective approach to strategic transformation is thus transferring base functions *among existing bases*, as with the 2006 proposed transformation of Camp Zama in the Tokyo area through transfer of U.S. Army I Corps command functions there.[51] This approach is more politically feasible in countries like Japan, where entrenched compensation politics prevails, than moving bases to new locations, as was attempted with the abortive 1996 plan for relocating the Futenma Marine Corps Air Station in Okinawa to a new Henoko mobile-basing facility.

Compensation politics, as we have seen, appears to be a relatively rare pattern of base politics when seen in comparative perspective. Yet in the countries, such as Japan, Italy, and Portugal where it is seriously pursued at the grassroots level, base relations are unusually stable, and local relations with the U.S. military are generally good, at least as long as substantial funding continues. Foreign assistance from allied third countries, in the form of strategic foreign aid, could potentially complement American efforts—in Central Asia or Africa, for example—to apply parts of the Japanese model elsewhere in the world.

3. EMPHASIZE THE LOCAL LEVEL, AND BUILD "INCENTIVES TO AGREEMENT" THERE. Base politics have traditionally been conducted among diplomats and military personnel, often quite confidentially, at an elite level in national capitals. One of the primary implications of regime shifts, especially democratic transitions, for base politics is that they frequently empower new non-elite groups, particularly at the local level. Such people have very different incentives than national politicians, military officers, and diplomats. They are often impacted by the negative aspects of bases, including crime and environmental problems, and have only limited stakes in the positive national-level values, such as national security and international economic advantage, that the presence of foreign forces can actually enhance.

Targeted support for local communities and regions hosting American bases is obviously an imperative in Iraq. It could be important there in creating local growth poles in the more stable parts of the country, such as Kurdistan, and even in contested Anbar Province, that could greatly aid stabilization and recovery in the nation as a whole.[52] Support for local civic action could also be an important tool elsewhere for finessing the long-term base-political dilemma, clearly apparent in Central Asia today, as previously in the Philippines and South Korea, of basing in nations with nondemocratic regimes.

Such support would at least permit, aside from the important welfare benefits, the discreet fostering of interpersonal networks with counterelites, who might someday succeed to power, easing the chronic challenge that regime shifts typically present to stable base presence, as discussed in chapter 2. Significant shares of aid in such cases should be directed to local-support programs. The financial support of allies such as Japan, Italy, and Britain, or multilateral financial institutions like the Asian Development Bank, could also be utilized effectively in such grassroots support efforts.

4. "ONE SIZE DOES NOT FIT ALL." There has been a recent trend in U.S. base-relations policy toward standardization—the adoption of fixed approaches both within nations, as in movement for application of the NATO SOFA at all American bases across Italy, and cross-nationally as well. The findings of this research suggest the need for caution in applying such rigid procedures. Nations—and, indeed, communities within nations—vary profoundly in their character, in the nature of interpersonal networks within them, and in their institutions. While a systemic approach is crucial, treating bases all as "one of a kind" is a recipe for disaster.

One profoundly important cross-national difference, by way of illustration, is ethnic diversity. Japan, Korea, and Germany—sites of America's largest overseas troop concentrations outside the Middle East—are quite homogeneous nations. Yet Afghanistan and Iraq—the recent loci of conflict—are emphatically not. Homogeneity makes common incentives—including finance—more effective. Heterogeneity conversely creates a more complex base-politics map.

Illustrations of the problems with "one size fits all" are legion. In the past, planning for a replacement facility for the Futenma MCAS in Okinawa, for example, clearly suffered from the application of generic "mobile-basing–facility" concepts outside of Washington D.C. These created massive potential windfalls for certain Japanese manufacturers, but were impractical in financial and logistical terms. Similarly, the generic application of the "joint-basing–facility" concept, and the notion of "dual-use facilities" in Japan over the past decade ignore politically important differences in local circumstances, as between Okinawa and mainland Japan.

Cross-nationally, there is obviously also a need to recognize the legitimacy of differences in both institutions and policy outcomes in base politics. This research has noted the existence of at least four unique varieties of base politics. Each tends to correspond to the political tradition of a particular nation or region, although the different varieties have manifestations cross-regionally as well.

Since these base-politics variants produce distinctive outcomes, with clearly contrasting implications for American policy, and since they are not purely path-dependent, U.S. policymakers can reasonably attempt to modify the perverse elements of local patterns through appropriate channels. They need *not* passively take *any* of these local patterns as a given. It is, however, crucial that policy-makers systematically understand through methodical thought processes the cross-national variation in base-politics institutions and outcomes. And it is equally important that *they have flexible tools, rather than invariably standardized maxims,* for dealing with any given variant to their advantage.

"Think globally, and act locally" is *not* only a maxim for business strategists. It is relevant for base-politics policymakers, too. The empirical findings of this volume suggest the following implications for customizing global base policymaking to the individual circumstances that each case confronts:

1. If base negotiations globally are handled by common negotiators, as seems appropriate from a U.S. policy standpoint, those negotiations should have more systematic orientations regarding the national and subnational politics of the individual countries with which they deal. At present this preparation appears to be decidedly ad hoc. Such orientations should identify the particular variants of politics prevailing in each host nation—be they compensation, bazaar, fiat, or affective politics—and the implications for American negotiating strategy.

2. The state and defense departments, either individually or hopefully in combination, through a mechanism like the NMPC discussed above, should have more *comparative* base-relations data bases, including comparative work on the institutions, interpersonal networks, and precedents for handling such base relations in various host countries. The more generic elements should be computerized, where appropriate, and accessible to authorized personnel online.

3. The military Foreign Area Officer program, now limited to the U.S. Army, needs to be expanded and broadened to include other services. Heretofore the army, due to its territorial orientation and relatively static fixed-basing policies, has had a need for community-relations officers and political-economic analysts not shared by the other services. Alumni of its training programs have made good use of their culture-specific training and area-studies background in defusing local base problems in Germany, South Korea, and, on secondment, in Okinawa as well. Others have applied their expertise usefully as military attaches, in think tanks, universities, and even on the National Security Council. Such expertise can and should be used more systematically at the national policy level.

As the military's involvement broadens geographically through the war on terrorism, especially in the Islamic world and amongst other non-Western cultures, there is a pressing need for *more area-studies expertise* applied to base-politics problems, but *not* just arcane, pedantic area-studies book learning. What is needed most is information that is specific and knowledgeable, but also *comparative*. It is through comparative analysis, after all, that one gains a clear picture of just what is distinctive about a particular nation, and how its problems differ from those of other cases that are superficially similar.

One way to get this expertise could be by voluntarily contracting area specialists, in arrangements analogous to the military reserve officer system. Zinni proposes an Inter-Agency Field Force, which would be "a deployable civilian capability that would join military forces in the field to handle the non-military dimensions of program implementation or post-conflict recovery and reconstruction."[53] Such mobilization of retired personnel or academics on contract could help prevent the sort of disastrous obliviousness to local realities that helped turn a potential "liberating occupation" in Iraq into the quagmire of ethnic violence that it ultimately has become.

What American base policy needs, in sum, is a new mixture of two long-standing imperatives: (1) general *strategy*, making optimal use of changing technology to meet the demands of an era of global terrorism, on the one hand, and (2) local *knowledge*, of country and area-specific political-economic conditions. The world is rapidly becoming one, in both the flow of information and in the surge of expectations. Yet local institutions and cultures naturally still remain and generate their own distinctive variants of base politics. U.S. policy fails to account for these cross-national and even subnational differences only at its peril.

IMPLICATIONS FOR THEORY

Base politics is, as we have seen, a rich yet virtually unexplored field in its own right. In addition to its substantial implications for policy, in the volatile global system now emerging, base politics also has significance for our understanding of both international affairs in general and of how politics operates in individual political systems. It is thus a subset of both comparative and international politics, with important, if also largely unexplored, theoretical implications for both subfields of political science. Base politics is a felicitous area where findings of importance for policy simultaneously enrich scholarship.

Aside from a preliminary effort at conceptualizing the new field of base politics itself, this work has focused on comparative examination of how host nations, across history and in the more than 150 countries where the United States currently has a military presence of some sort, respond to the presence of those bases.[54] It is a theory-driven enterprise that draws on a wide range of empirical materials from subnational, national, and transnational politics. It attempts to both generate and test concrete propositions about the policies that host nations adopt toward foreign forces on their soil, and why those policies take the particular form that they do.

In an argument of importance for both policy and theory, this book has contended, simply put, that "Strategy does not necessarily determine outcomes." It has found empirically that "high politics," in the form of national strategy, is profoundly constrained by "low politics," in the form of domestic political strategies for the use of compensation and coercion. In the final analysis it appears to be low politics, expressed in the form of compensation strategies toward domestic interest groups, that crucially determines the long-term political success in host nations of forward-deployment strategies. By implication, this work thus calls into question the sharp conventional distinction between "high" and "low" politics, providing some concrete suggestions as to how the two are related, in an area of importance for both policy and theory.

This work, while conceding the role of values in shaping perception, also casts doubt on the proposition that local values in host nations, such as "antimilitarism" or "strong national-security consciousness," consistently determine outcomes. We start with the working assumption that concrete, individual material interests determine political behavior to a greater extent than do abstract values, and find this proposition validated in the complex and contradictory course that base politics assumes in virtually every nation. If values were determining, base politics should be more stable and consistent within individual nations or culture areas than appears to be the case.

This book accordingly calls into question the utility of constructivist approaches in accounting for concrete policy outcomes, finding them generally underpredictive. It also finds the rational-choice perspective, although lacking a way to account for subtle cultural influences, surprisingly useful to an understanding of important matters relating to war and peace, as in the base-politics area, where values might be expected to hold sway. In parts of the world as diverse as Okinawa, Turkey, and Kyrgyzstan, the evidence is clear that policy outcomes, and even the responses of civil society to policy, often diverge sharply from deeply held values, and not simply due to the preeminence of powerful, unjust forces. It is also evident that security-policy outcomes vary significantly over short periods of time, even as values remain relatively constant.

There are, to be sure, cases such as Saudi Arabia, where values appear highly salient in determining how bases operate, both on a day-to-day basis and within the broader national political system. Yet even there values alone are clearly insufficient in explaining policy outcomes, this study has found. While values are generally considered to be constant, policy varies, sometimes sharply and discontinuously over time, as was evident in the abrupt American withdrawal from high-quality Saudi bases, with Saudi encouragement, following the occupation of Iraq in 2003.

Furthermore, the role of values themselves in determining policy outcomes must be considered within a structural-functional context. Formal Islamic values are politically important in Saudi base politics because the legitimacy of Wahhabi rule itself ultimately rests on fidelity to Koranic norms. Were the Saudi government to allow foreign bases formal standing, or permit foreign troops to openly drink alcohol or contravene other Islamic social strictures, it would, in the eyes of many Saudis, no longer be serving as "defender of the faith"—the state's underlying license to rule. Where norms do not play such important functional roles in politics as in Saudi Arabia, they are typically less important in base politics, even in conservative Islamic nations.

TRANSFORMATION AND BEYOND: THE CRUCIAL CONSTRAINT OF HOST-NATION POLITICS

Both in policy and in theoretical terms, this volume speaks to the important issue of *transformation*. As analysts of varied political persuasions have often maintained, the revolution in military affairs makes possible, and the advent of an escalated struggle against global terrorism seems to make necessary, a shift in basing policies—toward greater force mobility and flexibility in deployment. Operationally, technological change creates new opportunities for joint operations among air, land, and naval services, as evidenced in Afghanistan and Iraq, and also by a new premium on the battlefield itself for Special Operations Forces.

Transformation also has major potential implications for the configuration of America's worldwide security profile beyond Iraq. The shift toward a more extensive and diverse American global military presence, extending into the heart of the Middle East, Central Asia, Eastern Europe, and Africa—all areas where American forces had not ventured in strength before—exposes the United States to a range of new, perhaps inevitable, uncertainties. And the successful conduct of base politics in such often volatile and virtually ungoverned developing lands could have a major impact on global stability as well.

Transformation also, of course, opens the prospect of reconfiguring America's forward presence in the advanced industrial world, much of it frozen rigidly in place since the Korean War. New technology and communications, after all, not to mention post–Cold War geopolitical changes, make it easier to move forces more quickly, and to base more troops closer to home. No longer need they be deployed rigidly along Korea's DMZ, not to mention the now strategically irrelevant Fulda Gap in central Germany.

Yet, as in the redeployment of forces toward the Third World, it is important in the advanced nations also to take account of *local political-economic context*. American forces in Europe and Northeast Asia are not simply fighting machines. They are also simultaneously *political-economic guarantors*, who by their very presence reduce country risk, especially along major geographical fault lines. To move those forces in precipitous fashion is to undermine alliance relations—implicit guardians of economic and financial stability across the industrialized world since the Korean War.

In a world of overwhelming American military preeminence, the credibility of alliance commitments may well be a more substantial concern for host nations than for the United States.[55] Yet in a world of massive and often volatile capital flows, as well as interdependent financial markets, uncertainty in core security alliances can easily have broader, potentially perverse systemic implications. Precipitous troop movements can thus be disruptive, not only for domestic interests in host nations, but also for America's clear interest in global political-economic *system stability*, no matter how militarily attractive enhanced mobility may be.

As chronicled in the foregoing pages, the prognosis for successful conduct of base politics—sufficient to sustain the kind of comprehensive, global imperium apparently envisioned under the preemptive Bush doctrine—is *not* good. America's overseas garrisons are increasingly embattled, and likely to grow more so, as this country's controversial Middle East commitments are steadily redefined. The problem for U.S. foreign policy is, however, *not* merely the paucity of resources that realists and decline theorists such as Robert Gilpin and Paul Kennedy have stressed. It goes deeper, into the tensions between the Pentagon's ambitious goals of military transformation and global intervention, on the one hand, and the turbulent political contexts of nations in which America deigns to intervene, on the other.

To be sure, the United States is relying ever more heavily on compensation politics to sustain its global presence. That approach has clear resource limits, both for America and for major HNS providers such as Japan and South Korea, on whom the U.S. military relies for major financial and in-kind support. Yet the world political economy is too global, the U.S. geopolitical role too central, and American Middle Eastern intervention too important to allied nations for it to flounder on financial grounds alone.

There is a still deeper problem. It lies at the subnational level of both reality and analysis. It is the tension between two crucial variables: (1) the *ambitious goals* of military transformation and global intervention, as conceived by the Bush administration, especially former Defense Secretary Donald Rumsfeld and his staff, on the one hand; and (2) the *domestic political context*—both national and subnational—of many of the nations where the United States intervenes. The problems of coming to terms with the realities of Iraq are powerful testament to the formidable political optimism of those leaders, although the problem, as suggested in these pages, is clearly much larger, and extends back to our own failure to engage with the complex and often obscure realities of foreign civilizations.[56]

To succeed in the global struggle against terrorism, and in maintaining global preeminence in the world beyond Iraq, America needs a much clearer and more sophisticated *political* strategy, much as the British Empire developed a century ago. Technology and geopolitical might alone are not enough. This understanding flows from our focus on the subnational dimension—the trees in the analytical forest. That is a key analytical contribution of this volume, and of base-political analysis more generally, to the study of world affairs.

IN CONCLUSION

Human affairs, in the final analysis, need to be concerned with more than freedom from fear. They must also grapple seriously with freedom from want. To create a world of prosperity, nations together must find a means to reconcile global interdependence with stability and prosperity in individual countries as well. In a global world, some form of global governance could plausibly provide such a resolution, although doubtless requiring a redefinition of Pax Americana as it has been conventionally known.

It seems unlikely that America itself can avoid an expansive global political role as long as it remains a world superpower. Effectively it will need to be a global stabilizer. It will need to help insulate the "functioning core" of the global system from the persistent volatility at its less-integrated periphery—across the developing yet often thinly governed nations of Asia, Africa, and Latin America.

Such an international reassurance function will no doubt require some enduring form of forward military presence. Abstract rules alone, without geopolitically credible enforcement, cannot assure the stability required by the finely tuned global political economy of the twenty-first century. Yet precisely because it will remain so necessary, in the world beyond Iraq, that presence will need sensitivity to the local political, economic, and even historical context to which it is inextricably linked. The exigencies of terrorism and low-intensity conflict will likely make such a basing presence imperative, even as global geostrategic tensions hopefully begin to wane. And in an international community where transitions to and from democracy are frequent and unpredictable, and where the winds of populism blow strong, sustaining that forward role will require more vision, sensitivity, and willingness to engage in public diplomacy than the United States, or any great power, has typically shown in the past.

American outposts abroad may well be embattled garrisons. Yet, in an increasingly interdependent world, their functions will likely continue to be crucial to global stability. And that need will persist, amidst turbulence and ambivalence, as far into the future as we can see.

APPENDIX

BASE POLITICS PARADIGMS: SPECIFIC CASES

THROUGH 2006

CONFORMITY: FOREIGN WITHDRAWAL (YES)
AND REGIME SHIFT (YES)

U.S. Bases
Jamaica (1960)
Morocco (1963)
Guyana (1966)
Trinidad (1967)
Libya (1969)
South Vietnam (1975)
Bahrain[a] (1977)
Ethiopia (1977)
Barbados (1979)
Iran (1979)
Philippines (1992)
Panama (1999)

French Bases
Indochina (1954)
Morocco (1956)
Guinea (1959)
Algeria (1962)
Malagasy (1975)
Vanuatu[b] (1980)
Rwanda (1994)
Cent. Afric. Rep. (1998)

British Bases
Egypt (1954)
Ceylon (1956)
Iraq (1958)
Kenya (1964)
South Yemen (1967)
Malta (1979)
Vanuatu (1980)
Hong Kong (1997)

Russian Bases
Hungary (1991)
Czechoslovakia (1991)
Kyrgyzstan (1992)
Mongolia (1992)
Lithuania (1993)
Poland (1993)
Ukraine (1993)
Azerbaijan (1994)
Estonia (1994)
Germany (1994)
Uzbekistan (1994)
Latvia (1999)

SUCCESSFUL ACCOMMODATION: FOREIGN WITHDRAWAL (NO)
AND REGIME SHIFT (YES)

U.S. Bases
Portugal (1974)
Greece (1975)
Spain (1975)
Turkey (1983)
South Korea (1998)
Kyrgyzstan (2005)

Russian Bases
Moldova (1992)
Armenia (1995)
Georgia (1995)

STRATEGIC WITHDRAWAL: FOREIGN WITHDRAWAL (YES) AND REGIME SHIFT (NO)

British Bases
Jordan (1957)
South Africa (1962)
Libya (1966)
Malaysia (1967)
Singapore (1967)
Belize (1994)

U.S. Bases
France (1966)
Taiwan (1973)
Thailand (1976)
Saudi Arabia (2003)

Russian Bases
Egypt (1972)
Cuba (2001)
Vietnam (2001)

DORMANT VOLCANO? FOREIGN WITHDRAWAL (NO) AND REGIME SHIFT (NO)

U.S. Bases
Afghanistan
Australia
Bahrain
Belgium
BIOT[c]
Britain
Canada
Colombia
Cuba (Guantanamo)
Denmark/Greenland
Ecuador
Germany
Honduras
Iceland
Italy
Japan
Kuwait
Luxemburg
Netherlands
Oman
Qatar
Singapore

French Bases
Chad
Comoro Islands
Djibouti
Gabon
Germany
Ivory Coast
Senegal

Russian Bases
Belarus
Kazakhstan
Tajikistan
Kyrgyzstan[d]

British Bases
Brunei
Cyprus
Germany

Notes: Dates in parentheses indicate timing of withdrawal, where relevant, and of regime shift where withdrawal did not occur. Only cases of basing for over five years in a given nation are shown; U.S. bases established after 2002, including those in Iraq, are therefore not included.

a. U.S. troops left Bahrain in 1977 after a regime shift, returning in 1987.

b. Both French and British troops were stationed simultaneously in Vanuatu. while both U.S. and Russian troops are stationed in Kyrgyzstan.

c. BIOT stands for British Indian Ocean Territory, where Diego Garcia is located. (6)

d. Both the United States and Russia have sustained bases in Kyrgyzstan. The relevant regime shift for the Russians was independence in 1992; for the U.S., it was the democratic revolution of 2005. The Russians returned in 2004.

Source: David Lea and Anna Marie Rowe, *Political Chronologies of the World*. (London: Europa Publications, Ltd., 2001); supplementary press data.

Notes

Introduction

1. There are, of course, a few partial exceptions to the generalization about overseas basing in independent nations dating from the late 1930s that should be noted. In the American case, Pearl Harbor was leased to the United States by the Kingdom of Hawaii as a naval base in 1884, although the United States did not formally annex the Hawaiian Islands until 1898. Between 1903 and 1914, U.S. Marines were likewise stationed in the nominally independent Panamanian Republic to protect American interests during the building of the canal.

American troops thereafter returned intermittently to Panama, Haiti, and the Dominican Republic, to maintain order, although the most substantial presence came in 1942, under the U.S.-Panama Base Convention. That pact allowed the U.S. wartime use of one hundred new military communications facilities outside the Canal Zone. The United States sought to retain these at war's end, but its proposal was rejected by the Panamanian National Assembly.

The periodic pre–World War II American expeditions into Latin America, which involved only temporary basing, included the following: (1) a two-year Marine deployment to Panama during 1918–20; (2) a twelve-day U.S. Army deployment of 600 troops to Panama in 1925, to break a rent strike and guard U.S. property; (3) a 1915–34 deployment of roughly 600 Marines to Haiti, to forestall potential German influence and safeguard property; and (4) a 1916–26 deployment to the Dominican Republic. On the details, see *The Historical Basis of Anti-U.S. Sentiment in Panama: A Brief Summary, 1825–1985*, at http://www.skepticfiles.org/socialis/panamahs.html; and Christopher Sandars, *America's Overseas Garrisons*. Oxford: Oxford University Press, 2000, 28.

2. "American globalism" is defined here as an open, rule-based world political-economic order in which the United States exercises preponderant influence through its hegemonic political-military capabilities and related impact on national and corporate political-risk premiums.

3. I define "base politics" as the interaction between "basing nations" and "host nations" on matters relating to the operation of local military facilities in the host nations, together with related transnational interactions involving non-state actors. "Basing nations" are defined as nations deploying forces abroad, and "host nations" as those receiving such forces.

Chapter One
The Heritage of History

1. This agreement was concluded between the United States and South Korea, formally known as the Republic of Korea. Henceforth the term "Korea" will be understood to mean "South Korea," or "Republic of Korea," unless "North Korea" is explicitly specified.

2. *New York Times*, May 31, 2004.

3. *BBC Worldwide Monitoring*, May 9, 2006 and *Financial Times*, December 13, 2006. Due to the protests the United States and South Korea were considering postponing the relocation to as late as 2013.

4. "386" stands for South Koreans in their 30s, educated in the 1980s, and born in the 1960s. This tended to be a politically activist, socially radical group.

5. Aidan Foster-Carter, "Here There Be Monsters," *New York Times*, August 11, 2006.

6. Thucydides, *The Peleponnesian Wars*. Trans. R. Warner. Baltimore: Penguin Books, 1954, 447.

7. Robert E. Harkavy, *Bases Abroad: The Global Foreign Military Presence*. Oxford: Oxford University Press, 1989, 2; and Arnold Toynbee, *America and the World Revolution*. New York: Oxford University Press, 1962, 105–106.

8. Paul M. Kennedy, *The Rise and Fall of British Naval Mastery*. Amherst, NY: Prometheus Books, 1998, 151.

9. Ibid., 154.

10. On the details, see ibid., 239–98.

11. Ibid., 205–37.

12. Carl von Clausewitz, *On War*. Princeton: Princeton University Press, 1984; and Michael Howard, *Clausewitz*. New York: Oxford University Press, 1983.

13. For a concurring Soviet view, see Admiral S. G. Gorshakov, *Sea Power of the State*. Annapolis: U.S. Naval Institute Press, 1979. Imperial Russia, with huge reserves of troops, artillery, provisions, and naval power in Europe, was unable to project its power in Northeast Asia, or even smoothly resupply its Baltic fleet, en route to defeat off the Japanese coast.

14. Harkavy, *Bases Abroad*, 3, 23. German use of Libya at the onset of World War II was crucial to Rommel's attack on British forces in Egypt; Spanish bases provided to Germany in the Canary Islands were also reportedly important for refueling U-boats.

15. On the special problems, and functional role, of deployment across the developing world in an era of global interdependence, see Thomas P. M. Barnett, *The Pentagon's New Map: War and Peace in the Twenty-First Century*. New York: G. P. Putnam's Sons, 2004.

16. The nation deploying troops abroad is defined here as the "basing nation," and the recipient as the "host nation."

17. Britain occupied Ascension in 1815 and the Falkland Islands in 1833. St. Helena, where Napoleon was exiled under British military supervision following his defeat at Waterloo in 1815, only became a formal British colony in 1834, but it was owned privately from 1673 to 1834 by the East India Company.

18. See Christopher Sandars, *America's Overseas Garrisons: The Leasehold Empire*. Oxford: Oxford University Press, 2000, 51–52. Significantly, the British have only rarely allowed the United States to use their bases in Cyprus as a staging post for Middle Eastern operations, especially since the independence of Cyprus in 1960, although they appear to be more flexible about authorizing American intelligence-collecting flights.

19. *Los Angeles Times*, February 10, 2002, reporting General Tommy Frank's testimony before the Senate Armed Services Committee, February 10, 2002.

20. On the details, see Sandars, *America's Overseas Garrisons*, 42–47.

21. More on the DEW line is available at http://www.lswilson.ca/dewline.htm and http://www.lswilson.ca/dewhist-a.htm.

22. The GATT, International Monetary Fund, and World Bank are evidence of this common geoeconomic interest. On the rationale and process of foundation, see G. John Ikenberry, *After Victory*. Princeton: Princeton University Press, 2001, 163–214.

23. Roosevelt, as Henry Kissinger points out, also attached the sort of high strategic priority to the Atlantic that the British accorded to the English Channel. He, like Churchill, thus saw both strategic and ideological reasons for an Anglo-American "special relationship." See Henry Kissinger, *Diplomacy*. London: Simon and Schuster, 1994, 387.

24. Sandars, *America's Overseas Garrisons*, 28.

25. See ibid., 104–105.

26. The United States sent 150 troops from the USS *Boston* into Honolulu in January, 1893, leading ultimately to annexation, although that only occurred after the Spanish-American War. See Christine Wing, "The United States in the Pacific," in Joseph Gerson and Bruce Birchard, eds., *The Sun Never Sets: Confronting the Network of Foreign U.S. Military Bases*. Boston: South End Press, 1991, 123–24.

27. See Alfred T. Mahan, *The Influence of Sea Power upon History, 1660–1783*. Boston: Little Brown, 1906; T. Smith, *The Pattern of Imperialism*. Cambridge: Cambridge University Press, 1981; G. Hess, *The U.S. Emergence as a South East Asian Power*. New York: Columbia University Press, 1987; Stanley Karnow, *In Our Image: America's Empire in the Philippines*. London: Century, 1990; and James R. Holmes, *Theodore Roosevelt and World Order*. Washington, D.C.: Potomac Books, 2006.

28. Sandars, *America's Overseas Garrisons*, 131.

29. Ibid., 70–71.

30. On Roosevelt's evolving strategic vision, see James McGregor Burns, *Roosevelt: The Lion and the Fox*. Norwalk, CT: Easton Press, 1989.

31. See Elliott Vanveltner Converse, III, *United States Plans for a Postwar Overseas Military Base System, 1942–1948*. Unpublished Princeton University Ph.D. dissertation, 1984, 10. At the end of the Pacific War in August, 1945, the United States had around 8.3 million Army, 3.3 million Navy, and nearly 500,000 Marine Corps personnel deployed overseas. See U.S. Department of Defense data, available at: http://web1.infoplease.com?ipa/A0004598.html.

32. In February 1945, for example, Roosevelt met King Abdul Aziz of Saudi Arabia aboard the American cruiser *Quincy* in a meeting that laid the groundwork for the American air base at Dhahran, explicitly designed to help reinforce the stability of the Saudi monarchy, and thus to protect ready American access to the massive Saudi oil reserves. See Michael A. Palmer, *Guardians of the Gulf: A History of America's Expanding Role in the Persian Gulf, 1833–1992*. New York: Free Press, 1992, 27–29.

33. According to U.S. Navy data, there were 443 American overseas bases in all at the end of World War II: 228 in the Atlantic, 195 in the Pacific, and the balance in the Indian Ocean and the Middle East. See Sandars. *America's Overseas Garrisons*, 5.

34. James R. Blaker, *United States Overseas Basing*. New York: Praeger, 1990, 9, 37.

35. See David McCullough, *Truman*. New York: Simon and Schuster, 1992.

36. On these linkages between mercantilism and geopolitical conflict, see Albert O. Hirschman. *National Power and the Structure of Foreign Trade*. Berkeley: University of California Press, 1980.

37. *Public Papers of the President of the United States, Harry S. Truman, 1945*. Washington, D.C.: Office of the Federal Registrar, National Archives Records Service, 1961, 203, cited in Converse, *United States Plans*, 154–55, 184–85. Truman's Potsdam speech, which in early drafts mentioned only Pacific bases, grew increasingly assertive in subsequent versions, reportedly at the urging of Secretary of State James Byrnes, who saw a strong Truman reaffirmation regarding the importance of postwar American overseas bases as an effective way of countering escalating Soviet claims on Spitsbergen.

38. On the importance of a forward-deployed presence in Europe and Northeast Asia to the emerging American postwar strategic concept—in economic as well as security terms—see Nicholas John Spykman, *America's Strategy in World Politics: The United States and the Balance of Power*. New York: Harcourt Brace, 1942; and Melvyn P. Leffler, "The American Conception of National Security and the Beginning of the Cold War, 1945–1948," *American Historical Review* 89, 2 (April 1984): 349–56.

39. Converse, *United States Plans*, 262.

40. Ibid., 262.

41. Ibid., 109. The Panamanian Assembly decision was in 1947.

42. James R. Blaker, *United States Overseas Basing*, 32.

43. Converse, *United States Plans*, 145. South Asian and Middle Eastern bases were particularly valued for their proximity to Soviet oil fields around Baku, and industrial sites beyond the Urals, which B-29s could not reach from prospective British bases.

44. The occupations of Germany and Italy were multilateral—the others essentially unilateral. The United States also shared in the occupation of Austria for a decade (1945–55), but that experience had no lasting impact on base politics, as all foreign forces were withdrawn, and Austria was neutralized, in 1955. The United States also separately occupied the Japanese League of Nations–mandated territories in the South Pacific, including such major battlefields of World War II as Saipan and Tarawa. Some of these islands, organized as the Strategic Trust Territory of the Pacific, later became important in connection with American nuclear and missile-testing programs, but no major deployments were ever made there.

45. On Kennan's conception of containment, which focused on pragmatic, flexible attempts to maintain a positive balance of power with the Soviet Union and its allies, with the political-economic dimension of power given substantial precedence relative to the military, see John Lewis Gaddis, *Strategies of Containment: A Critical Appraisal of Postwar American National Security Policy*. Oxford: Oxford University Press, 1982, 25–53.

46. Converse, *United States Plans*, 173.

47. Sanders, *America's Overseas Garrisons*, 201.

48. Ibid., 201.

49. Michael Schaller, *The American Occupation of Japan*. Oxford: Oxford University Press, 1985, 54; and Sandars, *America's Overseas Garrisons*, 153.

50. F. Shiels, *America, Okinawa, and Japan*. Washington, D.C.: University Press of America, 1980, 85.

51. Sandars, *America's Overseas Garrisons*, 162.

52. Ibid., 154.

53. Ibid., 181.

54. John Lewis Gaddis, *The Long Peace*. Oxford: Oxford University Press, 1987, 76.

55. Sandars, *America's Overseas Garrisons*, 182.

56. This return to concern for ground-force deployments was also influenced by the Soviet acquisition of nuclear weapons, confirmed with the testing of the first Soviet atomic bomb in August 1949. In the face of an emerging Soviet nuclear-deterrent capacity, the United States arguably needed conventional, land-based defensive options, although American strategists of the 1950s and 1960s differed on the relative priority to assign to these options, as the contrasts in "New Look" and "flexible response" approaches suggest.

57. Truman noted shortly after the Chinese intervention that "it looks like World War III is here." See McCulloch, *Truman*, 1992, 825.

58. On the structure and evolution of the "San Francisco System," see Kent E. Calder, "Securing Security through Prosperity: The San Francisco System in Comparative Perspective," *Pacific Review* 17,1 (March 2004): 135–57.

59. See John Lewis Gaddis and Paul Nitze, "NSC-68 and the Soviet Threat Reconsidered, *International Security* 4, 4 (1980): 164–86. Kennan's pleas for pragmatic balance-of-power engagement were meeting with increasing skepticism.

60. Gaddis, *Strategies of Containment*, 91.

61. For the original text, see "NSC-68: United States Objectives and Programs for National Security, April 14, 1950," *Naval War College Review* 27 (May–June 1975): 51–108. Also in U.S. Department of State, *Foreign Relations of the United States: 1950*, 1

62. See Gaddis, *Strategies of Containment*, 97.

63. Ibid., 113.

64. Sandars, *America's Overseas Garrisons*.

65. T. J. McCormick, *America's Half Century*. Baltimore: Johns Hopkins University Press, 1995, 33.

66. Ted G. Carpenter, "U.S. NATO Policy at a Cross-Roads," *International History Review* (August 1986): 389–414.

67. Wing, "The United States in the Pacific," 130.

68. The appointment of John Foster Dulles as Special Advisor to the Secretary of State on the Japan Peace Treaty further intensified the strategic emphasis on Japan and support for its economic recovery. Both the San Francisco Peace Treaty and the subsequent bilateral Treaty of Commerce and Navigation greatly aided this political-economic effort. See Kent E. Calder, "Securing Security through Prosperity," and William S. Borden, *The Pacific Alliance: United States Foreign Economic Policy and Japanese Trade Recovery, 1947–1955*. Madison: University of Wisconsin Press, 1984, 143–65.

69. Wing, "The United States in the Pacific," 130.

70. Ibid., 131.

71. Robert Gilpin, *The Political Economy of International Relations*. Princeton: Princeton University Press, 1987.

72. The core of the military leverage generated by such bases was America's nuclear deterrent, but such bases had, as George Quester points out, important deterrent value even in the absence of nuclear weapons. The conventional destruction that air power could potentially cause had been amply demonstrated at Rotterdam, Dresden, and Tokyo during World War II. See George Quester, *Deterrence before Hiroshima: The Air Power Background of Modern Strategy*. New Brunswick, NJ: Transaction Publishers, 1986, chapter 1.

73. See Kurt Wayne Schake, *Strategic Frontier: American Bomber Command Bases Overseas, 1950–1960*. Trondheim, Norway: Norwegian University of Science and Technology, 1998, 46-79; and David Miller. *The Cold War: A Military History*. New York: St. Martin's Press, 1998, 124–35.

74. Schake, *Strategic Frontier*, 97.

75. Ibid., 175.

76. Ibid., 183.

77. Ibid., 70.

78. On the salience of nuclear issues in affecting the configuration of Allied security policy during the Cold War, including operational dimensions, see Miller. *The Cold War*, 319–57, 363–78.

79. In World War II, by contrast, 80 percent of the oil consumed by the Allies was pumped from stateside American fields. See Palmer, *Guardians of the Gulf*, 45.

80. Ibid., 17–19; and Stephen D. Krasner, *Defending the National Interest: Raw Materials Investments and U.S. Foreign Policy*. Princeton: Princeton University Press, 1978, 106–19.

81. Palmer, *Guardians of the Gulf*, 19.

82. Ibid., 23.

83. Ibid., 25–26.

84. Ibid., 28.

85. Ibid., 31.

86. Ibid., 43.

87. Established as Adana Air Force Base in 1951, this facility was renamed Incirlik in 1955, although the early name continued to be informally used thereafter.

88. See http://www.airpower.au.af.mil/airchronicles/aureview/1980/may-jun/brown.html and http://www.globalsecurity.org/military/facility/gaeta.htm.

89. The Piraeus carrier, unlike its counterpart in Japan, was withdrawn following the collapse of the Greek military regime in 1975.

90. On this strategic reassessment, see Charles A. Kupchan, *The Persian Gulf and the West: The Dilemmas of Security*. Boston: Allen and Unwin, 1987.

91. President Jimmy Carter, "State of the Union Address", January 23, 1980, in U.S. Department of State. *Basic Documents, 1977–1980*, #15.

92. On the reflagging operation, see Palmer, *Guardians of the Gulf*, 128–29.

93. The maintenance of a single carrier in the North Arabian Sea during the reflagging episode, for example, tied down six or seven of the U.S. Navy's fifteen carriers. See Palmer, *Guardians of the Gulf*, 137.

94. Chalmers Johnson, *The Sorrows of Empire*. New York: Metropolitan Books, 2004, 249.

95. The Qatar Joint Operations Center was reportedly established with the enthusiastic support of the emir, Sheik Hamad ibn Khalifa al Thani. When CENTCOM commander Tommy Franks first asked the emir how he might be helpful, Sheik Hamad reportedly asked for ten thousand American soldiers. See Tommy Franks, *American Soldier*. New York: HarperCollins, 2004, 386.

96. On the estimated dimensions of its reserves, see *New York Times*, December 22, 2005.

97. Ibid.

98. Sandars, *America's Overseas Garrisons*, 201.

99. See Robert Harkavy, *Bases Abroad*, 263–67.

100. John F. Kennedy's reported willingness during the 1962 Cuban missile crisis to implicitly trade American Jupiter missiles, deployed at bases in Turkey, for a withdrawal of Soviet missiles from Cuba was a reflection of this changing strategic environment. The Jupiter, with a range of only 1,500 miles, was the increasingly obsolete IRBM predecessor of the Atlas ICBM, with a range of over 5,000 miles. On this episode, see Graham Allison, *Essence of Decision*. New York: HarperCollins, 1971.

101. U.S. Department of Defense, *DoD Deployments of Military Personal by Country*, June 30, 1950 and June 30, 1953. Cited in Kawakami Takashi, *Beigun no Zenpō Tenkai to Nichibei Dōmei (American Military Forward Deployment and the U.S.-Japan Alliance)*. Tokyo: Dōbunkan Shuppan, 2004, 47.

102. In 2004 over 37,000 U.S. troops, mainly U.S. Army, remained in Korea, amidst plans for a 4,300-man redeployment to Iraq, with additional redeployments back from the DMZ.

103. Roughly 50,000 U.S. troops remain in Japan, including one of three Marine Expeditionary Forces worldwide, with about half of the total deployed in Okinawa. U.S. ground forces have largely withdrawn from mainland Japan, except for a headquarters contingent at Camp Zama, just outside Tokyo.

104. U.S. Department of Defense, *Base Structure Report*, 2006 edition.

105. Johnson, *The Sorrows of Empire*, 239–41.

106. Hudson Institute, *Dual Use and the Future of Yokota Air Base*. Washington, D.C.: The Hudson Institute, 2004, 2.

107. Ibid., 4.

108. See *New York Times*, August 17, 2004; Congressional Budget Office, *Options for Changing the Army's Overseas Basing*. Washington, D.C.: U.S. Government Printing Office, May 2004; testimony by Secretary of Defense Donald H. Rumsfield before the Senate Committee on Armed Services, "Global Posture Review of the Unites States Military Forces Stationed Overseas," September 23, 2004; President George W. Bush, "Remarks by the President at the 2002 Commencement Exercise of the U.S. Military Academy, West Point, New York"; and Paul Wolfowitz, "Thinking about the Imperatives of Defense Transformation," Heritage Lectures, April 30, 2004. The 2004 proposals involved returning 60,000–70,000 service members and their families to the United States over the ensuing decade—two-thirds from Europe, with the majority returning

from Germany. Over the ensuing three years, 12,500 soldiers were also scheduled to return from Korea, with many of those remaining in Korea repositioned.

Chapter Two
Deepening Vulnerablility

1. Harkavy, *Bases Abroad*, 3

2. U.S. Department of Defense statistics, available at: http://web1.infoplease .com/ipa/A0004598.html; and U.S. Department of Defence, Deployment of Military Personnel by Country, 1950 edition, available at http://siadapp.dior.whs.mil/ personnel/MILITARY/history//309hist.htm. In early 1950 the U.S. forward-deployment total fell as low as 660,000.

3. Joseph Gerson and Bruce Birchard, eds., *The Sun Never Sets*. Boston: South End Press, 1991, 281.

4. See Bruce Birchard, "The Rise and Decline of the Second Superpower," in Gerson and Birchard, *The Sun Never Sets*, 47–76. Soviet troops had previously been based in Czechoslovakia, Hungary, the Baltic States, Ukraine, and Moldova, as well as the GDR and Mongolia.

5. The Russians did, for example, reinforce their informal presence in the trans-Dniester portion of Moldova, as well as in the South Ossetia and Abkazian portions of Georgia, after 9/11. They also, as noted, began reestablishing a presence in Kyrgyzstan, one of the few nations in the world to host both U.S. and Russian forces, opening a major new air base at Kant, twenty miles from the capital Bishtek, in September 2003. And they retained their strategically important naval base at Sevastopol, located on nominally Russian soil, commanding the northern Black Sea, although largely surrounded by Ukrainian territory.

6. See Jeffrey Pickering, *Britain's Withdrawal from East of Suez*, 177–93.

7. Britain's only overseas deployments of over 1,000 troops in 2005, apart from Iraq, were in Germany (22,000); Northern Ireland (10,700); Cyprus (3,275); Serbia and Montenegro (1400); the Falkland Islands (1,200); in Brunei (1,120); and in Bosnia-Herzegovina (1,100). It also deployed 340 troops in Gibraltar. See International Institute for Strategic Studies, *The Military Balance*, 2005–2006 edition.

8. In 2005 the French economy comprised 4.8 percent of the global total in nominal terms, after the United States (28.1 percent); Japan (10.2 percent); Germany (6.3 percent), and the United Kingdom (4.9 percent). See World Bank, WDI Online available at: http://devdata.worldbank.org/dataonline/htm.

9. In 2005 France continued to maintain garrisons in Ivory Coast (3,800); Djibouti (2,850); New Caledonia (1,030); French Indian Ocean Territories (1,000); Gabon (800); Senegal (1,100); and several small colonies. See IISS, *The Military Balance*, 2005–2006 edition.

10. At the end of the Korean War, 1.6 million U.S. troops were deployed overseas, a figure that fell to around 700,000 by 1962, and then rose to over 1.2 million again by 1969, driven by the Vietnam War. After declining below 500,000 in the late 1970s, forward deployment rose beyond 60,000 for the Gulf War, fell below 200,000 by 2000, and then rose again following 9/11, as indicated in figure 3.1. On the details, see U.S. Department of Defense, *Directorate for*

Information on Operations and Reports, avaliable at http://www.globalpolicy
.org/empire/tables/militaryabroad.htm.

11. See http://www.globalsecurity.org.

12. IISS, *The Military Balance*, assorted editions.

13. For more on Philippine base negotiations and their ultimately unsuccessful outcome, see Fred Green, ed., *The Philippine Bases: Negotiating for the Future*. New York: Council on Foreign Relations, 1988; William E. Berry Jr., *U.S. Bases in the Philippines: The Evolution of the Special Relationship*, Boulder, Colorado: Westview Press, 1989; and H. W. Brands, *Bound to Empire: The United States and the Philippines*. New York: Oxford University Press, 1992.

14. Bonn International Center for Conversion, *Conversion Survey 1996: Global Disarmament, Demilitarization, and Demobilization*. Oxford: Oxford University Press, 1996, 191–92.

15. Even the Nazi German deployments on Italian and Spanish territory discussed in chapter 1 were in the overseas possessions of those nations—in Libya and the Canary Islands respectively. The American exceptions to this general pattern are discussed in the introduction.

16. See appendix for a full listing of countries and relevant dates for table 2.2.

17. A "regime shift" is defined as "a fundamental change in the organizational and representational rules of a political system." Examples could include transitions among feudal monarchic, military, noncompetitive one-party dominant, and competitive multiparty pluralist political orders, as well as transition from colonial rule to independence.

18. Program on International Policy Attitudes, "What Iraqi Public Wants – A WorldPublicOpinion.org poll," January 31, 2006, available at http://www.pipa .org/OnlineReports/Iraq/Iraq_Jan06_rpt.pdf. Many Iraq specialists, it should be noted, are skeptical of the reliability of polls taken under wartime conditions.

19. See *New York Times*, July 17, 2006.

20. In the Vietnamese case, U.S. congressional constraints on military action, together with the turbulence of the Watergate years, may well have undermined American resolve to remain in South Vietnam. But it was ultimately the fall of Saigon, of course, that terminated the U.S. military presence there.

21. Another interesting case of implicit strategic withdrawal, although too soon after initial deployment to meet the criteria of figure 2.3, is the American withdrawal from Uzbekistan at the end of 2005, following the Andijian massacre. In contrast to previous American strategic withdrawals, such as those from France, Taiwan, and Saudi Arabia, that from Uzbekistan appears to have been done on human rights grounds. Involving forthright condemnations of a domestic massacre in a host nation that the United States realized would lead to an Uzbek request that American forces leave. This prioritization of human rights over broader geostrategic considerations seems to indicate a distinctive idealism in the foreign policy of the second Bush administration, during its early days.

22. In Moldova, Russian troops remain in the trans-Dniester region, ostensibly to protect the local ethnic-Russian population. Russia agreed in 2005 to withdraw from Georgia by the end of 2007, but subsequently equivocated, as relations with Georgia deteriorated during 2006. See *Defense and Security*, March 4, 2005 and March 10, 2006.

23. U.S. base payments to fledgling democracies in southern Europe (Greece, Spain, Portugal, and Turkey) rose, for example, from under $200 million in 1975 to over $1.5 billion in 1987. See Thanos Veremis and Yannis Valinakis, *U.S. Bases in the Mediterranean: The Cases of Greece and Spain*. Athens: Hellenic Foundation for Defense and Foreign Policy, 1989, esp. 148.

24. "The Agenda," *Atlantic Monthly*, May 2003, 50.

25. Ibid., 51.

26. Ibid., 50.

27. Ibid., 51.

28. On the wide range of military intelligence, space, and communications facilities that have emerged since the dawn of the space age, with some basic discussion of their capabilities, see Harkavy, *Bases Abroad*, 149–230.

29. See Johnson, *The Sorrows of Empire*, 162–63.

30. Ibid., 161.

31. See Harkavy, *Bases Abroad*, 192–96.

32. Ibid., 198–99.

33. Ibid., 189–92.

34. Johnson, *The Sorrows of Empire*, 161, quoting Lt. General Michael V. Hayden, director, U.S. National Security Agency, before the Joint Inquiry of the Senate Select Committee on Intelligence, October 17, 2002.

35. See, for example, Paul Bracken, *Fire in the East: The Rise of Asian Military Power and the Second Nuclear Age*. New York: HarperCollins, 1999.

36. IISS, *The Military Balance*, 2001–2005 editions.

37. In 2003, as noted in figure 2.5, there was, to be sure, a small dip in the number of American troops deployed abroad, and in the American share of UN P-5 troops deployed abroad. This was the result of some redeployment of forces back to the United States after the end of conventional combat in Iraq. It was reversed during the ensuing insurgency there, as during the early 2007 surge in Baghdad-related deployment.

38. *Los Angeles Times*, January 7, 2002.

39. Combined, the United States and Britain had 160,000 troops in Iraq. See *New York Times*, May 30, 2003.

40. *Associated Press*, May 30, 2006.

41. IISS, *The Military Balance,* 2006 edition. London.

42. On the details, see U.S. Department of Defense, *Base Structure Report*. Washington, D.C.: U.S. Government Printing Office, annual.

43. On the "arc of instability" concept, see Thomas P. M. Barnett, *The Pentagon's New Map: War and Peace in the Twenty-First Century*. New York: G. P. Putnam's Sons, 2004.

44. Ibid., 191–245.

45. This discussion follows the testimony of General James Jones, Supreme Allied Commander Europe (SACEUR), and Commander, U.S. European Command (EUCOM), before the House of Representatives Armed Services Committee, on March 24, 2004, available at: http://www.globalsecurity.org/military/library/congress/2004_hr/04-03-24Jjones.htm.

46. Jon R. Anderson, "Transforming EUCOM, Part 1: Plan could shift leaner units closer to hot spots," *Stars and Stripes*, European edition, June 15, 2003,

available at: http://www.estripes.com/article.asp?section=&article=15472&archive=
true.

47. John Pike, "E.S. European Command Facilities," *GlobalSecurity.org*,
March 27, 2004, available at http://www.globalsecurity.org/military/facility/
eucom.htm.

48. Kensuke Ebata, *Beigun Saihen (U.S. Force Transformation)*. Tokyo: Business Sha, 2005, 118–20.

49. Statement of General James L. Jones, USMC Commander, U.S. EUCOM,
before the House Appropriations Subcommittee on Military Quality of Life and
Veterans Affairs, March 10, 2005, available at http://www.dod.mil/dodgc/olc/
docs/test05-03-10Jones.doc.

50. Ebata, *Beigun Saihen*, 118–20.

51. Mali and Algeria have been suggested as locales for periodic training or
possible antiterrorist deployment due to their proximity to large, ungoverned
areas that could be terrorist havens. Senegal and Uganda are representative locales where the United States has concluded aircraft refueling agreements. See
New York Times, July 5, 2003.

52. During Operation Enduring Freedom in Afghanistan, the U.S. military also
used bases at Bagram, Kandahar, Khost, Mazar-i-Sharif, and Pul-i-Kandahar in
Afghanistan; Chirchik and Tuzel in Uzbekistan; Dushanbe, Khujand, Kulyab,
and Kurgan-Tyube in Tajikistan; and a range of informal sites such as Jalal-
abad. More information is available at www.globalsecurity.org/military/facility/
centcom.htm.

53. *Financial Times*, October 22, 2006; and World Bank, *World Development
Indicators*.

54. *New York Times*, July 18, 2006.

55. *International Herald Tribune*, April 23, 2003; and UPI, October 18 2006.
In October 2006 there were also reports of major new base construction near
Arbil, in Iraqi Kurdistan.

56. Romania also sent four hundred infantry soldiers to Afghanistan, prior
to its formal entry into NATO in May, 2004. See *New York Times*, July 16,
2003.

57. Elizabeth Williamson, "Poland's Rent-a-Battlefields: Bring in the War
Games," *Wall Street Journal*, December 16, 2002.

58. See *New York Times*, August 17, 2004. The redeployment, expected to affect both the 60,000–70,000 troops in the two heavy divisions and an additional
100,000 military support staff and families, is to be completed by 2010, but one
of the heavy divisions to be deployed out of Germany back to the United States is
already in Iraq and not expected to return to Germany.

59. Bulgaria, for example, concluded a ten-year access and training agreement
with the United States in March, 2006. See *New York Times*, March 25, 2006.
Romania also concluded a ten-year agreement on access to several Romanian
military bases in December 2005. See the *Associated Press*, February 14, 2006.

60. *Agence France Presse*, May 26, 2006 and the *Associated Press*, February
14, 2006.

61. *New York Times*, July 5, 2003; and Robert Schlesinger, "U.S. remaking
look, location of bases abroad," *Boston Globe*, July 7, 2003.

62. Twenty-one Marines were actually assigned to Kenya as a formal duty station in 2004. The number had expanded to 153 by 2006. See Department of Defense. *Base Structure Report,* September 2005 and September 2006 editions.

63. See http://www.globalsecurity.org/military/ops/pan-sahel.htm.

64. The editors, "Military Bases and Empire," *Monthly Review,* March 2002, 5.

65. U.S. Department of Defense, *Worldwide Manpower Distribution by Geographical Area,* September 30, 2005, 5. Many personnel actually deployed in Iraq, Afghanistan, and elsewhere in the Middle East and Central Asia were in those locations in temporary duty ("TDY") status, and remained formally assigned elsewhere, with respect to their regular units abroad and Stateside, as well as with the National Guard. Figures are for personnel physically attached to regular units abroad and Stateside, as well as with the National Guard.

66. U.S. Department of Defense, *Base Structure Report,* 2006 edition.

67. U.S. Department of Defense, *Report on Allied Contributions to the Common Defense,* 2004 edition.

68. U.S. Department of Defense, *Base Structure Report,* 2006 edition.

69. *Associated Press,* September 27, 2006.

70. On details of Singapore's approach to defense relations with the United States and the relationship to base politics, see http://www.globalsecurity.org/military/facility/singapore.htm.

71. U.S. Department of Defense, *Base Structure Report,* 2005 edition.

Chapter Three
Base Politics: A Conceptual Introduction

1. See John Lindsay-Poland, "U.S. Military Bases in Latin America and the Caribbean," October 2001, avaliable at www.americaspolicy.org/briefs/2001/body_v6n35milbase.html.

2. This is a 2005 figure. See Energy Information Administration, U.S. Department of Energy, available at http://www.eia.doe.gov/emeu/international/contents.html.

3. See, for example, Anne-Marie Slaughter, *A New World Order,* Princeton: Princeton University Press, 2004; and G. John Ikenberry, *After Victory.* Princeton: Princeton University Press, 2001.

4. "Basing nations" are defined as nations deploying forces abroad, and "host nations" as those receiving such forces. "Nonstate actors" include nongovernmental organizations (NGOs) and multinational corporations (MNCs).

5. For a useful typology, see Harkavy, *Bases Abroad,* 17.

6. For a more detailed explication of definitional issues, see Harkavy, *Bases Abroad,* 7–8.

7. U.S. Department of the Army, *Counterinsurgency.* Washington, D.C.: Marine Corps War-Fighting Publications, December 2006. General David Petraeus, who became commander of the U.S. forces in Iraq in January 2007, was a principal coauthor of this manual.

8. See, for example, Robert Gilpin, *War and Change in International Politics.* Cambridge: Cambridge University Press, 1981.

9. Alan Cawson, *Organized Interests and the State: Studies in Meso-Corporatism*. Beverly Hills: Sage Publications, 1985.

10. See IISS, *The Military Balance*, 2003 edition.

11. On the general conceptual problems for conflict-resolution created by the existence of significant groups with "low costs for disagreement," see Thomas Romer and Howard Rosenthal, "Political Resource Allocation, Controlled Agendas, and the Status Quo," *Public Choice* 33, no. 4 (1978): 27–44.

12. On the psychological anxieties produced by the combination of dependence, respect, and resentment, see Neil J. Smelser, "The Rational and the Ambivalent in the Social Sciences," *American Sociological Review* 63. no. 1 (1998): 1–16.

13. This dimension of American involvement in Iraq was emphasized strongly by the Baker-Hamilton Commission. See James A. Baker and Lee H. Hamilton, cochairs, *The Iraq Study Group Report*. New York: Vintage Books, 2006, esp. 43–58.

14. Thomas Schelling, *The Strategy of Conflict*. Cambridge, Massachusetts: Harvard University Press, 1960.

15. Iraq was a member of the Baghdad Pact, which had only been founded in 1955, three years before the military coup that deposed the King Faisal regime, and led to forced British withdrawal from the RAF's strategic Habanniyah and Shaibah bases. On Britain's involvement with the Baghdad Pact, see C. J. Bartlett, *The Long Retreat: A Short History of British Defense Policy*. London: Macmillan, 1970, 117–20.

16. See, for example, Chalmers Johnson, *Blowback: The Costs and Consequences of American Empire*. New York: Metropolitan Books, 2000; and the more deeply researched sequel, *The Sorrows of Empire*. Similar studies alleging widespread local backlash against foreign (especially American) political-military presence were also common in Latin America during the 1980s, and in many nations during the Vietnam War.

17. See, for example, Gore Vidal, *The Decline and Fall of the American Empire*. Berkeley: Odonian Press, 1992; Andrew J. Bacevich, *American Empire: The Realities and Consequences of U.S. Diplomacy*. Cambridge, Massachusetts: Harvard University Press, 2002; Jim Garrison, *America as Empire: Global Leader or Rogue Power?* San Francisco: Berret-Koehler Publishers, 2004; William E. Odom and Robert Dujarric, *America's Inadvertent Empire*. New Haven: Yale University Press, 2004; and Niall Ferguson, *Colossus: The Price of America's Empire*. New York: Penguin, 2004.

18. See, for example, Paul Kennedy, *The Rise and Fall of the Great Powers: Economic Change and Military Conflict from 1500 to 2000*. New York: Random House, 1987, and Robert Gilpin, *The Political Economy of International Relations*. Princeton: Princeton University Press, 1987.

19. Niall Ferguson, *Empire: The Rise and Demise of the British World Order and the Lessons for Global Power*. New York: Basic, 2004.

20. Ferguson, for example, stresses the short-term benefits for the British Empire—albeit the long-term impracticability also—of minimalist, indirect imperial rule. See ibid., xxiv, 137–84.

21. See, for example, John W. McDonald, Jr., and Diane B. Bendahmane, *U.S. Bases Overseas: Negotiations with Spain, Greece, and the Philippines*. Boulder,

Colorado: Westview Press, 1990; and Geraldo M. C. Valero et al., *A Comparative Analysis of United States Military Base Agreements*. Manila: International Studies Institute of the Philippines, 1987; and Veremis and Valinakis, *U.S. Bases in the Mediterranean*.

22. See Harkavy, *Bases Abroad*, 320–72. For Harkavy, the types of foreign-military presence include large air, naval, and army bases, C4ISR installations, and technical facilities. Objects of bargaining include arms transfers, security assistance, overseas development assistance (ODA), base rentals, and offsets.

23. Sandars, for example, distinguishes among American bases emerging from wartime arrangements, colonial legacies, and World War II conquests. See Sandars, *America's Overseas Garrisons*.

24. See, for example, G. W. Boyd, *Images of America: McGuire Air Force Base*. Charleston, SC: Arcadia Publishing, 2003; Dan Walker, *San Diego: Home Base for Freedom*. San Diego: Premier Publishing, 2003; and Roger Ricardo, *Guantanamo: The Bay of Discord*. Melbourne, Australia: Ocean Press, 1994.

25. Roger W. Lotchin, *Fortress California, 1910–1961: From Warfare to Welfare*. Urbana: University of Illinois Press, 1962.

26. Catherine Lutz, *Homefront: A Military City and the American Twentieth Century*. Boston: Beacon Press, 2001. This is a well-crafted study of the relationship between Fayetteville, North Carolina and the U.S. Army's Fort Bragg, home to the 82nd Airborne Division. The book won the 2002 Anthony Leeds Prize in Urban Anthropology.

27. See, for example, David S. Sorenson, *Shutting Down the Cold War: The Politics of Military Base Closure*. New York: St. Martin's Press, 1998; Lilly J. Goren and P. Whitney Lackenbauer, *The Comparative Politics of Military Base Closures: How Congress Balances Geographic and General Interests*. Orono, MA: University of Maine Canadian-American Center, 2000; and Lilly J. Goren, *BRAC to the Future: Evasive Delegation and Blame Avoidance in Base Closings*. Ph.D. diss., Department of Political Science, Boston College, 1998.

28. See especially Goren and Lackenbauer, *The Comparative Politics of Military Base Closures*.

29. Ibid., 3–4.

30. Seventy-one percent of new U.S. bases established between 1995 and 2002 were created in the Islamic world. Figures for 1995 are from CRS Report to the U.S. Congress, "Military Base Closure: Where Do We Stand?" Washington, D.C.: Congressional Research Service, 1999. Figures for 2000–2004 are from the U.S. Department of Defense, *Base Structure Report*, 2001, 2003, and 2005 editions.

31. "Basing nation" is defined as the country supplying troops for deployment in the host nation.

32. The study includes ninety-seven cases, as noted in chapter 2 in greater detail, but only eighty-six countries, because: (a) Germany, Morocco, Kyrgyzstan, Libya, Vietnam, Egypt, Singapore, and Vanuatu hosted troops of multiple nations; and (b) Bahrain expelled U.S. forces in 1977, following a regime shift, and subsequently invited them back, in 1987. Kyrgyzstan similarly expelled the Russians in 1992 and invited them back in 2004. More detailed information is provided in the appendix of the present volume.

Chapter Four
The Nature of the Contest

1. See Peter Katzenstein, ed., *The Culture of National Security: Norms and Identity in World Politics*. New York: Columbia University Press, 1996.

2. Thomas U. Berger, *Cultures of Anti-Militarism: National Security in Germany and Japan*. Baltimore: Johns Hopkins University Press, 1998 and Pater J. Katzenstein, *Cultural Norms and National Security: Police and Military in Postwar Japan*. Ithaca: Cornell University Press, 1996.

3. Bernard Lewis, *What Went Wrong: Western Impact and Middle Eastern Response*. New York: Oxford University Press. 2002.

4. On this point, see Jeffery Checkel, "The Constructivist Turn in International Relations Theory: A Review Essay," *World Politics* 50, 2 (1998): 324–48.

5. See Kent Calder and Min Ye, "Regionalism and Critical Junctures: Explaining the 'Organization Gap' in Northeast Asia," *Journal of East Asian Studies* 4 (2004): 191–226, esp. 219–21.

6. See Laura Hein and Mark Selden, eds., *Islands of Discontent: Okinawan Responses to Japanese and American Power*. Oxford: Rowan and Littlefield, 2003; Chalmers Johnson, ed., *Okinawa: Cold War Island*. Japan Policy Research Institute, 1999; and Chalmers Johnson, *Blowback*.

7. See Alexander Cooley and Kimberly Zisk Marten, "Base Bargains: The Political Economy of Okinawa's Anti-Militarism." *Armed Forces and Society*, July 2006, 566–83.

8. For examples of this genre, see Fritz W. Scharpf, *Games Real Actors Play: Actor-Centered Institutionalism in Policy Research*. Boulder, Colorado: Westview Press, 1997.

9. On this concept, see Thomas Romer and Howard Rosenthal, "Political Resource Allocation, Controlled Agendas, and the Status Quo," *Public Choice* 33, 4 (1978): 27–44.

10. For a simple explanation, see George Tsebelis, *Nested Games: Rational Choice in Comparative Politics*. Berkeley: University of California Press, 1990, 72–78.

11. For an exploration of the relevance of this notion in international relations, see Robert Putnam, "Diplomacy and Domestic Politics," *International Organization* 42, 3 (Summer 1988): 427–60; and Peter B. Evans, Harold K. Jacobson, and Robert Putnam, eds., *Double Edged Diplomacy: International Bargaining and Domestic Politics*. Berkeley: University of California Press. 1993.

12. Francis Fukuyama, *The End of History and the Last Man*. London: Hamish Hamilton, 1992.

13. Okinawa, twice as close to Shanghai as to Tokyo, has a per capita income 30 percent below Japan's average, and unemployment nearly twice as high. The unemployment rates in Japan and in Okinawa as of June 2006 were 4.2 percent and 8.1 percent, and per capita GDP-GPP in 2002 were ¥2,916,000 and ¥2,031,000 respectively, according to The Ministry of Internal Affairs and Communications Statistics Bureau, and the Statistics Department of Okinawa Prefecture. Data available at http://www.stat.go.jp/ and http://www.pref.okinawa.jp/toukeika/.

14. In this incident, twenty tourists died in the Italian Alps when a U.S. Marine Corps EA-6B Prowler jet, flying only three hundred feet above the ground, severed a sky-lift cable line, sending the tourists to their deaths. President Bill Clinton apologized, and Italian Prime Minister d'Alema made a pro forma demand for a review of related NATO accords. The crew was ultimately acquitted in American military court, and Italian public opinion was outraged, but the actual policy response of the leftist d'Alema government was nevertheless minimal. On the details of the case, see "D'Alema, Clinton meet amid rising US-European tensions," *Agence France Presse*, March 5, 1999.

15. On the general conceptual problems for conflict-resolution that the existence of significant groups with incentives to nonagreement creates, see Romer and Rosenthal, "Political Resource Allocation.

16. See Sook-jong Lee, "The Rise of Korean Youth as a Political Force: Implications for the U.S.-Korea Alliance," in Richard C. Bush, Sharon Yanagi, and Kevin Scott, eds., *Brookings Northeast Asia Survey*, 2003–2004 edition. Washington, D.C.: Brookings Institution Center for Northeast Asian Policy Studies, 2004, 15–30.

17. Sidney Tarrow, *The New Transnational Activism*. Cambridge: Cambridge University Press, 2005, 29.

18. Jeffrey D. Boutwell, "NATO Theater Nuclear Forces: The Third Phase, 1977–1985," in *The Nuclear Confrontation in Europe*, ed. Jeffrey D. Boutwell, Paul Doty, and Gregory F. Treverton. London: Croom Helm and Dover, MA: Auburn House, 1985, 150.

19. See Josef Joffe, "Peace and Populism: Why the European Anti-Nuclear Movement Failed," *International Security* 11, no. 4 (Spring, 1987): 19.

20. Russell Watson, "Battle over Missiles," *Business Week*, December 21, 1981, 59.

21. Lee, "The Rise of Korean Youth as a Political Force."

22. Pippa Norris, *Democratic Phoenix*. Cambridge, U.K.: Cambridge University Press, 2002.

23. In 1997 South Korean Internet usage was 36.2 per 1000 people, compared to 221.3 in the United States, and 91.6 in Japan. By 2002 South Korean usage had risen to 551.9, passing the United States at 551.4, and Japan, at 448.9. See World Bank, *World Development Indicators*, 2004 edition.

24. Literally, in English, Solidarity for Peace and Reunification of Korea (SPARK), or, in Korean, Pyong'wha'wa Tong'il'eul Yonun Saramdeul.

25. See also Hyug Baeg Im, "Korean Democracy after Transition: Challenges and Opportunities" in Cheong-Si Ahn, ed., *Democracy in Asia, Europe, and the World*. Seoul: Korean Association of International Studies, 2004, 222–46, on the impact of new technology in fueling NGO protest behavior in Korea.

26. The Okinawan antibase movement, for example, has been energized by the success of its counterpart in Vieques, Puerto Rico, although similar outcomes did not occur in Okinawa due to the "compensation politics" pursued by the Japanese government there.

27. *Oh, My! News*, June 2004.

28. In 1988, for example, the United States provided $435 million, $265 million, $235 million, and $40 million, respectively, in concessionary FMS aid to

Greece, Spain, Turkey, and Portugal, with Israel, Egypt, and Pakistan being the only other large recipients. See Harkavy, *Bases Abroad*, 340–54.

29. For a detailed examination of Japanese host-nation support policies from a comparative perspective, see Kent E. Calder, "Beneath the Eagle's Wings? Japanese Burden-sharing Policies in Comparative Perspective," *Asian Security* 2, no. 3 (October 2006), 148–73.

30. In one such 2003 study, for example, 43.5 percent of respondents indicated "inconvenience in exercising property rights caused by granted land" as the greatest reason for conflict between local communities and U.S. forces in Korea. See Il-Young Kim and Seong-Ryoul Cho, *Chuhan Mikyu* (*The U.S. Forces in Korea*). Seoul: Hanyol, 2003.

31. Kent E. Calder, "Securing Security through Prosperity: The San Francisco System in Comparative Perspective," *The Pacific Review* 17, no. 1 (March 2004): 135–57.

32. U.S. Department of Defense, *National Manpower Survey*, 2005 edition.

33. Marni McEntee and Lisa Horn, "U.S. adds $1 billion to Kaiserslautern economy," *Stars and Stripes*, European edition, February 20, 2004.

34. Schweinfurt, a city of 55,000 German residents in northern Bavaria, near the old Cold War zone boundary with East Germany, hosted 12,000 American members of the First Infantry Division, family members, and Department of Defense civilians in mid-2004. Local unemployment was 10.2 percent, and the Americans spent $31 million annually in Schweinfurt, or roughly 5 percent of local retail sales. The town, isolated geographically and heavily dependent on declining ball-bearing industry sales, had virtually no diversification opportunities, and desperately wanted to keep the strategically irrelevant American base. See *New York Times*, August 22, 2004.

35. See, for example, *Financial Times*, January 14, 2003 and Hans Greimel, "Pro-U.S. crowd finds voice in South Korea as nuclear standoff intensifies," *Associated Press*, February 22, 2003.

36. Lee, "The Rise of Korean Youth as a Political Force."

Chapter Five
The Base-Politics Environment: Comparative Perspectives

1. See, for example, Lotchin, *Fortress California 1910–1961*; Lutz, *Homefront*; Walker. *San Digo*; and Anni Baker, *Wiesbaden and the Americans, 1945–2003: The Social, Economic, and Political Impact of the U.S. Forces in Wiesbaden*. Wiesbaden, Germany: Druckerei Zeidler, 2004.

2. See, for example, Ferguson, *Colossus*; Bacevich, *American Empire*; Odom and Dujarric, *America's Inadvertent Empire*; and Michael Mandelbaum, *The Case for Goliath*. New York: Public Affairs, 2005.

3. British forces also remain in Brunei, but it is little more than a city-state, although an energy-rich one.

4. Akrotiri is a major RAF airfield in the southwest of the island, and Dhekelia a British Army garrison in the southeast. See Sandars, *America's Overseas Garrisons*, 51.

5. In Cyprus, the Sovereign Base Areas are written into a "Treaty Concerning the Establishment of the Republic of Cyprus," formalized at the time of independence in 1960. In Oman the dimensions of British involvement have never been so formalized. On the history of British geopolitical involvement in Oman, see Omani Information Resources, "Treaties with the British," available at http://reference.allrefer.com/country-guide-study/oman/oman15.html.

6. See Roger Ricardo, *Guantanamo: Bay of Discord*. Melbourne, Australia: Ocean Press, 1994.

7. On the latter case, see Larry Diamond, *Squandered Victory*. New York: Times Books, 2005 and Thomas Ricks, *Fiasco*. New York: Penguin Press, 2006.

8. On the complex, and at times bitter, Manglapus relationship with the United States, see Stanley Karnow, *In Our Image: American Empire in the Philippines*. New York: Random House, 1989, 24, 353, and 363.

9. Paul Bremer, longtime managing director of Kissinger Associates, had served during his state department career as ambassador to the Netherlands, director of the State Department's Office of Counter-Terrorism, and as special or executive assistant to six secretaries of State, including Henry Kissinger. Yet he had never been posted in the Arab world before suddenly arriving there in May 2003 as director of the Coalition Provisional Authority—effectively, the viceroy of Iraq. On these details, see Michael R. Gordon and Bernard E. Trainor, *Cobra II: The Inside Story of the Invasion and Occupation of Iraq*. New York: Pantheon Books, 2006, 475.

10. Around 500,000 Japanese, for example, died in the American wartime air raids on Japan, only 22 percent of which were conducted against precision industrial targets. In one memorable March 10, 1945, fire bombing of Tokyo, 1,700 tons of incendiary ordnance were unloaded on Japan's capital, burning an area half the size of Manhattan, and killing roughly 100,000 people, with the flames of the conflagration visible 250 kilometers out to sea. During the last nine months of the war, 24 percent of Japan's housing supply was burned to the ground; in Germany around 300,000 people were killed in U.S. air raids, and 28 percent of the national housing stock destroyed. See Thomas R. H. Havens, *Valley of Darkness: The Japanese People and World War II*. New York: W. W. Norton and Company, 1978, 176–77.

11. One must, of course, be sensitive to historical differences also. Most conspicuously, both occupier and occupied, in the early postwar cases, were coming out of a major world war, and had unusually strong mutual incentives, reinforced by geopolitical logic, to make the various occupations succeed. See Kimberley Zisk Marten, *Enforcing the Peace: Learning from the Imperial Past*. New York: Columbia University Press, 2004, 149–51.

12. On this pre-1931 liberal tradition of interwar Japan, and its implications for that country's overall political evolution, see Edwin O. Reischauer, *Japan: The Story of a Nation*. New York: Knopf, 1970; Peter Duus, *Party Rivalry and Political Change in Taishō Japan*. Cambridge, Massachusetts: Harvard University Press, 1968; Akira Iriye, *After Imperialism: The Search for a New Order in the Far East, 1921–1931*. Cambridge, Massachusetts: Harvard University Press, 1965.

13. Heine, for example, represented this liberal internationalist tradition in Germany, as Mazzini and Garibaldi did in Italy. See Charles Sabine, *A History of Political Theory*. Hinsdale, Illinois: Dryden Press, 1973.

14. In Iraq, Italy supplied the third-largest contingent of allied forces for more than two years, from 2003 to 2005. Italian Prime Minister Silvio Berlusconi adamantly refused to withdraw Italian forces from Iraq in 2004, even after major insurgent attacks that on one occasion killed 17 of 300 Italian *carbanieri* stationed in the country. On Italy's role in Iraq, see, for example, Iraqwatch.org, whose Web site is available at http://www.iraqwatch.org/government/Italy/italy-mfa-mantica-041503.html.

15. Sandars, *America's Overseas Garrisons*, 228.

16. Ibid. In 1979, the United States maintained 11,350 troops in Italy, compared to 8,750 in Spain, 4,500 in Turkey, and 3,500 in Greece.

17. For more information, see http://encyclopedia.thefreedictionary.com/Alps%20ski-lift%20air%20disaster.

18. As Bruce Cumings points out, "there was no middle in Korea, thanks to the Japanese," so the United States occupation forces had a difficult choice between an establishment replete with collaborations and a mass public too radical for U.S. liking. The United States also, of course, relied quite heavily on the existing power structure in Japan, engaging in only a relatively mild and superficial purge even there. The difference, however, was that Korea had been a *colony*, so that many of the existing authorities were *collaborators* of Japan. See Bruce Cumings, *Korea's Place in the Sun: A Modern History*. New York: W. W. Norton and Company, 1997, 192–202, especially 194, and idem, *The Origins of the Korean War: Liberation and the Emergence of Separate Regimes, 1945–1947*. Princeton: Princeton University Press, 1981, 185–236.

19. Cumings, *Korea's Place in the Sun*, 185–224, and *The Origins of the Korean War*, Volume II. 237–90.

20. On the details, see Mark Lynch, "Anti-Americanism in the Arab World," in Peter J. Katzenstein and Robert O. Keohane, eds., *Anti-Americanisms in World Politics*. Ithaca: Cornell University Press, 2007, 196–24.

21. Ibid., 210.

22. The acronym IFOR denotes "Intervention Force," while ISAF indicates "International Security Assistance Force." Both efforts were broadly multilateral, with a central NATO role.

23. According to the Associated Press, on November 13, 2003, seven months after the fall of Baghdad, about thirty countries other than the United States were stationing their troops in Iraq, although the American contingent was by far the largest. These nations were topped by the United Kingdom (7,400), Italy (3,000), Poland (2,400), Ukraine (1,640), and Spain (1,300). Historical accidents, as well as design, to be sure, were also partly at work in sustaining the near unilateralism prevailing in Iraq. UN Special Representative Sergio de Mello, with whom the United States broadly cooperated, was killed in Baghdad by a car bomb in August 2003, only four months into the occupation, leading to a wholesale withdrawal of the UN's local presence in Iraq. On the implications, see Bremer, *My Year in Iraq*, 86, 94–95.

24. Bremer had, it is important to note, both served as Henry Kissinger's chief of staff and as director of the Office of Counter-Terrorism at the State Department, but these highly responsible posts still did not provide him with much relevant historical or cultural background relating to Iraq. On Bremer's tenure as

director of the Coalition Provisional Authority (CPA) and the critical role that it played in Iraq's political evolution, see Bremer, *My Year in Iraq*, and Rajiv Chandrasekaran, *Imperial Life in the Emerald City*. New York: Alfred A. Knopf, 2007, esp. 58–80.

25. Bremer, *My Year in Iraq*, 94.

26. See Sumantra Bose, *Bosnia after Dayton: Nationalist Partition and International Intervention*. Oxford: Oxford University Press, 2002.

27. Bremer, *My Year in Iraq*, 37.

28. The numbers were substantially lower even than in the Balkans, not to mention Japan and Germany. To safeguard the peace in the Balkans, NATO had deployed about twenty peacekeepers per thousand civilians. The CPA in Iraq maintained only one-third that ratio. See Gordon and Trainor, *Cobra II*, 477.

29. Bremer, *My Year in Iraq*, 10, 37.

30. Andrew F. Krepinevich, "How to Win in Iraq," *Foreign Affairs* 84, no. 5 (September–October 2005): 87; and Peter W. Galbraith, *The End of Iraq*. New York: Simon and Schuster, 2006, 221.

31. Survey conducted by the independent Iraqi Center for Research and Strategic Studies, cited in Diamond, *Squandered Victory*, 51, 340.

32. U.S. Department of the Army, *Counterinsurgency*.

33. On the critical failings of the first six months of the occupation, which prevented the United States from being credibly viewed as an "occupying liberator" in Iraq, see Diamond. *Squandered Victory*; Gordon and Trainor, *Cobra II*, 475–512; Anthony Shadid, *Night Draws Near*. New York: Henry Holt and Company, 2005, 118–40; and Galbraith, *The End of Iraq*, 112–30.

34. For a useful overview, see Kenneth Waltz, *Man, the State, and War*. New York: Columbia University Press, 1959.

35. See Robert D. Putnam, "Diplomacy and Domestic Politics," *American Political Science Review* 42, no. 3 (Summer 1998), 427–60.

36. Simon Duke, *United States Military Forces and Installations in Europe*. Oxford: Oxford University Press: 1989, 260–64.

37. Ibid., 167–74.

38. *Agence France Presse*, July 14, 2006.

39 Atlantic Council, "U.S. Challenges and Choices in the Gulf" and "Turkey, Iraq and Regional Security." Atlantic Council of the United States, Washington, D.C., 2003.

40. Al-Maliki, for example, demanded the removal of American checkpoints in Baghdad during late 2006, in an apparent attempt to curry favor with the residents and power brokers of Sadr City. See, for example, *New York Times*, November 1, 2006.

41. See, for example, Mark Peceny, "Two Paths to the Promotion of Democracy during U.S. Military Interventions," *International Studies Quarterly* 39, no. 3 (September 1995): 371–401; and Jeanne Kirkpatrick, *Dictatorship and Double Standards: Rationalism and Reason in Politics*. New York: Simon and Schuster, 1982. Peceny notes that although initial presidential choices do have a conservative, security-oriented bias, they are often moderated by liberal attacks from Congress, which tends to be less oriented toward dictatorships than the White House.

42. Peceny, "Two Paths to the Promotion of Democracy," 386–88.

43. See, for example, Johnson, *The Sorrows of the Empire*, 170–72.

44. See Donald Oberdorfer, *The Two Koreas: A Contemporary History*. Reading, MA: Addison-Wesley, 1997, 85–94.

45. Fred Greene, ed., *The Philippine Bases: Negotiating for the Future, American and Philippine Perspectives*. New York: Council on Foreign Relations, 1979.

46. John C. K. Daly, Kurk H. Meppen, Vladimir Socor, and S. Frederick Starr, *Anatomy of a Crisis: U.S.-Uzbekistan Relations, 2001–2005*. Washington, D.C.: SAIS Central Asia- Caucasus Institute, 44–65.

47. Stanley Karnow, *In Our Image*, 418–23.

48. Bruce Cumings, *Korea's Place in the Sun*, 344–45.

49. On the Freedom House scale, 1 represents complete democracy and 7 complete dictatorship. The calculation made here for countries hosting U.S. bases excludes Cuba, where the United States has a base at Guantanamo Bay but no working relationship with the host government.

50. Freedom House, *Freedom in the World*, 2003 edition, available at: http://www.freedomhouse.org, 720–21. The higher the score a nation received, the more authoritarian it was regarded to be.

51. U.S. Department of State, *Foreign Relations of the United States* vol. 4, 1951, 773–871.

52. These relationships were more delicate than often appreciated. A Spanish Republican government in exile, for example, continued to exist in Mexico until the late 1950s, while Britain was at odds with Franco over Gibraltar, and France over Moroccan issues, not to mention human rights concerns that troubled many nations.

53. U.S. Department of State, *Foreign Relations of the United States*, volume 6, 1952–54, 1777–2001.

54. Franco, for example, was convinced that the wartime Allies would fall out, and manipulated tensions between the British and Americans, on the one hand, and the Soviet Union, on the other, to assure the continuity of his own regime, established with Nazi and fascist support during the 1936–39 Spanish Civil War. He noted to Churchill in 1944, for example, that neutral Spain, unravaged by war, would be a haven of stability on a disintegrated European continent at war's end. See Mark Byrnes, "Unfinished Business: The United States and Franco's Spain, 1944–1947," *Diplomacy and Statecraft* 11, no. 1 (March 2000): 129–62.

55. Stanley Payne notes, for example, that Franco's regime, in its latter years, was a pragmatic authoritarian system, without clear-cut ideological boundaries, characterized by limited but undeniable pluralism. See Stanley G. Payne, "In the Twilight of the Franco Era," *Foreign Affairs* 49, no. 2 (January 1971): 342.

56. Paul Preston, "Franco: The Patient Dictator," *History Today* 35, no. 11 (November 1985): 8–9.

57. Cumings, *Korea's Place in the Sun*, 358–59.

58. See Oberdorfer, *The Two Koreas*, 37–41.

59. In 2004, approximately 288,000 American troops were deployed outside the United States, of which more than 155,000 were formally posted in the four nations in question. See U.S. Department of Defense, *Worldwide Manpower Distribution by Geographical Area*, 2004 edition.

60. Yokosuka is homeport to the USS *Kitty Hawk*, the only U.S. aircraft carrier home-ported outside the United States, with a contingent of over 11,000 sailors, while Yokota Air Base has over 3,300 U.S. military personnel. See U.S. Department of Defense, *Base Structure Report*, 2005 edition.

61. See Center for Strategic and International Studies, *Path to an Agreement: The U.S.-Republic of Korea Status of Forces Agreement Revision Process*. Washington, D.C.: C.S.I.S., 2001.

62. This proposition, of course, has prospective relevance for the future of Iraq, now a democratic nation with a decentralized, federalist bias.

Chapter Six
Base Politics Deconstructed: Four Paradigms

1. Regarding the relationship of culture and rationality, including the implications for comparative research, see Frank Dobbin, *Forging Industrial Policy: The United States, Britain, and France in the Industrial Age*. Cambridge: Cambridge University Press, 1994, 1–27.

2. Douglass C. North, *Institutions, Institutional Change, and Economic Performance*. Cambridge: Cambridge University Press, 1990.

3. Charles Tilly, ed., *The Formation of Nation States in Western Europe*. Princeton: Princeton University Press, 1975; Alexander Gerschenkron, *Economic Backwardness in Historical Perspective*. Cambridge, Massachusetts: Harvard University Press, 1960; and Stephen Skowronek, *Building a New American State: The Expansion of National Administrative Capabilities, 1877–1920*. Cambridge: Cambridge University Press, 1982.

4. See, for example, Gerschenkron, *Economic Backwardness in Historical Perspective*, and Peter Hall and David Soskice, eds., *Varieties of Capitalism*. Oxford: Oxford University Press, 2001, 1–70.

5. See, for example, Kennedy, *The Rise and Fall of British Naval Mastery*; Kennedy, *Rise and Fall of the Great Powers*; Gilpin, *The Political Economy of International Relations*; Gilpin, *War and Change in World Politics*; and E. E. Schattschneider, *Politics, Pressure, and the Tariff*. New York: Prentice-Hall, 1935.

6. See, for example, Sheldon Garon, *Molding Japanese Minds: The State in Everyday Life*. Princeton: Princeton University Press, 1997, 70–84; and Helen Hardacre, "Creating State Shinto: The Great Promulgation Campaign and the New Religions," *Journal of Japanese Studies* 12, no. 1 (Winter 1986): 29–63.

7. On the sobering details of that savage, inter-cultural conflict, see John Dower, *War without Mercy*. New York: Pantheon Books, 1986.

8. See Marius Jansen, *The Making of Modern Japan*. Cambridge, MA: Harvard University Press, 2000.

9. Peter Katzenstein, "Same War—Different Views: Germany, Japan, and Counterterrorism," *International Organization* 57, no. 4 (2003): 731–60.

10. See John Dower, *Embracing Defeat*. New York: W. W. Norton, 1999.

11. Calder, *Crisis and Compensation*, 160.

12. Ibid.

13. On the details, see U.S. Department of Defense, *Report on Allied Contributions to the Common Defense*. Washington, D.C.: U.S. Government Publications Office, annual.

14. Joseph P. Keddell, Jr., *The Politics of Defense in Japan: Managing Internal and External Pressures*. Armonk, New York: M. E. Sharpe, 1993, 155 and Japan Defense Agency, *Defense of Japan*, assorted issues.

15. More information is available at http://www.dfaa.go.jp/en/profile/role.html.

16. Refer to the DFAA Web site, available at http://www.dfaa.go.jp/yosan_kessan/yosan/17_souhyou.pdf; and Japan's Ministry of Finance Web site, available at http://www.mof.go.jp/seifuan17/yosan015-5.pdf. This budget provided support for the Japanese Self Defense Force, as well as American and joint-use bases.

17. From January 2007, the Japanese Self-Defense Agency became formally known as the Ministry of Defense.

18. See, for example, "Dangō Bōshi: Bōei Shisetsu Chō kara no Seiyakusho ni Shirigomi: Genekon Kaku Sha" ("Cartel Countermeasures: General Contractors Hesitate to Bid for DFAA Contracts"), *Mainichi Shimbun*, February 1, 2007; *Tō Oku Shimbun*, January 30, 2006; *Tō Oku Shimbun*, February 21, 2006; and *Kyōdō Tsūshin*, May 29, 2006.

19. SACO's fiscal 2006 budget, separate from that of the DFAA, but functionally related to it, was ¥23.3 billion, or around $210 million annually. See Japan's Ministry of Finance Web site, available at http://www.mof.go.jp/seifuan17/yosan015-5.pdf.

20. The regionally targeted nature of the compensation process, and its configuration toward local needs, appears to broadly parallel patterns in Italy and the Portuguese Azores, for example.

21. See Calder, *Crisis and Compensation*, 188–90; Tetsuo Najita. *Hara Kei in the Politics of Compromise, 1905–1915*. Cambridge, MA: Harvard University Press, 1967; and Nathaniel B. Thayer, *How the Conservatives Rule Japan*. Princeton: Princeton University Press, 1969, 268–304.

22. In Germany, as early post–World War II Japanese Prime Minister Yoshida Shigeru pointed out, the Basic Law lays down the principle that political parties whose aims and acts are inimical to free and democratic social order are unconstitutional; this allowed the possibility of banning radical groups by juridical means. In Japan, by contrast, this had to be done through the passage of specific laws, a much more politically delicate operation. See Yoshida Shigeru, *The Yoshida Memoirs: The Story of Japan in Crisis*. London: Heinemann, 1961, 237.

23. *Nippon Times*, April 27, 1951.

24. Yoshida, *The Yoshida Memoirs*, 234; and Kurt Steiner, *Local Government in Japan*. Stanford: Stanford University Press, 1965, 255.

25. For Kishi's views on the Police Bill struggle, see Kishi Nobusuke, *Kishi Nobusuke Kaikoroku: Hoshu Gōdō to Ampo Kaitei*. Tokyo: Kōsaidō, 1983, 436–46.

26. See, for example, State Army to DOS (Top Secret), "Conditions in Japan," April 7, 1949.

27. On the transnational politics of Japanese labor union relationships with the state, see Ehud Harari, *The Politics of Labor Legislation in Japan*. Berkeley: University of California Press, 1973.

28. On efforts at changing the electoral system see, for example, Calder, *Crisis and Compensation*, 169–71.

29. For more detail on how the "defense dividend" in Japan was diverted to political stabilization rather than to industrial support, as commonly alleged, see Calder, *Crisis and Compensation*, 172–82, 411–39.

30. In Italy, there was an eight-year hiatus (1943–1951) between the Allied occupation and conclusion of the London Peace treaty, during which vigorous working relations between local governments and resident U.S. forces developed. In the Azores, geographical distance from Lisbon and the establishment of close working relations between the Lajes Air Base and local communities during World War II, when Anglo-American influence was magnified by wartime imperatives, as well as the legal standing of the Azores as an autonomous region of Portugal all helped produce a similar responsiveness to grassroots concerns.

31. Interview discussions with former U.S. State Department base negotiators, and the *New York Times*, November 25, 2005.

32. The United States provided substantial assistance until the late 1990s, with Portugal receiving $48.7 million in the fiscal year 1998. See U.S. A.I.D., *U.S. Overseas Loans and Grants* (Green Book), 2005 edition and http://globalsecurity .org/military/facility/lajes.htm.

33. See, for example, Alga Oliker and David A. Shlapak, *U.S. Interests in Central Asia: Policy Priorities and Military Roles*. Santa Monica, California: Rand Project Air Force, 2005, 11–19.

34. Lenore G. Martin and Dimitris Keridis, eds., *The Future of Turkish Foreign Policy*. Cambridge, MA: MIT Press, 2004, 87–88. The recent flashpoint has been U.S. congressional ambivalence regarding the sale of attack helicopters and main battle tanks, due to persistent human-rights concerns relating to repression of the Kurds.

35. On the importance of this imbalance between political participation and political institutionalization, see Samuel P. Huntington, *Political Order in Changing Societies*. New Haven: Yale University Press, 1968.

36. See U.S. Agency for International Development, *Green Book*, 2003 edition.

37. *Agence France Presse*, July 14, 2006.

38. For a good survey of the details of the case, see Bill Park, "Strategic Location, Political Dislocation: Turkey, the United States, and Northern Iraq", *Middle East Review of International Affairs* 7, no. 2 (June 2003): 1–13.

39. *Washington Post*, December 3, 2002.

40. International Institute for Strategic Studies, "Turkey in Flux," *Strategic Survey*, 2003–2004 edition. London: I.I.S.S., 2003, 138.

41. *Washington Post*, March 10, 2003.

42. In January 1997 the Turkish Army sent troops into the streets of suburban Ankara to break up violent anti-Israel celebrations of Jerusalem Day. At a climactic meeting the next month of Turkey's powerful National Security Council, Islamist Prime Minister Erbakan was obliged to sign antiactivist measures that put him in conflict with his own militants, and that ultimately caused his coalition government to fall. See Giles Kepel, *Jihad: The Trail of Political Islam*. Cambridge, MA: Harvard University Press, 2002, 354–60.

43. Martin and Keridis, ed., *The Future of Turkish Foreign Policy*, 48.

44. *Financial Times*, March 22, 2005.

45. On the interests involved in this case and their inter-relationships, see "Turkey in Flux," *Strategic Survey*, 2003–2004 edition, 129–46.

46. In Spain, for example, five-year U.S. base-rental payments soared 20-fold during 1970–1983, from $100 million in 1970 to $2 billion in 1983. See McDonald and Bendahmane, *U.S. Bases Overseas: Negotiations with Spain, Greece, and the Philippines*, 123.

47. H. W. Brands, *Bound to Empire: The United States and the Philippines*. New York: Oxford University Press, 1992.

48. The 1987 Filipino Constitution indicates in Section 25 of Article 18: Transitory Provisions, "After the expiration in 1991 of the Agreement between the Republic of the Philippines and the United States of America concerning military bases, foreign military bases, troops, or facilities shall not be allowed in the Philippines except under a treaty duly concurred in by the Senate and, when the Congress so requires, ratified by a majority of the votes cast by the people in a national referendum held for that purpose, and recognized as a treaty by the other contracting State." See Republic of the Philippines Web site, available at http://www.gov.ph/aboutphil/constitution.asp.

49. In South Korea, for example, 19.4 percent of the land requisitioned for the use of American military forces under SOFA land grants in 2002, with an estimated value of roughly $200 million, was private land, yet the ROK government had never paid rent to the landowners. See Nam Chang-hee, "Relocating USFK Bases: Background and Implications," *East Asian Review* 15, no. 3 (Autumn 2003): 113.

50. Translation of Article 2, Republic of Korea National Security Law.

51. On this general problem, see Robert O. Keohane, "The Big Influence of Small Allies," *Foreign Policy* no. 2 (1971): 161–82.

52. See Donald W. Boose, Barbara Y. Hwang, Patrick Morgan, and Andrew Scobell, eds., *Recalibrating the U.S.-ROK Alliance*. Carlisle, PA: U.S. Army War College Strategic Studies Institute, 2003, 38.

53. Nineteen thousand Spanish volunteers served with the Spanish Blue Division (Division Azul), a part of the Wehrmacht's 250th Infantry Division, from 1941–43, under a Spanish commander. When Franco recalled the force in 1943, 3,000 disobeyed his orders and remained on the Russian front, attached to the Waffen SS, and renamed the Blue Legion. In this capacity, they fought to the bitter end of World War II, to defend Berlin from the Soviet onslaught. See Paul Stuart and Vicky Short, "Spain: Socialist Party government moves to rehabilitate Francoite fascists" *World Socialist Web site*, October 20, 2004, available at http://www.wsws.org/articles/2004/oct2004/spai-020.shtml.

54. See Ellis Krauss, *Japanese Radicals Revisited*. Berkeley, University of California Press, 1974.

55. See Sook Jong Lee, "The Rise of Korean Youth as a Political Force," 15–30.

56. On the general problem of stabilizing the aftermath of dictatorship, see Huntingon, *Political Order in Changing Societies*.

57. See, for example, Michael A. Palmer, *Guardians of the Gulf: A History of America's Expanding Role in the Persian Gulf, 1833–1992*. New York: Free Press, 1992, 29–32; and Rachel Bronson, *Thicker than Oil: America's Uneasy Partnership with Saudi Arabia*. Oxford: Oxford University Press, 2006, 46–49.

58. The British established major bases in Egypt for defense of the Suez Canal in 1882, and in Iraq and Palestine following World War I. The French were active in Lebanon and Syria between the World Wars.

59. Bernard Lewis, *What Went Wrong: Western Impact and Middle Eastern Response*. New York: Maxwell MacMillan International, 1995.

60. Bronson, *Thicker than Oil*, 47.

61. Johnson. *Sorrows of the Empire*, 219; and Bronson, *Thicker than Oil*, 79.

62. Bronson, *Thicker than Oil*, 194–95.

63. Ibid., 195.

64. Johnson, *The Sorrows of Empire*, 242.

65. Ibid., 241.

66. Ibid., 238.

67. Said Aburish, *The Rise, Corruption, and Coming Fall of the House of Saud*. New York: St. Martin's Press, 1995, 27.

68. Giles Kepel, *Jihad: The Trail of Political Islam*. Cambridge: Harvard University Press, 2002, 50.

69. Ibid.

70. Stephen Schwartz, *The Two Faces of Islam: The House of Sa'ud from Tradition to Terror*. New York: Doubleday, 2002, 75.

71. Kepel. *Jihad*, 75.

72. This figure of 600 represents half of all the mosques now operating in the United States. See Stephen Schwartz, "Wahhabism and Islam in the U.S.," *National Review*, June 30, 2003.

73. Kepel, *Jihad*, 53.

74. A decade earlier, the fall of the Shah of Iran and the marginalization of Anwar Sadat in the Arab world had also eroded the regional political bases for moderate Saudi base policies. See Charles Kupchan, *Persian Gulf and the West: The Dilemma of Security*. Boston: Allen and Unwin, 1987.

75. Mohammed al-Masari, a member of the Committee for the Defense of Legitimate Rights, for example, engaged in caustic criticism of the Saudi regime from London in the early 1990s. See Kepel, *Jihad*, 215–16.

76. In a classified addendum to the December 30, 1966 U.S.-U.K. agreement to make Diego Garcia and surrounding islands available for fifty years for common defense purposes, the United States agreed to provide up to half of British detachment costs, up to $14 million, through a waiver of the 5 percent research and development surcharge on Polaris submarine sales to Britain. This finessed the need for a regular congressional appropriation. See Vyautas Blaise Bandjunis, *Diego Garcia: The Navy's Best Kept Secret*. San Jose, CA: Writer's Showcase, 2001, 26–27.

77. On these facilities, see John Baker and Douglas H. Paal, "The U.S.-Australian Alliance," in Robert D. Blackwill and Paul Dibb, eds., *America's Asian Alliances*. Cambridge, MA: MIT Press, 2000, 88–89.

78. Desmond Ball, *A Suitable Piece of Real Estate: American Installations in Australia*. Sydney: Hale and Iremonger, 1980, 15–16.

79. Gerson and Birchard, *The Sun Never Sets*, 138.

80. Ibid.

81. Johnson, *The Sorrows of Empire*, 162–63.

82. Gerson and Birchard, *The Sun Never Sets*.

83. For details of the dispute, see Ted Galen Carpenter, "Pursuing a Strategic Divorce: The U.S. and the ANZUS Alliance," *Cato Policy Analysis*, no. 67, available at http://www.cato.org/cgi-bin/scripts/printtech.pubs/pas/pa067/html.

Chapter Seven
Base-Politics Management: The Subnational Dimension

1. Johnson, *Blowback: The Costs and Consequences of American Empire*, 36.

2. During the eighty-two days of the Battle of Okinawa, 234,000 people were killed, including 147,000 Okinawans, over 72,000 mainland Japanese, and more than 12,000 Americans. The U.S. Navy lost more men at Okinawa than in any other battle in its entire history. On the details, see Aloysius O'neill, *Okinawa and its Role in the U.S.-Japan Alliance*. Washington, D.C.: Reischauer Center for East Asian Studies, 2007, 4; and Ōta Masahide, *Kore ga Okinawasen da Globalsecurity .org; Kaiteiban: Shashin Kiroku* (This is the Definitive Version of the Battle of Okinawa: Photo Record). Naha, Okinawa: Naha Shuppan Sha, 1998.

3. Sandars, *America's Overseas Garrisons*, 162.

4. Nicholas Evan Sarantakes, *Keystone: The American Occupation of Okinawa and U.S.-Japanese Relations*. College Station: Texas A & M University Press, 2000.

5. The two local Okinawan dailies have subscriptions of around 200,000 each, while all the Tokyo dailies combined have a subscription in Okinawa of less than 10,000. See O'neill, *Okinawa and its Role in the U.S.-Japan Alliance*, 8.

6. On the general background of the Futenma problem against the backdrop of Okinawan antimilitarist sentiments, see Muramichi Sebastian Inoue, John Purves, and Mark Selden, "Okinawa Citizens, U.S. Bases, and the Dugong," *Bulletin of Critical Asian Studies* 29, no. 4 (1997), available at http://csf.colorado.edu/bcas/ campaign/okinawa.htm.

7. *Yomiuri Shimbun*, July 18, 2004.

8. The Security Consultative Committee, also known as the "2 + 2 Committee."

9. MOFA Japan Web site, available at http://www.mofa.go.jp/region/n-america/ us/security/scc/doc0510.html.

10. *Kyōdō News*, February 5, 2006.

11. *Ryūkyū Shimpō*, February 20, 2006.

12. *Kyōdō News*, January 23, 2006.

13. The United States and Japan finally agreed on May 1, 2006, to locate the Futenma Replacement Facility in a configuration combining a portion of Camp Schwab together with some reclaimed land in adjacent waters, providing two runways, each having a length of 1,800 meters plus 200-meter overruns, aligned in a V-shape. See *Japan Times*, May 18, 2006.

14. Chalmers Johnson, "The Heliport, Nago, and the End of the Ota Era," in Chalmers Johnson ed., *Okinawa: Cold War Island*. Tokyo: Japan Policy Research Institute, 1999, 230.

15. *Daily Yomiuri*, September 16, 2005.

16. *Jiji Press*, October 26, 2005.

17. This figure for military-related income includes military-base rental fees (for both the U.S. military and the Japanese Self-Defense Forces), wages of base employees, and consumption expenditures by the bases, military personnel, and their families.

18. Okinawa Prefecture, Statistics Office Web site, available at http://www .pref.okinawa.jp/toukeika/accounts/2002/acc4_2.xls.

19. Hiroshi Kakazu, *Thriving Locally in the Global Economy: The Case of Okinawa*. Naha, Okinawa: Okinawa Development Finance Corporation, 2000, 14.

20. Defense Facilities Administration Agency, *Progress of the SACO Final Report*. Unpublished memorandum. Tokyo, 2003, 8.

21. Aloysius O'neill, *Okinawa and its Role in the U.S.-Japan Alliance*, 8.

22. Okinawan commercial land prices themselves fell by fully one-third between 1998 and 2004. See Ministry of Land, Infrastructure, and Transport, *Todofuken Chika Chosa (Research Report on Prefectural Land Prices)*, available at http://tochi.mlit.go.jp.

23. Robert Eldridge, "The 1996 Okinawa Referendum on U.S. Base Reductions: One Question, Several Answers," *Asian Survey* 37, no. 10 (October 1997): 896–97.

24. On the concept of the veto player, see George Tsebelis, *Veto Players: How Political Institutions Work*. Princeton: Princeton University Press, 2002.

25. Indeed, the long-time chairman of the JSP, Ishibashi Masashi, was an early member of Zenchūrō. See Keddell, *The Politics of Defense in Japan*, 68.

26. Ibid.

27. Ibid., 17, 68, 144.

28. *Okinawa Times* reported that United States Forces Japan calculated its "consumption," including base-related contracts as ¥73.7 billion for FY2003, according to its report "Economic Impact of the U.S. Forces on Okinawa," 2005 edition. Okinawa Prefecture calculated USFJ local "consumption" expenditures for 2002 to be only ¥52.3 billion.

29. Naha Defense Facilities Administration Branch, Defense Facilities Administration Agency Web site, available at http://www.naha.dfab.dfaa.go.jp/kensetsu/naha/index.html.

30. Okinawa Prefecture, Statistics Office Web site, available at http://www .pref.okinawa.jp/toukeika/accounts/2003/toukeihyo.xls.

31. Ministry of Internal Affairs and Communications Statistics Bureau Web site, available at http://www.stat.go.jp/data/nihon/zuhyou/n0300800.xls.

32. *Daily Yomiuri*, October 27, 2005.

33. For a detailed chronological overview of the Vieques protest movement, with some attention to cultural and social context also, see Katherine T. McCaffrey, *Military Power and Popular Protest: The U.S. Navy in Vieques, Puerto Rico*. New Brunswick, NJ: Rutgers University Press, 2002.

34. Vieques citizens, especially organized groups with special economic concerns, did, to be sure, periodically oppose specific military operations on or around their island, as during the Fishermen's War of 1978–83. Yet local divisions on the island, and the difficulty of generating support beyond Vieques, made these intermittent efforts unsustainable. See McCaffrey, *Military Power and Popular Protest*, 67–123, for example.

35. See Fellowship of Reconciliation, *Vieques Issue Brief*, 2001, 3.

36. The term "transnational" is used here in a specialized sense. Puerto Rico is, of course, a Commonwealth affiliated with the United States, rather than an independent nation. Yet it is not an American state, it does not vote in U.S. presidential elections, and it is culturally distinct from the American mainland. It is thus a largely distinct political system, quasinational in character, so the term "transnational" seems appropriate in discussing its base-political relations with the U.S. mainland.

37. *New York Times*, June 15, 2001.

38. *Washington Post*, June 12, 2001.

39. On the radar site (ROTHR) controversy of 1994–97, see McCaffrey, *Military Power and Popular Protest*, 138–45.

40. *Washington Post*, June 12, 1999.

41. Two prominent retired navy admirals, John Shanahan and Eugene Carroll, for example, testified in support of the Vieques movement in a U.S. district court, arguing that the training the navy was conducting in Vieques was neither unique nor necessary for contemporary amphibious warfare, and that the kind of short-range gunfire support and close-in bombing that the navy rehearsed in Vieques were in themselves becoming obsolete as the military shifted to cruise missiles and other more powerful "stand-off" weapons fired from long ranges. On the broadening range of legitimators for the Vieques movement, see McCaffrey, *Military Power and Popular Protest*, 167–77.

42. *New York Times*, June 15, 2001.

43. Ibid.

44. John Lindsay-Poland, "U.S. Military Bases in Latin America and the Caribbean," *Foreign Policy in Focus*, August 2004.

45. Vytautas Blaise Bandjunis, *Diego Garcia*, 1.

46. Ibid., 12.

47. K. S. Kawatkar, *Diego Garcia in International Diplomacy*. London: Sangam, 1982.

48. Wilson announced to the House of Commons on January 16, 1968, that the British military disengagement from Singapore, Malaysia, and the Persian Gulf would be complete by the end of 1971. For details of the policy shift, see C. J. Bartlett, *The Long Retreat: A Short History of British Defense Policy, 1945–1970*. London: The Macmillan Press, 1972, 215–63.

49. Bandjunis, *Diego Garcia*, 3.

50. Ibid., 45–46.

51. On these issues, see Christopher Sandars, *America's Overseas Garrisons*, 55–59.

52. Ibid., 56.

53. It was later revealed, in U.S. House of Representatives Committee on International Relations hearings in 1975, that Britain received a $14 million waiver of the normal research and development levies on Polaris missile sales, in return for this provision. See ibid., 57.

54. Ibid.

55. William Pomeroy, "Diego Garcia: For U.S. defense and security, from the people," *Diego Garcia: For U*, available at http://www.pww.org/past-week-2000/Diego%20Garcia.htm.

56. Bandjunis. *Diego Garcia*, 110.

57. Ibid., 119–24.

58. Ibid., 128–29.

59. In 1977 Mansfield was named U.S. Ambassador to Japan by President Jimmy Carter, in which position he remained for twelve years. See Don Oberdorfer, *Senator Mansfield*. Washington, D.C.: Smithsonian Books, 2003, 457–502.

60. Bandjunis, *Diego Garcia*, 3.

61. *Agence France Presse*, November 3, 2000. Many workers, of course, had been only temporary, but some families had resided in the Chagos Archipelago for as long as two generations.

62. *Associated Press*, October 9, 2003.

63. "LALIT Communique on Diego Garcia," *Workers' Liberty*, June 23, 2004, available at http://www.workersliberty.org/node/View.

Chapter Eight
The Financial Equations: Local Equities, Base Stability, and Burden Sharing

1. The relocation cost is expected to be around $8 billion, with well over half of the total expenses likely to be covered by Japan. See *Ryūkyū Shimpō*, March 1, 2006.

2. See Harold Lasswell, *Politics: Who Gets What, When, How*. New York: McGraw-Hill Books, 1936.

3. Most U.S. military personnel in nations like Turkey, Kyrgyzstan, Romania, Poland, Hungary, and Bulgaria, it should be noted, are in temporary duty (TDY) status, obscuring the substantial American "on-the-ground" commitments in all of the nations concerned.

4. Japanese "strategic foreign aid" to the Philippines in the late 1980s, or to Central Asian nations since 9/11, has, for example, filled this supportive function. For details, see Japanese Foreign Ministry, *Diplomatic Blue Book*, annual.

5. Japanese provision of around 500,000 kiloliters of fuel oil for American and other allied naval forces engaged in Indian Ocean antiterrorist operations during the first five years after 9/11 is one conspicuous exception. So were large Japanese, Saudi, and Kuwaiti operational-support payments for U.S. forces during the 1991 Gulf War.

6. See, for example, Peter Katzenstein and Christopher Hemmer, "Why Is There No NATO in Asia?" *International Organization* 56, 3 (2001): 575–607.

7. Japan's population decreased by nearly six thousand in 2005—the first peacetime decline in its modern history. See *Asahi Shimbun*, February 20, 2006. Meanwhile, the Self Defense Agency's peacekeeping-operations budget rose by around 9 percent in the same year.

8. Defense Facilities Administration Agency, *Change in Host Nation Support*, 2005 edition.

9. "Direct" support includes costs borne by host nations in support of stationed U.S. forces for rent on privately owned land and facilities, labor, utilities, and vicinity improvements. "Indirect" costs include foregone rents and revenues, including rents on government-owned land and facilities occupied or used by

U.S. forces at no or reduced cost to the United States, and tax concessions or customs duties waived by the host nation.

10. Donald W. Boose et al., eds., *Recalibrating the U.S.-ROK Alliance.* Carlisle, PA: U.S. Army War College Strategic Studies Institute, 2003, 58.

11. As mentioned above, roughly 75 percent of the land on which U.S. military bases in Okinawa stand is leased from more than 27,000 local land owners, while in Korea most U.S. bases stand on Korean government land, with no rental payments to local interests involved. This contrast is among the most striking and consequential differences between the political economy of HNS in Korea and in Japan.

12. *British Broadcasting Corporation*, December 17, 2004.

13. Ibid., June 1, 2006; *Financial Times*, February 7, 2006.

14. Those being relocated from Pyeongtaek due to expansion of the U.S. military base there were to be offered (1) land for housing and business, or a residence for lease; (2) special relocation allowances of up to U.S.$15,000 per household; and (3) stabilization-of-livelihood special support of U.S $2,500 per person, through a special Presidential Decree. See *Yonhap News Agency Wire Service*, March 22, 2005.

15. *British Broadcasting Corporation*, October 4, 2003; *Korean Herald*, January 19, 2005 and November 25, 2005.

16. Boose et al., *Recalibrating the U.S.-ROK Alliance*, 38.

17. On the details, see Joel S. Wit, Daniel B. Poneman, and Robert Gallucci, *Going Critical: The First North Korean Nuclear Crisis*. Washington, D.C.: The Brookings Institution, 2004.

18. Korean figures, it must be noted, treat liaison staff on secondment with USFK, as well as inputted labor costs, in a different fashion than do American statistics. See Boose et al., *Re-Calibrating the U.S.-ROK Alliance*, 40.

19. The tragic deaths of two Korean middle-school students during the summer of 2002 in an accident with a U.S. military vehicle might have been expected to have had analogous implications, since they stirred a massive anti-U.S. military backlash in South Korea. Yet the proximity of the South Korean presidential elections, and the election of a government not notably sympathetic to improving the local standing of the U.S. military, diluted the impact on new HNS-related programs in Korea.

20. See Calder and Ye, "Regionalism and Critical Junctures: Explaining the 'Organization Gap' in Northeast Asia," 198–99.

21. Simon W. Duke and Wolfgang Krieger, eds., *U.S. Military Forces in Europe: The Early Years, 1945–1970*. Boulder, Colorado: Westview Press, 1993; and Simon Duke, *United States Military Forces and Installations in Europe*. Solna, Sweden: SIPRI, 1989.

22. German HNS support for American forces in Germany rose from $862 million in 2001 to $1.563 billion in 2002. See U.S. Department of Defense, *Report on Allied Contributions*. 2004 edition.

23. Lajes Air Force Base lies 2,700 miles from the U.S. east coast, 1,100 mile from Gibraltar, and around 3,000 miles from Israel.

24. *Agence France Presse*, July 14, 2006. Unfortunately there was not enough *Green Book* data to include Kyrgyzstan in table 8.7, although admittedly incomplete evidence strongly suggests that its case clearly fits the argument being made here.

25. Japanese Ministry of Foreign Affairs, *Diplomatic Blue Book*, annual, available at http://www.mofa.go.jp/policy/other/bluebook/index.html; and Ministry of Foreign Affairs Economic Cooperation Bureau, *ODA White Paper*, annual, available at http://mofa/go/jp/policy/oda/white/index.html. During 2000–2004 Japan was consistently the largest or second largest donor to Kyrgyzstan, Uzbekistan, and Kazakhstan—two of which hosted U.S. bases and all of which were strategically important to the United States.

26. Anup Shah, "The U.S. and Foreign Aid Assistance," *Global Issues*, July 11, 2004, available at: http://www.globalissues.org/images/USAid20012002.gif.

27. Kennedy, *The Rise and Fall of Great Powers*.

28. Barnett, *The Pentagon's New Map*, 107–90.

29. *Kyōdō News*, May 1, 2006.

30. Johnson, *The Sorrows of Empire*, 238–41.

Chapter Nine
Bases and American Strategy: Emerging Options

1. This figure, of $118 billion, was the "plant replacement value" (PRV) of all American bases overseas as of September 2006. The Department of Defense defines the PRV of a given base as "the reported cost of replacing the facility using today's costs (labor and materials), and standards (methods and codes)." For base-specific calculations, see U.S. Department of Defense, *Base Structure Report*, 2006 edition.

2. Over $400 billion in mid-2006 and rising at over $5 billion a month—not including long-term veterans' assistance costs, which are projected to bring the long-term cost of the war to over $1 trillion. See *United Press International*, June 27, 2006. Figures from the Department of Defense.

3. George F. Kennan, *Around the Cragged Hill: A Personal and Political Philosophy*. New York: W. W. Norton, 1993, 183.

4. On the general logic of retrenchment from large-scale American commitments overseas in the post–Cold War world, see Christopher Layne, "From Preponderance to Offshore Balancing: America's Future Grand Strategy," *International Security* 22, no. 1 (Summer 1997): 86–124.

5. On the details of "offshore balancing," see ibid., 112–19.

6. William E. Odom and Robert Dujarric, *America's Inadvertent Empire*. New Haven: Yale University Press, 2004.

7. Michael Mandelbaum, *The Case for Goliath: How America Acts as the World's Government in the Twenty-First Century*. New York: Public Affairs, 2005.

8. Jim Garrison, *America as Empire: Global Leader or Rogue Power?* San Francisco: Berret-Koehler Publishers, 2004.

9. The B-2s landed for recovery at Diego Garcia, 3,000 miles south of Afghanistan. On landing at Diego, the planes kept their engines running: fresh crews came aboard, and took off for the long flight back to Missouri. For more details on the Afghan air campaign, including its long-range dimensions, see John A. Tirpak, "Enduring Freedom," *Air Force Magazine* (February 2002): 32–39.

10. Daniel Bayman, "Do Targeted Killings Work?" *Foreign Affairs* 85, no. 2 (March–April 2006): 95.

11. *CNN.com*, on December 30, 2002, available at http://www.cnn.com/2002/WORLD/meast/12/30/sproject.irq.predator.irap/.

12. *Newsweek*, January 30, 2006.

13. Tirpak, "Enduring Freedom," 34. Also Anthony J. Cordesman, *The Lessons of Afghanistan*. Washington, D.C.: CSIS Press, 2002, 4–11.

14. International Institute for Strategic Studies, *The Military Balance*, 2005–2006 edition.

15. The B-2A (stealth) bomber has an unfueled range of 6,900 miles, the B-1B (nonstealth) bomber a range of 8,050 miles, and the B-52H a range of 8,800 miles. See Council for a Livable World Web site, available at http://64.177.207.201/pages/8_75.html.

16. On the Predator, see http://www.campusprogram.com/reference/en/wolo[edoa/r/rq/rq_l_predator.

17. On the Global Hawk, see the U.S. Air Force Web site, available at http://www.af.mil/factsheets/factsheet_print.asp?fsID=175&page=1.

18. Elinor Sloan, *The Revolution in Military Affairs*. Montreal: McGill-Queens University Press, 2002, 44.

19. RATTLRS denotes "Revolutionary Approach to Time-Critical Long-Range Strike Aircraft." On the details of this program, see *Defense and Foreign Affairs Daily*, August 12, 2004.

20. David Talbott, "The Ascent of the Robotic Attack Jet," *Technology Review* 108, no. 3 (March 2005): 56–60.

21. On sea basing, see Jane G. Dalton, "Future Navies—Present Issues," *Naval War College Review* 59, no. 1 (Winter 2006): 17–39; and Charles Hazard, "Sea Basing: Chasing the Dream," *U.S. Naval Institute Proceeding* 131, no. 7 (July 2005): 65–66.

22. Quoted in Michael O'Hanlon, "Can High Technology Bring U.S. Troops Home?' *Foreign Policy* (Winter 1998–99): 73.

23. Ibid.

24. Ibid.

25. The U.S. national defense budget for 2006 was $441.8 billion, a 4.4 percent increase over 2005 spending.

26. Cordesman, *The Lessons of Afghanistan*, 6.

27. Ibid.

28. Paul Bracken, *Fire in the East*. New York: HarperCollins, 1999, 63–70.

29. See, for example, Doug Bandow, and Ted Galen Carpenter, eds., *The U.S.-South Korean Alliance: Time for a Change*. New Brunswick, NJ: Transaction Books, 1992.

30. O'Hanlon, "Can High Technology Bring U.S. Troops Home?" 73–74.

31. See Layne, "From Preponderance to Offshore Balancing," 108 and Bracken. *Fire in the East*.

32. Chalmers Johnson, *Blowback*. New York: Metropolitan Books, 2000.

33. Layne, "From Preponderance to Offshore Balancing," 108.

34. Talbott, "The Ascent of the Robotic Attack Jet."

35. *Associated Press*, January 14, 2006.

36. Mark Mazzetti, "PAX AMERICANA," *U.S. News and World Report*, October 6, 2003.

37. The concept of "Classic Pax Americana" presented here is similar to Layne's characterization of post–World War II U.S. grand strategy. See Layne, "From Preponderance to Offshore Balancing: America's Future Grand Strategy,"86–124.

38. Wolfram Hanrieder, *Germany, Europe, and America*. New Haven: Yale University Press, 1989.

39. Extended deterrence involves active efforts by a major power (the defender) to deter another challenging state from launching a significant military attack upon a friend or ally.

40. As Thomas Schelling points out, persuading enemies or allies requires more than military capability; it requires projecting *intentions*. And the local presence of U.S. troops, especially in tripwire situations, such as the DMZ in Korea or the Fulda Gap in Cold War Europe, clearly conveyed the intention of U.S. commitment. See Thomas Schelling, *Arms and Influence*. Cambridge, MA: Harvard University Press, 1960, 36.

41. See, for example, Gilpin, *War and Change in World Politics* ; Kennedy, *The Rise and Fall of the Great Powers*; and David Calleo, *The Imperious Economy*. Cambridge, MA: Harvard University Press, 1982.

42. Christopher Layne, "Less is More: Realist Foreign Policy for East Asia," *National Interest* (Spring 1996), available at http://www.findarticles.com/p/articles/mi_m2751/is_n43/ai_18298481.

43. See, for example, O'Hanlon, "Can High Technology Bring American Troops Home?," 72–86.

44. Ibid., 74.

45. See also Kurt M. Campbell and Celeste Johnson Ward, "New Battle Stations?" *Foreign Affairs* (September–October 2003): 95–103.

46. O'Hanlon, "Can High Technology Bring American Troops Home?," 81.

47. See Campbell and Ward, "New Battle Stations?," 100–101.

48. See, for example, Anthony Arnove, *Iraq: The Logic of Withdrawl*. New York: The New Press, 2006 and Eugene Gholi, Daryl G. Press, and Benjamin Valentino, "Time to Offshore Our Troops," *New York Times*, December 12, 2006.

49. The core security problem with respect to Persian Gulf energy access is perceived to be responding to Iranian mines, or cruise-missile attacks on oil tankers. Prospective American response would be carried out largely by submarines, surface ships, and naval aircraft—all of which could be stationed in the Indian Ocean during peacetime, it is argued. See Gholi, Press, and Valentino, "Time to Offshore Our Troops."

50. President George W. Bush, "Remarks by the President at 2002 Graduation Exercise of the U.S. Military Academy, West Point, New York", available at http://www.whitehouse.gov/news/releases/2002/06/print/20020601-3.html.

51. Former Deputy Defense Secretary Paul Wolfowitz, among others, was very explicit about this linkage, maintaining that "we need to think about transformation in the context of the global war on terrorism. One area that we have

neglected, as a country and as a military, is the area of irregular warfare." See Paul Wolfowitz, "Thinking about the Imperatives of Defense Transformation," *Heritage Lectures*, April 30, 2004, 1.

52. Bush, "Remarks," 2.

53. Jim Garamone, "War and Transformation: The U.S. Military's Story," *American Forces Information Service*, February 14, 2003, available at http://www.dod.gov/news/Feb2003/n02142003_200302142.html.

54. Wolfowitz, "Thinking about the Imperatives of Defense Transformation," 2.

55. U.S. Secretary of Defense, *Annual Report to the President and the Congress*. Washington, D.C.: U.S. Government Printing Office, 2003, 8.

56. Wolfowitz, "Thinking about the Imperative of Defense Transformation," 2–4.

57. "U.S. Military Transformation Necessary, but Path Not Smooth," *JINSA Online*, July 9, 2004, available at http://www.jinsa.org/articles/print.html/documentid/2602.

58. Wolfowitz, "Thinking about the Imperative of Defense Transformation," 2–4.

59. Ibid.

60. Paul D. Wolfowitz, Testimony before the House Budget Committee, Washington, D.C., February 12, 2002.

61. Steve Liewer, "Plans Slow for Base Closures in Europe," *The Stars and Stripes* (European edition), December 8, 2003.

62. The U.S. European Command (EUCOM) is, for example, expected to reduce its personnel strength of 112,000 in 2005 by 40 percent over the coming decade, with the majority of the troop cuts made from forces currently stationed in Germany. See the United States European Command Web site, available at http://www.eucom.mil/English/Transformation/Transform_Blue.asp.

63. Michael O'Hanlon calculates, for example, that new bases typically cost $5–7 billion in initial investment, which is recouped over an average of 7–10 years. See Michael E. O'Hanlon, *Defense Strategies for the Post-Saddam Era*. Washington, D.C.: The Brookings Institution, 2005, 62–63; and Frances Lussier, *Options for Changing the Army's Overseas Basing*. Washington, D.C.: Congressional Budget Office, 2004, xiv.

Chapter Ten
Implications for Policy and Theory

1. Anni Baker, *Wiesbaden and the Americans, 1945–2003*. Wiesbaden: Druckerei Zeidler, 2004.

2. This is an interesting contrast to the muted American response to the May 1980 Kwangju massacre in also strategic South Korea, during the Carter administration, although the Cold War geopolitical context was markedly different.

3. By comparison, the British defense budget was $51.5 billion, the Japanese $44.7 billion, the French $41.6 billion, the German $30.2 billion, the Chinese $29.5 billion, and the Russian $18.8 billion. See International Institute for Strategic Studies, *The Military Balance*, 2005–2006 edition.

4. On the massive capital flows that allowed the Reagan administration to sustain huge deficits without sharp interest-rate increases during the 1980s, see Robert Gilpin, *The Political Economy of International Relations*. Princeton: Princeton University Press, 1987.

5. Ferguson, *Colossus*, 224. France, for example, was represented on the Egyptian Caisse de la Dette Publique, which had been set up to administer Egyptian finances after the 1876 default.

6. Ibid., 221.

7. On the attractiveness of such sites, see also Roger Cliff, Sam J. Tangredi, and Christine E. Wormuth, "The Future of U.S. Overseas Presence," in Michele A. Flournoy (editor), *QDR 2001: Strategy Driven Choices for America's Security*. Washington, D.C.: National Defense University Press, 2001, 235–62.

8. Anderson Air Base in Guam reportedly stores more jet fuel than any other military base in the United States, amid indications that the United States indeed may contemplate a major long-term buildup on Guam to counter rising Chinese regional capabilities. See *Daily Yomiuri*, August 25, 2002.

9. Donald Rumsfeld gave Special Forces development substantial priority, doubling the special operations budget between fiscal 2001 and fiscal 2007. See *Wall Street Journal*, February 18, 2006. Similarly Harold Brown, Jimmy Carter's Defense Secretary, helped create the Rapid Deployment Force over a quarter century earlier.

10. See Department of the Army, *Counterinsurgency*, 8–5.

11. Alexander Cooley, "Base Politics: Redeploying U.S. Troops," *Foreign Affairs* 84, no. 6 (November–December 2005): 79–92.

12. See Timothy J. Paris, *Britain, the Hashemites, and Arab Rule, 1920–1925*. London: Frank Cass, 2003; and Joel Rayburn, "How the British Quit Mesopotamia," *Foreign Affairs*, (March–April 2006), 29–41.

13. Fouad Ajami, *The Foreigner's Gift: The Americans, the Arabs and the Iraqis in Iraq*. New York: Free Press, 2006.

14. For a particularly concise and authoritative chronicle from a participant in the CPA of the tactical mistakes that turned a potential "liberating occupation" into a neocolonialist manifestation inspiring popular resistance, see Larry Diamond, *Squandered Victory*.

15. See Shadid, *Night Draws Near*.

16. See International Institute for Strategic Studies, "U.S. Forces in the Persian Gulf: Options for the Post-Saddam Era," *Strategic Comments* 9, no. 3 (May 2003).

17. On the more general issue of privatized warfare, and the mixed incentives it creates, see P. W. Singer, *Corporate Warriors: The Rise of the Privatized Military Industry*. Ithaca: Cornell University Press, 2003; and Alexander Cooley, *Logics of Hierarchy: The Organization of Empires, States, and Military Occupations*. Ithaca: Cornell University Press, 2005, 143–56.

18. *New York Times*, January 7, 2007; Department of the Army, *Counterinsurgency*, 2–12; and Steven W. Simon, *After the Surge*. New York: Council on Foreign Relations Special Study no. 23 (February 2007): 3–4. The PRTs had successful antecedents in Afghanistan and Vietnam. As of early 2007, however, the United States had authorized only 167 civilian and 178 military PRT positions

for Iraq. In 1969 there were 1,700 State Department and 6,400 military personnel respectively serving in PRT positions in South Vietnam.

19. Tony Zinni and Tony Koltz. *The Battle for Peace*. New York: Macmillan
Palgrave, 2006, pp. 177–208, especially p. 193.

20. They can, of course, be partially compromised by counter-trends, such as
Afghanistan's reviving the drug trade, which weakened Karzai, who opposed it,
after 2004. Indeed, as much as 90 percent of world opium trade was estimated to
have passed through Afghanistan in 2006 (*New York Times*, February 4, 2007).
Karzai was also undermined by the occasional undeclared willingness of Pakistani intelligence services to allow their country to be used as a haven for insur-
gents operating against the Afghan government, and the frequent diversion of
American support toward Iraq. Those dynamics, however, do not negate the underlying value of "liberating occupations" more generally, or of the initial impact
of "liberating occupation" on Afghanistan, in particular. Different origins give
the Afghan insurgency a decidedly different and more hopeful potential trajec-
tory from Iraq. See *Financial Times*, February 1, 2007.

21. Robert Thompson, *Defeating Communist Insurgency*. St. Petersburg, FL:
Hailer Publishing, 2005.

22. See C. J. Bartlett, *The Long Retreat*, 105–28; and Richard Neustadt, *Alliance Politics*. New York: Columbia University Press, 1970, 8–29.

23. U.S. Department of Defense, *Base Structure Report*, 2005 edition.

24. Bruce Falconer, "U.S. Military Logistics," *Atlantic Monthly* 291, no. 4
(May 2003): 51.

25. Sidney Tarrow, *The New Transnational Activism*. Cambridge: Cambridge
University Press, 2005, 29.

26. The Pentagon's long-standing "no-confirm-or-deny" policies with respect
to nuclear-weapons deployment, and its resistance to arbitrary time limits on
basing, as in opposing a fifteen-year time limit on the Futenma replacement facility in Okinawa, have a clear and justifiable political-military logic, for example.

27. These included the Russian Republic itself, together with Armenia, Georgia, Kyrgyzstan, Moldova, Tajikistan, and Belarus.

28. Zinni and Koltz, *The Battle for Peace*, 184.

29. See Anni Baker, *Wiesbaden and the Americans, 1945–2003*.

30. Charlie Coon, "Kaiserslautern Office Aids American, German Concerns,"
Stars and Stripes, European edition, August 31, 2003.

31. *Haisai* (Hi) (published by Naha branch, Defense Facility Administration
Agency), July 2006 and June 2004 editions.

32. For more details, see Defense Facilities Administration, Naha Branch, Web
site, available at http://www.naha.dfab.dfaa.go.jp/chura/jpn/chura0.html.

33. Zinni and Koltz, *The Battle for Peace*, 129–42.

34. Ricks, *Fiasco*, 255–58.

35. U.S. Department of the Army, *Counterinsurgency*.

36. A similar approach has been suggested as a vehicle for strategic military
disengagement in time of war as well. See Edward Luttwak, "To Help Iraq, Let It
Fend for Herself," *New York Times*, February 6, 2007.

37. For evidence on this point, see Baker, *American Soldiers Overseas*, especially 110–65.

38. On the latter concept, see Simon, *After the Surge*, 41.

39. U.S. Department of the Army, *Counterinsurgency*, 8–5.

40. See Anni P. Baker, *American Soldiers Overseas: The Global Military Presence*. Westport, CT: Praeger, 2004, 58–60. In Okinawa, base-community interaction emerged much later than in Germany, but was prominent during U.S.-Japan festivities relating to the 2000 Okinawa Summit, for example.

41. See James A. Baker and Lee H. Hamilton, cochairs, *The Iraq Study Group Report*, 49.

42. Bremer, *My Year in Iraq*, 10.

43. Ferguson, *Empire*, 209.

44. *Christian Science Monitor*, May 20, 2003.

45. *New York Times*, August 20, 2005.

46. Fifty-thousand contractors reportedly supported 130,000 troops—a ratio matched in the United States only once before, during the Korean War. See T. Christian Miller, *Blood Money*. New York: Little, Brown, and Company, 2006, 76.

47. The proximate cause of the rebellion was introduction of the Enfield rifle amid rumors that its distinctive reloading system involved biting cartridges greased with lard or tallow, against which both Hindus and Muslims had religious scruples. See Wikipedia.com, available at http://en.wikipedia.org/wiki/Indian_rebellion_of_1857.

48. Ferguson, *Empire*, 210.

49. Ibid., 215.

50. Ibid.

51. The redeployment of refueling aircraft from the Futenma MCAS in Okinawa to the already established Kanoya Base of the Japanese Self-Defense Forces would be another example.

52. See, for example, *New York Times*, January 3, 2007, on Kurdistan's relative success in attracting outside aid and investment; and *New York Times*, August 19, 2007, on the use of compensation politics with the tribes of Anbar Province.

53. Zinni and Koltz, *The Battle for Peace*, 172–73.

54. As of Septembe r 2005, there were formally established forward American military facilities in 156 nations. See U.S. Department of Defense, *Worldwide Manpower Distribution by Geographical Area*, September 2005 edition.

55. See Stephen M. Walt, *Taming American Power: The Global Response to U.S. Primacy*. New York: W. W. Norton, 2005, 242.

56. Andrew Kohut and Bruce Stokes, *America against the World*. New York: Times Books, 2006, 220–25; and Walt, *Taming American Power*, 246.

Abramowitz, Morton (ed.), *The United States and Turkey: Allies in Need*. New York: The Century Foundation Press, 2003.

Aburish, Said., *The Rise, Corruption, and Coming Fall of the House of Saud*. New York: St. Martin's Press, 1995.

Ahn, Cheong-Si. (ed.), *Democracy in Asia, Europe, and the World*. Seoul: Korean Association of International Studies, 2004.

Ajami, Fouad, *The Foreigner's Gift: The Americans, the Arabs, and the Iraqis in Iraq*. New York; Free Press, 2006.

Aketagawa Tooru, *Nichibei Gyōsei: Kyōtei no Seiji Shi* (A Political History of U.S.-Japan Administrative Agreements). Tokyo: Hōsei Daigaku Shuppan, 1999.

Allison, Graham, *Essence of Decision*. New York: HarperCollins, 1971.

Arms Control Association, "The Intermediate-Range Nuclear Forces Treaty at a Glance." *Arms Control Association*, Feb 2003, at http://www.armscontrol.org/factsheets/IMFtreaty.asp.

Armstrong, Charles K., *Korean Society: Civil Society, Democracy, and the State*. London: Routledge, 2002.

Asahi Shimbun Sha (ed.), *Japan Almanac*. Tokyo: Asahi Shimbun Sha, annual.

Atlantic Council, *U.S. Challenges and Choices in the Gulf: Turkey, Iraq, and Regional Security*. Washington, DC: Atlantic Council of the United States, 2002.

Bacevich, Andrew J., *American Empire: The Realities and Consequences of U.S. Diplomacy*. Cambridge, MA: Harvard University Press, 2002.

———, *The New American Militarism: How Americans are Seduced by War*. Oxford: Oxford University Press, 2005.

Baker, Anni P., *American Soldiers Overseas: The Global Military Presence*. Westport, CT: Praeger, 2004.

———, *Wiesbaden and the Americans, 1945–2003*. Wiesbaden: Druckerei Zeidler, 2004.

Baker, James A., and Lee Hamilton (cochairs), *The Iraq Study Group Report*. New York: Vintage Books, 2006.

Ball, Desmond, *A Suitable Piece of Real Estate: American Installations in Australia*. Sydney: Hale and Iremonger, 1980.

Bandjunis, Vyautas Blaise, *Diego Garcia: The Navy's Best-Kept Secret*. San Jose, CA: Writers' Showcase, 2001.

Bandow, Doug, and Ted Galen Carpenter (eds.), *The U.S.-South Korean Alliance: Time for a Change*. New Brunswick, NJ: Transaction Books, 1992.

Barnett, Thomas P. M., *Blueprint for Action: A Future Worth Creating*. New York: G. P. Putnam's Sons, 2005.

———, *The Pentagon's New Map: War and Peace in the Twenty-First Century*. New York: G. P. Putnam's Sons, 2004.

Bartlett, C. J., *The Long Retreat: A Short History of British Defense Policy, 1945–1970*. London: Macmillan Press, 1972.

Bengzon, Alfredo A., and Raul Rodrigo, *A Matter of Honor: The Story of the 1990–1991 RP-US Base Talks*. Manila: Anvil Publishing, 1997.

Berger, Thomas U., *Cultures of Anti-Militarism: National Security in Germany and Japan*. Baltimore: Johns Hopkins University Press, 1998.

Berry, William E., Jr., *U.S. Bases in the Philippines: The Evolution of the Special Relationship*. Boulder, CO: Westview Press, 1989.

Blackwill, Robert D., and Paul Dibb (eds.), *America's Asian Alliances*. Cambridge, MA: MIT Press, 2000.

Blaker, James R., *United States Overseas Basing*. New York: Praeger, 1990.

Bonn International Center for Conversion. *Conversion Survey, 1994–2004* editions. Bonn: Bonn International Center for Conversion, 1994–2004.

Boose, Donald W., Balbina Y. Hwang, Patrick Morgan, and Andrew Scobell (eds.), *Recalibrating the U.S.-ROK Alliance*. Carlisle, PA: U.S. Army War College Strategic Studies Institute, May, 2003.

Borden, William S., *The Pacific Alliance: United States Foreign Economic Policy and Japanese Trade Recovery, 1947–1955*. Madison: University of Wisconsin Press, 1984.

Bose, Sumantra., *Bosnia after Dayton: Nationalist Partition and International Intervention*. Oxford: Oxford University Press, 2002.

Boutwell, Jeffrey D., Paul Doty, and Gregory F. Treverton. (eds.), *The Nuclear Confrontation in Europe*. Dover, MA: Auburn House, 1985.

Boyd, G. W., *Images of America: McGuire Air Force Base*. Charleston, SC: Arcadia Publishing, 2003.

Bracken, Paul, *Fire in the East: The Rise of Asian Military Power and the Second Nuclear Age*. New York: HarperCollins, 1999.

Brands, H. W., *Bound to Empire: The United States and the Philippines*. New York: Oxford University Press, 1992.

Bremer, L. Paul III, *My Year in Iraq: The Struggle to Build a Future of Hope*. New York: Simon and Schuster, 2005.

Bronson, Rachel, *Thicker than Oil: America's Uneasy Partnership with Saudi Arabia*. Oxford: Oxford University Press, 2006.

Burns, James McGregor, *Roosevelt: The Lion and the Fox*. Norwalk, CT: Easton Press, 1989.

Bush, George W., "Remarks by the President at the 2002 Commencement Exercises of the U.S. Military Academy." West Point, NY: June 2002, at http://www.whitehouse.gov/news/releases/2002/06/print/20020601-3.html.

Byrnes, Mark, "Unfinished Business: The United States and Franco's Spain, 1944–1947." *Diplomacy and Statecraft*, vol. 11, No. 1 (March 2000), pp. 129–62.

Calder, Kent E., "Beneath the Eagle's Wings? Japanese Burdensharing Policies in Comparative Perspective," *Asian Security*, vol. 2, no.3 (October 2006), pp. 148–73.

———, "Securing Security through Prosperity: The San Francisco System in Comparative Perspective." *Pacific Review*, vol. 17, no. 1 (March 2004), pp. 135–57.

———, "The New Face of Northeast Asia." *Foreign Affairs* (January–February 2001), pp. 1–16.

————, *Crisis and Compensation: Public Policy and Political Stability in Japan*. Princeton: Princeton University Press, 1988.

————, "Japanese Foreign Economic Policy Formation: Explaining the Reactive State." *World Politics*, vol. 40, no. 4 (July 1988): 517–41.

Calder, Kent, and Min Ye, "Critical Junctures and Northeast Asian Regionalism." *Journal of East Asian Studies*, vol. 4, no. 2 (May–August 2004), pp. 191–226.

Calleo, David, *The Imperious Economy*. Cambridge, MA.: Harvard University Press, 1982.

Campbell, Kurt M., and Celeste Johnson Ward, "New Battle Stations?" *Foreign Affairs*, vol. 82, no. 5 (September–October 2003), pp. 95–103.

Carpenter, Ted G., *A Search for Enemies: America's Alliances after the Cold War*. Washington, DC: Cato Institute, 1992.

————, "Pursuing A Strategic Divorce: The U.S. and the ANZUS Alliance." CATO Policy Analysis, no. 67.

————, "U.S. NATO Policy at a Cross-Roads." *International History Review* (August 1986), pp. 389–414.

Carpenter, Ted G., and Doug Bandow, *The Korean Conundrum: America's Troubled Relations with North and South Korea*. New York: Palgrave Macmillan, 2004.

Cawson, Alan, *Organized Interests and the State: Studies in Meso-Corporatism*. Beverly Hills: Sage Publications, 1985.

Center for Defense Information, "Post–Sept. 11 Arms Sales and Military Aid Demonstrate Dangerous Trend." CDI Information, June 18 2003, at http://www.cdi.org/friendlyversion/printversion.cfm?documentID=454.

Center for Strategic and International Studies, *Path to an Agreement: The U.S.-Republic of Korea Status of Forces Agreement Revision Process*. Washington, DC: CSIS, July 2001.

Chandrasekaran, Rajiv, *Imperial Life in the Emerald City: Inside Iraq's Green Zone*. New York: Alfred A. Knopf, 2007.

Checkel, Jeffrey, "The Constructivist Turn in International Relations Theory." *World Politics*, vol. 50, no. 2 (1998), pp. 324–48.

Clausewitz, Carl von, *On War*. Princeton: Princeton University Press, 1984.

Cohen, Eliot A., "Defending America in the Twenty-First Century." *Foreign Affairs*, vol. 79, no. 6 (November–December 2000), at http://www.foreignpolicy 2000.org/transcripts/t_cohen.html.

Coniff, Michael I., *Panama and the United States: The Forced Alliance*. Athens: University of Georgia Press, 1992.

Converse, Elliott Vanveltner III, "United States Plans for a Post-War Overseas Basing System, 1942–1948. "Unpublished Princeton University Ph.D. thesis, January 1984.

Cooley, Alexander, *Logics of Hierarchy: The Organization of States, Empires, and Military Occupations*. Ithaca: Cornell University Press, 2005.

————, "Base Politics: Redeploying U.S. Troops." *Foreign Affairs*, 84, no. 6 (November–December 2005), pp. 79–92.

Cooley, Alexander, and Kimberly Zisk Marten, "Base Bargains: The Political Economy of Okinawa's Anti-Militarism." *Armed Forces and Society*, July 2006, pp. 566–83.

Copper, John F., and Daniel S. Papp, *Communist Nations' Military Assistance*. Boulder, CO: Westview Press, 1983.

Corbin, Marcus, *Honing the Sword: Strategy and Forces after 9/11*. Washington, DC: Center for Defense Information, February 2003.

Cordesman, Anthony H., *The Lessons of Afghanistan: War Fighting, Intelligence, and Force Transformation*. Washington, DC: CSIS Press, 2002.

———, *The War after the War: Strategic Lessons of Iraq and Afghanistan*. Washington, DC: CSIS Press, 2004.

Cumings, Bruce, *Korea's Place in the Sun: A Modern History*. New York: W. W. Norton, 1997.

———, *The Origins of the Korean War: Liberation and the Emergence of Separate Regimes*, 1945–1947. Princeton: Princeton University Press, 1981.

Diamond, Larry, *Squandered Victory: The American Occupation and the Bungled Effort to Bring Democracy to Iraq*. New York: Times Books, 2005.

Dobbin, Frank, *Forging Industrial Policy: The United States, Britain, and France in the Railway Age*. Cambridge: Cambridge University Press, 1994.

Dower, John, *War without Mercy*. New York: Pantheon Books, 1986.

———, *Embracing Defeat*. New York: W. W. Norton /The New Press, 1999.

Duke, Simon. *United States Military Forces and Installations in Europe*. Oxford: Oxford University Press, 1989.

Duke, Simon W., and Wolfgang Krieger (eds.), *U.S. Military Forces in Europe: The Early Years, 1945–1970*. Boulder, CO: Westview Press, 1993.

Duus, Peter, *Party Rivalry and Political Change in Taishō Japan*. Cambridge, MA: Harvard University Press, 1968.

Ebata, Kensuke, *Beigun Saihen* (U.S. Military Force Transformation). Tokyo: Business Sha, 2005.

Ek, Richard, "A Revolution in Military Geo-Politics?", *Political Geography*, vol. 19 (2000), pp. 841–74.

Eldridge, Robert, "The 1996 Okinawa Referendum on U.S. Base Reductions," *Asian Survey*, vol. 37, no. 10 (1997), pp. 879–904.

Evans, Peter B., Harold K. Jacobson, and Robert D. Putnam (eds.). *Double-Edged Diplomacy: International Bargaining and Domestic Politics*. Berkeley: University of California Press, 1993.

Fellowship of Reconciliation, *Vieques Issue Brief*, Fall 2001.

Ferguson, Niall, *Colossus: The Price of America's Empire*. New York: Penguin Press, 2004.

———, *Empire: The Rise and Demise of the British World Order and the Lessons for Global Power*. New York: Basic Books, 2004.

Flournoy, Michele A. (ed.), *QDR 2001: Strategy Driven Choices for America's Security*. Washington, DC: National Defense University Press, 2001.

Franks, Tommy, *American Soldier*. New York: Harper Collins, 2004.

Freedom House, *Freedom in the World*, annual, at http://www.freedomhouse.org.

Fukuyama, Francis, *The End of History and the Last Man*. Toronto: Maxwell Macmillan Canada, 1992.

Gabe, Masaaki, *Sekai no naka no Okinawa—Okinawa no naka no Nihon* (The Okinawa Inside of the World; The Japan Inside of Okinawa). Yokohama: Seori Shobō, 2003.

Gaddis, John Lewis, *Strategies of Containment: A Critical Appraisal of Postwar American National Security Policy*. Oxford: Oxford University Press, 1982.

Gaddis, John Lewis, and Paul Nitze, "NSC 68 and the Soviet Threat Reconsidered." *International Security*, vol. 4, no. 4 (1980), pp. 164–86.

Gaddis, John L., *The Long Peace*. Oxford: Oxford University Press, 1987.

Galbraith, Peter W., *The End of Iraq: How American Incompetence Created A War without End*. New York: Simon and Schuster, 2006.

Garon, Sheldon, *Molding Japanese Minds: The State in Everyday Life*. Princeton: Princeton University Press, 1997.

Garrison, Jim, *America as Empire: Global Leader or Rogue Power?* San Francisco: Berret-Koehler Publishers, 2004.

Gerschenkron, Alexander, *Economic Backwardness in Historical Perspective*. Cambridge, MA: Belknap Press of Harvard University Press, 1962.

Gerson, Joseph, and Bruce Birchard (eds.), *The Sun Never Sets: Confronting the Network of Foreign U.S. Military Bases*. Boston: South End Press, 1991.

Gilpin, Robert, *The Political Economy of International Relations*. Princeton: Princeton University Press, 1987.

———, *War and Change in World Politics*. Cambridge: Cambridge University Press, 1981.

Glantz, Aaron, *How America Lost Iraq*. New York: The Penguin Group, 2005.

Gordon, Michael R., and Bernard E. Trainor, *Cobra II: The Inside Story of the Invasion and Occupation of Iraq*. New York: Pantheon Books, 2006.

Goren, Lilly J., "BRAC to the Future: Evasive Delegation and Blame Avoidance in Base Closings." Unpublished Ph.D. dissertation in Political Science, Boston College, 1998.

Goren, Lilly J., and P. Whitgney Lackenbauer. *The Comparative Politics of Military Base Closures: How Congress Balances Geographic and General Interests*. Orono, ME: University of Maine Canadian-American Center Canadian-American Public Policy Seriew Occasional Paper Number 43, September, 2000.

Gorschakov, S. G., *Sea Power of the State*. Annapolis: U.S. Naval Institute Press, 1979.

Greene, Fred (ed.), *The Philippine Bases: Negotiating for the Future*. New York: Council on Foreign Relations, 1988.

Greider, William, *Fortress America*. New York: Public Affairs Press, 1998.

Hadwiger, C. D., "Military Base Closures: How Congress Balances Geographic and General Interests." Berkeley: University of California Ph.D. dissertation, 1993.

Hahei Checku Henshū Iinkai (ed.), *Kore ga Beigun e no Omoiyari Yosan da* (This is the U.S. Military's Sympathy Budget). Tokyo: Shakai Hyōron Sha, 1997.

Hall, Peter, and David Soskice, *Varieties of Capitalism*. Oxford: Oxford University Press, 2001.

Hanrieder, Wolfram, *Germany, Europe, and America*. New Haven: Yale University Press, 1989.

Harari, Ehud, *The Politics of Labor Legislation in Japan*. Berkeley: University of California Press, 1973.

Hardacre, Helen, "Creating State Shintō: The Great Promulgation Campaign and the New Religions." *Journal of Japanese Studies*, vol. 12, no. 1 (Winter 1986), pp. 29–63.

Harkavy, Robert E., *Bases Abroad: The Global Foreign Military Presence*. Oxford: Oxford University Press, 1989.

Harkavy, Robert E., *Great Power Competition for Overseas Bases: The Geopolitics of Access Diplomacy*. New York: Pergamon Press, 1982.

Havens, Thomas R. H., *Valley of Darkness: The Japanese People and World War II*. New York: W. W. Norton and Company, 1978.

Hein, Laura, and Mark Selden (eds.). *Islands of Discontent: Okinawan Responses to Japanese and American Power*. Oxford: Rowan & Littlefield, 2003.

Hess, G., *The U.S. Emergence as a South East Asian Power*. New York: Columbia University Press, 1987.

Hirschman, Albert O., *National Power and the Structure of Foreign Trade*. Berkeley: University of California Press, 1980.

Howard, Michael, *Clausewitz*. New York: Oxford University Press, 1983.

Hudson Institute, *Dual Use and the Future of Yokota Air Base*. Washington, DC: The Hudson Institute, 2004.

Huntington, Samuel P., *Political Order in Changing Societies*. New Haven: Yale University Press, 1968.

Ignatieff, Michael, *Empire Lite: Nation-Building in Bosnia, Kosovo, and Afghanistan*. Toronto: The Penguin Group, 2003.

Ikenberry, G. John, *After Victory*. Princeton: Princeton University Press, 2001.

Inoue, Muramichi Sebastian, John Purves, and Mark Selden, "Okinawa Citizens, U.S. Bases, and the Dugong." *Bulletin of Critical Asian Studies*, vol. 29, no. 4, 1997, at http://csf.colorado.edu/bcas/campaign/Okinawa.html.

International Energy Agency, *Energy Statistics of OECD Countries*. Paris: OECD/IEA, annual.

International Institute for Strategic Studies, *The Military Balance*. Assorted issues.

Iriye, Akira, *After Imperialism: The Search for a New Order in the Far East, 1921–1931*. Cambridge, MA: Harvard University Press, 1965.

Jansen, Marius, The Making of Modern Japan. Cambridge, MA: Harvard University Press, 2000.

Japan Defense Agency, *Defense of Japan*. Assorted issues, Tokyo.

Joffe, Josef, "Peace and Populism: Why the European Anti-Nuclear Movement Failed." *International Security*, vol. 11, no. 4 (Spring 1987), pp. 3–40.

Johnson, Chalmers, *Blowback: The Costs and Consequences of American Empire*. New York: Metropolitan Books, 2000.

———, *The Sorrows of Empire*. New York: Metropolitan Books, 2004.

Johnson, Chalmers (ed.), *Okinawa: Cold War Island*. Encinitas, CA: Japan Policy Research Institute. 1999.

Kakazu, Hiroshi, *Thriving Locally in the Global Economy: The Case of Okinawa*. Naha: Okinawa Development Finance Corporation, 2000.

Karnow, Stanley, *In Our Image: American Empire in the Philippines*. New York: Random House, 1989.

Katzenstein, Peter J., *Cultural Norms and National Security: Police and Military in Postwar Japan*. Ithaca: Cornell University Press, 1996.

——— "Same War—Different Views: Germany, Japan, and Counterterrorism." *International Organization*, vol. 57, no. 4 (2003), pp. 731–60.

Katzenstein, Peter J. (ed.), *The Culture of National Security: Norms and Identity in World Politics*. New York: Columbia University Press, 1996.

Katzenstein, Peter J., and Christopher Hemmer, "Why is There No NATO in Asia?" *International Organization*, vol. 56, no. 3 (2001), pp. 575–607.

Katzenstein, Peter J., and Robert O. Keohane (eds.), *Anti-Americanism in World Politics*. Ithaca: Cornell University Press, 2007.

Kawakami, Takashi, *Beigun no Zenpō Tenkai to Nichibei Dōmei* (U.S. Military Forward Deployment and the US-Japan Alliance). Tokyo: Dōbunkan Shuppan, 2004.

Kawatkar, *Diego Garcia in International Diplomacy*. London: Sangam, 1982.

Keaney, Thomas A., "The Linkage of Air and Ground Power in the Future of Conflict." *International Security*, vol. 22, no. 2 (Autumn 1997), pp. 147–50.

Keck, Margaret E., and Kathryn Sikkink, *Activists beyond Borders*. Ithaca: Cornell University Press, 1998.

Keddell, Joseph P., *The Politics of Defense in Japan: Managing Internal and External Pressures*. Armonk, NY: M. W. Sharpe, 1993.

Kennan, George F., *Around the Cragged Hill: A Personal and Political Philosophy*. New York: W. W. Norton, 1993.

Kennedy, Paul M., *The Rise and Fall of British Naval Mastery*. Amherst, NY: Prometheus Books, 1998.

———, *The Rise and Fall of the Great Powers: Economic Change and Military Conflict from 1500 to 2000*. New York: Random House, 1987.

Keohane, Robert O., "The Big Influence of Small Allies." *Foreign Policy*, no. 2 (1971), pp. 161–82.

———, "American Policy and the Trade-Growth Struggle." *International Security*, vol. 3, no. 3 (Autumn 1978), pp. 20–43.

Kepel, Giles, *Jihad: The Trail of Political Islam*. Cambridge, MA: Harvard University Press, 2002.

Kim, Il-Young, and Seong Ryol Cho, *Chuhan Mikyu* (U.S. Forces in Korea). Seoul: Hanyol, 2003.

Kim, Sunhyak, *The Politics of Democratization in Korea: The Role of Civil Society*. Pittsburgh: University of Pittsburgh Press, 2000.

Kirk, Robin, *More Terrible Than Death: Violence, Drugs, and America's War in Colombia*. New York: Perseus Book Group, 2003.

Kirkpatrick, Jeanne, "Dictatorship and Double Standards." *Commentary*, vol. 68, no. 36 (November 1979), at http://www.commentarymagazine.com.

Kishi, Nobusuke, *Kishi Nobusuke Kaikoroku: Hoshu Gōdō to Ampo Kaitei* (The Conservative Merger and the Security Treaty Revision). Tokyo: Kōsaidō, 1983.

Kissinger, Henry, *Diplomacy*. London: Simon and Schuster, 1994.

Klare, Michael T., *Blood and Oil: The Dangers and Consequences of America's Growing Petroleum Dependency*. New York: Metropolitan Books, 2004.

Kohut, Andrew, and Bruce Stokes, *America against the World: How We Are Different and How We Are Disliked*. New York: Times Books, 2006.

Kōsaka, Masataka (ed.), *Sengo Nichibei Kankei Nenpyō, 1945–1983* (A Chronology of Postwar U.S.-Japan Relations, 1945–1983). Tokyo: PHP Kenkyū Jo, 1985.

Krasner, Stephen D., *Defending the National Interest: Raw Materials Investments and U.S. Foreign Policy*. Princeton: Princeton University Press, 1978.

———, "Trade Conflicts and the Common Defense: The United States and Japan." *Political Science Quarterly*, vol. 101, no. 5 (1986), pp. 787–806.

Krauss, Ellis, *Japanese Radicals Revisited*. Berkeley, University of California Press, 1974.

Krepinevich, Andrew F., "Cavalry to Computer: The Pattern of Military Revolutions." *The National Interest*, Fall 1994, pp. 30–42.

Krepinevich, Andrew F., "How to Win in Iraq." *Foreign Affairs*, vol. 84, no. 5 (September–October 2005), pp. 87–104.

———, *Transforming America's Alliances*. Washington, DC: Center for Strategic and Budgetary Assessments, February, 2000.

Kupchan, Charles A., *The Persian Gulf and the West: The Dilemmas of Security*. Boston: Allen & Unwin, 1987.

Lasswell, Harold, Politics: *Who Gets What, When, How*. New York: Whittlesey House, McGraw-Hill Book Company, 1936.

Layne, Christopher, "From Preponderance to Offshore Balancing: America's Future Grand Strategy." *International Security*, vol. 22, no. 1 (Summer 1997), pp. 86–124.

Lea, David, and Anna Marie Rowe, *Political Chronologies of the World*. London: Europa Publications, Ltd., 2001.

Lee, Sook-Jong, "The Rise of Korean Youth as a Political Force," in Bush, Yanagi, and Scott (eds.), *Brookings Northeast Asia Survey*, 2003–2004 ed. Washington, DC: The Brookings Institution, 2004, pp. 15–30.

Lewis, Bernard, *What Went Wrong: Western Impact and Middle Eastern Response*. Oxford and New York: Oxford University Press, 2002.

Lotchin, Roger W., *Fortress California, 1910–1961: From Warfare to Welfare*. Urbana: University of Illinois Press, 1962.

Lussier, Frances, *Options for Changing the Army's Overseas Basing*. Washington, DC: Congressional Budget Office, 2004.

Lutz, Catherine, *Homefront: A Military City and the American Twentieth Century*. Boston: Beacon Press, 2001.

MacDougall, Terry E. (ed.), *Political Leadership in Contemporary Japan*. Ann Arbor: University of Michigan Center for Japanese Studies, 1982.

Mahan, Alfred T., *The Influence of Sea Power upon History, 1660–1783*. Boston: Little Brown, 1906.

Mandelbaum, Michael, *The Case for Goliath*. New York: Public Affairs, 2005.

March, James G., and Johan P. Olsen, *Rediscovering Institutions: The Organizational Base of Politics*. New York: Free Press, 1989.

Marten, Kimberley Zisk, *Enforcing the Peace: Learning from the Imperial Past*. New York: Columbia University Press, 2004.

Martin, Lenore G., and Dimitris Keridis (eds.), *The Future of Turkish Foreign Policy*. Cambridge, MA: MIT Press, 2004.

McCaffrey, Katherine T., *Military Power and Popular Protest: The U.S. Navy in Vieques, Puerto Rico*. New Brunswick, NJ: Rutgers University Press, 2002.

McCormick, T. J., *America's Half Century*. Baltimore: Johns Hopkins University Press, 1995.

McCullough, David, *Truman*. New York: Simon and Schuster, 1992.

McDonald, John W., and Diane B. Bendahmane, *U.S. Bases Overseas: Negotiations with Spain, Greece, and the Philippines*. Boulder, CO: Westview Press, 1990.

Merrill, John, Korea: *The Peninsular Origins of the War*. Newark: University of Delaware Press, 1989.

Meyer, David S., "Social Movements and Nested Institutions: International Constraints on Political Efficacy." Cambridge, MA: Harvard University Weatherhead Center for International Affairs Program on Non-Violent Sanctions, Fall, 1994.

Miller, David, *The Cold War: A Military History*. New York: St. Martin's Press, 1998.

Miller, T. Christian, *Blood Money*. New York: Little, Brown, and Co., 2006.

Moon, Katherine, H. S., "South Korean Movements against Militarized Sexual Labor." *Asian Survey*, March–April 2002, 49:2, pp. 310–27.

Morris, Aldous, and Carol M. Mueller, *Frontiers and Social Movement Theory*. New Haven: Yale University Press, 1992.

Morrow, James D., "Arms versus Allies: Trade-Offs in the Search for Security?" *International Organization*, vol. 47, no. 2 (Spring 1993), pp. 207–33.

Najita, Tetsuo, *Hara Kei in the Politics of Compromise, 1905–1915*. Cambridge, MA: Harvard University Press, 1967.

Neustadt, Richard, *Alliance Politics*. New York: Columbia University Press, 1970.

Norris, Pippa, *Democratic Phoenix*. Cambridge: Cambridge University Press, 2002.

North, Douglass C., *Institutions, Institutional Change, and Economic Performance*. Cambridge: Cambridge University Press, 1990.

"NSC 68: United States Objectives and Programs", *Naval War College Review*, vol. 27, (May–June), 1975, pp. 51–108.

Nye, Joseph, *The Paradox of American Power*. Oxford: Oxford University Press, 2002.

Oberdorfer, Don, *Senator Mansfield*. Washington, DC: Smithsonian Books, 2003.

———, *The Two Koreas: A Contemporary History*. Reading, MA: Addison-Wesley, 1997.

Odom, William E., and Robert Dujarric, *America's Inadvertent Empire*. New Haven: Yale University Press, 2004.

O'Hanlon, Michael E., *Defense Strategies for the Post-Saddam Era*. Washington, DC: The Brookings Institution, 2005.

———, "Can High Technology Bring U.S. Troops Home?" *Foreign Policy*, no. 113 (Winter, 1998–1999), pp. 72–86.

Oliker, Olga, and David A. Shlapak, *U.S. Interests in Central Asia: Policy Priorities and Military Roles*. Santa Monica: Rand Corporation, 2005.

Olson, Mancur, *The Logic of Collective Action*. Cambridge, MA: Harvard University Press, 1965.

Oneill, Aloysius, *Okinawa and Its Role in the U.S.-Japan Alliance*. Washington, DC: Reischauer Center for East Asian Studies, 2007.

Ōta Masahide, *Kore ga Okinawa Sen da Kaiteiban: Shashin Kiroku* (This is the Definitive Version of the Battle of Okinawa: Photo Record). Naha: Naha Shuppan Sha, 1998.

Ostrom, Elinor, Roy Gardner, and James Walter, *Rules, Games, and Common-Pool Resources*. Ann Arbor, Michigan: University of Michigan Press, 1994.

Olson, Mancur, and Richard Zeckhauser, "An Economic Theory of Alliances." *The Review of Economics and Statistics*, vol. 48, no. 3, (1966), pp. 266–79.

Packer, George, *The Assassin's Gate*. New York: Farrar, Strauss, Giroux, 2005.

Palmer, Michael A., *Guardians of the Gulf: A History of America's Expanding Role in the Persian Gulf, 1833–1992*. New York: Free Press, 1992.

Park, Bill, "Strategic Location, Political Dislocation: Turkey, the United States, and Northern Iraq." *Middle East Review of International Affairs*, vol. 7, no. 2 (June 2003), pp. 1–13.

Paul, Roland A., *American Military Commitments Abroad*. New Brunswick, NJ: Rutgers University Press, 1973.

Payne, Stanley G., "In the Twilight of the Franco Era." *Foreign Affairs*, vol. 49, no. 2 (January 1971), p. 342.

Peceny, Mark, "Two Paths to the Promotion of Democracy during U.S. Military Interventions." *International Studies Quarterly*, vol. 39, no.3 (September 1995), pp. 371–401.

Phillips, David L., *Losing Iraq: Inside the Postwar Reconstruction Fiasco*. Boulder, CO: Westview Press, 2005.

Pickering, Jeffrey, *Britain's Withdrawal from East of Suez*. Hampshire: Macmillan, 1998.

Preston, Paul, "Franco: The Patient Dictator." *History Today*, vol. 35, issue 11 (November, 1985), pp. 8–9.

Przeworski, Adam, *Democracy and the Market*. Cambridge: Cambridge University Press, 1991.

Putnam, Robert D., "Diplomacy and Domestic Politics: The Logic of Two-Level Games." *International Organization* 42 (Summer 1988), pp. 427–60.

Putnam, Robert D., et. al. (eds.), *Double-Edged Diplomacy: International Bargaining and Domestic Politics*. Berkeley: University of California Press, 1993.

Quester, George, *Deterrence before Hiroshima: The Air Power Background of Modern Strategy*. New Brunswick, NJ: Transaction Publishers, 1986.

Ratner, Michael, and Ellen Ray, *Guantanamo: What the World Should Know*. White River Junction, VT: Chelsea Green Publishing, 2004.

Reischauer, Edwin O., *Japan: The Story of a Nation*. New York: Alfred A. Knopf, 1970.

Ricardo, Roger, *Guantanamo: The Bay of Discord*. Melbourne: Ocean Press, 1994.

Richards, Chester W., *A Swift, Elusive Sword: What If Sun Tzu and John Boyd Did a National Defense Review?* (2d ed.). Washington, DC: Center for Defense Information, February 2003.

Ricks, Thomas E., *Fiasco: The American Military Adventure in Iraq.* New York: Penguin Press, 2006.

Romer, Thomas, and Howard Rosenthal, "Political Resource Allocation, Controlled Agendas, and the Status Quo." *Public Choice*, vol. 33, no. 4 (1978), pp. 27–44.

Rumer, Boris (ed.), *Central Asia: The Gathering Storm.* Armonk, NY: M. E. Sharpe, 2002.

Sabine, Charles, *A History of Political Theory.* Hinsdale, IL: Dryden Press, 1973.

Sandars, Christopher, *America's Overseas Garrisons: The Leasehold Empire.* Oxford: Oxford University Press, 2000.

Sarantakes, Nicholas Even, *Keystone: The American Occupation of Okinawa and U.S.-Japan Relations.* College Station: Texas A. & M. University Press, 2000.

Schake, Kurt Wayne, *Strategic Frontier: American Bomber Command Bases Overseas, 1950–1960.* Trondheim: Norwegian University of Science and Technology, 1998.

Schaller, Michael, *Douglas MacArthur: The Far-Eastern General.* New York: Oxford University Press, 1989.

———, *The American Occupation of Japan.* Oxford: Oxford University Press, 1985.

Scharpf, Fritz W., *Games Real Actors Play: Actor-Centered Institutionalism in Policy Research.* Boulder, CO: Westview Press, 1997.

Schattschneider, E. E., *Politics, Pressure, and the Tariff.* New York: Prentice-Hall, 1935.

Schelling, Thomas, *Arms and Influence.* New Haven: Yale University Press, 1966.

———, *The Strategy of Conflict.* Cambridge, MA: Harvard University Press. 1960.

Schlesinger, Jacob, *Shadow Shogun.* New York: Simon and Schuster, 1997.

Schwartz, Frank J., and Susan J. Pharr, *The State of Civil Society in Japan.* Cambridge: Cambridge University Press, 2003.

Schwartz, Stephen, "Wahhabism in the United States." *National Review*, June 30, 2003.

———, *The Two Faces of Islam: The House of Sa'ud from Tradition to Terror.* New York: Doubleday, 2002.

Secretary of Defense, Annual Report to the President and the Congress. Washington, DC: U.S. Government Publishing Office, annual.

Secretary of Defense, Report on Allied Contributions to the Common Defense, 1995–2003. Washington, DC: U.S. Government Publishing Office, annual.

Seig, Julia E., *Friendly Fire: Losing Friends and Making Enemies in the Anti-American Century.* New York: Perseus Book Group, 2006.

Shadid, Anthony, *Night Draws Near.* New York: Henry Holt and Company, 2005.

Shah, Anup, "The United States and Foreign Aid Assistance." *Global Issues*, July 11, 2004.

Shlapak, David A., John Stillion, Olga Oliker, and Tanya Carlick Paley, *A Global Strategy for the U.S. Air Force.* Santa Monica: Rand Project Air Force, 2002.

Shiels, F., *America, Okinawa, and Japan*. Washington, DC: University Press of America, 1980.

Simon, Steven, *After the Surge*. New York: Council on Foreign Relations Special Study, no. 23 (February 2007).

Singer, P. W., *Corporate Warriors: The Rise of the Privatized Military Industry*. Ithaca: Cornell University Press, 2003.

Skowronek, Stephen, *Building a New American State: The Expansion of National Administrative Capabilities, 1877–1920*. Cambridge: Cambridge University Press, 1982.

Slaughter, Anne-Marie, *A New World Order*. Princeton: Princeton University Press, 2004.

Sloan, Elinor C., *The Revolution in Military Affairs*. Montreal: McGill-Queens University Press, 2002.

Smith, Sheila A., *Shifting Terrain: The Domestic Politics of the U.S. Military Presence in Asia*. Honolulu: East-West Center Special Reports, March, 2006.

Smith, T., *The Pattern of Imperialism*. Cambridge: Cambridge University Press, 1981.

Sorenson, David S., *Shutting Down the Cold War: The Politics of Military Base Closure*. New York: St. Martin's Press, 1998.

Spykman, Nicholas John, *America's Strategy in World Politics: The United States and the Balance of Power*. New York: Harcourt Brace, 1942.

Steiner, Kurt, *Local Government in Japan*. Stanford: Stanford University Press, 1965.

Stueck, William, *Rethinking the Korean War: A New Diplomatic and Strategic History*. Princeton: Princeton University Press, 2002.

Tarrow, Sidney, *The New Transnational Activism*. Cambridge: Cambridge University Press, 2005.

Thayer, Nathaniel B., *How the Conservatives Rule Japan*. Princeton: Princeton University Press, 1969.

Thucydides, *The Peloponnesian War*, transl. R. Warner. Baltimore: Penguin Press, 1954.

Tilly, Charles (ed.), *The Formation of Nation States in Western Europe*. Princeton: Princeton University Press, 1975.

Thompson, Robert, *Defeating Communist Insurgency*. St. Petersburg, FL: Hailer Publishing, 2005.

Tirpak, John A., "Enduring Freedom." *Air Force Magazine*, February 2002, pp. 32–39.

Toynbee, Arnold, *America and the World Revolution*. New York: Oxford University Press, 1962.

Tsebelis, George, *Veto Players: How Political Institutions Work*. Princeton: Princeton University Press, 2002.

———, *Nested Games: Rational Choice in Comparative Politics*. Berkeley: University of California Press, 1990.

U.S. Agency for International Development, *U.S. Overseas Loans and Grants (Green Book)*, 2003 and 2004 editions. Washington, DC: U.S. Government Publishing Office, 2003 and 2004.

U.S. Congressional Budget Office, *Options for Changing the Army's Overseas Basing*. Washington, DC: U.S. Government Publishing Office, May, 2004.

U.S. Department of the Army, *Counterinsurgency*. Washington, DC: Marine Corps War-Fighting Publications, December 2006.

U.S. Department of Defense, *The United States Security Strategy for the East Asia-Pacific Region*, 1998 edition. Washington, DC: U.S. Government Publishing Office, 1998.

———, *Base Structure Report*. Washington, DC: U.S. Government Publishing Office, annual.

———, *Report on Allied Contributions to the Common Defense*. Washington, DC: U.S. Government Publishing Office, annual.

———, *Total Military, Civilian, and Dependent Strengths, by Regional Areas and by Country*. Washington, DC: U.S. Department of Defense Directorate for Information, Operations, and Reports, annual.

———, *World Manpower Distribution by Geographic Area*. Washington, DC: U.S. Government Publishing Office, annual.

U.S. Department of State, *Foreign Relations of the United States*, assorted issues. Washington, DC: U.S. Government Publishing Office, annual.

"U.S. Military Bases and Empire." *Monthly Review*, vol. 53, no. 10 (March, 2002), at http://www.monthlyreview.org/0302editr.htm.

Valero, Geraldo M. C., et al., *A Comparative Analysis of United States Military Base Agreements*. Manila: International Study Institute of the Philippines, 1987.

Veremis, Thanos, and Yannis Valinakis, *U.S. Bases in the Mediterranean: The Cases of Greece and Spain*. Athens: Hellenic Foundation for Defense and Foreign Policy, 1989.

Vidal, Gore, *The Decline and Fall of the American Empire*. Berkeley: Odonian Press, 1992.

Wakamiya Yoshibumi, *The Postwar Conservative View of Asia*. Tokyo: International Library Foundation, 1998.

Walker, Dan, *San Diego: Home Base for Freedom*. San Diego: Premier Publishing, 2003.

Walt, Stephen M., *Taming American Power: The Global Response to U.S. Primacy*. New York: W. W. Norton, 2005.

Weller, George, *Bases Overseas: An American Trusteeship in Power*. New York: Harcourt, Brace, and Co., 1944.

Wendt, Alexander, "The Social Construction of Power Politics." *International Organization* vol. 46, no. 2 (Spring 1992), pp. 391–425.

Wit, Joel S., Daniel B. Poneman, and Robert Gallucci, *Going Critical: The First North Korean Nuclear Crisis*. Washington, DC: The Brookings Institution, 2004.

Wolfowitz, Paul, "Thinking about the Imperatives of Defense Transformation." *Heritage Lectures*, April 30, 2004.

World Bank Group, *Expanded Trade and Investment Holds Promise for Millions of Jobs in the Middle East*. Washington, DC: The World Bank, 2001.

Yoshida, Shigeru, *The Yoshida Memoirs: The Story of Japan in Crisis*. Transl. Yoshida Kenichi. London: William Heinemann, 1961.

Zinni, Tony, and Tony Koltz, *The Battle for Peace: A Frontline Vision of America's Power and Purpose*. New York: Palgrave Macmillan, 2006.

Index